RESEARCH IN ORGANIZATIONAL BEHAVIOR

RESEARCH IN ORGANIZATIONAL BEHAVIOR

Series Editors: Barry M. Staw and L. L. Cummings

Volumes 1–20: Research in Organizational Behavior – An Annual Series of Analytical Essays and Critical Reviews

Series Editors: Barry M. Staw and Robert I. Sutton

Volumes 21–23: Research in Organizational Behavior – An Annual Series of Analytical Essays and Critical Reviews

Series Editors: Barry M. Staw and Roderick M. Kramer

Volume 24: Research in Organizational Behavior – An Annual Series of Analytical Essays and Critical Reviews

Volume 25: Research in Organizational Behavior – An Annual Series of Analytical Essays and Critical Reviews

Volume 26: Research in Organizational Behavior – An Annual Series ofAnalytical Essays and Critical Reviews

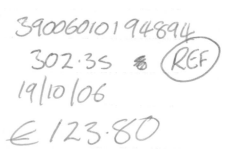

RESEARCH IN ORGANIZATIONAL BEHAVIOR

AN ANNUAL SERIES OF ANALYTICAL ESSAYS AND CRITICAL REVIEWS

EDITED BY

BARRY M. STAW

Haas School of Business, University of California, USA

ELSEVIER
JAI

Amsterdam – Boston – Heidelberg – London – New York – Oxford
Paris – San Diego – San Francisco – Singapore – Sydney – Tokyo

JAI Press is an imprint of Elsevier

JAI Press is an imprint of Elsevier
The Boulevard, Langford Lane, Kidlington, Oxford OX5 1GB, UK
Radarweg 29, PO Box 211, 1000 AE Amsterdam, The Netherlands
525 B Street, Suite 1900, San Diego, CA 92101-4495, USA

First edition 2006

British Library Cataloguing in Publication Data
A catalogue record for this book is available from the British Library

ISBN-13:   978-0-7623-1335-8
ISBN-10:   0-7623-1335-8
ISSN: 0191-3085 (Series)

For information on all JAI Press publications
visit our website at books.elsevier.com

Printed and bound in The Netherlands

06 07 08 09 10 10 9 8 7 6 5 4 3 2 1

Working together to grow
libraries in developing countries

www.elsevier.com | www.bookaid.org | www.sabre.org

ELSEVIER   BOOK AID
             International   Sabre Foundation

CONTENTS

LIST OF CONTRIBUTORS

Allen C. Bluedorn	Department of Management, University of Missouri – Columbia, Columbia, MO, USA
Eliza Byington	School of Business, University of Washington, Seattle, WA, USA (student)
Gilad Chen	Robert H. Smith School of Business, University of Maryland, MD, USA
Roy Yong-Joo Chua	Columbia Business School, Columbia University, New York, NY, USA
Jeannette A. Colyvas	School of Education, Stanford University, Stanford, CA, USA
Will Felps	School of Business, University of Washington, Seattle, WA, USA
Francis J. Flynn	Columbia Business School, New York, NY, USA
Simona Giorgi	Kellogg School of Management, Northwestern University, USA
Sheena S. Iyengar	Columbia Business School, Columbia University, New York, NY, USA
Ruth Kanfer	School of Psychology, Georgia Institute of Technology, Atlanta, GA, USA
Charalampos Mainemelis	Department of Organizational Behavior, London Business School, London, UK
Terence R. Mitchell	School of Business, University of Washington, WA, USA
Walter W. Powell	School of Education, Stanford University, Stanford, CA, USA

Hayagreeva Rao   Stanford Graduate School of Business,
                         Stanford University, Stanford, CA, USA

Brent W. Roberts   Department of Psychology, University of
                         Illinois, Champaign, IL, USA

Sarah Ronson   Department of Organizational Behavior,
                         London Business School, London, UK

Mary J. Waller   School of Economics and Business
                         Administration, University of Maastricht,
                         Maastricht, The Netherlands

PREFACE

This 27th volume of Research in Organizational Behavior carries forward the tradition of high-level scholarship on a broad array of organizational topics. Like many previous volumes, this collection is truly interdisciplinary. It contains chapters ranging from personality and decision making in organizations, to interpersonal dynamics such as helping and group process, to organizational-level analyses of legitimization and change.

The volume begins with three chapters that reformulate some long-standing issues concerning individual behavior in organizations. In the first chapter, Brent Roberts takes a fresh look at personality development and change over the life-course. Instead of the usual dichotomy of person vs. situation effects, Roberts addresses both the continuity and development of personality as individuals enter and interact with organizations over time. With a new theoretical model, the neo-socioanalytic framework, this chapter resolves person-situation debates by elaborating the appropriate unit of analysis for individual differences as well as the paths by which individuals and situations mutually influence each other.

In the second chapter, Roy Chua and Sheena Iyengar re-examine the role of choice in organizational life. Although much psychological theory and research touts the positive role of choice, suggesting that it confers personal agency and intrinsic motivation, Chua and Iyengar note how people's decision making and well-being may be impaired by too much choice. They show that, when confronted with a set of undesirable or stressful choices, people tend to delay choosing, shift the responsibility to others, or opt not to choose at all. Even when there are equally attractive alternatives from which to choose, people tend to defer decisions or rely on the default option. Thus, while Americans and other Westerners widely endorse the idea that "more choice is better," the actual consequences of choice may not so benign, with important implications for issues such as job design, procedural justice, and leadership.

For the third chapter, Charalampos Mainemelis and Sarah Ronson discuss the many ways play and creativity are inextricably bound. They persuasively argue that play, either as a form of engagement with work tasks or as a form of diversion from work, can help to stimulate creativity. By suspending ordinary conventions, structural obligations, and functional pressures, and by encouraging behaviors whose value may not be immediately evident, play may stimulate and facilitate creativity in organizations.

At this point in the volume attention turns to some important questions in interpersonal relations. In Chapter 4, Francis Flynn describes a fascinating program of research on helping behavior in organizations. Although past research on interpersonal cooperation has always assumed that there is agreement on the value of help given and received, Flynn shows how the subjective evaluations of giving and receiving help often diverge. Many people inflate the value of help they give and depreciate the value of help they receive, creating problems for balancing future obligations and reciprocity. The value of favors also depends on many characteristics of the person and the exchange relationship itself, such as the relative status of the parties, frequency of the exchange, and perceived indebted of the participants. Relying upon both past theory and recent research, Flynn draws implications for managing cooperation in organizational life.

In the fifth chapter, Will Felps, Terence Mitchell, and Eliza Byington explore the notion that one problematic group member can have a dramatically negative effect on group attitudes and behavior. They review prior theory and research supporting the notion that "bad apples can spoil the barrel." They convincingly show how one negative group member can induce negative psychological states of teammates, such as reduced trust and perceptions of inequity, and contribute to a general decline in group cooperation and creativity.

In Chapter 6, Gilad Chen and Ruth Kanfer propose a multi-level theory of motivation. They identify parallel, or functionally similar, constructs and relationships that underlie motivational processes at both the individual and team levels. They compare similarities and differences in the determinants and outcomes of motivation across levels, and they examine cross-level influences between individual and team motivation. These cross-level effects include top-down effects of the team on individual cognition and behavior as well as bottom-up effects of individual cognition and behavior on team processes. This multi-level model sheds important new light on the system of relationships underpinning member and team effectiveness.

The volume closes with three provocative chapters on macro or organizational processes. In Chapter 7, Hayagreeva Rao and Simona Giorgi address the paradox of social stability and change in institutional theory. Although much of institutional theory highlights the place of rules, norms, and cognition in perpetuating a homogeneous social order, institutional change can and does occur. Rao and Giorgi show how institutional entrepreneurs generate change through the deft deployment of pre-existing cultural logics, classifying these change strategies into modes of cultural subversion, appropriation, integration and insurgency. By elaborating some interesting yet relevant examples of each change strategy, they explain exactly how institutions can be successfully altered across a range of industries and cultures.

In Chapter 8, Jeannette Colyvas and Walter Powell illustrate how institutional change can be created, not by exogenous shocks, but by endogenous practices and understandings. They show how legitimacy and taken-for-grantedness can be built over time by tracing the commercialization of science as it moved from an unusual activity to a routine undertaking. By using archival materials on technology transfer at a leading research university, Colyvas and Powell demonstrate how science and property, two spheres that were formerly distinct, could be fused over time. Their archival study provides a vivid example for researchers seeking to operationalize both the level and mode of institutionalization, clarifying processes that are generally opaque in nature.

In the final chapter, Allen Bluedorn and Mary Waller explore the idea of a temporal commons – the shared conceptualization of time, including a set of values, beliefs, and behaviors regarding time. They argue that, just as physical resources have been altered by early efforts to enclose and privatize the public greens or commons, intangible resources such temporal commons are being altered over time. Bluedorn and Waller trace such changes at the civilization, societal, organizational, and group levels, illustrating the important consequences of these developments on people's behavior. They conclude by arguing that such changes should be made with caution and deliberation rather than being left to those with special interests.

As a collection, this set of nine essays covers a very diverse set of topics. At the same time, each of these essays has a common quality that should make it a welcome addition to organizational scholarship. Each of the essays is well-reasoned, thoughtful, and provocative – proving, once again, that the field of organizational behavior is flourishing in both its depth and breadth.

Barry M. Staw
Editor

PERSONALITY DEVELOPMENT AND ORGANIZATIONAL BEHAVIOR

Brent W. Roberts

ABSTRACT

This chapter provides an overview of a new theoretical framework that serves to integrate personality psychology and other fields, such as organizational behavior. The first section describes a structural model of personality that incorporates traits, motives, abilities, and narratives, with social roles. The second section describes basic patterns of continuity and change in personality and how this might be relevant to organizational behavior. The third section describes the ASTMA model of person–organization transaction (attraction, selection, transformation, manipulation, and attrition), which describes the primary transactions between personality and organizational experiences across the life course. The goal for the chapter is to build a bridge between modern personality psychology and organizational behavior, such that the two fields can better inform one another.

Research in Organizational Behavior: An Annual Series of Analytical Essays and Critical Reviews
Research in Organizational Behavior, Volume 27, 1–40
Copyright © 2006 by Elsevier Ltd.
ISSN: 0191-3085/doi:10.1016/S0191-3085(06)27001-1

The goal of this chapter is to present a new model of personality psychology. This new model has grown out of a program of research in which both persons and organizations have been studied over long periods of time (Roberts, 1997; Roberts & Chapman, 2000; Roberts, Caspi, & Moffitt, 2003; Roberts & Robins, 2004). What is clear in reviewing the findings from these studies is that existing models of personality, which tend to be dispersive and non-integrative (Mayer, 2005), are inadequate for understanding personality, personality development, and the interface between personality and organizations. My hope is that this model can provide a focal point through which a more fruitful and productive integration can be made between personality psychology and organizational behavior.

The fields of personality psychology and organizational behavior have had an ambivalent relationship over the last several decades. On the positive side, there has been a resurgence of research on the role personality plays in affecting organizational outcomes, such as job performance (Hogan & Holland, 2003), job satisfaction (Judge, Heller, & Mount, 2002), leadership (Judge, Bono, Ilies, & Gerhardt, 2002), and person–organization fit (PO Fit) (Roberts & Robins, 2004). On the other hand, there is an inherent tension between personality psychology and the study of organizational behavior, as the latter has focused more on situational influences on job attitudes and behaviors (e.g., Mowday & Sutton, 1993). This focus on situational influences is clearly appropriate as organizational researchers are often motivated to provide concrete advice to managers on how to improve their organizations. Intrinsic to the typical approach to organizational behavior is the assumption that thoughts, feelings, and behaviors are changeable and can be shaped or created by organizational experiences alone. A position which, at first blush, appears to conflict with the typical way personality is conceptualized in organizational studies – as personality traits. Personality traits are the relatively enduring patterns of thoughts, feelings, and behaviors that differentiate individuals from one another. The idea that traits cause organizational behaviors has in the past been a point of controversy (Davis-Blake & Pfeffer, 1989), primarily because it is difficult to reconcile behavior being changeable by organizational factors and simultaneously caused by stable individual differences.

The tension between personality psychology and the field of organizational behavior is symptomatic of the broader person–situation debate that has beleaguered psychology intermittently for the last 100 years. The most recent incarnation, which raged in the 1960s and 1970s, played a significant role in shaping both personality psychology and organizational behavior. In personality psychology, the study of traits almost disappeared, as researchers and academic institutions responded to Mischel's (1968) critique by emphasizing the importance of social situations and examining alternative units of analysis to traits.[1] Similarly, the field of organizational behavior followed the zeitgeist of the times and de-emphasized the importance of stable individual differences in organizational life (see Staw & Cohen-Charash, 2005 for a review).

The person–situation debate was in many ways misguided. It was misguided because in hindsight, all of the arguments made against personality traits were either factually or interpretively incorrect (Hogan & Roberts, 2000; Roberts, 2005). For example, Mischel (1968) raised four critical points: (a) traits had limited utility in predicting behavior (i.e., the infamous "personality coefficient" of 0.3); (b) Stability was a fiction in the mind of the observer; (c) behavior was not stable across situations; and (d) if there is stability it is attributable to the situation, not the person.

In the intervening decades, research has shown that each of these arguments is false or misleading. First, there is no such thing as a "personality coefficient." Rather, there is the "psychological coefficient." The large majority of effect sizes in psychology are between 0.1 and 0.3 on a correlational scale (Meyer et al., 2001). It turns out that there is nothing unique about the effect sizes in personality psychology. Moreover, the vaunted "power of the situation" was also overstated. When uninformative test statistics (e.g., F and t-tests) are transformed into effect sizes, situational manipulations were found to be no bigger than the effects of personality traits (Funder & Ozer, 1983). In addition, well-run studies in which different people rated the same person across time and age showed that stable individual differences did exist (Block, 1993). Therefore, personality was not a semantic fiction of our busy minds. Also, the original estimates of behavioral stability across situations were found to be underestimates (see Borkenau, Mauer, Riemann, Spinath, & Angleitner, 2004, for evidence and insights as to why). Nonetheless, it should be noted that no personality psychologist other than Mischel ever went on record claiming that the cross-situational consistency of behavior should be high. This was a straw man from the start and immaterial to the viability of the personality trait construct (see Roberts & Pomerantz, 2004). Finally, longitudinal research has shown that stable environments are not always associated with stability (e.g., Roberts & Robins, 2004), and that genetic factors also play a significant role in personality trait stability (McGue, Bacon, & Lykken, 1993). In sum, all of the primary criticisms of personality psychology that derive from the person–situation debate have been refuted.

At this point in history the person–situation debate is best considered dead, not because it was ever successfully resolved, but most likely because young scholars have grown tired of the bickering of their elders. The present situation can be best described as a sleepy détente rather than a full-fledged resolution. This leaves the field of personality psychology at a crossroad. Trait psychology has made a successful return, which is, in many ways, the legacy of the field of organizational behavior from which many of the most impressive tests of the predictive validity of personality traits have come (Judge, Higgins, Thoresen, & Barrick, 1999). Social cognitive approaches to personality have many adherents and also constitute a coherent and viable model of individual differences (Cervone & Shoda, 1999). Situationism has not gone away, as it is clear that situations are just as important as personality in determining behavior and personality. Nonetheless, adherents to the different camps tend to focus on research that substantiates their worldview rather than searching for a true reconciliation (e.g., Cervone, Shadel, & Jencius, 2001; Lewis, 1999; McCrae, 2004).

What is needed at this juncture is a model of personality that can achieve several goals at once. First, this new model must successfully integrate trait and social cognitive approaches to personality. Second, it needs to take situations seriously and fully integrate them into a conceptualization of the person and their life context. Third, it must account for the wealth of findings gathered over the last few decades on the consistency and changeability of personality over time and the effect of contexts on patterns of continuity and change. If successful, this model can serve as a fulcrum for a more successful integration of personality psychology with other fields, such as organizational behavior.

My goal for this chapter is to provide an overview of a model of personality that I believe achieves all of these goals. First, I will describe a new theoretical framework that serves to integrate personality psychology and other fields, such as organizational behavior. Second, I will review what we know about personality continuity and change over the life course. In this section, I will describe the relationship between personality traits and organizational experiences and how these relationships guide personality development over time. In the context of this review, I will introduce a new model of the ways in which people can interact with organizations over time and how these processes can affect both the organization and the individual. My hope is to build a bridge between modern personality psychology and organizational behavior, such that the two fields can better inform one another.

A NEO-SOCIOANALYTIC FRAMEWORK FOR PERSONALITY PSYCHOLOGY

Interestingly, much of the work facilitating the re-emergence of personality psychology has come from organizational psychology (e.g., Barrick & Mount, 1991; Hough & Ones, 2002; Staw & Ross, 1985). However, the version of personality psychology adopted in organizational psychology has proven to be overly static. Personality is conceptualized as traits, and traits are typically conceptualized as causal forces used to predict outcomes and are not themselves subject to change. If combined with situations, they are typically seen to interact with situational contingencies (e.g., Porter et al., 2003). Unfortunately, this take on personality psychology ignores the fact that personality traits have to develop and can change, even in adulthood (Roberts, Walton, & Viechtbauer, 2006). It is this fact that makes the interface of personality psychology and organizational behavior so interesting, as trait models that do not incorporate the transactions between personality and situation over time fail to account for conceptual or empirical findings of personality development (Fraley & Roberts, 2005).

In order to better understand how personality transacts with situations over time, a framework is needed that can address the tension between continuity and change in behavior and what role situations play in shaping behavior and thus personality. The following theoretical model, described as the neo-socioanalytic model of personality is an attempt to provide an integrative framework for personality psychology that has been explicated in several other outlets (Roberts & Caspi, 2003; Roberts, Harms, Smith, Wood, & Webb, 2006; Roberts & Wood, 2006). It includes a reorganization of the basic units of analysis, a description of the typical patterns of continuity and change in personality over time, and the types of transactions found between persons and organizations. First, we will discuss the units of analysis in personality psychology.

The Units of Analysis

Fig. 1 depicts the primary domains in the neo-socioanalytic theory. The first thing to note about Fig. 1 is that there are four "units of analysis" or domains that make up the core of personality: traits, values/motives, abilities, and narratives. These four domains are intended to subsume most of the important categories of individual differences.

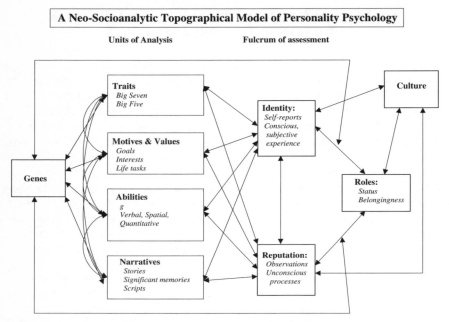

Fig. 1. A Seo-Socioanalytic Topographical Model of Personality Psychology.

The first domain, traits, is defined as the enduring patterns of thoughts, feelings, and behaviors that people exhibit. Much attention has been dedicated to finding a working taxonomy of traits, and many accept the Big Five, extraversion, agreeableness, conscientiousness, emotional stability, and openness to experience, as a minimal number of domains (Goldberg, 1993). Recent research has begun to show that the rush to accept the Big Five may be premature. The empirical foundation of the Big Five was based primarily on western samples. And, although the Big Five structure appears to replicate across many different cultures (McCrae & Costa, 1997), this finding is inconsequential because it was based on a measure designed only to assess the Big Five (e.g., the NEO-PI-R, Costa & McCrae, 1994). Alternatively, a meticulous examination of the structure of natural language lexicons that derive from many different cultures show that the Big Six (Ashton et al., 2004) or Multi-Language Seven (ML7; Saucier, 2003), may be better representations of the trait domain.

In terms of the Big Five, the Big Six or ML7 are not radical alternatives. Rather, these systems add one or two dimensions to the Big Five and, most importantly, shift the meaning of the Big Five slightly, but significantly. For example, in these systems agreeableness contrasts warmth and gentleness with hostility and aggressiveness, whereas in the typical Big Five System, hostility and aggressiveness are found on the negative end of emotional stability. Emotional stability also changes and contrasts insecurity and anxiousness with toughness and bravery. The latter are not part of emotional stability in the Big Five. Added to the Big Five are a positive evaluation or honesty factor (Ashton et al., 2004) and a global negative evaluation. Both of these dimensions would have obvious application to organizational issues, such as counterproductive work behaviors and performance feedback systems. Also, these additional dimensions bring two evaluative dimensions that are missing to the Big Five system. Finally, in contrast to the Big Five, the Big Six and ML-7 appear to replicate more readily across different cultures and emerge in both emic and etic approaches to scale development.

Values and motives constitute the second domain of personality. These dimensions reflect all of the things that people feel are desirable – that is, what people want to do or would like to have in their life. Thus, this category includes the classic notion of motives and needs (e.g., Murray, 1938), in addition to values, interests, preferences, and goals. This category is explicitly hierarchical, and the structure of goals and motives has been discussed by numerous researchers (Austin & Vancouver, 1996; Emmons, 1986). The hierarchy described here is unlike that proposed by Maslow (1968), in that it is one of conceptual breadth, rather than one of priorities. Maslow's theory, one of the foundations of the humanistic tradition in psychology and in organizational behavior, posits that people move systematically from lower-level needs, such as the need for safety, to higher-level needs, such as the need for self-actualization. Ostensibly people attempt to satisfy lower-order needs before moving on to higher-order needs. Maslow's theory has served as the basis for many influential perspectives in personality psychology and organizational behavior, presumably because of how optimistic and hopeful Maslow's version of human nature was in contrast to those found in psychoanalytic theory or behaviorism. Unfortunately, empirical tests of Maslow's theory have been equivocal at best, with many finding little support for the hierarchy (Wahba & Bridwell, 1976). This should not have been a great surprise, as reading Maslow's original writings (e.g., Maslow, 1968) shows that the need hierarchy is more of a prescription for human nature than a description. It represents Maslow's vision of what humans could be rather than how they are.

In contrast, the hierarchy proposed here is agnostic when it comes to the preference for which need, goal, or motive should have priority, and utilizes a hierarchical structure to indicate that some motivational components are broader and more inclusive than narrower components. Furthermore, if there are two thematically dominant needs they are not the need for safety or self-actualization but rather the need for status and the need for belonging (Hogan, 1982). Status motives subsume the desires for social status, money, fame, and social regard. Belongingness motives subsume desires to have a family, close friendships, and some form of identification with a social group or groups (Baumeister & Leary, 1995). Although clearly insufficient to capture the entire spectrum of values/motivation, it is also clear that these two dimensions show up across implicit motives (e.g., nPower, nAffiliation), explicit goals (Roberts & Robins, 2000), and values (Schwartz, 1992), and work values (Hofstede, Bond, & Luk, 1993). These motives are dominant over other needs because if satisfied, they provide the more basic needs. If one has a group to belong to and a position of importance in that community, then basic needs such as for food and safety are provided for. If a person lacks a supporting group, be it a family or community, then basic needs are much more difficult to come by.

The third domain reflects abilities and the hierarchical models identified by what people can do (Lubinski, 2000). Although still somewhat controversial, the hierarchical model of g, which subsumes verbal, quantitative, and spatial intelligence, is a widely accepted model that encompasses the majority of the domains of existing intelligence measures (Gray & Thompson, 2004). The hierarchical model of g clearly does not capture the full range of ability variables that are important for organizational functioning. For example, Ackerman's PPIK theory, integrates intelligence-as-process (e.g., g), personality, interest, and intelligence-as-knowledge (Ackerman & Heggestad, 1997). Tests of the PPIK model have shown that domain knowledge, though related to general intelligence, is also distinct (Rolfhus & Ackerman, 1999). Thus, people can develop domain-based abilities that are distinct from their general intelligence. This should be highly relevant to organizational studies, as expertise in specific domains can be shaped through training and practice.

The final domain focuses on the devices people employ to tell the stories and narratives they use to understand themselves and their environments (McAdams, 1993). A critical point to consider in any model of personality is that while individuals can be classified in terms of traits, goals, and abilities, they often (if not generally) communicate information about themselves quite differently than suggested by nomothetic classification systems. One common strategy is the use of illustrative stories (McAdams, 1993) or scripts (de St. Aubin, 1999). People find it very easy to tell stories about themselves, others, and their environments. These narratives, in turn, help people create meaning and purpose in their lives and predictability in the events they observe and experience, and provide explanations of how people have come to be in their present circumstances.

At first blush, narratives may appear to be superfluous fluff compared to traits, motives, and abilities, but this conclusion would be naive. First, the information gleaned from narratives is simply unavailable from the other approaches. The particular details about a person's life, reflected for example in concepts such as biodata in job interviews, have unknown ramifications for a person's experiences, accomplishments, and self-evaluations. For example, narratives of personal growth predict well-being above and beyond personality traits (Bauer & McAdams, 2004), suggesting that narrative information provides unique information in the prediction of self-evaluations.

Another reason not to dismiss the narrative component of personality is that it provides an avenue to successfully incorporate information at the level of an individual life. This is directly analogous to case study approaches in other fields, including organizational behavior. For example, case studies of organizational practices have illuminated many fundamental organizational principles and practices, including how organizations create meaning for their employees (Pratt, 2000). This type of information can and is used to create new understanding of human nature and organizations, to test theories, and to simply add new information to our science. Narrative information provides a direct conduit to the phenomenology of everyday life, which is simply not captured in other approaches to personality assessment.

The components of personality are both manifested and organized around two psychological and methodological entities: identity (or self-reports) and reputation (observer reports). From a methodological perspective, there are two privileged, yet flawed ways to access information about people – what they say about themselves and what others say about them. Personality inventories represent typical self-report methods. This category also includes basic trait ratings, self-concept measures, such as self-esteem, as well as measures of goals and values. Observer methods encompass observer ratings of behavior, projective tests, implicit measures, and even physiological tests. Typically, self-reports are derogated for being biased by response sets, such as social desirability responding (cf. Piedmont, McCrae, Riemann, & Angleitner, 2000). Observer methods are afforded greater respect within personality psychology, but in I/O psychology where they are used more often, it is widely known that they suffer from biases such as halo error (Viswesvaran, Schmidt, & Ones, 2005). When researchers bother to assess both self-reports and observer ratings of personality, they often find that both perspectives predict organizational outcomes (Mount, Barrick, & Strauss, 1994).

These two methods of assessment correspond to two global psychological constructs, identity and reputation, which have meaning above and beyond the methods themselves. Identity reflects the sum total of opinions that are cognitively available to a person across the four units of analysis described above. The first domain of these cognitions would be the content of identity – whether a person considers themselves shy or creative, for example. Identity also pertains to the metacognitive perception of those same self-perceptions. Specifically, people can simultaneously see themselves as "outgoing" and a "carpenter" (content) and feel more or less confident and invested (metaperception) in those self-perceptions.

This conceptualization of identity is both consistent with and different from classic social psychological perspectives on social identity (e.g., Stryker & Serpe, 1982). Similar to social identity theory, it is assumed that the content of identity is shaped by social interactions and that these interactions are organized according to specific social categories, such as roles (Tajfel & Turner, 1979). Clearly, organizations provide a context in which work roles are structured and defined. Role experiences should affect people's experiences and thus their self-perceptions (Salancik & Pfeffer, 1978). For example, organizations can affect the symbols used in work roles and their significance, which in turn should affect the content of identity (Pratt & Rafaeli, 1997). Similarly, receiving different versions of the symbolic white coat is used to mark status transitions in the process of moving from a medical student to a full-fledged doctor. Presumably, receiving these symbols facilitates shifts in a medical student's identity.

Where the neo-socioanalytic conceptualization of identity adds to the conceptualization offered by social identity theory is in the assumption that traits also cause the content of identity. On its face, this is not a radical departure from social identity theory. For example, there is no reason why a person cannot retain an identity over time in a dispositional fashion. A person may come to see herself as a "tough worker" because of experiencing a highly competitive work environment. This new self-perception may perpetuate simply because the person remains in the environment. Nonetheless, we would propose that something more than social context is needed to understand a person's experience at work and that internal, temperament factors are additional influences on variation in social identity. Specifically, underlying trait-like patterns derive in part from genetic and physiological factors that contribute to continuity over time (Johnson, McGue, & Krueger, 2005). These underlying physiological systems may provide a strong countervailing force against the influence of the environment. For example, a dispositionally inhibited, or shy individual, may always have a readiness to respond to social interactions with reticence, despite social pressures to do otherwise.

A second feature of the neo-socioanalytic framework that is distinct from most personality, social cognitive, and social identity theories is the inclusion of reputation. Reputation is the perspective on the part of others about a person's traits, motives, abilities, and narratives. Consistent with the "looking glass self," reputation is conceptualized as affecting identity. People will come to see themselves differently depending on how other people define them. On the other hand, underlying dispositions can affect reputation directly without being mediated through identity. This reflects the fact that people are not always aware of their own behavior and that others may see patterns in their behavior that they do not. Given the arrow pointing from identity to reputation, we also propose that people actively shape their reputation. It is a fact of social interaction that people do not share all of their self-perceptions and actively attempt to persuade others of their desirable qualities (Goffman, 1959). Reputations are clearly important from an organizational perspective. People are hired, fired, promoted, and demoted, in part, because of their reputation. Presumably, the better a person is at managing their reputation, the better they should do in an organization.

Social roles also play a prominent function in our model and serve to explicitly incorporate the social environment (Hogan & Roberts, 2000). Social roles tend to fall in two broad domains that correspond closely to the two primary motives highlighted above: Status and belongingness roles. Status roles encompass work and social position roles, such as being a CEO, supervisor, PTA president, and so forth. Belongingness roles encompass friendship, family, and community roles, such as being a father, mother, and friend. Although, work is often associated with status hierarchies, both status and belongingness roles can be found within work. Clearly, the person who aspires for and achieves the CEO position has acquired a high-status role. On the other hand, many friendships are made and fostered through work and serve to provide meaning and support even within a network of relationships in which status is so salient.

Integrating Stable Dispositions and Variable Behaviors, Thoughts, and Feelings

One of the challenges for this framework is to successfully address the question of how behaviors can change from situation to situation, but still

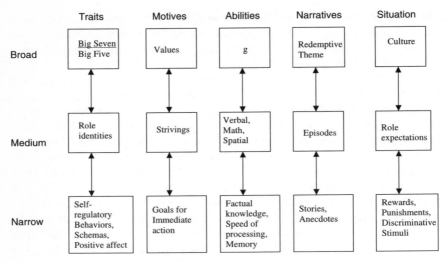

Fig. 2. A Hierarchical Model of Personality and Situation.

be trait-like. It is useful to distill these issues through a hierarchical structure (Roberts & Pomerantz, 2004). Specifically personality constructs and situational constructs can be ordered from broad to narrow (see Fig. 2). For example, on the person side of the equation, traits are often considered broad constructs because they entail aggregation of thoughts, feelings, and behaviors across many situations. Implicit in this idea is that the trait is a broader concept than specific behaviors, thoughts, and feelings. That is, from the top down, one can see that behavior is a reflection of the trait. From the bottom up, one can see the behavior as a constituent element of the superordinate trait. What is most important about making the hierarchy explicit is that it clearly shows that traits are not isomorphic with thoughts, feelings, and behaviors. Traits reflect the common variance among representative thoughts, feelings, and behaviors. In turn, thoughts, feelings, and behaviors are most likely overdetermined. That is, many factors, including traits, motives, and the situation may influence whether thoughts, feelings, and behaviors happen.

The classic form of the trait hierarchy may be traced to Eysenck's (1970) multi-level personality structure, where supertraits (e.g., extraversion) can be decomposed into intercorrelated but conceptually distinct narrower traits (e.g., sociability, activity, excitability). These narrower traits are made up of habits, which in turn are related to "stimulus–response" patterns, or what might be described as the behaviors manifested in specific situations. What is interesting about the classic trait hierarchy is the unwillingness to discuss the role of context in the definition of the hierarchy. For example, the differences between extraversion and its constituent elements of sociability and dominance is context. Extraversion is typically a generic term applying to most if not all social situations and whether a person acts in an agentic fashion in these situations. On the other hand, sociability is particular to benign social settings and dominance is particular to power situations. Individual differences in a person's level of gregariousness (sociability) can be best seen in informal social settings, like in a group of friends or at a party. Individual differences in dominance can be best seen in social settings where power is being exchanged. For example, when a person asserts themselves at a work meeting in which their performance will dictate their future pay and position, this is an act of dominance. Of course, people can act sociable in power settings and act dominant in social settings, but these actions are less common and may even be punished by one's social group – no one likes a person who cannot turn it off when he gets to the bar.

As an alternative to the classic trait hierarchy, we recently proposed the Personality Role-Identity Structural Model (PRISM; Wood & Roberts, 2006). The PRISM largely parallels the structure of a trait hierarchy, in that the PRISM can be thought of as a hierarchy with multiple levels of varying breadth: (a) the *general identity*, representing how the person sees oneself in general, (b) *role identities*, which represent perceptions of narrower, context-specific dispositions (e.g., "how I see myself as a worker"), (c) aggregated role outcomes, such as general thoughts, feelings, and behavioral patterns occurring within the role, and (d) single occurrences of outcomes occurring in a given role. Research has shown repeatedly that people see systematic differences in themselves across various roles (Donahue & Harary, 1998; Roberts & Donahue, 1994; Wood & Roberts, in press) and that using lower-order constructs, like role-identities improves predictive validity (Roberts & Donahue, 1994).

As noted earlier in this chapter, and as shown in Fig. 2, each of the major domains of personality and social situations can be organized hierarchically. For example, values may be seen as a broad manifestation of motives, as they represent relatively decontextualized principles of what is deemed desirable. Strivings, which tend to be concrete manifestations of broad principles enacted in a short time frame, are excellent examples of mid-level constructs (Emmons, 1986). At the lowest level would be goals for actions in the present situation (Ford & Nichols, 1987). Similar hierarchical organizations of abilities and narratives are also possible. For example, the act of telling stories is often constrained to specific episodes and is also tailored to one's audience (Fiese, Hooker, Kotary, Schwagler, & Rimmer, 1995).[2]

Unlike many theories of personality, we also view the situation hierarchically. Broad situations are represented with concepts such as culture in a country or social climate in a community (Bronfrenbrenner, 1979). Medium-level situational factors can be represented as role-based phenomena, such as role expectations, which are the demands others have for how we should act in certain social roles. At the lowest level of breadth, we would find the concrete discriminative stimuli, rewards, or punishers, which shape behavior.

How does this hierarchical elaboration address the apparent contradiction of changing behavior and stable dispositions? Most situationally driven research, such as that focusing on the effect of experimental manipulations, is focused at the lower level of abstraction on specific types of thoughts, feelings, or behaviors (Roberts & Pomerantz, 2004). Researchers studying personality traits, on the other hand, focus on aggregations of thoughts, feelings, and behaviors across many situations. This is one reason why trait psychologists and those who study the effect of experiments appear to talk past one another. They study similar phenomena at different levels of abstraction. Specifically, behaviors are both outcomes of traits and causes of traits. Moreover, the effect of the situation on a trait, which directly impacts behavior, is mediated by one or more layers of the hierarchy. Thus, the effect of a situation on a trait is filtered and diluted. A simple change in behavior will not result in change to a trait, which reflects a broad aggregation of behaviors across many situations. Rather, a change in behavior will register like a rock thrown into a pond. The changing behavior may cause a ripple in the surface of the pond, but is unlikely to affect the depth of the water. Likewise, the effect of a trait on a situationally constrained behavior is filtered through multiple levels and therefore its effect is watered down. Because of the multiple levels of breadth that a trait must move through, it is reasonable to assume that the relationship between behavior and a disposition should be modest at best.

Take Fig. 3 as an example. Fig. 3 shows a hypothetical scenario detailing the relationship between work experiences and the trait of conscientiousness (Roberts, in press). In this example, the woman has taken her first job right out of high school or college. The new work role brings with it a press to work harder than she did in school. These changes in behavior may be noted and integrated into her identity, but these changes would not necessarily affect the inferences associated with the trait of conscientiousness. Rather, they would first affect the role identity of conscientiousness. That is, this

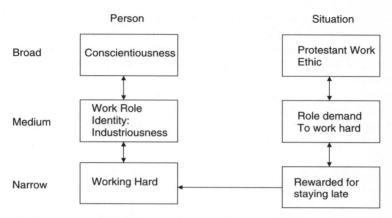

Fig. 3. A Hierarchical Model of the Work Socialization Process.

new employee may, after a few weeks of demanding work and active effort to match these demands, come to see herself as a "hard worker" but not necessarily as "industrious" (Wood & Roberts, 2006). Over time, with more consistent experiences, a person may internalize and generalize these lower-level attributions into something broader, like a dispositional inference. For example, observing oneself doing something different is one of the key mechanisms of the learning generalization hypothesis, in which it is proposed that work experiences are internalized and then generalized to other domains (Kohn & Schooler, 1978). For example, people may see themselves acting more intellectual at work, and by doing so come to see themselves as more intellectual, and then generalize this change by adopting more intellectually engaging hobbies, such as chess.

This integration of the topographical neo-socioanalytic model and the hierarchical model in Fig. 2 also helps to identify many of the mechanisms responsible for personality change that we have outlined elsewhere (Caspi & Roberts, 1999; Roberts & Caspi, 2003; Roberts & Wood, 2006). For example, role expectations are embedded in the roles that people acquire. They act as discriminative stimuli, signaling to people what behaviors are called for in specific contexts. Presumably, acting in accordance with role expectations can lead to change in personality (Roberts, Wood, & Smith, 2005). Feedback mechanisms in which people are told how to change or how they are acting also come as part of a role. For example, supervisors provide concrete messages concerning which behaviors are acceptable and unacceptable. Presumably, supervisors also have the power to administer rewards for certain behaviors (raises), and punishment for other behaviors (demotions and firings). One of the key mediators of the influence of expectations and contingencies on change in personality may be the extent to which the job and the people communicating expectations and contingencies are well liked (Roberts & Wood, 2006). For example, children tend to respond more willingly to parental expectations for probity when the child has a more positive relationship with the parent (Kochanska & Murray, 2000). Likewise, the ability of supervisors to influence the long-term behavior patterns of their protégés may be dependent on whether they are liked by their subordinates. Similarly, peers may have more power to influence their friends if they are well liked.

Countering these change processes are mechanisms on the person side of the equation that might inoculate or nullify the press to change. For example, to the extent that top–down heuristic processing takes place, certain people may not notice or acknowledge the press to change because they will lack the schemas to register the press (Roberts & Caspi, 2003). Alternatively, people may use more active means to avoid changing by avoiding the situation, or using more strategic information processing mechanisms, like undermining the change message by painting the person pressing for change as unskilled or ignorant. Of course, more psychodynamic processes are possible as people may simply deny the press for change or project the press back to the messenger (see Roberts & Caspi, 2003; Roberts & Wood, 2006, for a full description of these mechanisms).

In summary, the neo-socioanalytic framework, brings together the full range of individual differences and provides a clear conduit for understanding how social contexts will affect those dispositions. In addition, one can locate many of the core issues within OB in the interface between role and identity. Organizational climate dictates the nature of the roles experienced at work (Haslam, Alexander, Postmes, & Ellemers, 2003). Job design reflects how one's work role is configured by the organization (Ilgen & Hollenbeck, 1991). PO fit reflects how well one's attributes fit with the role defined by the organization (Chatman, 1991). Of course, leadership is a role. Probably more relevant to most people is the role of follower – a relatively understudied phenomena. Needless to say, this model affords us the opportunity to see a constructive interface between the two fields. Based on this conceptualization, personality affects organizational phenomena and is affected by organizational experiences. If this is the case, we should see systematic relationships between personality and organizational factors. For example, as we will see below, we should find that certain personality traits will affect organizational outcomes and that organizational experiences should be related to changes in personality traits.

PERSONALITY DEVELOPMENT IN THE NEO-SOCIOANALYTIC FRAMEWORK

Before we embark on a description of the relations between people and organizations it is important to understand how people develop in terms of personality traits across adulthood. If there is no continuity in personality traits, then it would be clear that the relationship would be a one-way street from organization to person. If there is no change in personality, then we would expect the opposite – personality should only affect organizational experiences. Understanding the overall patterns of continuity and change in personality provides a foundation on which the subsequent study of person–environment transactions can be understood.

Continuity is most often indexed by correlations between personality scores across two points in time (i.e., test–retest correlations). These differential, or rank-order stability correlations, reflect the degree to which the relative ordering of individuals on a given trait is maintained over time. Our recent meta-analysis of the rank-order stability of personality (organized according to the Five-Factor Model) revealed six major conclusions (Roberts & DelVecchio, 2000): Test–retest correlations over time (a) are moderate in magnitude, even from childhood to early adulthood. (b) Rank-order stability increases with age. Test–retest correlations (unadjusted for measurement error) increased from 0.41 in childhood to 0.55 at age 30, and then reached a plateau around 0.70 between ages 50 and 70. Rank-order consistency (c) decreases as the time interval between observations increases, and does not vary markedly (d) across the Big Five traits nor (e) according to assessment method (i.e., self-reports, observer ratings, and projective tests), or (f) by gender.

Several observations can be drawn from this meta-analysis. First, the magnitude of rank-order consistency, although not unity, is still remarkably high. The only psychological constructs more consistent than personality traits are measures of cognitive ability (Schuerger & Witt, 1989). Second, the level of continuity in childhood and adolescence is much higher than originally expected (Lewis, 1999), especially after age three. Even more impressive is the fact that the level of stability increases in a relatively linear fashion through adolescence and young adulthood. Young adulthood has been described as demographically dense, in that it involves more life-changing roles and identity decisions than any other period in the life course (Arnett, 2000). Yet, despite these dramatic contextual changes, personality differences remain remarkably consistent during this time period. Third, personality continuity in adulthood peaks later than expected. According to one prominent perspective, personality traits are essentially fixed and unchanging after age 30 (McCrae & Costa, 1994). However, the meta-analytic findings show that rank-order consistency peaks some time after age 50, but at a level well below unity. Finally, the levels of consistency found in this recent meta-analysis replicated smaller studies dating back to the early part of the 20th century. There have been few if any cohort shifts in the level of rank-order stability in personality traits in recent history.

The obvious question that arises from this meta-analysis is why does personality consistency increase with age? There are several obvious candidate mechanisms embedded in the neo-socioanalytic model. For example, genetic and environmental factors have been implicated in maintaining personality continuity over time (Fraley & Roberts, 2005). The best evidence for the role of genes in maintaining consistency has been provided by longitudinal studies that track monozygotic and dizygotic twins over time. For example, McGue et al. (1993) administered personality tests to monozygotic and dyzygotic twins over a 10-year period. Their estimates of overall consistency were similar to other studies (ranging from 0.4 to 0.7) showing that there was a balance of consistency and change. Most interestingly, the authors estimated that 80% of the personality consistency demonstrated by their sample of twins was attributable to genetic influences (see also, Johnson, McGue, & Krueger, 2005).

Of course, the environment itself has often been invoked to explain consistency. Presumably, people experience more consistent environments as they age and this, in turn, should promote greater continuity over time (Mischel, 1968). Unfortunately, there are very few studies that directly test this idea. There is some indirect evidence. For example, a longitudinal study of adult twins showed that a significant portion of continuity in personality traits over time was attributable to shared environmental experiences (Johnson et al., 2005). Unfortunately, like many twin studies, the actual environment was not assessed, so a direct test of the idea was not provided. In contrast, there is a tremendous amount of evidence to the contrary. For example, the level of rank-order stability in a study of American college students going through little or no serious environmental transitions (Robins, Fraley, Roberts, & Trzesniewski, 2001) was identical to the rank-order stability found in a heterogeneous sample of New Zealanders, most of whom made major shifts from their family of origin to independent living (Roberts, Caspi, & Moffitt, 2001). The evidence for environmental consistency promoting personality consistency is weak at best.

Identity development is another factor that has been proposed as a contributor to increasing personality continuity with age (Roberts & Caspi,

2003). With age, the process of developing, committing to, and maintaining an identity leads to greater personality consistency (Roberts & Caspi, 2003). Implicit in this idea is the process of finding one's niche. People will select roles that on their face appear to fit with their dispositions, values, and abilities and this selection process should facilitate continuity over time (Roberts & DelVecchio, 2000). Assuming that most roles will not fit perfectly, people will be motivated to shape the features of their roles so that they do fit better than before. Thus, through building an optimal or satisfying niche, people will inevitably create an environment that facilitates continuity over time.

Although one's identity is made up of constituent elements, such as traits and goals, it also consists of meta-cognitive elements which reflect people's perceptions of their own attributes. For example, with age people become clearer about their own personality attributes, interests, abilities, and life story (Helson, Stewart, & Ostrove, 1995). This increase in identity clarity may also contribute to increasing consistency with age. For example, having an achieved identity was found to be related to higher levels of psychological well-being (Helson et al., 1995). Identity achievement has also been shown to be related to higher levels of self-esteem, autonomy, and moral reasoning, and to lower levels of anxiety (see Marcia, 1980). Therefore, identity, and aspects of identity – such as achievement, are linked to higher levels of psychological well-being and adjustment, which in turn are related to higher levels of personality trait consistency (Roberts & Caspi, 2003).

Having a well-developed identity may promote other personality consistency mechanisms. For example, to the extent that a person's identity becomes known to others in the form of a reputation (Hogan & Roberts, 2000), other people may react to a person in a way that is consistent with his or her personality. For example, if a person has a reputation of being outgoing, other people may invite him or her to social engagements more often. Or, if a person has a reputation for being domineering, others may avoid that person or act submissive in his or her presence, which in turn engenders more domineering behavior.

The existence of rank-order stability does not preclude other types of change (see Block, 1971). For example, populations can shift up or down on a personality trait, even when there is perfect rank-order stability (Caspi & Roberts, 1999). Given this possibility, we conducted a second meta-analysis of longitudinal studies of mean-level change in personality traits (Roberts et al., 2006). We examined patterns of change across 92 different longitudinal studies covering the life course from age 10 to 101. Across these studies, we found that people became more socially dominant (a facet of extraversion), especially in young adulthood. They became more conscientious and emotionally stable through midlife. Although much of the change on agreeableness was positive, the increase was only statistically significant in old age. Finally, we found that individuals demonstrated gains in social vitality (a second facet of extraversion) and openness to experience in adolescence and then equivalent declines in old age for both of these trait domains. Clearly, change in personality traits is possible at all ages of the life course, with the preponderance of change occurring in young adulthood from ages 20 to 40.

Much like the meta-analysis of longitudinal consistency, several factors conspicuously did not affect patterns of mean-level change across the life course. First, men and women did not differ in their patterns of mean-level change in personality traits. Although reliable sex differences exist on several personality trait dimensions (Feingold, 1994), it appears that there are no reliable sex differences in the way these traits develop over time. Interestingly, like rank-order consistency, time had a positive effect on change in mean-levels. That is, longitudinal studies that follow participants for a longer period of time tend to report higher mean-level change estimates.

We also we found that cohort standing was related to differential patterns of mean-level change. Younger cohorts had larger standardized mean-level changes in terms of social dominance. The changes in social dominance were consistent with the cross-sectional patterns which indicate that younger cohorts are more assertive (e.g., Twenge, 2001). In addition, we found curvilinear relationships between cohort standing and both agreeableness and conscientiousness. This pattern indicated that studies focusing on samples drawn from the 1950s and 1960s tended not to increase as much as samples drawn from before and after this period of the 20th century, a pattern first identified by Helson, Jones, and Kwan (2002). These cohort findings point to the importance both of social context and the more inclusive social climate or culture of the people living in a particular period of history. Presumably, social climate affects the way roles are enacted and the behaviors rewarded in those roles, which then affects personality trait development (see Fig. 1).

Of course, rank-order consistency and mean-level change are not the only ways in which to track continuity and change (Caspi & Roberts, 1999). Continuity and change in the factor structure of personality traits over time can be examined, as well as individual differences in change. The latter reflects the fact that each person may have his or her own unique pattern of change despite the population level trends captured in global indices, such as rank-order consistency and mean-level change. Individual differences in personality trait change are especially relevant to the interface of the person and organization. As organizational experiences are particular to each individual, the assumption would be that distinct organizational experiences will be related to, if not the cause of unique patterns of personality trait change. Therefore correlations between individual differences in personality trait change and organizationally base experiences would both support the idea of individual differences in change and the idea that organizational experiences are critical predictors of those changes. As we will see below, it appears that these patterns exist.

PERSONALITY DEVELOPMENT AND ORGANIZATIONAL EXPERIENCES

Within the neo-socioanalytic framework, personality traits and organizational experiences are in constant transaction across the life span. To better understand how these transactions affect development, I will build upon Schneider's attraction–selection–attrition model (ASA; Schneider, Smith, Taylor, & Fleenor, 1998). In this model, organizations become more homogeneous over time because people with common characteristics seek out organizations that will reward their proclivities. In turn, organizations seek out individuals who match the culture of the organization and will hire individuals with a certain personality in disproportionate numbers. Finally, people who do not fit in with the organizational culture will have a tendency to leave the organization, accentuating the homogeneity effect.

Although, clearly more comprehensive and dynamic than most models of person–organization transactions, this model overlooks several ways of interacting with organizations that dovetail with the developmental patterns we see in personality traits. For example, in the original ASA model there is little room for people to change either themselves or their organization. That is to say, that the ASA framework overlooks socialization processes and any attempts made by the individual to shape their work to better suit their needs. To capture these types of transactions requires that we add two more ways of transacting with organizations, transformation and manipulation, resulting in the ASTMA model of person–organization transactions (attraction, selection, transformation, manipulation, and attrition). Transformation refers to the fact that people may be changed by their organizational experiences. Manipulation, on the other hand, reflects the fact that people are not helpless in the face of organizational demands. Consciously or unconsciously they may attempt to shape their organizational experiences in order to maximize fit. Thus, they will change the organization at the level of their interactions. Below, I will review evidence for each step of the ASTMA model and how transactions in each step will play out in terms of personality development. I should note that though the model is sequential in its structure, it is clear that individuals spiral through these steps many times within an organizational experience and can skip stages or slightly change their order (e.g., manipulation before transformation).

Attraction and Selection: How do Personality Traits Affect Organizational Outcomes?

One of the consistent themes across organizational, social, developmental, and personality psychology is the perspective that people actively seek out situations that fit with their personality (Snyder & Ickes, 1985). Of course, organizations are not simply unwitting victims of the selection process. They, in turn, will seek to select individuals who share certain qualities that they believe match their climate or value system (Schneider et al., 1998). For example, selection of workers into management positions appears to be dictated early in the employment process when an individual gains the reputation of being a good performer (Graen, Novak, & Summerkamp, 1982).

One of the best ways to test for attraction and selection effects is to see if personality traits, or other units of personality, predict organizational experiences later in life. This test requires longitudinal data in which people have been followed, preferably for many decades. Fortunately, there are now a handful of longitudinal studies in which this type of question has been addressed. Some of the longest running longitudinal studies of this sort are those housed in the Institute of Human Development at U.C. Berkeley (Eichorn, Clausen, Haan, Honzik, & Mussen, 1981). One of the most well-known organizational studies to come out of these data is Staw, Bell, and Clausen's (1986) study showing that dispositional affect measured in early adolescence predicted job attitudes in young adulthood and middle age. Thus, happy people tend to be more satisfied in their jobs. This study sparked a resurgence in research on the role of individual differences in organizations, reestablishing the possibility that personality traits influence work outcomes (Schneider & Smith, 2004).

Several additional studies drawn from the IHD data have demonstrated equally impressive selection effects. For example, participants from the IHD samples who were ill-tempered as children had more erratic work lives in young adulthood and were less successful according to objective indicators of occupational attainment (Caspi, Elder, & Bem, 1987). Analogously, participants who were shyer in childhood initiated their careers at a later age (Caspi, Elder, & Bem, 1988). Recently, Judge et al. (1999) used the IHD data to test how adolescent Big Five scores and measures of cognitive ability predicted occupational attainment and satisfaction in late middle age – a time span of 46 years. Despite the four-decade gap between the assessment of personality and occupational attainment, they found that participants who were more conscientious and extraverted and less neurotic and agreeable were more successful in their careers in late middle age. In addition, these effects were independent of cognitive ability, which also predicted success.

Similar findings have emerged from the Mills Longitudinal Study of women. In this study, a group of women deemed to be creative in college was followed for 40 years along with a control group of women who were not nominated as creative. In one study, measures of personality assessed in college were used to predict occupational creativity at age 52 (Helson, Roberts, & Agronick, 1995). Occupational creativity was defined as being in a prestigious occupation that was also categorized as artistic on Holland's RIASEC system (Holland, 1985). A number of personality traits predicted this outcome 30 years later, but the best predictor was the creative temperament scale, which correlated 0.49 with success in creative careers 30 years later (Helson et al., 1995). Moreover, this effect remained quite high even when controlling for the influence of cognitive ability.

In a recent longitudinal study following a sample of New Zealanders from age 18 to 26, we replicated many of these effects and extended the analysis to a broader set of occupational outcomes (Roberts et al., 2003). In addition to the standard outcome of occupational attainment and job satisfaction, we examined who acquired more resource power (control of hiring, firing, and salary changes), who was more involved in their work, who had stronger feelings of financial security, who had more autonomy at work (decision latitude), and who were more stimulated by their work (learning new things on the job). We found that adolescents who scored high on neuroticism experienced a turbulent and unsuccessful transition into the world of work. By age 26, they occupied lower prestige jobs, were less satisfied with their jobs, and reported difficulties in paying bills and making ends meet. Adolescents who scored high on traits from the domain of sociability/agreeableness had the opposite experience. By age 26, according to multiple measures, they achieved work success, experienced fewer financial problems, and were happier in their jobs. They also acquired more stimulating work by age 26. It appears that, at least in the case of young New Zealanders, nice men and women do not finish last. The predictive correlates of extraversion were similar to agreeableness, with one exception: By age 26, adolescents who were more socially dominant also achieved more resource power. As they entered the world of work, adolescents who were forceful and decisive, fond of leadership roles, and willing to work hard rose to positions where they had direct control over other people. Adolescents who scored high on traits from the domain of conscientiousness were more likely than other adolescents to achieve higher occupational attainment, to be satisfied with their job, to evidence higher levels of work commitment, and to be financially independent. These findings are consistent with previous research demonstrating the importance of traits from the domain of conscientiousness to work outcomes (Judge et al., 1999). The strongest pattern of relations with conscientiousness-related traits was with work involvement, indicating that conventional adolescents with good impulse control make stronger emotional and psychological commitments to their work than other adolescents.

Most of these studies focused on individual achievement and not organizational-level variables. Two recent longitudinal studies have examined the intersection of personality and one of the mainstays of organizational psychology – person–organization fit. According to theoretical models of person–organization fit, individuals should be drawn to and thrive in the environments that share their characteristics (Chatman, 1991). Thus, rather than expecting a universal pattern of predictions from personality traits, the predictive relationships between personality and PO fit should be driven by the nature of the organization itself. For example, it should not be the case that all emotionally stable people fit well in an environment. Rather, if the organization calls for and values emotional stability, then people who are emotionally stable should fit better with that organization. Consistent with this perspective, different personality traits predicted fit in different organizations. In the first study, the organization was a university and the culture was described as unsupportive and competitive. Based on this description, it was expected that fit would be related to emotional stability and low agreeableness and this is what was found (Roberts & Robins, 2004). In the second study, the organization was also a university, but one described by students as valuing intellectual pursuits and the expansion of knowledge and insight. Consistent with this value system, students who were more open to experience fit better with the university's organizational culture (Harms, Roberts, & Winter, in press).

These studies leave little doubt that personality traits help to shape the types of organizational experiences people have across their life course. Of course, it is unclear how these relationships play out and whether organizations are being selected or are selecting the individuals. Obviously, these two processes are not mutually exclusive. Interestingly, if these mechanisms are in place across the life course, we should find that PO fit should increase with age, a hypothesis that has yet to be tested.

Transformation: How do Experiences in Organizations Affect Personality Traits?

Complementing the findings that organizational experiences are in part dictated by personality traits, a number of studies have shown that the reverse is also true. Experiences in social organizations appear to promote change in personality traits. Analogous to the type of study needed to find support for the attraction and selection effects, a particular type of longitudinal analysis is necessary to infer a relationship between organizational experiences and change in personality. Specifically, one needs a longitudinal study in which organizational experiences are tracked over time and personality traits are assessed at least twice. Assessing personality multiple times allows one to track change in personality over time and to control for the selection effects we described above. The majority of studies described below utilized this type of design.

For example, men who achieved more than their fathers became more dependable and responsible, independent, and motivated for success over time (Elder, 1969). Mortimer and Lorence (1979) reported that men who experienced greater autonomy in work increased in competence in the 10-year period following graduation from college. Brousseau and Prince (1981) found that job characteristics were related to changes in personality in a longitudinal study of male engineers. Specifically, being called upon to use a wider variety of skills on the job was related to increases in emotional stability and task significance was related to increases in social dominance.

Several studies have also examined the relation between work experiences and personality change in women. Women who had high labor force participation increased in self-confidence from adolescence to midlife (Clausen & Gilens, 1990). Similarly, women who achieved higher levels of occupational attainment in work tended to increase on achievement, responsibility, and self-control; demonstrating that more continuous investment in work is related to increases in facets from the domain of conscientiousness (Roberts, 1997). Interestingly, despite the "dispositional" nature of job satisfaction, experiencing more satisfying work is related to changes in personality traits.

Specifically, work satisfaction is associated with increases in measures of emotional stability (Roberts & Chapman, 2000).

In our study of the relationship between work experiences and personality traits described above (Roberts et al., 2003), we also tested whether work experiences were related to changes in personality traits. We found that the pattern of associations between work experiences and change in personality was strongest for traits from the domains of neuroticism and extraversion. Young adults decreased faster in neuroticism if they were in higher-status jobs that were more satisfying and if they achieved financial security. Similarly, young adults increased in facets of extraversion if they were in higher status, more satisfying jobs that provided enough money to make ends meet. Moreover, increases in social dominance, a facet of extraversion, were also associated with experiencing more resource power and greater work involvement. Young adults who gained power became more confident and harder working. Finally, young adults increased on facets of conscientiousness if they were more involved in their jobs and financially secure.

In our longitudinal studies we have also found that PO fit is related to change in personality. In the first study in which the university called for emotional stability and disagreeableness, higher levels of fit over time were related to increases in emotional stability and decreases in agreeableness (Roberts & Robins, 2004). In the second study in which the university called for openness to experience we found that higher levels of fit over time were related to increases in openness (Harms et al., in press).

Because all of these studies are passive longitudinal studies, it is impossible to discern the exact causal direction of the transactions between persons and organizations. We can conclude only that change in personality is associated with work experiences. This leaves two possible interpretations. First, changes in personality may be causing people to achieve more or have different experiences at work. For example, becoming more dominant may lead to choosing to fight for positions of power and acquiring them. Second, life experiences may actually be changing personality traits. At this point in time, this conclusion can be preferred only through the examination of indirect factors. For example, we know from intervention studies that personality traits can be changed, often close to a half of standard deviation over relatively short periods of time (De Fruyt, Leeuwen, Bagby, Rolland, & Rouillon, 2006). Moreover, there are studies examining other life experiences, such as marriage and antisocial activities that have been shown to have prospective effects on change in personality traits (Roberts & Bogg, 2004). Unfortunately, at this point in time, the appropriate intervention study or passive longitudinal study examining work experiences has yet to be run in order to substantiate the inference that work experiences are actually causing change in personality traits.

If one looks across the predictive and change relationships found in many of the longitudinal studies that we have described, a systematic pattern emerges. The traits that "selected" people into specific work experiences, whatever the process, were the same traits that changed in response to those same work experiences. We have described this pattern as "corresponsive" and believe that this is the most probable type of personality change that occurs over the life course (Roberts & Caspi, 2003; Roberts & Wood, 2006). That is, life experiences do not impinge themselves on people in a random fashion causing widespread transformation in personality structure. Rather, the traits that people already possess will be deepened and elaborated by trait-correlated experiences.

Manipulation and Attrition: The Understudied Phenomena

The last two ways people may interface with an organization would be by changing their organization and/or leaving their organization. Presumably, both would result in greater continuity in personality over time. In terms of changing an organization, one would assume that the organization would be changed in order to better match a person's personality or to match their ideal vision, which would presumably reflect their personality. Two mechanisms are most likely involved in this process. First, one way in which an organization would change is through "evocative" processes (Caspi & Roberts, 1999). That is, people tend to evoke personality consistent responses from others, and this process can occur outside of conscious awareness. For example, aggression typically evokes hostility from others (Dodge & Tomlin, 1987), which would convince the aggressive person that it was a "dog-eat-dog" world and reinforce his aggressive tendencies. Presumably, adding an aggressive person to an organization would change the organization to become a more aggressive place because of these reciprocal processes. Likewise, dominant behavior is typically responded to with submissive responses (Thorne, 1987). Thus, a dominant person, by evoking more submissive responses from others would find their perception that they are leadership material reinforced. As people make up the primary interface with an organization, presumably evocative transactions would largely define the way in which an organization is experienced and how it would be changed over time. Moreover, since personality traits appear to change with age, a person's organizational experience may change in concert with these developmental trends. If a group of workers becomes more conscientious over time, then these personality changes may translate into changes in their work experiences and their work environment.

The second way in which a person may "manipulate" the organization is to change it in some way over time. Influencing the organization can occur from the bottom up or the top down. For example, leaders have tremendous power to shape the nature of the organization by hiring, firing, and promoting individuals. Through these perquisites of power, a person can wield tremendous influence over the culture of an organization from the top down. For example, cross-sectional studies of groups have shown that leader's conscientiousness and cognitive ability affect decision making and treatment of subordinates (LePine, Hollenbeck, Ilgen, & Hedlund, 1997). Presumably over a long period of time, these qualities of a leader would affect the culture and climate of an organization.

Of course, most people do not wield much power and their attempts to change their organization have gone unexamined. In fact, more often than not, organizations are treated as static entities that do not change over time. Rather, they are the socializing agents, not the target of socialization. In contrast, the idea of job crafting (Wrzesniewski & Dutton, 2001) or job sculpting (Bell & Staw, 1989) reflects the perspective that individuals are active agents in their relationships to organizations. They can affect change in their day-to-day work experience from the bottom up through changing the tasks they do, organizing their work differently, or changing the nature of the relationships they maintain with others (Wrzesniewski & Dutton, 2001). Unfortunately, none of these ideas has been tested in a true longitudinal study in which the organization can be seen shifting over time.

In fact, there is a surprising paucity of research examining continuity and change in the psychological meaning of organizational characteristics over time. However, in a recent study, we provided one of the first glimpses into how perceptions of an organization can and do change over time (Harms et al., in press). As noted above, in this study perceptions of the ideal and actual university environment were tracked over a four-year period for a large group of Harvard undergraduates. Although not a direct reflection of evocative or manipulative strategies of changing an organization, these perceptions do constitute one of the few instances when the perception of an organization on psychologically meaningful constructs has been tracked in a longitudinal study. The resulting patterns are at least informative for addressing the question of whether there are changes in perceptions of the organization over time. Surprisingly, we found several large changes for perceptions of the presses in the environment over time, while the changes in corresponding needs were found less often and to a smaller degree. That is, people were more likely to change their perceptions of their environment than their self-perceptions.

The nature of the changes in perceived environment and in needs appeared quite consistent with the transition made by the students from freshman to senior years in college. Students found the university to be less playful, energetic, risky, and introspective as they progressed toward graduation. In essence, the school moved from being fun to being a more sober and serious place. In contrast, the students found the university to become more hedonistic, aggressive, dominant, and focused on future achievement. These changes are consistent with the worldview of a graduating senior who has been readied for the world by an organization designed to facilitate the attainment of status and recognition. Changes in personal needs were similar in content, but far fewer in number and magnitude.

To our knowledge, this is one of the first studies to track and report changes on dimensions of the environment and the person that were designed to be commensurate in nature. This makes the comparison of change more meaningful, such that we can state with more confidence that perceptions of the environment changed more than personal needs. This finding has important implications for our understanding of development, as stereotypically the environment has been portrayed as a stable influence on personality (e.g., Feldman, 1981). If, however, the perceptions of the environment are more dynamic than self-perceptions, then more attention should be paid to the mechanisms through which people avoid changing in response to a more dynamic environment (Roberts & Wood, 2006). For example, through the use of strategic information processing mechanisms, or more euphemistically – defense mechanisms – people may inoculate themselves from the effect of a changing environment. People may suppress or deny the meaning of job changes, such as the hiring of a new supervisor or the impact of a demotion, in order to protect their self-worth and through this process maintain a consistent personality despite changes in the environment.

If research on the continuity and change in the psychological meaning of organizations is rare, then research on the effect of attrition on personality is relatively non-existent. This is quite understandable as the organization is often the point of contact for our research. Once someone leaves the organization, they also leave our study. Thus, the study of the effect of leaving an organization or type of organization remains an entirely untapped research domain. Nonetheless, one would assume that transitions into and out of different organizations would provide critical turning points and opportunities for both change and consistency.

A Life Course Integration of the ASTMA Model

In summary, the ASTMA model provides a relatively complete description of the key transactions between persons and organizations that are relevant to personality and personality development. Several key questions remain, such as how these mechanisms interact with one another, and how they play out across the life course.

As a general gestalt of person–organization transactions, the ASTMA model makes clear that the predominant personality-related phenomenon is continuity rather than change. The attraction, selection, and manipulation transactions serve to bolster continuity over time as they reflect unconscious or active attempts to create a personal niche that reflects one's attributes. The effect of attrition should be evenly split between continuity and change. If someone leaves an organization by choice to go to a more optimal organizational setting, this should promote continuity. On the other hand, if the transition is not within their control due to being laid off, then a person's ability to move to a more optimal organization may be hindered. Given the fact that the majority of transactions with organizations promote continuity, we should find increasing personality continuity with age, which is what repeated studies have found (Roberts & DelVecchio, 2000). In turn, because the continuity mechanisms clearly outweigh the change mechanisms, changes in personality should be modest. Evidence for this appears to already exist in the base rate of personality change. For example, the modal number of traits showing dramatic change in young adulthood appears to be 1 out of 5 (Roberts et al., 2001).

As the life course progresses, continuity factors should begin to take precedent over change factors. Individuals should become better at selecting environments that fit with their personality as they age and avoiding problematic environments. With the natural accumulation of status that comes with experience, people should also get more opportunities to define their work and thus better manipulate their work place to fit their predilections. In terms of organizational outcomes, these patterns should result in a general increase in PO fit over the life course as well as a general increase in job satisfaction (e.g., Clark, Oswald, & Warr, 1996).

In terms of the change in personality, multiple factors from the ASTMA model and the neo-socioanalytic framework converge on young adulthood being the key developmental period for personality traits. Young adulthood is the period when people are exposed to more serious role demands, and thus transformational processes should be at a peak during this period. Specifically, people move from being dependent on others in adolescence to becoming both independent and responsible in young adulthood as they initiate their careers and start a family. Acquiring independence, while simultaneously becoming responsible for others would naturally call for people to be more confident, conscientiousness, and calm in the face of stress. Thus, as we have found in several longitudinal studies, investments in conventional social institutions are related to increasing scores on measures of social dominance, agreeableness, conscientiousness, and emotional stability (Roberts et al., 2005).

A second factor that would facilitate transformational mechanisms taking precedence in young adulthood is that up until that point in the life course, people's identities are provisional. The adolescent identity is a composite of potentials that better reflect possible selves rather than actual selves. Of course, possible selves may still have an effect on development (Roberts, O'Donnell, & Robins, 2004). Nonetheless, a provisional identity can be shed more easily than one that has been committed to or one that has been invested in for a long period of time. A third contributing factor to young adulthood being the fulcrum period of personality trait development is that it is the time when people make their first serious commitments to work. By making these commitments, people inevitably expose themselves to the new forces of change that come with the transformational transactions (Roberts et al., 2005). They will meet a set of expectations, demands, and contingencies that call for new or improved behavior patterns.

From this transactional model of continuity and change, we can also better understand certain seemingly non-intuitive findings. For example, life events, though stressful, do not always impart change in personality (Caspi & Moffitt, 1993). For example, a typical feature of socialization models is the assumption that simple life events, demographic changes, or large life events are the locus of change. The ASTMA model and the neo-socioanalytic model provide a compelling alternative hypothesis. It is not the significant life event that changes an individual. It is the long-term environment that presses on the individual over years and decades that imparts change, not the loss of a job or existence of a seemingly dramatic transition. If change is dependent on being exposed to contingencies and being committed to the social milieu in which they come, then a transition or life event, by definition cannot impart much change. What becomes much more important is the nature of the environment over time after the event, not the event itself.

The long, slow model of change has important implications for training programs in organizations. Many training programs are born out of a behaviorist worldview, which assumes that short interventions focused on changing discrete behaviors are appropriate. For many issues, such as learning how to use a new computer program, this assumption is fine. On the other hand, many organizations attempt to train employees to be better managers and leaders. As personality traits, motives, and abilities play a significant role in managerial and leadership success, attempting to train a person to become a better manager or leader constitutes changing his or her personality. This is not an unreasonable venture, but given the nature of personality change, applying a behavioristic model to the training intervention is inappropriate. That is, most training programs, regardless of their focus, are too brief to successfully change a person to become a better manager or leader. In contrast, if one takes a long view of training people in ways that would inevitably change their personality, then training programs would be designed to work over months and years, rather than days and weeks. This would have the added benefit of communicating to the employee that the organization is committed to the employee improving his or her management skills. One would assume that this would enhance the effectiveness of the training program and improve the employee's outlook on the organization.

The long-term perspective on change is also relevant to training older employees. One of the basic propositions of the neo-socioanalytic framework is that people remain open systems even in old age (Roberts & Wood, 2006). Thus, change is still possible if not inevitable. The mistake that is often made is to assume that older individuals cannot change, as it is difficult to "teach an old dog new tricks." In actuality, it is difficult to teach any dog a new trick. Given the long-term perspective engendered by the neo-socioanalytic model, changing older workers is most likely just as difficult as changing younger employees. Of course, given the different contingencies in young adulthood versus middle age, the younger employee might be more receptive to the training. Nonetheless, the assumption that older workers cannot be trained does not correspond well with the longitudinal research showing that entrenched phenomena, like personality traits, can and do change in old age. If personality traits can change, then why not other syndromes or skill sets related to organizational performance? Again, the primary caveat being that without a long-term investment in change, transformation will most likely not come about whether the employee is young or old.

CONCLUSION

In this chapter, I have attempted to outline a general theory of personality that can inform a richer, more accurate picture of personality development and facilitate a more fruitful interface between personality psychology and organizational behavior. Several features of the theoretical model deserve emphasis. First, I see a number of theoretical and empirical benefits of integrating social roles into a model of personality. This integration provides a well-organized conduit through which features of the organization act on an individual's personality, and in turn where personality may act on an organization. I also hold out hope that the inculcation of roles, combined with a hierarchical approach to all of the domains of personality, can facilitate a productive integration of long simmering divisions within personality psychology and organizational behavior. Specifically, the neo-socioanalytic model of personality can successfully resolve person–situation debates that have been predicated on a misunderstanding of both person and situation.

Second, the integration of trait and social cognitive approaches to personality psychology also provides an important leverage point for a better relationship between personality psychology and organizational behavior. Social cognitive mechanisms are necessary to explain why personality traits change and continue to develop in adulthood. Social cognitive mechanisms are also more amenable to organizational influences – it is simpler to shape a behavior or low-level goal than to transform a trait. Nonetheless, given the goal of most organizational interventions, which is to shape behavior in the long term, it is clear that shaping social cognitive units will be the first step in long-term socialization processes that will change both personality and the organization.

One reason to aspire to a productive reconciliation between personality psychology and organizational behavior is that so much work still needs to be done. The pattern of relationships between personality traits and organizational experiences begs the question of how and why these relationships occur. What are the intervening mechanisms that facilitate a dominant person being more likely to assume a position of power in an organization? Why do certain experiences impart change for individuals? What are the intervening mechanisms that enhance or detract from change occurring? The answers to these and related questions lie in a broader reconciliation between traditional trait and social cognitive approaches to personality psychology, as well as a keen understanding of organizational dynamics (Roberts, in press; Roberts & Caspi, 2003). The mechanisms linking personality traits and organizational factors have to be the micro-analytic components of social cognitive models, such as schemas, moods, cognitive processing styles, and beliefs. Of course, organizational theory can provide useful insights into how situational constraints and demands can shape a person's thoughts, feelings, and behaviors and subsequently their personality.

NOTES

1. At U.C. Berkeley in the late 1980s, the term "trait" was off limits. One could study "folk concepts," "dispositions," or "personal resources," but not traits, despite the fact that these concepts, when operationalized, are indistinguishable from traits.

2. It is also assumed that all of the units of analysis are interrelated. These paths are not included in Fig. 2 for aesthetic reasons only.

ACKNOWLEDGMENTS

Preparation of this paper was supported by grants from the National Institute of Aging (AG19414). I would like to thank Teresa Cardador for helpful comments on an earlier draft of this manuscript.

REFERENCES

Ackerman, P. L., & Heggestad, E. D. (1997). Intelligence, personality, and interests: Evidence for overlapping traits. *Psychological Bulletin, 121*, 219–245.

Arnett, J. J. (2000). Emerging adulthood: A theory of development from the late teens through the twenties. *American Psychologist, 55*, 469–480.

Ashton, M. C., Lee, K., Perugini, M., Szarota, P., de Vries, R. E., Di Blas, L., Boies, K., & De Raad, B. (2004). A six-factor structure of personality-descriptive adjectives: Solutions from psycholexical studies in seven languages. *Journal of Personality and Social Psychology, 86*, 356–366.

Austin, J. T., & Vancouver, J. B. (1996). Goal constructs in psychology: Structure, process and content. *Psychological Bulletin, 120*, 338–375.

Barrick, M. R., & Mount, M. K. (1991). The Big Five personality dimensions and job performance: A meta-analysis. *Personnel Psychology, 44*, 1–26.

Bauer, J. J., & McAdams, D. P. (2004). Personal growth in adults' stories of life transitions. *Journal of Personality, 72*, 573–602.

Baumeister, R. F., & Leary, M. R. (1995). The need to belong: Desire for interpersonal attachments as a fundamental human motivation. *Psychological Bulletin, 117*, 497–529.

Bell, N. E., & Staw, B. M. (1989). People as sculptors versus sculpture: The roles of personality and personal control in organizations. In: M. B. Arthur, D. T. Hall & B. S. Lawrence (Eds), *Handbook of career theory*. New York, NY: Cambridge University Press.

Block, J. (1971). *Lives through time*. Berkeley, CA: Bancroft.

Block, J. (1993). Studying personality the long way. In: D. C. Funder, R. D. Parke, C. Tomlinson-Keasey & K. Widaman (Eds), *Studying lives through time*, (Vol. 27, pp. 9–41). Washington, DC: American Psychological Association.

Borkenau, P., Mauer, N., Riemann, R., Spinath, F. M., & Angleitner, A. (2004). Thin slices of behavior as cues of personality and intelligence. *Journal of Personality and Social Psychology, 86*, 599–614.

Bronfrenbrenner, U. (1979). *The ecology of human development: Experiments by nature and design.* Cambridge, MA: Harvard University Press.

Brousseau, K. R., & Prince, J. B. (1981). Job-person dynamics: An extension of longitudinal research. *Journal of Applied Psychology, 66,* 59–62.

Caspi, A., Elder, G. H., & Bem, D. J. (1987). Moving against the world: Life-course patterns of explosive children. *Developmental Psychology, 23,* 308–313.

Caspi, A., Elder, G. H., & Bem, D. J. (1988). Moving away from the world: Life-course patterns of shy children. *Developmental Psychology, 24,* 824–831.

Caspi, A., & Moffitt, T. E. (1993). When do individual differences matter? A paradoxical theory of personality coherence. *Psychological Inquiry, 4,* 247–271.

Caspi, A., & Roberts, B. W. (1999). Personality continuity and change across the life course. In: L. A. Pervin & O. P. John (Eds), *Handbook of personality: Theory and research* (2nd ed., pp. 154–196). New York, NY: Guilford.

Cervone, D., Shadel, W. G., & Jencius, S. (2001). Social-cognitive theory of personality assessment. *Personality and Social Psychology Review, 5,* 33–51.

Cervone, D., & Shoda, Y. (1999). *The coherence of personality.* New York, NY: The Guilford Press.

Chatman, J. (1991). Matching people and organizations: Selection and socialization in public accounting firms. *Administrative Science Quarterly, 36,* 459–484.

Clark, A., Oswald, A., & Warr, P. (1996). Is job satisfaction U-shaped in age? *Journal of Occupational and Organizational Psychology, 69,* 57–81.

Clausen, J. A., & Gilens, M. (1990). Personality and labor force participation across the life course: A longitudinal study of women's careers. *Sociological Forum, 5,* 595–618.

Costa, P. T., Jr., & McCrae, R. R. (1994). *Revised NEO Personality Inventory (NEO-PI-R) and NEO-Five-Factor Inventory (NEO-FFI) Professional Manual.* Odessa, FL: Psychological Assessment Resources.

Davis-Blake, A., & Pfeffer, J. (1989). Just a mirage: The search for dispositional effects in organizational research. *Academy of Management Review, 14,* 385–400.

De Fruyt, F., Van Leeuwen, K., Bagby, R. M., Rolland, J., & Rouillon, F. (2006). Assessing and interpreting personality change and continuity in patients treated for major depression. *Psychological Assessment, 18,* 71–80.

de St. Aubin (Ed). (1999). Personal ideology: The intersection of personality and religious beliefs. *Journal of Personality, 67,* 1105–1139.

Dodge, K. A., & Tomlin, A. M. (1987). Utilization of self-schemas as mechanisms of interpretational bias in aggressive children. *Social Cognition, 5,* 280–300.

Donahue, E. M., & Harary, K. (1998). The patterned inconsistency of traits: Mapping the differential effects of social roles on self-perceptions of the Big Five. *Personality and Social Psychology Bulletin, 24,* 610–619.

Eichorn, D. H., Clausen, J. A., Haan, N., Honzik, M. P., & Mussen, P. H. (1981). *Present and past in middle life.* New York: Academic Press.

Elder, G. H. (1969). Occupational mobility, life patterns, and personality. *Journal of Health and Social Behavior, 10,* 308–323.

Emmons, R. A. (1986). Personal strivings: An approach to personality and subjective well-being. *Journal of Personality and Social Psychology, 51,* 1058–1068.

Eysenck, H. J. (1970). *The structure of human personality.* New York, NY: Methuen.

Feingold, A. (1994). Gender differences in personality: A meta-analysis. *Psychological Bulletin, 116,* 429–456.

Feldman, D. C. (1981). The multiple socialization of organizational members. *Academy of Management Review, 6*, 309–318.

Fiese, B. H., Hooker, K. A., Kotary, L., Schwagler, J., & Rimmer, M. (1995). Family stories in the early stages of parenthood. *Journal of Marriage & the Family, 57*, 763–770.

Ford, M. E., & Nichols, C. W. (1987). A taxonomy of human goals and some possible applications. In: M. Ford & D. Ford (Eds), *Humans as self-constructing living systems: Putting the framework to work* (pp. 289–311). Hillsdale, NJ: Lawrence Erlbaum Associates, Publishers.

Fraley, C., & Roberts, B. W. (2005). Patterns of continuity: A dynamic model for conceptualizing the stability of individual differences in psychological constructs across the life course. *Psychological Review, 112*, 60–74.

Funder, D. C., & Ozer, D. J. (1983). Behavior as a function of the situation. *Journal of Personality and Social Psychology, 44*, 107–112.

Goffman, E. (1959). *The presentation of self in everyday life.* New York, NY: Doubleday.

Goldberg, L. R. (1993). The structure of phenotypic personality traits. *American Psychologist, 48*, 26–34.

Graen, G. B., Novak, M. A., & Summerkamp, P. (1982). The effects of leader-member exchange and job design on productivity and satisfaction: Testing a dual attachment model. *Organizational Behavior and Human Decision Processes, 30*, 109–131.

Gray, J. R., & Thompson, P. M. (2004). Neurobiology of intelligence: Science and ethics. *Nature Neuroscience, 5*, 471–482.

Harms, P. D., Roberts, B. W., & Winter, D. (in press). Becoming the Harvard Man: Person-Environment Fit, Personality Development, and Academic Success. *Personality and Social Psychology Bulletin.*

Haslam, S., Alexander, D., Postmes, T., & Ellemers, N. (2003). More than a metaphor: Organizational identity makes organizational life possible. *British Journal of Management, 14*, 357–369.

Helson, R., Jones, C., & Kwan, V. S. Y. (2002). Personality change over 40 years of adulthood: Hierarchical linear modeling analyses of two longitudinal samples. *Journal of Personality & Social Psychology, 83*, 752–766.

Helson, R., Roberts, B. W., & Agronick, G. (1995). Enduringness and change in creative personality and the prediction of occupational creativity. *Journal of Personality and Social Psychology, 69*, 1173–1183.

Helson, R., Stewart, A. J., & Ostrove, J. (1995). Identity in three cohorts of midlife women. *Journal of Personality and Social Psychology, 69*, 544–557.

Hofstede, G., Bond, M. H., & Luk, C. (1993). Individual perceptions of organizational cultures: A methodological treatise on levels of analysis. *Organization Studies, 14*, 483–503.

Hogan, J., & Holland, B. (2003). Using theory to evaluate personality and job-performance relations: A socioanalytic perspective. *Journal of Applied Psychology, 88*, 100–112.

Hogan, R. T. (1982). A socioanalytic theory of personality. In: *Nebraska Symposium on Motivation* (pp. 55–89). Lincoln, Nebraska: University of Nebraska Press.

Hogan, R. T., & Roberts, B. W. (2000). A socioanalytic perspective on person/environment interaction. In: W. B. Walsh, K. H. Craik & R. H. Price (Eds), *New directions in person-environment psychology* (pp. 1–24). Mahwah, NJ: Earlbaum.

Holland, J. L. (1985). *Making vocational choices: A theory of vocational personalities and work environments.* Englewood Cliffs, NJ: Prentice-Hall.

Hough, L. M., & Ones, D. S. (2002). The structure, measurement, validity, and use of personality variables in industrial, work, and organizational psychology. In: N. Anderson, D. S. Ones, H. K. Sinangil, & C. Viswesvaran (Eds), *Handbook of industrial, work and organizational psychology: Personnel psychology* (Vol. 1, pp. 233–277). Thousand Oaks, CA: Sage.

Ilgen, D. R., & Hollenbeck, J. R. (1991). The structure of work: Job design and roles. In: M. D. Dunnette & L. M. Hough (Eds), *Handbook of industrial and organizational psychology.* (2nd ed., Vol. 2, pp. 165–207). Palo Alto, CA, US: Consulting Psychologists Press, Inc.

Johnson, W., McGue, M., & Krueger, R. F. (2005). Personality stability in late adulthood: A behavioral genetic analysis. *Journal of Personality, 73,* 523–551.

Judge, T. A., Bono, J. E., Ilies, R., & Gerhardt, M. W. (2002). Personality and leadership: A qualitative and quantitative review. *Journal of Applied Psychology, 87*(4), 765–780.

Judge, T. A., Heller, D., & Mount, M. K. (2002). Five-factor model of personality and job satisfaction: A meta-analysis. *Journal of Applied Psychology, 87,* 530–541.

Judge, T. A., Higgins, C. A., Thoresen, C. J., & Barrick, M. R. (1999). The big five personality traits, general mental ability, and career success across the life span. *Personnel Psychology, 52,* 621–652.

Kochanska, G., & Murray, K. T. (2000). Mother–child mutually responsive orientation and conscience development: From toddler to early school age. *Developmental Psychology, 71,* 417–431.

Kohn, M. L., & Schooler, C. (1978). The reciprocal effects of the substantive complexity of work and intellectual flexibility: A longitudinal assessment. *American Journal of Sociology, 84,* 24–52.

LePine, J. A., Hollenbeck, J. R., Ilgen, D. R., & Hedlund, J. (1997). Effects of individual differences on the performance of hierarchical decision-making teams: Much more than g. *Journal of Applied Psychology, 82,* 803–811.

Lewis, M. (1999). On the development of personality. In: L. A. Pervin & O. P. John (Eds), *Handbook of personality: Theory and research,* (2nd ed., pp. 327–346). New York, NY: Guilford.

Lubinski, D. (2000). Scientific and social significance of assessing individual differences: Sinking shafts at a few critical points. *Annual Review of Psychology, 51,* 405–444.

Marcia, J. E. (1980). Identity in adolescence. In: J. Adelson (Ed.), *Handbook of adolescent psychology* (pp. 159–187). New York: Wiley.

Maslow, A. H. (1968). *Toward a psychology of being* (2nd ed.). New York, NY: Van Nostrand.

Mayer, J. D. (2005). A tale of two visions: Can a new view of personality help integrate psychology. *American Psychologist, 60,* 294–307.

McAdams, D. P. (1993). *The stories we live by: Personal myths and the making of the self.* New York, NY: William Morrow.

McCrae, R. R. (2004). Human nature and culture: A trait perspective. *Journal of Research in Personality, 38,* 3–14.

McCrae, R. R., & Costa, P. T. (1994). The stability of personality: Observation and evaluations. *Current Directions in Psychological Science, 3,* 173–175.

McCrae, R. R., & Costa, P. T., Jr. (1997). Personality trait structure as a human universal. *American Psychologist, 52,* 509–516.

McGue, M., Bacon, S., & Lykken, D. T. (1993). Personality stability and change in early adulthood: A behavioral genetic analysis. *Developmental Psychology, 29,* 96–109.

Meyer, G. J., Finn, S. E., Eyde, L. D., Kay, G. G., Moreland, K. L., Dies, R. R., Eisman, E. J., Kubiszyn, T. W., & Reed, G. M. (2001). Psychological testing and psychological assessment. *American Psychologist, 56*, 128–165.

Mischel, W. (1968). *Personality and assessment.* New York: Wiley.

Mortimer, J. T., & Lorence, J. (1979). Occupational experience and the self-concept – A longitudinal study. *Social Psychology Quarterly, 42*, 307–323.

Mount, M. K., Barrick, M. R., & Strauss, J. P. (1994). Validity of observer ratings of the big five personality factors. *Journal of Applied Psychology, 79*, 272–280.

Mowday, R. T., & Sutton, R. I. (1993). Organizational behavior: Linking individuals and groups to organizational contexts. *Annual Review of Psychology, 44*, 195–229.

Murray, H. A. (1938). *Explorations in personality.* New York: Oxford University Press.

Piedmont, R. L., McCrae, R. R., Riemann, R., & Angleitner, A. (2000). On the invalidity of validity scales: Evidence from self-reports and observer ratings in volunteer samples. *Journal of Personality and Social Psychology, 78*, 582–593.

Porter, C., Hollenbeck, J. R., Ilgen, D. R., Ellis, A. P. J., West, B. J., & Moon, H. (2003). Backing up behaviors in teams: The role of personality and legitimacy of need. *Journal of Applied Psychology, 88*, 391–403.

Pratt, M. G. (2000). The good, the bad, and the ambivalent: Managing identification among Amway distributors. *Administrative Science Quarterly, 45*, 456–493.

Pratt, M. G., & Rafaeli, A. (1997). Organizational dress as a symbol of multilayered social identities. *Academy of Management Journal, 40*, 862–898.

Roberts, B. W. (1997). Plaster or plasticity: Are work experiences associated with personality change in women? *Journal of Personality, 65*, 205–232.

Roberts, B. W. (2005). Blessings, banes, and possibilities in the study of childhood personality. *Merrill Palmer Quarterly, 51*, 367–378.

Roberts, B. W. (in press). From kindling to conflagration: Self-regulation and personality change. In: K. W. Schaie & L. L. Carstensen (Eds), *Social structures, aging and self-regulation in the elderly.*

Roberts, B. W., & Bogg, T. (2004). A 30-year longitudinal study of the relationships between conscientiousness-related traits, and the family structure and health-behavior factors that affect health. *Journal of Personality, 72*, 325–354.

Roberts, B. W., & Caspi, A. (2003). The cumulative continuity model of personality development: Striking a balance between continuity and change in personality traits across the life course. In: R. M. Staudinger & U. Lindenberger (Eds), *Understanding human development: Lifespan psychology in exchange with other disciplines* (pp. 183–214). Dordrecht, NL: Kluwer Academic Publishers.

Roberts, B. W., Caspi, A., & Moffitt, T. (2001). The kids are alright: Growth and stability in personality development from adolescence to adulthood. *Journal of Personality and Social Psychology, 81*, 670–683.

Roberts, B. W., Caspi, A., & Moffitt, T. (2003). Work experiences and personality development in young adulthood. *Journal of Personality and Social Psychology, 84*, 582–593.

Roberts, B. W., & Chapman, C. (2000). Change in dispositional well-being and its relation to role quality: A 30-year longitudinal study. *Journal of Research in Personality, 34*, 26–41.

Roberts, B. W., & DelVecchio, W. F. (2000). The rank-order consistency of personality from childhood to old age: A quantitative review of longitudinal studies. *Psychological Bulletin, 126*, 3–25.

Roberts, B. W., & Donahue, E. M. (1994). One personality, multiple selves: Integrating personality and social roles. *Journal of Personality, 62*, 201–218.

Roberts, B. W., Harms, P. D., Smith, J., Wood, D., & Webb, M. (2006). Methods in personality psychology. In: Eid, M. & Diener, E. (Eds), *Handbook of psychological assessment: A multimethod perspective* (Chap. 22, pp. 321–335). Washington, DC.: American Psychological Association.

Roberts, B. W., O'Donnell, M., & Robins, R. W. (2004). Goal and personality development. *Journal of Personality and Social Psychology, 87*, 541–550.

Roberts, B. W., & Pomerantz, E. M. (2004). On traits, situations, and their integration: A developmental perspective. *Personality and Social Psychology Review, 8*, 402–416.

Roberts, B. W., & Robins, R. W. (2000). Broad dispositions, broad aspirations: The intersection of the Big Five dimensions and major life goals. *Personality and Social Psychology Bulletin, 26*, 1284–1296.

Roberts, B. W., & Robins, R. W. (2004). A longitudinal study of person-environment fit and personality development. *Journal of Personality, 72*, 89–110.

Roberts, B. W., Walton, K., & Viechtbauer, W. (2006). Patterns of mean-level change in personality traits across the life course: A meta-analysis of longitudinal studies. *Psychological Bulletin.*

Roberts, B. W., & Wood, D. (2006). Personality development in the context of the neo-socioanalytic model of personality. In: D. Mroczek & T. Little (Eds), *Handbook of Personality Development* (Chapter 2, pp. 11–39). Mahwah, NJ: Erlbaum.

Roberts, B. W., Wood, D., & Smith, J. L. (2005). Evaluating Five Factor Theory and social investment perspectives on personality trait development. *Journal of Research in Personality, 39*, 166–184.

Robins, R. W., Fraley, C., Roberts, B. W., & Trzesniewski, K. (2001). A longitudinal study of personality change in young adulthood. *Journal of Personality, 69*, 617–640.

Rolfhus, E., & Ackerman, P. L. (1999). Assessing individual differences in knowledge: Knowledge, intelligence, and related traits. *Journal of Education Psychology, 91*, 511–526.

Salancik, G. R., & Pfeffer, J. (1978). A social information processing approach to job attitudes and task design. *Administrative Science Quarterly, 23*, 224–253.

Saucier, G. (2003). An alternative multi-language structure of personality attributes. *European Journal of Personality, 17*, 179–205.

Schneider, B., & Smith, D. B. (2004). *Personality and organizations*. Mahwah, NJ: LEA.

Schneider, B., Smith, D. B., Taylor, S., & Fleenor, J. (1998). Personality and organizations: A test of the homogeneity of personality hypothesis. *Journal of Applied Psychology, 83*, 462–470.

Schuerger, J. M., & Witt, A. C. (1989). The temporal stability of individually tested intelligence. *Journal of Clinical Psychology, 45*, 294–302.

Schwartz, S. H. (1992). Universals in the content and structure of values: Theoretical advances and empirical tests in 20 countries. *Advances in Experimental Social Psychology, 25*, 1–65.

Snyder, M., & Ickes, W. (1985). Personality and social behaviour. In: E. Aronson & G. Lindzey (Eds), *Handbook of social psychology* (pp. 248–305). New York: Random House.

Staw, B. M., Bell, N. E., & Clausen, J. A. (1986). The dispositional approach to job attitudes: A lifetime longitudinal test. *Administrative Science Quarterly, 31*, 56–77.

Staw, B. M., & Cohen-Charash, Y. (2005). The dispositional approach to job satisfaction: More than a mirage, but not yet an oasis: Comment. *Journal of Organizational Behavior, 26*, 59–78.

Staw, B. M., & Ross, J. (1985). Stability in the midst of change: A dispositional approach to job attitudes. *Journal of Applied Psychology, 70,* 469–480.

Stryker, S., & Serpe, R. T. (1982). Commitment, identity salience, and role behavior: Theory and research example. In: W. Ickers & E. Knowles (Eds), *Personality, roles and social behavior* (pp. 199–219). New York: Springer.

Tajfel, H., & Turner, J. C. (1979). An integrative theory of intergroup conflict. In: G. Worchel (Ed.), *Social psychology of group relations* (pp. 33–47). Monterey, CA: Brooks-Cole.

Thorne, A. (1987). The press of personality: A study of conversations between introverts and extraverts. *Journal of Personality & Social Psychology, 53,* 718–726.

Twenge, J. M. (2001). Changes in women's assertiveness in response to status and roles: A cross-temporal meta-analysis, 1931–1993. *Journal of Personality and Social Psychology, 81,* 133–145.

Viswesvaran, C., Schmidt, F. L., & Ones, D. S. (2005). Is there a general factor in ratings of job performance? A meta-analytic framework for disentangling substantive and error influences. *Journal of Applied Psychology, 90,* 108–131.

Wahba, M. A., & Bridwell, L. T. (1976). Maslow reconsidered. A review of research on the need hierarchy theory. *Organizational Behavior and Human Performance, 15,* 212–240.

Wood, D., & Roberts, B. W. (2006). Cross-sectional and longitudinal tests of the personality and role identity structural model (PRISM). *Journal of Personality, 74,* 779–809.

Wrzesniewski, A., & Dutton, J. E. (2001). Crafting a job: Revisioning employees as active crafters of their work. *Academy of Management Review, 26,* 179–201.

EMPOWERMENT THROUGH CHOICE? A CRITICAL ANALYSIS OF THE EFFECTS OF CHOICE IN ORGANIZATIONS

Roy Yong-Joo Chua and Sheena S. Iyengar

ABSTRACT

The provision of choice is one of the most common vehicles through which managers empower employees in organizations. Although past psychological and organizational research persuasively suggests that choice confers personal agency, and is thus intrinsically motivating, emerging research indicates that there could be potential pitfalls. In this chapter, we examine the various factors that could influence the effects of choice. Specifically, we examine individual-level factors such as the chooser's socioeconomic status and cultural background. We also examine situational factors such as the content of choice and the number of choices offered. We then expand our discussion on the effect of giving employees extensive choice by looking at its influence on creative performance. In the second half of this chapter, we discuss implications for future organizational behavior research and examine how emerging research on choice making can inform specific managerial practices.

Research in Organizational Behavior: An Annual Series of Analytical Essays and Critical Reviews
Research in Organizational Behavior, Volume 27, 41–79
ISSN: 0191-3085/doi:10.1016/S0191-3085(06)27002-3

INTRODUCTION

Douglas McGregor's (1960) specification of Theory X and Theory Y beliefs about human motivation at the workplace has left a lasting impact in management research and practices. Instead of viewing employees as work-avoiding individuals who dislike responsibilities, McGregor proposed that employees are individuals who can be counted on to make decisions about their work and contribute actively to the organization. Today, concepts such as employee empowerment and participative management are ubiquitous not only in the organizational research literature but also in the day-to-day modus operandi of modern-day managers.

Among the many ways in which employees can be empowered in their work (e.g., participation in decision making, goal setting, and ownership in organizational outcomes), giving employees choice in how they approach their work is probably one of the simplest and yet most powerful tactics. The underlying idea is simple. Choice gives people a sense of personal control and agency, which in turns enhances their intrinsic motivation toward their work. The results include increased employee morale, higher creativity and innovation, better performance, greater organizational commitment, and lower turnover.

Yet empowering employees is not as simple as it seems. For instance, Locke and Schweiger (1979) cautioned that employee participation in decision making does not always lead to positive results. Specifically, the effectiveness of employee participation hinges on numerous contextual factors such as individual differences, organizational characteristics (e.g., organization size), and situational demands (e.g., time pressure). Similarly, empowering employees through the provision of choice is context sensitive. Although most managers generally understand the importance of empowering employees by giving them choice, they may not be equipped with the necessary knowledge on how to administer choice effectively, nor are they aware of the potential pitfalls. Indiscriminatingly giving employees choice may result in the expected beneficial effects, but it may also have detrimental outcomes.

Considering these potentially detrimental outcomes, managers need to ask several critical questions before empowering employees through the provision of choice. At the broadest level, the question is, of course, whether or not to give employees choice in the first place. Is having choice always motivating to every individual? Under what circumstances is choice de-motivating or counter-effective? At the next level, if a manager should decide that some form of choice is to be given, how much choice should he or she offer to the employee? Is more always better? Finally, does the choice-making process end after one or more choices have been made? What if people have to do more with the chosen options (e.g., create something out of them) and if so, what consequences do we expect to see?

In this chapter, we attempt to answer these important questions about giving employees choice in the workplace by drawing on past psychological and organizational research on choice making. First, we will contemplate the issue of when to give people choice. Specifically, we will review past research that argues for the provision of choice and then modify this perspective by examining recent studies which explored the boundary conditions of such a prescription. Second, we will look at the effects of giving people extensive choices on motivational and behavioral outcomes. This will help us understand whether giving more choice is always better. Finally, we go beyond the act of choosing and examine how the extent of choice in task materials and initial resources influence creative performance. Specifically, we will revisit the conventional wisdom that the more flexibility employees have at work, the more creative they are likely to be.

In the second half of this chapter, we propose future directions for research by discussing potential factors that could affect the choice-making process but have not yet been systematically studied by organizational scholars. Examples include individual difference variables such as the importance of having the appropriate knowledge to make a choice and personality variables such as one's need for closure. In closing, we will also discuss how the expanded view on choice making can inform specific managerial practices.

CHOICE VERSUS NO CHOICE

The idea that choice confers personal agency and control to the chooser, and is thus intrinsically motivating, can be traced back to early psychological research on choice and self-determination. As the American psychologist Richard deCharms (1968) postulated, "Looking at both sides of the coin, we may hypothesize that when a man perceives his behavior as stemming from his own choice, he will cherish that behavior and its results; when he perceives his behavior as stemming from the dictates of external forces, that behavior and its results, although identical in other respects to behavior of his own choosing, will be devalued" (p. 273). Repeatedly, across many domains of inquiry, other psychologists have also contended that the provision of choice will increase an individual's sense of personal control (e.g., Lefcourt, 1973; Rotter, 1966; Taylor, 1989; Taylor & Brown, 1988) and feelings of intrinsic motivation (e.g., deCharms, 1968; Deci, 1981; Deci & Ryan, 1985).

Drawing in part on earlier work by deCharms (1968), Deci and his colleagues (e.g., Deci, 1981; Deci & Ryan, 1985) have argued that individuals, because of their desire for certainty, are like actors seeking to exercise and validate a sense of control over their external environments. As a result, they are likely to enjoy, prefer, and persist at activities that provide them with opportunities to make choices, to control their own outcomes, and to determine their own fates (Condry, 1977; Condry & Chambers, 1978; Deci, 1971, 1975, 1981; Deci, Driver, Hotchkiss, Robbins & Wilson, 1993; Deci & Ryan, 1985, 1991; Malone & Lepper, 1987; Nuttin, 1973; Ryan, 1982; Zuckerman, Porac, Lathin, Smith, & Deci, 1978). Conversely, the absence of choice and control has been hypothesized and shown to produce a variety of detrimental effects on intrinsic motivation, life satisfaction, and health status (e.g., Deci, Speigel, Ryan, Koestner, & Kaufman, 1982; Schultz & Hanusa, 1978; Seligman, 1975).

In a classic example, Zuckerman et al. (1978) found that college students who were given choices over which puzzles to solve and how much time to allocate to solving each puzzle were more intrinsically motivated during a subsequent period than those who were not given such choices. In a more organizational context, various psychologists and designers (e.g., Averill, 1973; Gifford, 1987; Barnes, 1981) have found that the provision of choice in the physical work environment (e.g., the ability to choose office lighting or stop environmental noise) can lead to desirable outcomes such as improved mood and job performance.

The beneficial effects of choice have also been of central importance to creativity research. A large number of studies have demonstrated that creativity is enhanced when individuals are given autonomy and freedom in their work (e.g., Amabile, 1983; Smeltz & Cross, 1984; Amabile & Gitomer, 1984; Amabile & Gryskiewicz, 1987, 1989; Witt & Beorkrem, 1989; Shalley, 1991; Greenberg, 1992; Zhou, 1998). For instance, Amabile and Gitomer (1984) found that children who were given choices in which task materials to use when creating a collage produced collages that were assessed to be more creative than those produced by children given no choice. Similarly, work by Greenberg (1992) found that subjects who were given choice in selecting which problems to work on produced more creative outputs. More recent studies by Zhou (1998) and Shalley (1991) that considered multiple situational factors also found high task autonomy to be a necessary condition for creative performance. Common to all of this research is the key idea that choice confers freedom and agency on the creator and thus enhances his or her intrinsic motivation on the task, a critical antecedent for creative performance (e.g., Amabile, 1979, 1983; Amabile, Hennessey, & Grossman, 1986).

According to this formulation then, managers who want to empower their employees by giving them a greater sense of control over their work should seriously consider offering all employees some form of choice whenever possible. However, recent research has begun to modify this view from a more cautious perspective. In this section, we will discuss three streams of emerging research that take a more contextualized perspective in evaluating the effects of choice. Specifically, we will discuss how (a) socioeconomic status and (b) cultural background can influence the effects of offering choice. Here, the idea is that choice may not be perceived in the same way by everyone. Whereas choice is linked to personal agency and therefore motivating for some people, this may not be so for others. Next, we move on to examine the effects of choosing from undesirable options. This is an important contextual variable because in an organizational context, employees need not always be presented with neutral or attractive options. Oftentimes, because of organizational demands or difficulties, employees may be confronted with unattractive options. In situations like these, giving employees choice may actually be counter-effective.

The Effect of Differences in Socioeconomic Status

One reality of modern organizations is that people from all walks of life come together to help advance a common organizational goal. In such an organization, managers often have to supervise both well-educated professionals as well as employees of lower socioeconomic status (e.g., factory production workers and store helpers). The question then becomes, are findings from the choice research reviewed thus far relevant and applicable to individuals of varied socioeconomic status?

In a recent series of studies, Snibbe and Markus (2005) found evidence that college graduates (i.e., those with a college degree or higher) have different models of agency than high school graduates (i.e., those without a college degree). Specifically, these researchers argue that the model of agency for college graduates tends to emphasize the expression of uniqueness and the exertion of environmental control, whereas the model for high school graduates tends to emphasize the maintenance of personal integrity (e.g., honesty, loyalty, etc.) and the exertion of self-control. Choice is therefore especially relevant to the model of agency held by college graduates, as choosing is an expression of unique preferences and an exercise of personal control over one's environment. Conversely, the absence of choice may threaten one's sense of agency and incur negative psychological effects. For high school graduates however, choice is less critical to the model of agency, because these students are less concerned about expressing uniqueness and control. Due to these differences in models of agency, college graduates and high school graduates are expected to respond differently to the provision of choice.

To illustrate these ideas, Snibbe and Markus (2005) recruited high school and college graduates to participate in a marketing research study. The high school graduates worked as firefighters, construction workers, and maintenance workers whereas the college graduates included post baccalaureate or post-doctoral students and employees. All subjects were first presented with a list of 10 popular, recently released music CDs and asked to rank the CDs according to how much they thought they would like them. Subjects were specifically told that their ranking of the CDs would determine which CD they would eventually get to keep. Moments later, the experimenter told the subjects that they had run out of some CDs and offered each subject a choice of his or her fifth or sixth ranked CD instead. After subjects chose their desired CD, they were given a filler survey and then asked to re-rank the list of CDs. As expected, subjects who held college degrees improved the ranking of the chosen CD, exhibiting the classic dissonance effect of evaluating the chosen object more positively and the rejected objects less positively. This effect, however, was not found among those subjects who were high school graduates; for these subjects, their ranking of the chosen CD remained unchanged.

In a second study, subjects were approached outside of discount shopping centers and airports. They were invited to take part in a school project involving writing instruments in exchange for $2 and a pen. Subjects in the free-choice condition chose a pen that they liked from among five types of pens. They then tested out the pen and completed a pen evaluation survey. The same procedure was followed for subjects in the no-choice condition, however in this condition, the experimenter interrupted subjects before they could complete the pen evaluation survey. The experimenter told the subject that because the chosen pen was the last of its kind, it could not be given to him or her. The subject was then offered a different pen and subsequently tested out this pen and proceeded to complete the pen evaluation survey. The results indicate that college graduate subjects in the no-choice condition evaluated their pens less favorably than those in the free-choice condition. Conversely, high school graduate subjects evaluated their pens equally favorably irrespective of the experimental condition.

These two studies illustrate the differences in perceptions of choice held by individuals from different socioeconomic status. Specifically, because choosing is central to the agency model held by high socioeconomic status individuals, these individuals revised their attitudes toward the chosen object to make it appear as though they had made good decisions. Because choice does not take on a similar meaning for those with lower socioeconomic status, such attitude changes were not found. Thus, managers seeking to empower employees through the provision of choice may want to consider how choice is perceived by employees of different socioeconomic status; whereas choice is likely to be welcomed, or even sought after, by well-educated white collar employees, this may not be so for the less-educated blue collar employees. More importantly, the absence of choice could prove to be especially de-motivating for well-educated employees, while this may not hold for less-educated employees.

The Effect of Cultural Differences

Organizations today are often staffed by employees with diverse cultural backgrounds. As organizations become more globalized and multicultural, another important contextual factor that warrants our attention is that of cultural differences. For example, does providing choice to a Chinese employee elicit as strong a feeling of personal agency and intrinsic motivation as it does for an American employee?

The seminal cultural analysis provided by Markus and Kitayama (1991) suggests that because Western cultures are characterized as independent and individualistic (Triandis, 1990, 1995), the provision and perception of choice may be of particular intrinsic value to members of these cultures. Westerners, Markus and Kitayama (1991) theorized, possess a model of the self as fundamentally independent. Such individuals strive for independence, desire a sense of autonomy, and seek to express their internal attributes in order to establish their uniqueness from others within their environments. Thus, the perception that one has chosen is integrally linked to one's intrinsic motivation. This is because choice allows for the expression of personal preferences, control, and internal attributes, in turn allowing one to establish oneself as a volitional agent and to fulfill the goal of being independent (Nix, Ryan, Manly, & Deci, 1999).

In contrast, members of non-Western cultures are theorized to possess an interdependent model of the self (Markus & Kitayama, 1991). Specifically, for these individuals, the super-ordinate goal is a sense of interconnectedness and belongingness with one's social ingroup, rather than direct personal control over social situations. The mechanism through which this goal is fulfilled involves acting in accordance with one's social obligations to others, which also allows for the intermediate goal of maintaining social harmony (De Vos, 1985; Hsu, 1985; Miller, 1988; Shweder & Bourne, 1984; Triandis, 1990, 1995). Thus, for members of non-Western cultures, the perception of having chosen may be of little intrinsic value. This is because choice-making contexts may be conceived of, not as searches for personal preference matches and agency, but rather as a search for options which conform to the socially sanctioned standards of one's reference group, in turn allowing for the fulfillment of one's responsibilities.

These cultural differences regarding the value of choice are echoed by cross-cultural research examining the concept of agency. For instance, Menon, Morris, Chiu, and Hong (1999) found that Singapore students, compared to American students, were less likely to believe in the autonomy of individual persons. Similarly, Ames and Fu (2000) found that Americans believe a wider range of individual acts are intentional than do Chinese. Rather than believing that agency lies largely within the individual, members of interdependent cultures tend to believe in groups as having more agency and power. Thus, personal choice may not hold as much importance for individuals from interdependent cultures as it does for those from independent cultures.

In fact, in some situations, the exercise of personal choice might even pose a threat to interdependent individuals whose personal preferences are at odds with those of their reference group. Interdependent-selves, therefore, might actually prefer to have their choices made for them. This is especially true if it enables these individuals to be both relieved of the "burden" associated with identifying the socially sanctioned option and, at the same time, fulfills the superordinate cultural goal of belongingness. For instance, it is observed that Japanese workers are often proud in pointing out their bosses' role in the decision-making process. For members of interdependent cultures then, it is not the exercise of choice per se that is necessary for intrinsic motivation. Rather, motivation is derived from the perception of themselves as responsible members acting to fulfill their duties and obligations toward their reference groups. This leads to the hypothesis that for members of independent cultures (e.g., Americans), the traditional choice condition should be more intrinsically motivating than the traditional no-choice condition, whereas for members of interdependent cultures (e.g., East Asians), other-choice contexts should be more intrinsically motivating, especially if the choosers are identified as members of their reference group.

To examine the hypothesis that personal versus other-made choices would be perceived differently by members of contrasting cultural groups, Iyengar and Lepper (1999) first conducted an ethnographic study with Japanese and American students. These students were asked to catalog the choices they made during one normal workday and to rate how important each choice was to them. The results indicated that American students perceived themselves as having nearly 50% more choices than their Japanese counterparts. Furthermore, the American students rated their choices as significantly more important than the Japanese students did. The students were also asked to list the occasions in which they would wish not to have a choice. The results were striking. Nearly 30% of the American students said they wished to have choices *all* of the time. More than 50% of the American students said that they could not imagine a circumstance in which they would prefer not to have a choice. In contrast, none of the Japanese students expressed these sentiments at all.

Two further experimental studies conducted by Iyengar and Lepper (1999) provided more direct empirical evidence. In the traditional choice paradigm, first employed by Zuckerman et al. (1978), the chooser in the no-choice condition was typically an unknown experimenter. Iyengar and Lepper (1999) extended this paradigm to include choosers in the no-choice condition who were members and non-members of the participants' reference groups. As members of interdependent cultures were theorized to make distinctions between social ingroup and outgroup members, varying the identity of the chooser to reflect this distinction was hypothesized to significantly influence interdependent participants' responses to others' choices (Iyengar, Ross, & Lepper, 1999; Triandis, 1988, 1989, 1990; Triandis, Bontempo, Villareal, Asai, & Lucca, 1988; Triandis, Marin, Lisansky, & Betancourt, 1984). Furthermore, it was predicted that the preference for relinquishing choice would be exhibited by interdependent-selves when the chooser was identified as a member of a relevant social ingroup.

In the first experiment, a yoked design was employed in which both European and Asian American children (seven to nine years old) were either asked to choose for themselves or were told that someone else had chosen for them. In the personal choice condition, participants were allowed to select one of six activities they wished to undertake, whereas in two no-choice conditions, participants were assigned this same activity. For half of the students in the assigned-choice conditions, the person making the choice for them was a previously never encountered before adult (i.e., the experimenter), while for the other half of the students in the assigned-choice condition, the person making the choice was one with whom participants shared a close and interdependent relationship (i.e., their mothers). Subsequently, the students' performance at the activity and their intrinsic motivation to engage in the same activity during a later free-play period, were measured. As earlier research would predict, the findings suggest that European Americans were most highly motivated and performed best when given a personal choice, as compared to when choices were made for them either by the experimenter or by their own mothers. Asian Americans, by contrast, were most motivated and performed the best when their mothers had made the selection, and did significantly worse when they had made the choice themselves. Like their European American counterparts, however, Asian Americans performed least well when an unfamiliar experimenter made choices for them.

The second experimental study by Iyengar and Lepper (1999) provides evidence of comparable and even more powerful cultural differences under circumstances in which the actual choices involved are quite trivial, and choices were made for students by peers rather than parents. This second experiment employs a paradigm adapted from Cordova and Lepper (1996). Here, both Asian and European American fifth graders engage in a computer math game under one of three conditions. In the personal choice condition, participants are given half a dozen instructionally irrelevant and seemingly trivial options (e.g., "Which icon would you like to have be your game piece?"). In two yoked no-choice conditions, students were told that they were being assigned to these choices on the basis of a vote taken amongst either their own classmates (ingroup condition) or amongst slightly younger children at a rival school (outgroup condition).

As in the first study, the findings were striking. European American children preferred more challenging math problems, showed increased task engagement, and actually learned more when they had been allowed to make their own choices, as compared to either of the other conditions in which choices had been made for them. In contrast, Asian American children were more intrinsically motivated and learned better when these choices were made by their classmates than when they made their own choices, and performed worst when the choices were made for them by unfamiliar and lower status others. One explanation for the observed differences in intrinsic motivation exhibited by Asian American children across ingroup and outgroup contexts may be that the ingroup's choice elicited greater perceptions of responsibility than the outgroup's choice, suggesting that perceptions of responsibility may be the mediating mechanism underlying the relationship between no-choice and intrinsic motivation among interdependent cultural members.

To test whether the above findings observed among children from contrasting cultural backgrounds can be generalized to adults from a variety of independent and interdependent cultures, a field study was conducted. Specifically, an extensive questionnaire study was conducted with Citigroup employees to examine whether variations in perceived choice versus perceived responsibility could actually predict significant factors such as job satisfaction, intrinsic motivation, and job performance. Citigroup bank tellers and sales representatives were selected from nine different countries whose cultures varied in their individualism scores (Hofstede, 1980, 1991; Triandis, 1995). A total of 2,399 Citigroup employees from Taiwan ($n = 183$), Singapore ($n = 89$), the Philippines ($n = 96$), Japan ($n = 100$), Australia ($n = 62$), Argentina ($n = 150$), Brazil ($n = 200$), Mexico ($n = 150$), and the United States (including New York ($n = 880$), Los Angeles ($n = 150$), and Chicago ($n = 339$)) participated in this questionnaire study. Specifically, this survey instrument included measures of (a) perceived choice, in which employees rated the prevalence of choice in various aspects of their jobs; (b) intrinsic and extrinsic motivation (adapted from prior research, e.g., Deci, Eghrari, Patrick, & Leone, 1994; Harter, 1981); (c) job satisfaction; (d) perceptions of fairness of treatment on the job (Lind & Tyler, 1988; Tylor, 1989; Tyler & Smith, 1999); and (e) perceptions of duty and responsibility at work. In addition to employee questionnaire responses, performance data for each participant was obtained from their managers and subsequently matched with participants' individual responses.

The findings were consistent with those observed from the investigations with European and Asian American children. The results suggest that, first, perceptions of choice predict job satisfaction, intrinsic motivation, perceptions of fair treatment at work, and job performance significantly better for employees in the United States as compared to employees in Asian countries. Second, comparisons among various ethnic groups in the United States indicate that the perception of choice was a stronger predictor of these dependent measures for European, African, and Hispanic Americans as compared to Asian Americans. Third, the results suggest that among Asian participants – from both Asia and the United States – perceptions of duty and responsibility were more positively correlated with perceptions of choice, intrinsic motivation, and job satisfaction and performance, suggesting that perceptions of choice may be integrally linked to perceptions of responsibility for Asians (Iyengar, Lepper, Hernandez, DeVoe, & Alpert, 2001).

Taken together, the findings from these studies are of theoretical significance in that they starkly challenge one of our most fundamental assumptions regarding human motivation and personal agency. They suggest that among cultures fostering social interdependence, individuals seeking to fulfill their social responsibilities and obligations may be more intrinsically motivated by having their choices made for them – particularly when the chooser is someone from their social ingroup (e.g., a family member or an ingroup peer) – as compared to contexts in which they make their own choices. The previously assumed link between choice and perceptions of individual agency and control should thus be restricted to cultures that emphasize self-independence.

Examining the effects of culture from a different perspective, Kim and Drolet (2003) studied cultural differences in variety-seeking tendency during choice making. Instead of focusing on choices among items, these researchers extended choice research to the choosing of "choice rules" (Drolet, 2002). When faced with a choice problem, it is believed that people rely on various rules to help them make a decision. For example, when choosing which electronic product to buy, people may either choose price over quality or quality over price. These heuristics are referred to as choice rules. The choice rule that people select from their repertoire of rules depends on various characteristics of the choice problem they encounter (e.g., framing).

Research by Drolet (2002) found that people tend to vary their use of choice rules independent of their choice problem characteristics. In other words, the use of a particular choice rule on one occasion decreases the probability of use of the same rule on a subsequent occasion. Interestingly, recent work by Kim and Drolet (2003) suggests that such variety-seeking tendencies in employing different choice rules across multiple occasions appears to be culturally bound. In a study involving a series of choices of consumer products, Korean subjects varied their use of choice rules significantly less than American subjects did. Specifically, American subjects who chose the "compromise" rule (e.g., a compromise between price and quality) in earlier decisions tended not to choose the same rule in a subsequent choice-making exercise. However, there was no such effect for Koreans. The results suggest that Americans see choice as an act of self-expression and agency; by not adhering to a set of fixed rules, they are signaling their individual freedom to follow their own minds. By contrast, individuals from East Asian cultures are not encouraged to express individual uniqueness to such a large extent (Kim & Markus, 1999), and as a result, exhibit lower tendencies to vary their patterns of decision-making behavior as a means of expressing individuality and personal agency.

Drawing on this cross-cultural body of choice research, we advocate that managers be mindful of the cultural background of the employees to whom they are giving choices. Whereas choice is a reflection of agency and self-expression for individuals from independent cultures such as the U.S., this does not appear to be true for individuals from interdependent cultures. For such interdependent employees, choice may not have its purported desirable effects.

The Effects of Choosing among Undesirable Options

Organizational life is not always a bed of roses. In times of organizational difficulties or when faced with unexpected business demands, painful decisions often have to be made. Should managers give employees choices in these decisions as well? Traditional choice research does not have much to contribute to answering this question. Most research on the observed benefits of personally made choices as compared to externally dictated choices has been limited to contexts in which the choice sets included are either attractive or neutral options. But what if choosers are required to make a selection from a variety of options – all of which are associated with unwanted outcomes? For example, during an organizational downsizing operation, some employees must be laid off. Does it make sense to offer these employees a choice of compensation packages? Would choosers still welcome such agency and experience more satisfaction than non-choosers even if they expected the outcomes to be negative?

At the outset, one might expect choosers to necessarily be happier than non-choosers, regardless of whether the options included in the choice set have a positive or a negative valence. The obvious rationale behind such an assumption is that choosing for oneself ought to allow for utility maximization across contexts in which choice sets include either attractive or unattractive alternatives. Hence, when choice sets have positive valence, choosers can select "the best of the best," and when choice sets have negative valence, choosers can select "the least worst." However, this analysis assumes that the benefits from choosing stem solely from one's ability to engage in preference matching, and the analysis ignores the affective experiences associated with the act of choosing. Can the pleasure of exercising personal control be instead replaced with anxiety or pain when the choice is to be made among unwanted outcomes? For example, are laid off employees necessarily able to cope better if they can choose for themselves which severance package to accept? Or will the mere acting of choosing accentuate the pain of being laid off?

A large body of research has shown that when confronted with a set of undesirable or stressful choices, people tend to delay choosing, resort to the default, shift the responsibility of making the decision onto others, and often opt not to choose at all (Beattie, Baron, Hershey, & Spranca, 1994; Burger, 1989; Dhar, 1997; Janis & Mann, 1977; Iyengar & Lepper, 2000; Lewin, 1951; Luce, 1998; Miller, 1959; Shafir, Simonson, & Tversky, 1993; Simonson, 1992). For instance, Luce (1998) demonstrated that the process of making trade-offs between choice attributes linked to highly valued goals (e.g., safety features versus the purchase price of a car) increases the level of conflict experienced by the decision maker, and gives rise to avoidant responses such as maintaining the status quo, choosing a dominant alternative, and prolonging the search. These findings suggest that, although the presence of choice confers personal agency over a situation, such agency is not necessarily welcomed. Specifically, to the extent that personal agency generates conflict, stress, and anxiety, people may actually prefer to avoid it.

More recent research by Botti and Iyengar (2004) provides convincing evidence that, whereas choosers are more satisfied than non-choosers when selecting from among attractive alternatives, non-choosers are more satisfied with the decision outcome than choosers when selecting from among unattractive alternatives. In one laboratory study involving the selection of yogurt flavors, participants were assigned the role of either choosers or non-choosers, and were then exposed to either appealing yogurt flavors (e.g., mint, cocoa, cinnamon, and brown sugar) or unappealing yogurt flavors (e.g., sage, chili powder, tarragon, and celery seed). After participants selected the yogurt of their choice, they completed a pre-survey concerning their expected satisfaction with the selected yogurt. Participants were then given the opportunity to eat as much as they wanted of the selected yogurt. The amount of yogurt consumed served as a behavioral measure of satisfaction. Finally, a second questionnaire (post-survey) was administered to measure participants' preferences for choosing and their experienced satisfaction with the sampled yogurt.

The results were telling. Although all of the subjects preferred to choose for themselves as opposed to relinquishing choice-making control to external forces (an indication of preference for personal control), choosers reported greater satisfaction than non-choosers only when the yogurt options were appealing. When the yogurt options were unappealing, choosers were less satisfied than non-choosers. Furthermore, when sampling appealing yogurt flavors, choosers and non-choosers consumed similar quantities of yogurt, but when the yogurt flavors were unappealing, choosers ate less yogurt than non-choosers. In addition, measurements of satisfaction taken before and after the yogurt tasting were highly correlated, suggesting that the effect of choice on outcome satisfaction may have depended on psychological mechanisms that took place during the very act of choosing, even before the actual decision outcome has been experienced (i.e., tasting the yogurt).

The research described above demonstrates that when they are confronted by unattractive alternatives, choosers experience "choice-outcome aversion." In other words, the very act of choosing detrimentally affects choosers' anticipated and experienced satisfaction as compared to non-choosers. Ethnographic studies conducted in naturalistic settings suggest that the potency of the observed "choice-outcome aversion" phenomenon can be extended to more consequential real-life events. For instance, recent interviews with French and American parents of chronically ill infants, conducted at the MacLean Center for Clinical Medical Ethics, have shown that French parents were better able to cope with the death of their newborn infants than American parents (Orfali & Gordon, 2004). In France, current medical practices put physicians in charge of deciding which treatments are in a patient's best interest, while medical practices in the United States leave patients, or their families, with the responsibility of deciding which treatments to undergo. Follow-up interviews with parents up to six months later revealed better coping abilities in the French parents, who were served by a paternalistic medical system, as compared to the American parents, who were served by an autonomous medical system.

Drawing on this body of research, it seems that the positive effects of choice are limited to choosing from among positive or at least neutral alternatives. Although choice confers agency on the chooser, such agency may not always be welcomed and, more importantly, not in the best interest of the chooser. Perhaps in situations in which the available options are undesirable, managers should consider simply making the decision for their employees and not offering any choice at all.

CHOICE: IS MORE ALWAYS BETTER?

Now, suppose a manager has considered the various factors discussed so far (specifically, the socioeconomic status of the employee, cultural influences, and choice content) and decided that he or she would still like to give the employee some form of choice in a given situation. A natural question, then, is how much choice to give. Is more always better? In this section, we will discuss research that examines the effects of providing people with extensive choice sets. In addition, we will consider a related topic on the choice-making strategies that people use, and the effect of these strategies on people's preference for more or fewer options.

The Effects of Extensive Choice

We first consider the effects of providing people with extensive choice. Recall that research on intrinsic motivation suggests that, at least among North Americans, the provision of choice allows for self-determination and intrinsic motivation, regardless of the challenges that the choice-making process imposes (e.g., deCharms, 1968; Deci & Ryan, 1985, 1991; Zuckerman et al., 1978). On the other hand, research examining the behavior of choosers confronted by equally attractive and risky options finds that choosers exhibit a greater tendency to choose sub-optimally. Choosers also tend to delay making a choice and demonstrate lower levels of intrinsic motivation (Higgins, Trope, & Kwon, 1999; Mischel & Ebbesen, 1970; Shafir et al., 1993; Seligman, 1975; Shafir & Tversky, 1992; Yates & Mischel, 1979; see also Kahneman & Tversky, 1984). As the attractiveness of these alternatives rises, individuals experience added conflict as to which is the best option. As a result, they tend to defer decisions, search for new alternatives, choose the default option, or simply opt not to choose. In addition, consumer research suggests that as the number of options and the information about options increases, people tend to consider fewer choices and process smaller percentages of the overall information regarding their choices (Hauser & Wernerfelt, 1990).

How does one reconcile these two opposing sets of findings? The answer could lie in the number of choices offered. Drawing upon both research traditions, recent findings have shown that while members of independent cultures are intrinsically motivated by the provision of extensive choices, the act of making a selection from an excessive number of options might result in "choice overload." This in turn lessens both their motivation to choose and their subsequent motivation to commit to a choice. In a series of studies, Iyengar and Lepper (2000) extended the traditional choice paradigm by adding a choice condition in which the choice set was extensive. Field and laboratory experiments were conducted to compare the intrinsic motivation of participants encountering limited as opposed to extensive choice sets. In one field experiment, a tasting booth for exotic jams was arranged at a neighborhood grocery store. As consumers passed the tasting booth, they encountered a display with either 6 (limited choice condition) or 24 (extensive choice condition) different flavored jams. The number of passersby who approached the tasting booth and the number of purchases made in these two conditions served as dependent variables. The results suggested that although extensive choice proved initially more enticing than limited choice, limited choice was ultimately more motivating. Thus, 60% of the passersby approached the table in the extensive-choice condition, as compared to only 40% in the limited-choice condition. However, 30% of the consumers who encountered the limited selection actually purchased a jam, whereas only 3% of those exposed to the extensive selection made a purchase. Another field study revealed that students in an introductory college level course were more likely to write an essay for extra credit when they were provided a list of only 6, rather than 30, potential essay topics. Moreover, even after having chosen to write an essay, students wrote higher quality essays if their essay topic had been picked from a smaller choice set.

Laboratory experiments provide further evidence for the "choice overload" phenomenon and lend us some insight into the potential mediators of this phenomenon. In another study by Iyengar and Lepper (2000), participants were exposed to a choice (choice versus no-choice) by options (limited versus extensive) experimental design. Participants either sampled a chosen Godiva chocolate from a selection of 6 or 30, or were given a chocolate to sample from a selection of six or 30. At the time of choice, participants reported enjoying the process of choosing a chocolate more from a display of 30 than from a display of 6. Subsequently, however, participants in the extensive choice condition proved least satisfied and most regretful with their sampled chocolates, whereas participants in the limited choice condition proved most satisfied and least regretful about the chocolates they sampled. Satisfaction and regret ratings for no-choice participants fell in the middle. Parallel findings on a behavioral measure of intrinsic motivation were reflected in participants' subsequent preference for chocolate or money as compensation for their participation in the study.

Collectively, these findings are consistent with the hypothesis that American independent-selves desire and value the provision of choice, as such contexts ideally allow for the fulfillment of personal preferences and the exercise of personal control. Yet, at the same time, choosing from an extensive choice context may thwart choosers' satisfaction when the complexity of such choice-making situations elicits uncertainty regarding one's personal preferences. Thus, although the provision of extensive choices may initially be perceived as desirable, the actual exercise of choice in such decision-making contexts could attenuate rather than enhance choosers' intrinsic motivation; instead of having a sense of agency or control over the choice scenario, a chooser may actually feel confused and overwhelmed by the large number of options.

To test these ideas in a more organizational context, Iyengar, Jiang, and Huberman (2004) conducted a field study using data from 647 company retirement plans run by the Vanguard Group. The key independent variable in this study was the extensiveness of choice in retirement plan options given to employees, whereas the outcome measure was the rate of participation by employees in the available plans. The results showed that, when employers increased the number of investment options available to employees for voluntary 401(k) investments, the rate of participation actually went down; for every 10 funds offered, participation rates declined by 2 percent. And this was true even when employers matched employee contributions to the plans. More specifically, these researchers found that 401(k) participation peaked at 75 percent when a retirement plan offered only two investment options, while participation dropped dramatically to 60 percent when investors had 60 choices. This study provides further field evidence that too much choice can have an unanticipated negative impact.

All in all, the combined results from this series of studies provide some important theoretical implications. First, the provision of choice may not be valued to the same extent as was previously theorized when the number of options to be considered becomes extensive. Second, even when people demonstrate a desire for the provision of choice, they paradoxically do not experience higher intrinsic motivation and satisfaction after exercising their choice. Third, and worse still, people may even avoid choosing altogether because the large number of options simply confuses or overwhelms them.

The Effects of Individuals' Choice-making Strategies

Closely related to the question of how much choice to offer employees is the type of choice-making strategy to be employed by these individuals. By considering individuals' choice-making strategies, we hope to provide a more nuanced perspective on the effects of having extensive choice. Specifically, we extend our earlier discussion that extensive choice can lead to cognitive overload and confusion by surveying another stream of research, which argues that there are certain individuals who actively seek out extensive options. Interestingly, these individuals actually do well by pursuing such an approach.

According to Simon (1955, 1956, 1957), one important distinction between people's choice-making strategies is that of "maximizing" versus "satisficing." For a maximizer, the strategy is to seek out the best, a strategy that requires an exhaustive search of all possibilities. For a satisficer, the strategy is to seek "good enough," searching until an option is encountered that crosses the threshold of acceptability. One distinctive behavioral tendency of the maximizer is to engage in an exhaustive search of all available options (Schwartz et al., 2002). Maximizers are likely to focus on increasing their choice sets by exploring multiple options, presumably because expanded choice sets allow for greater possibilities to seek out and find the "best" option.

In a recent study by Iyengar, Wells, and Schwartz (2006), it was found that maximizers actually performed better in the job search process than satisficers. Graduating university students were first administered a scale that measured maximizing tendencies, and then followed over the course of the year as they searched for jobs. The maximizing scale was drawn from Schwartz et al. (2002) and included items such as "When I am in the car listening to the radio, I often check other stations to see if something better is playing, even if I am relatively satisfied with what I'm listening to," and "When shopping, I have a hard time finding clothes that I really love."

The results indicated that graduating college students who scored high on the maximizing scale (Schwartz et al., 2002) earned starting salaries that were 20% higher than those who scored low on the scale. This is likely to be the result of maximizers applying to more jobs, pursuing both realized and un-realized options to a greater degree, and relying on more external sources of information than satisficers. In an organizational context, this suggests that managers may want to give employees with maximizing tendencies greater flexibility in exploring large number of options and alternatives in getting their work done, as this could result in better job performance. Yet, this approach should be taken with care. Consistent with the earlier described research which shows that too much choice can be overwhelming, Iyengar et al. (2006) also found that despite their relative success, maximizers were less satisfied with the outcomes of their job searches. Specifically, they were reportedly more "pessimistic," "stressed," "tired," "anxious," "wor-ried," "overwhelmed," and "depressed" throughout the entire process. Maximizers' decreased satisfaction and increased negative affect with their resulting jobs are thought to result from their pursuit of the elusive "best," a strategy which induces them to consider a large number of possibilities, and creates unrealistically high expectations which cannot be easily fulfilled, thus increasing their potential for regret and/or anticipated regret.

Taken together, these two streams of research on extensive choice sets and choice-making strategies have significant managerial implications. First, giving employees extensive choice does not always empower them. Instead of feeling a heightened sense of personal control and agency, most people become confused and avoid choosing. Second, even if certain individuals with maximizing choice-making strategies welcome extensive options and can actually deliver enhanced performances, they may suffer associated psychological costs, such as lower satisfaction, regret, and even depression.

Thus, managers need to be cognizant of this trade-off when giving employees extensive choice or autonomy in their work. Managers must decide which to prioritize – the subjective well-being of the employee, or the improved organizational performance that could result from giving maximizing employees free reign in pursuing extensive alternatives in their work.

BEYOND CHOOSING: THE EFFECTS OF EXTENSIVE CHOICE ON CREATIVE PROBLEM SOLVING

In this section, we further expand our discussion on the effects of giving employees extensive choice by looking at its effect on creative performance. Although there has been some prior research on the effects of giving people choice and flexibility on creative performance during a problem-solving task (e.g., Amabile & Gitomer, 1984; Greenberg, 1992), no research has yet examined the effect of the number of initial resources on intrinsic motivation and creativity during problem-solving tasks. The following discussion moves beyond a consideration of the mere act of choosing, and examines situations in which individuals actually have to make choices from among a given set of options and create something out of these choices. Does giving employees more choice in terms of task materials and initial resources necessarily beget more creative performance?

This question is especially relevant to organizations that require their employees to engage in creative endeavors. For instance, when asking a chef to create a new dish, should a restaurant manager provide him with an extensive or a limited set of ingredients to begin with? Similarly, should a fashion designer be given greater or fewer choices of fabrics to work with when designing a new dress? One can easily think of other examples in real-life organizations in which the set of initial resources given to problem solvers to generate potential solutions can be either expansive or limited. In such a paradigm, task autonomy and freedom are a function of the problem solver's flexibility in combining the given resources to generate potential solutions. The larger the initial choice set of elements one has to work from, the more combinatorial flexibility there is in generating potential solutions. Hence, one would expect that the problem solver would be more intrinsically motivated and produce more creative products given greater flexibility. On the other hand, could the increased combinatorial flexibility and larger number of possibilities also lead to disorientation and cognitive overload? If so, giving a problem solver an extensive choice of initial resources may actually be de-motivating and hence detrimental to creativity.

In studying this issue, Chua and Iyengar (2005a) theorized that the larger the choice set of initial resources given to people during problem-solving tasks, the more likely they are to experience information overload due to the increased number of possible option combinations, which in turn, renders the creativity process de-motivating. As a result, people are unlikely to consider unconventional alternatives in addition to the given options, as doing so will further increase the search space and accentuate the information overload effect. In addition, a large choice set of initial resources may give the problem solver a false illusion that the solution he or she is seeking can be formulated using the given resources. This limits the problem solver's mode of creative thought, in that he or she will focus on generating combinations using the given resources, ignoring the wider possibilities that exist outside of the choice set.

In contrast, when individuals are given limited options, combinatorial flexibility may be more restricted but the search space for a creative solution is more manageable. In addition, problem solvers are less likely to think that the given resources are sufficient for the formulation of a solution. As a result, they may be more motivated to search for ideas outside of the given options. In other words, when the parameters of the problem are fewer, people may begin to think more expansively as opposed to more restrictively.

To test this idea, Chua and Iyengar (2005a) conducted a laboratory experiment in which undergraduate students from Columbia University were recruited to participate in a gift-wrapping study. Subjects were assigned to either a high-choice condition, in which they were given six types of ribbon and four types of wrapping paper, or a low-choice condition in which they were given only two types of ribbon and two types of wrapping paper. A set of five other unusual materials typically unrelated to gift-wrapping (i.e., newspaper, kitchen aluminum foil, metal wire, sponge, and cotton twine) were also provided to all subjects in equal amounts. The task was to wrap a square gift box. Participants were told that they could use as much or as little of the materials as they wished. There was also no restriction on how the gift was wrapped. For each of the choice conditions, half of the subjects were told that the objective of the task was to come up with as creative a gift wrap as possible (creativity goal) while the other half of the subjects were simply told to do their "best" in the gift-wrapping task (non-creativity goal). In addition, a creative self-efficacy questionnaire (Tierney & Farmer, 2002) was administered to all subjects at the beginning of the experiment. This questionnaire taps the belief that one has the ability to produce creative outputs. The key dependent variable in this study was the subject's level of divergent thinking, which was measured by counting the number of unusual gift-wrapping materials (e.g., newspaper, sponge, and cotton twine) used in each gift wrap.

The results were consistent with Chua and Iyengar's (2005a) hypothesis that larger choice sets result in lower levels of divergent thinking; however, creative self-efficacy and gift-wrapping goal were found to moderate these hypothesized effects. Specifically, there was a choice by creative self-efficacy interaction effect such that subjects with low creative self-efficacy were more likely to think divergently (i.e., use more unusual materials in gift wrapping) when given low choice as opposed to high choice. In contrast, subjects with high creative self-efficacy were not significantly affected by the complexities associated with a large choice set. More interestingly, subsequent analyses revealed that for subjects with low creative self-efficacy, lower choice actually led to more divergent thinking, regardless of the goal they were given. However, for subjects with high creative self-efficacy, there was an interaction effect between choice and goal, such that low choice led to more divergent thinking given a performance goal, but high choice led to more divergent thinking given a creativity goal. These results suggest that extensive choice enhances divergent thinking only under limited circumstances, i.e., for individuals with high creative self-efficacy given a creativity goal. Given a non-creativity goal, even an individual with high creative self-efficacy might not see the need to expend the additional effort necessary to engage in divergent thinking, as this type of thinking involves a conscious effort to explore options which deviate from convention and thus requires extra cognition.

This study directly challenges both conventional wisdom and past research which suggest that task flexibility, as defined by an increased number of choices during problem-solving tasks, is necessarily conducive to human creativity. Results from the gift-wrapping study demonstrate that the simplistic idea that more choice confers more combinatorial flexibility and thus leads to higher creativity is a limited one. For the most part, it appears that too much choice is actually detrimental to creativity.

To better understand the mechanism underlying the relationship between choice and creativity, Chua and Iyengar conducted a second study (Chua & Iyengar, 2005b) involving the creation of print advertisements. As in the previous study, the key experimental conditions were degree of choice and type of goal (creativity versus performance goal). In the high-choice condition, college student subjects were given 10 themes as starting points from which to generate ideas for a print advertisement. Examples of themes included broad categories such as "school," "music," and "romance." In the low-choice condition, subjects were randomly given two of the 10 possible themes. Subjects were asked to generate as many ideas as possible using the given themes but were not restricted to them. For each choice condition, half of the subjects were asked to be as creative as possible when generating ideas (creativity goal), while the other half were asked to be as persuasive as possible when generating ideas (non-creativity goal). Unlike the previous study, subjects' perceptions of the idea generation process was also measured at the end of the experiment. Specifically, subjects were asked the extent to which they felt frustrated during the idea generation process and how interested they would be in participating in a similar study in the future. The main dependent variable in this study was the number of ideas generated that did not conform to the given themes.[1]

The results indicated that when subjects were given an extensive choice of initial themes from which to generate ideas, they were less inclined to think outside of the box and explore divergent ideas not suggested by these themes, as compared to those who were given fewer themes. More importantly, it was found that subjects given the creativity goal reported more frustration when given an extensive choice of themes than when given a limited choice of themes. This finding is consistent with the idea that extensive choice sets of initial resources during creative problem-solving tasks can lead to information overload, due to the large number of possible alternative solutions. In order to avoid adding to the current complexity, people are therefore less inclined to explore additional ideas.[2] This is especially so when a large choice set could give people the perception that a creative solution can be formulated within the given resources.

Perhaps the most striking and counter-intuitive results come from the measure of how interested subjects would be in participating in a similar study in the future. There was a clear main effect of choice such that subjects in the low-choice condition reported more interest in participating in similar future studies than those in the high-choice condition, an effect that was especially salient when subjects were given a creativity goal. This result again challenges the idea that choice and flexibility during problem-solving tasks necessarily increase enjoyment and intrinsic motivation.

Taken together, these recent studies suggest that the effects of providing extensive choice in creative problem-solving tasks, and the resulting autonomy and flexibility that such choice sets allow, may not be as straightforward as one would otherwise imagine. While traditional creativity research suggested that giving people choice and flexibility in choosing which problems to solve would serve to enhance their intrinsic motivation, it has since been found that giving people too many choices in the initial resources needed to solve a problem may actually be detrimental to creativity.

PUSHING THE FRONTIER OF CHOICE RESEARCH IN ORGANIZATIONS

In the second half of this chapter, we will switch our focus from reviewing extant research to theorizing about the potential implications of yet unexamined contextual factors on organizational behavior research. Although we have discussed several streams of emerging research that have taken a more nuanced and critical look at the effects and consequences of empowering people through the provision of choice, this is, in our view, hardly comprehensive or exhaustive. We believe that there is room for more research that probes the boundary conditions under which choice may or may not have its purported beneficial effects. Furthermore, scholars may want to revisit some key organizational theories that advocate the benefits of choice and autonomy, and examine how emerging choice research could inform these theories. In this section, we will discuss four areas which, in our view, warrant more attention: (a) individual differences that could influence the effects of choice, (b) the effect of choice on job design theories, (c) the consequences of giving people choice on procedural justice, and (d) how ideas explored in choice research could be extended to the area of power and leadership. Such research, if conducted, could further enhance managers' abilities to effectively administer choice to their employees.

Individual Differences

One area that is clearly lacking in the choice research discussed so far is the impact of individual differences. Earlier in this chapter, we saw that individuals' socioeconomic status can influence how choice is perceived. Do other individual differences also influence the effects of choice? As Kofi Annan, secretary general of the United Nations and 2001 Nobel peace prize winner, once said, "To live is to choose. But to choose well, you must know who you are and what you stand for, where you want to go and why you want to get there." All too often, choice research tends to assume that people have (a) accurate self-knowledge (i.e., they know what they want) and (b) sufficient knowledge to evaluate the options they are choosing from. This is consistent with the idea that choice confers personal agency; to the extent that one knows what he or she wants and is knowledgeable about making a choice, having the ability to choose can indeed make one feel more empowered.

However, do people really know what they want in a world that offers a large and sometimes unfathomable number of options? Although it is possible that some people do indeed have a clear idea of what they are looking for, much research has shown that people may actually be limited in their ability to acquire self-knowledge (e.g., Silvia & Gendella, 2001; Wilson, 2002; Wilson & Dunn, 2004). It is likely that as the number of options increases, people who do not have a good sense of what they are looking for are going to feel much more confused and frustrated than those who do. Thus, it is plausible that the documented detrimental effects of having too much choice are exacerbated in individuals who do not have clear ideas about their own preferences. In a job search context for instance, to the extent that a job seeker is not sure about his or her employment preferences, the more job opportunities there are to choose from, the more frustrating and overwhelming the choice-making process becomes. For any given chosen option, there are likely to be other plausible and attractive options that must be given up, thus leading to much post-decision dissonance. Hence, the job seeker without clear preferences is more likely to face the question "what if I had chosen job B or C instead of job A?" On the other hand, if the job seeker is clear about his or her career directions and preferences, the seemingly large choice set can be more easily trimmed down to a manageable size from which a decision can then be made.

Another related dimension of individual differences involves having the knowledge and expertise to evaluate one's options. Consider the earlier 401(k) retirement plan study by Iyengar et al. (2004). If the chooser is unfamiliar with the various investment plans, he or she is unlikely to be able to evaluate the plans effectively. As the number of investment plans increases, the non-savvy employee is probably going to have a more difficult time making a decision. This may lead the individual to avoid making a decision, or make a wrong investment decision, which can be costly. The same logic can be applied to choosing which company stock or securities to buy. An uninformed investor is likely to be so overwhelmed by the large number of stocks that, rather than feeling empowered, he or she may decide not to enter the market at all. In contrast, an experienced investor is likely to be less overwhelmed by the large number of choices. Thus, we posit that the lack of knowledge (both self-knowledge about one's preferences and knowledge about evaluating the available options) can exacerbate the negative effects brought about by an extensive choice set. This effect of knowledge on choice is consistent with Locke and Schweiger's (1979) discussion on the importance of having relevant knowledge before one can successfully participate in decision-making tasks.

Yet another individual difference variable that could potentially influence the choice-making experience is one's need for closure (Kruglanski &

Webster, 1996). As a dispositional construct, the need for cognitive closure is conceptualized as a latent variable manifested in several ways, including one's desire for predictability, one's preference for order and structure, one's discomfort with ambiguity, one's level of decisiveness, and one's close-mindedness. Thus, a person with a high need for closure desires to be able to make a decision quickly (seizing) and then stick with it (freezing). When confronted with an extensive choice set, such an individual is likely to experience more frustration than one who has a relatively lower need for closure. A large option set renders making a final decision more difficult, and may thus lead an individual with a high need for closure to either avoid the act of choosing altogether or to employ some form of heuristic to quickly reach a decision. Conversely, for individuals with a low need for closure, an extensive choice set may cause even more deliberation over the various options, and lead this individual to take even longer to reach a decision than he or she would otherwise. Furthermore, because an individual with low need for closure is less likely to "freeze" a given decision, the large number of options will accentuate the perception that a better option is out there and thus lower his or her commitment to the chosen option.

It is important to note that these differential effects of choice on individuals with different levels of need for closure are not necessarily always detrimental or beneficial to organizational outcomes. For instance, during an early stage of business idea brainstorming, not freezing a decision too early could be a good thing as it allows for an exploration of more potential alternatives. Conversely, during business implementation with tight deadlines, not being able to make a choice and stick with it could hurt the entire execution of the business operation. Future research could examine the effects of choice and need for closure under different situational demands.

Finally, an individual's regulatory focus (Higgins, 1998) may also influence how choice is perceived. According to the regulatory focus theory (Higgins, 1998), all goal-directed behaviors are regulated by two distinct motivational systems: promotion and prevention focus. Briefly, promotion-focused individuals are driven by nurturance needs and are concerned with accomplishment and advancement. They tend to focus on ideals, aspirations, and hopes, and use an "approach" strategy to decision making. In other words, such individuals tend to ensure hits and ensure against error of omissions. Thus, they are especially sensitive to gain versus non-gain situations. Conversely, prevention-focused individuals are driven more by security needs and are concerned with safety and fulfillment of responsibilities. They tend to focus on "oughts," duties, and obligations and use an "avoidance" strategy toward decision making. In other words, such individuals tend to ensure correct rejections and ensure against errors of commission. Thus, they are especially sensitive to non-loss versus loss situations.

Drawing on the prevention–promotion regulatory distinction, we hypothesize that individuals with a promotion-focus motivational orientation are more likely to relish having a large number of options to choose from, and are more energized by this choice set than those with a prevention-focus motivational orientation. For the former, having more choice means more opportunities to fulfill their hopes and dreams. Having more choices also satisfies their tendency to insure hits and guard against possible omissions. In addition, the increased freedom to choose gives them a heightened sense of control and agency, which is consistent with their "approach" strategy toward decision making. In contrast, prevention-focused individuals may not welcome an extensive choice set to the same degree; they are more concerned with security and taking care not to make mistakes or incur losses, and too many choices simply increases the probability that a wrong decision is made.

Job Design

In an organizational context, job design is often used as a means to increase the intrinsic motivation of employees. According to the Job Characteristics Model, two of the ways to achieve this objective are by increasing task variety and giving people autonomy in the work that they do (Hackman & Oldham, 1976). Implicit in this formulation is that variety in the dimensions of one's job and having the freedom and personal control to choose how to do one's work would have an energizing effect on people. Not only would work be less boring given more variety, the associated flexibility and autonomy could also increase one's sense of responsibility toward the assigned task. As a consequence, employees in such conditions would likely become more intrinsically motivated in their work.

While the Job Characteristics Model makes the broad prescription of increasing task variety and autonomy, it is relatively uninformative about boundary conditions (other than the growth strength needs of the individuals involved). For example, will giving people autonomy in their work increase intrinsic motivation in East Asia as much as it does in the U.S.? To address this question, we turn to our earlier discussion regarding the effect of culture on the perception of choice. Recall that in an experiment by Iyengar and Lepper (1999), European Americans were most highly motivated and performed best when given a personal choice in deciding which activity to engage in, whereas Asians were more motivated when choices

were made for them by their own mothers. Drawing on this body of research, we argue that giving employees autonomy in terms of deciding how
to go about doing their work could have similar effects. For instance, various scholars have written about the relatively paternalistic management
style used in Chinese companies (e.g., Farh & Cheng, 2000). Here, management often retains tight control over how lower-level subordinates do
their work. While such a lack of autonomy and personal agency could easily
be perceived as a lack of trust in the West, and lead to low levels of employee
intrinsic motivation, it would likely have an opposite effect in China. Tight
management control could be perceived by Chinese employees as offering
clear direction and support for their work. Such a management style could
also signal a high degree of top-level involvement and interest. Seen in this
light, lack of choice can actually be motivating.

Consider next the suggestion of giving employees more variety in their
work as a way of enhancing intrinsic motivation. Here, we believe that
the research on choice overload could be relevant. While we agree with
Hackman and Oldham (1976) that giving employees some variety in their
work tasks could render the job more interesting and meaningful, we argue
that care must be taken to determine the degree of task variety that should
be given to employees. Drawing on the extensive choice research reviewed
earlier, we propose that by giving employees more variety in their work,
managers could easily risk overloading them. Specifically, as the number of
diverse tasks a person has on his or her work portfolio increases, it becomes
increasingly difficult to juggle them. This increase in difficulty need not come
from a large increase in task variety. Rather, increasing one's work portfolio
by just one task could have an overwhelming effect; even when the overall
workload is kept constant, an additional new task means that more cognitive switching from task to task is required. When the number of diverse
tasks is small, such switching can provide relief from the boredom associated with managing only one task. However, as the number of diverse
tasks increases, the cognitive shifting of attention and mental frameworks
among different tasks can become confusing and/or de-motivating.

Procedural Justice

Over the past three decades, scholars in organizational research have identified three key conceptualizations of justice: distributive, procedural, and
interactional (Brockner & Wiesenfeld, 1996). Of notable relevance to our
current discussion is that of procedural justice, which focuses on the process

by which decisions are made. One way to increase procedural justice is to give people some form of process control or voice (Thibaut & Walker, 1975). Another way to increase procedural justice is to give people some form of decision control through participation via the selection or veto of procedural options (e.g., offering a choice of procedures to accomplish a task). For instance, Earley and Lind (1987) showed that giving people choice in terms of which tasks to work on and which procedures to employ enhances their judgments of procedural justice.

However, research that examines choice as a means of increasing perceived procedural justice has not considered the potential downsides to such an approach. Can giving people choice in decision processes actually lead to lower perceptions of procedural justice? Consider the scenario in which a company is experiencing financial difficulties and needs to implement cost-cutting measures. To reduce human resources expenditure, it offers employees the options of either receiving a substantial pay cut or being laid off with a severance package. Although justice research would suggest that such a gesture should improve perceived procedural fairness, as the affected employees are being given choice and the opportunity to participate in the process, we would argue that research on the "choice-outcome aversion" effect (e.g., Botti & Iyengar, 2004) might suggest otherwise. Specifically, we hypothesize that the act of having to choose between two very painful options could actually lead the employees to reminisce and deliberate over their unfortunate fate and cause even greater resentment toward the company. Rather than feeling that the cost-cutting process is a fair one because they were involved in it, employees may even reject such a process as a poor and futile attempt to cushion the unfavorable outcome. Hence, the pleasure of choosing is supplanted by pain and resentment.

Power and Leadership

Although having choice has been linked to an increased sense of personal control and agency (e.g., Lefcourt, 1973; Rotter, 1966; Taylor, 1989; Taylor & Brown, 1988), the role of choice in the context of power and leadership has not yet been researched. Does having more choices in a specific domain give people the perception of being more powerful in that domain? We posit that, to the extent that choice increases one's perception of control, the more choices one has, the more powerful they are likely to feel. This feeling, in turn, could translate into behaviors characterized by more automatic information processing, approach-related tendencies, and reduced inhibition (Keltner, Gruenfeld, & Anderson, 2003). However, if prior research regarding the increased complexity of extensive choice sets is to be considered, it seems likely that having too many choices may cease to elevate one's perception of power. Rather, the overwhelming nature of too many choices may lead those given extensive options to actually feel less powerful, since they are less able to make a decision and be satisfied with this decision. In short, we argue that there could be a curvilinear relationship between the number of choices one has and one's perception of power. In other words, an individual given a moderate number of options is likely to feel more powerful than another who is given a greater number of options.

With respect to leadership, it would be interesting to explore how subordinates' perceptions of a leader are shaped by the number of options offered to them by the leader. When a leader routinely gives his or her subordinates some form of choice in various aspects of their work, such a leader is likely to be perceived as having a consultative or participative leadership style and less likely to be seen as an authoritarian figure. Thus, subordinates' positive perceptions of the leader should increase as the leader gives them more choices in their work. However, when a leader starts giving subordinates a sizable number of choices (e.g., five different projects to choose from instead of just two), he or she could actually be perceived as indecisive or weak. While some choice is welcomed, giving subordinates choices beyond a certain level may cause the subordinates to think that a leader does not have a clearly thought-out agenda. In this case, we believe that the number of choices offered need not even reach an extensive level for the negative impact to occur. For instance, if the norm is to have no options or very few options, offering subordinates any additional options beyond this norm may elicit the above-mentioned negative effect. Further research should examine how choices offered by leaders affect subordinates' perception of both leadership qualities as well as overall impressions of character.

PRACTICAL APPLICATIONS

Next, we briefly discuss a few examples to illustrate how managers can draw upon the emerging choice research reviewed in this chapter to make better decisions and more effectively motivate employees in practice.

Imagine that the human resources department of a company has decided to implement a flexible benefits scheme for its employees. Instead of giving all employees the same set of benefits, management wants to give them choices over the benefits they receive. In a typical flexible benefits program, employees are given a fixed number of points every year. They can then exchange these points for their desired benefits from a larger set of benefits provided by the company. By giving employees choice, it is often hoped that they will be more satisfied with the benefits package since it can now be customized to suit an individual's personal needs. Conventional wisdom therefore suggests that the more benefit options employees have, the more satisfied they will be. However, research that highlights the flip side of extensive choice (e.g., Iyengar & Lepper, 2000) suggests that this proposition may have to be more carefully evaluated. When the number of available benefits becomes large, employees are more likely to experience conflict over how to choose their desired benefits. For every benefit chosen, there is another equally attractive one forgone. Thus, although employees may have more flexibility in customizing their benefits packages, they are not necessarily more satisfied. Worse, they may even feel that the company is not giving them enough benefit points so that they can obtain all of the benefits that they think they need.

In the area of personnel selection and recruitment, ideas from emerging choice research are also applicable. Whenever a job position is advertised or a search for a job opening is conducted, it is often considered desirable to have as many available applicants as possible. Not only does this signal a huge demand for the available position, the company also has the advantage of a large number of potential candidates to choose from. So intuitive is this idea that oftentimes, recruitment or head-hunting strategies are formulated to attract as many applicants as possible. Is this necessarily a good strategy? Drawing again on "choice overload" research, we argue that having too many applicants has at least one major drawback – it is difficult to effectively screen through the large number of applicants to select the right one(s). Unless the company can invest extra resources to facilitate the search process, the typical solution is to use some form of heuristics as a screening mechanism. For instance, MBA admissions often use standardized test scores such as the GMAT to sift through large numbers of applications. Only those applications that meet the cutoff are given a more serious read. Yet this is hardly the best strategy, as otherwise good candidates may be eliminated as a result of the crude heuristics used. A better strategy may be to formulate a more targeted recruitment pitch so that only a manageable number of well-qualified applicants need to be evaluated. In this way, not only does the recruiting company save precious resources and time, a more effective selection process can be employed to choose the most suitable candidate(s).

Finally, in a knowledge-based economy, harnessing employee creativity has increasingly become an important concern for managers. The studies by

Chua and Iyengar (2005a, 2005b) highlight the potential pitfalls that managers may encounter when giving employees increased choices on tasks requiring creativity. Specifically, managers need to pay attention to whom they give extensive options on jobs requiring creativity. If extensive options are given to employees with high creative self-efficacy and a goal of creativity, one could potentially see the desired results. However, a potentially dangerous situation arises when a manager gives an employee with low creative self-efficacy extensive choices when solving a creativity-related problem. Not only will the employee probably not deliver a creative output, he or she might be de-motivated and discouraged by the complexity involved in the problem-solving process. Hence, not only would we lose out on the expected positive results, there could also be potential negative repercussions from such a strategy.

CONCLUSION

In organizational life, managers often struggle with the question of how to empower employees. In this chapter, we considered one of the most common vehicles through which individuals could be empowered – the provision of choice. Although past psychological and organizational research persuasively suggests that choice confers personal agency and is thus intrinsically motivating, emerging research suggests that things are not quite as straightforward.

The research we have reviewed suggests to managers that they have to pay careful attention to individual and cultural differences when administering choices to employees. For instance, individuals from lower socioeconomic status may not perceive the provision of choice as critical to their sense of personal agency because their focus is not on expressing uniqueness and control. Thus, whereas high socioeconomic status employees may react negatively when denied the opportunity to choose, those from lower socioeconomic status may not care whether or not they get to choose. With regard to cultural differences, first, it appears that individuals from interdependent cultures tend not to place as much emphasis on the provision of choice as individuals from independent cultures. In fact, when choices were made by significant authority figures (e.g., mothers or well-respected bosses), the effect was often more positive than when it was made personally.

Second, even for individuals from independent cultures who perceive having choice as an important form of personal control, the content of the options offered needs to be considered. When the alternatives are undesirable, the pleasure of choosing could be replaced by pain and anxiety. Thus, instead of embracing the agency and control that choice confers, people may actually avoid it. People who have choice over undesirable alternatives are also likely to be less satisfied with the options they choose compared to those who do not have choice.

Third, in the event that choice is to be offered, managers must be aware of the misconception that more is necessarily better. It is easy to think that if choice gives people a sense of control and autonomy, then more is always welcomed. In fact, the research we examined suggests that too much choice can lead to experiences of choice overload. Instead of feeling empowered, employees may become confused, avoid choosing, and experience less satisfaction than they otherwise would have, given fewer options.

Finally, although conventional wisdom suggests that in order to unleash employee creativity, people should be given as much flexibility and autonomy as possible, recent research indicates that managers may want to take a more cautious stance. When given extensive choices in terms of task materials and initial resources, individuals can become frustrated and overwhelmed because the combinatorial possibility of using the large number of options can be daunting. This may result, not only in less divergent thinking during the problem-solving process, but also in reduced intrinsic motivation during the task.

Taken together, this body of new research highlights to managers the limits of choice. Under many circumstances, choice not only fails to provide the expected benefits, it can also be detrimental to job performance and the psychological well-being of the individuals involved. Thus, rather than over-romanticizing the notion that choice empowers people, managers should carefully consider various situational factors before deciding whether to empower employees through the provision of choice.

In closing, we return to McGregor's (1960) challenge to managers to think of organizations, not as machines driven by authority figures at the top with employees as interchangeable cogs in a large wheel, but rather as human enterprises. This vision has had an influential legacy in management thinking today, with hundreds of companies now practicing different forms of employee involvement and empowerment. Top management control is increasingly decentralized and employees are given more choice and autonomy in their work because they are being recognized as individuals with very different values, needs, and goals.

This approach to management is consistent with various theories propounded by other influential management scholars of the human relations tradition such as Herzberg (Herzberg, Mausner, & Snyderman, 1959),

Maslow (1954), and Mayo (1933). Specifically, Herzberg and Maslow emphasized that people are not motivated merely by economic and security needs, but also by the need to grow and achieve various personal and social goals. Furthermore, Mayo highlighted the importance of socio-psychological factors in human behavior. According to Mayo, people's psychological states and behaviors are, to a large extent, shaped by their social context and interpersonal relations. In this chapter, we have brought together these key ideas in understanding the effects of choice in organizations. In the same spirit of these early scholars' visions of building more humanistic organizations, we argue that even when empowering employees through the provision of choice, managers should resist any attempts to use an overly simplistic one-size-fits-all approach. It is important to consider both individual differences as well as socio-cultural factors.

NOTES

1. An alternative dependent variable is the number of ideas that were not within the 10 themes used in the study. Separate analysis using this variable yielded similar results.

2. An alternative response to the increased frustration could be to abandon the creativity goal (as opposed to seeking it) so that one does not have to search expansively for a novel solution. However, doing so would mean directly undermining the creativity of any output produced. This is not likely to be the dominant strategy as it contradicts the given goal.

REFERENCES

Amabile, T. M. (1979). Effects of external evaluation on artistic creativity. *Journal of Personality and Social Psychology, 37*, 221–233.

Amabile, T. M. (1983). The social psychology of creativity: A componential conceptualization. *Journal of Personality and Social Psychology, 45*(2), 357–376.

Amabile, T. M., & Gitomer, J. (1984). Children's artistic creativity: Effect of choice in task materials. *Personality and Social Psychology Bulletin, 10*, 209–215.

Amabile, T. M., & Gryskiewicz, N. D. (1989). The creative environment work scales: Work environment inventory. *Creativity Research Journal, 21*, 231–254.

Amabile, T. M., & Gryskiewicz, S. S. (1987). *Creativity in the R&D laboratory*. Technical Report no. 30. Center for Creative Leadership, Greensbro, NC.

Amabile, T. M., Hennessey, B. A., & Grossman, B. S. (1986). Social influence on creativity: The effects of contract-for rewards. *Journal of Personality and Social Psychology, 50*, 14–23.

Ames, D. R., & Fu, J. H. (2000). Unpublished data. Stanford University, Graduate School of Business, Stanford, CA.

Averill, J. R. (1973). Personal control over aversive stimuli and its relationship to stress. *Psychological Bulletin, 80,* 286–303.

Barnes, R. D. (1981). Perceived freedom and control in the built environment. In: J. H. Harvey (Ed.), *Cognition, Social Behavior, and the Environment* (pp. 409–422). Hillsdale, NJ: Erlbaum.

Beattie, J., Baron, J., Hershey, J. C., & Spranca, M. (1994). Determinants of decision seeking and decision aversion. *Journal of Behavioral Decision Making, 7,* 129–144.

Botti, S., & Iyengar, S. (2004). The psychological pleasure and pain of choosing: When people prefer choosing at the cost of subsequent satisfaction. *Journal of Personality and Social Psychology, 87,* 312–326.

Brockner, J., & Wiesenfeld, B. M. (1996). An integrative framework for explaining reactions to decisions: Interactive effects of outcomes and procedures. *Psychological Bulletin, 120*(2), 189–208.

Burger, J. (1989). Negative reactions to perceived increases in personal control. *Journal of Personality and Social Psychology, 56,* 246–256.

Chua R. Y. J., & Iyengar, S. (2005a). The effects of choice, goal, and creative self-efficacy on divergent thinking and creative outcomes. Academy of Management Conference. Hawaii.

Chua, R. Y. J., & Iyengar, S. (2005b). *When more choice interferes divergent thinking: The effects of choice and goal on divergent thinking.* Unpublished manuscript. Columbia University.

Condry, J. (1977). Enemies of exploration: Self-initiated versus other-initiated learning. *Journal of Personality and Social Psychology, 35,* 459–477.

Condry, J. C., & Chambers, J. C. (1978). Intrinsic motivation and the process of learning. In: M. R. Lepper & D. Greene (Eds), *The hidden costs of reward* (pp. 61–84). Hillsdale, NJ: Erlbaum.

Cordova, D. I., & Lepper, M. R. (1996). Intrinsic motivation and the process of learning: Beneficial effects of contextualization, personalization, and choice. *Journal of Educational Psychology, 88,* 715–730.

deCharms, R. (1968). *Personal causation.* New York: Academic Press.

Deci, E. L. (1971). Effects of externally mediated reward on intrinsic motivation. *Journal of Personality and Social Psychology, 18,* 105–115.

Deci, E. L. (1975). *Intrinsic motivation.* New York: Plenum Press.

Deci, E. L. (1981). *The psychology of self-determination.* Lexington, MA: Heaths.

Deci, E. L., Driver, R. E., Hotchkiss, L., Robbins, R. J., & Wilson, T. D. (1993). The relation of mothers' controlling vocalization to children's intrinsic motivation. *Journal of Experimental Child Psychology, 55,* 151–162.

Deci, E. L., Eghrari, H., Patrick, B. C., & Leone, D. (1994). Facilitating internalization: The self-determination theory perspective. *Journal of Personality, 62,* 119–142.

Deci, E. L., & Ryan, R. M. (1985). *Intrinsic motivation and self-determination in human behavior.* New York: Plenum Press.

Deci, E. L., & Ryan, R. M. (1991). A motivational approach to self: Integration in personality. In: R. Dienstbier (Ed.), *Nebraska Symposium on Motivation: Perspectives on motivation* (Vol. 38, pp. 237–288). Lincoln: University of Nebraska Press.

Deci, E. L., Speigel, N. H., Ryan, R. M., Koestner, R., & Kaufman, M. (1982). The effects of performance standards on teaching styles: The behavior of controlling teachers. *Journal of Educational Psychology, 74,* 852–859.

Dhar, R. (1997). Consumer preference for a no-choice option. *Journal of Consumer Research, 24*, 215–231.

Drolet, A. (2002). Inherent rule variability in consumer choice: Changing rules for change's sake. *Journal of Consumer Research, 29*, 199–209.

De Vos, G. A. (1985). Dimensions of the self in Japanese culture. In: A. Marsella, G. De Vos & F. L. K. Hsu (Eds), *Culture and self* (pp. 149–184). London: Tavistock.

Earley, P. C., & Lind, E. A. (1987). Procedural justice and participation in task selection: The role of control in mediating justice judgments. *Journal of Personality and Social Psychology, 52*(6), 1148–1160.

Farh, J. L., & Cheng, B. S. (2000). A cultural analysis of paternalistic leadership in Chinese organizations. In: J. T. Li, A. S. Tsui & E. Weldon (Eds), *Management and organizations in the Chinese context* (pp. 84–127). London: Macmillan.

Gifford, R. (1987). *Environmental psychology: Principles and practice*. Boston: Allyn & Bacon.

Greenberg, E. (1992). Creativity, autonomy, and evaluation of creative work: Artistic workers in organizations. *Journal of Creative Behavior, 26*(2), 75–80.

Hackman, J., & Oldham, G. (1976). Motivation through the design of work: Test of a theory. *Organizational Behavior and Human Performance, 16*, 250–279.

Harter, S. (1981). A new self-report scale of intrinsic versus extrinsic orientation in the classroom: Motivational and informational components. *Developmental Psychology, 17*, 300–312.

Hauser, J. R., & Wernerfelt, B. (1990). An evaluation cost model of consideration sets. *Journal of Consumer Research, 16*, 393–408.

Herzberg, F., Mausner, B., & Snyderman, B. (1959). *The motivation to work* (2nd ed.). New York: Wiley.

Higgins, T. E. (1998). Promotion and prevention: Regulatory focus as a motivational principle. In: M. P. Zanna (Ed.), *Advances in Experimental Social Psychology* (Vol. 30). New York, NY: Academic Press.

Higgins, E. T., Trope, Y., & Kwon, J. (1999). Augmenting and undermining interest from combining activities: The role of choice in activity engagement theory. *Journal of Experimental Social Psychology, 35*, 285–307.

Hofstede, G. (1980). *Culture's consequences: International differences in work-related values*. Newbury Park, CA: Sage.

Hofstede, G. (1991). *Cultures and organizations: Software of the mind*. London: McGraw-Hill.

Hsu, F. L. K. (1985). The self in cross-cultural perspective. In: A. J. Marsella, G. De Vos & F. L. K. Hsu (Eds), *Culture and self* (pp. 24–55). London: Tavistock.

Iyengar, S. S., Jiang, W., & Huberman, G. (2004). How much choice is too much: Determinants of individual contributions in 401K retirement plans. In: O. S. Mitchell & Utkus (Eds), *Pension design and structure: New lessons from behavioral finance* (pp. 83–97). Oxford: Oxford University Press.

Iyengar, S. S., & Lepper, M. (1999). Rethinking the value of choice: A cultural perspective on intrinsic motivation. *Journal of Personality and Social Psychology, 76*, 349–366.

Iyengar, S. S., & Lepper, M. (2000). When choice is demotivating: Can one desire too much of a good thing? *Journal of Personality and Social Psychology, 79*, 995–1006.

Iyengar, S. S., Lepper, M., Hernandez, M. R., DeVoe, S. E., & Alpert, B. (2001). *Rethinking the consequences of choice: Cultural perspectives on intrinsic motivation, personal control, and job performance*. Manuscript submitted for publication.

Iyengar, S. S., Ross, L., & Lepper, M. (1999). Independence from whom? Interdependence with whom? Cultural perspectives on ingroups versus outgroups. In: D. Miller (Ed.), *Cultural divides: The social psychology of cultural identity* (pp. 273–301). New York: Sage.

Iyengar, S. S., Wells, R., & Schwartz, B. (2006). Doing better but feeling worse: Looking for the "best" job undermines satisfaction. *Psychological Science, 17*(2), 143–150.

Janis, I., & Mann, L. (1977). *Decision making: A psychological analysis of conflict, choice and commitment.* New York: Free Press.

Kahneman, D., & Tversky, A. (1984). Choices, value, and frames. *American Psychologist, 39,* 341–350.

Keltner, D., Gruenfeld, D. H., & Anderson, C. (2003). Power, approach, and inhibition. *Psychological Review, 110*(2), 265–284.

Kim, H. S., & Drolet, A. (2003). Choice and self-expression: A cultural analysis of variety seeking. *Journal of Personality and Social Psychology, 85*(2), 373–382.

Kim, H. S., & Markus, H. R. (1999). Deviance or uniqueness, harmony or conformity? A cultural analysis. *Journal of Personality and Social Psychology, 77,* 785–800.

Kruglanski, A. W., & Webster, D. M. (1996). Motivated closing of the mind: "Seizing" and "freezing." *Psychological Review, 103,* 263–283.

Lefcourt, H. M. (1973). The function of the illusions of control and freedom. *American Psychologist, 28,* 417–425.

Lewin, K. (1951). *Field theory in social science.* Chicago: University of Chicago Press.

Lind, E. A., & Tyler, T. R. (1988). *The social psychology of procedural justice.* New York: Plenum.

Locke, E. A., & Schweiger, D. M. (1979). Participation in decision-making: One more look. *Research in Organizational Behavior, 1,* 265–339.

Luce, M. F. (1998). Choosing to avoid: Coping with negatively emotion-laden consumer decisions. *Journal of Consumer Research, 24*(4), 409–433.

Malone, T. W., & Lepper, M. R. (1987). Making learning fun: A taxonomy of intrinsic motivations for learning. In: R. E. Snow & M. J. Farr (Eds), *Aptitude, learning and instruction: Cognitive and affective process analysis* (Vol. 3, pp. 223–253). Hillsdale, NJ: Erlbaum.

Markus, H., & Kitayama, S. (1991). Culture and the self: Implications for cognition, emotion and motivation. *Psychological Review, 98,* 224–253.

Maslow, A. (1954). *Motivation and personality.* New York: Harper & Row.

Mayo, E. (1933). *The human problems of an industrial civilization.* New York: Macmillan.

McGregor, D. (1960). *The human side of enterprise.* New York: McGraw-Hill.

Menon, T., Morris, M. W., Chiu, C. Y., & Hong, Y. Y. (1999). Culture and the construal of agency: Attribution to individual versus group dispositions. *Journal of Personality and Social Psychology, 76,* 701–717.

Miller, J. G. (1988). Bridging the content-structure dichotomy: Culture and the self. In: M. H. Bond (Ed.), *The cross-cultural challenge to social psychology* (pp. 266–281). Beverly Hills, CA: Sage.

Miller, N. E. (1959). Liberalization of basic S-R concepts: Extension to conflict behavior, motivation and social learning. In: S. Koch (Ed.), *Psychology: A study of a science.* New York: McGraw-Hill.

Mischel, W., & Ebbesen, E. (1970). Attention in the delay of gratification. *Journal of Personality and Social Psychology, 16,* 329–337.

Nix, G. A., Ryan, R. M., Manly, J. B., & Deci, E. L. (1999). Revitalization through self-regulation: The effects of autonomous and controlled motivation on happiness and vitality. *Journal of Experimental Social Psychology, 35*, 266–284.

Nuttin, J. R. (1973). Pleasure and reward in human motivation and learning. In: D. E. Berlyne & K. B. Madsen (Eds), *Pleasure, reward, preference* (pp. 243–274). New York: Academic Press.

Orfali, K., & Gordon, E. J. (2004). Autonomy gone awry: A cross-cultural study of parents' experiences in neonatal intensive care unit. *Theoretical Medicine and Bioethics, 25*(4), 329–365.

Rotter, J. B. (1966). Generalized expectancies for internal versus external locus of control of reinforcement. *Psychological Monographs, 80*, 1–28.

Ryan, R. M. (1982). Control and information in the interpersonal sphere: An extension of cognitive evaluation theory. *Journal of Personality and Social Psychology, 43*, 450–461.

Schultz, R., & Hanusa, B. H. (1978). Long-term effects of control and predictability-enhancing interventions: Findings and ethical issues. *Journal of Personality and Social Psychology, 36*, 1194–1201.

Schwartz, B., Ward, A., Monterosso, J., Lyubomirsky, S., White, K., & Lehman, D. R. (2002). Maximizing versus satisficing: Happiness is a matter of choice. *Journal of Personality and Social Psychology, 83*, 1178–1197.

Seligman, M. E. (1975). *Helplessness: On depression, development, and death.* San Francisco: Freeman.

Shafir, E., Simonson, I., & Tversky, A. (1993). Reason-based choice. *Cognition, 49*, 11–36.

Shafir, E., & Tversky, A. (1992). Thinking through uncertainty: Non-consequential reasoning and choice. *Cognitive Psychology, 24*, 449–474.

Shalley, C. E. (1991). Effects of productivity goals, creativity goals, and personal discretion on individual creativity. *Journal of Applied Psychology, 76*, 179–185.

Shweder, R. A., & Bourne, E. J. (1984). Does the concept of the person vary cross-culturally? In: R. A. Shweder & R. A. LeVine (Eds), *Culture theory: Essays on mind, self, and emotion* (pp. 158–199). Cambridge, England: Cambridge University Press.

Silvia, P. J., & Gendella, G. H. E. (2001). On introspection and self-perception: Does self-focused attention enable accurate self-knowledge? *Review of General Psychology, 5*, 241–269.

Simon, H. A. (1955). A behavioral model of rational choice. *Quarterly Journal of Economics, 59*, 99–118.

Simon, H. A. (1956). Rational choice and the structure of the environment. *Psychological Review, 63*, 129–138.

Simon, H. A. (1957). *Models of man, social and rational: Mathematical essays on rational human behavior.* New York: Wiley.

Simonson, I. (1992). The influence of anticipating regret and responsibility on purchase decision. *Journal of Consumer Research, 19*, 1–14.

Smeltz, W., & Cross, B. (1984). Toward a profile of the creative R&D professional. *IEEE Transactions on Engineering Management, EM-31*, 22–25.

Snibbe, A. C., & Markus, H. R. (2005). You can't always get what you want: Educational attainment, agency, and choice. *Journal of Personality and Social Psychology, 88*(4), 703–720.

Taylor, S. E. (1989). *Positive illusions: Creative self-deception and the healthy mind.* New York: Basic Books.

Taylor, S. E., & Brown, J. D. (1988). Illusion and well-being: A social-psychological perspective on mental health. *Psychological Bulletin, 103*, 193–210.

Thibaut, J., & Walker, L. (1975). *Procedural justice: A psychological analysis.* Hillsdale, NJ: Erlbaum.

Tierney, P., & Farmer, S. M. (2002). Creative self-efficacy: Potential antecedents and relationship to creative performance. *Academy of Management Journal, 145*(6), 1137–1148.

Triandis, H. C. (1988). Collectivism and individualism: A reconceptualization of a basic concept in cross-cultural social psychology. In: G. K. Verma & C. Bagely (Eds), *Personality, attitudes, and cognitions* (pp. 60–95). London: Macmillan.

Triandis, H. C. (1989). The self and social behavior in differing cultural contexts. *Psychological Review, 96*, 506–520.

Triandis, H. C. (1990). Cross-cultural studies of individualism and collectivism. In: J. Berman (Ed.), *Nebraska symposium of motivation* (Vol. XX, pp. 41–133). Lincoln: University of Nebraska Press.

Triandis, H. C. (1995). *Individualism and collectivism.* Boulder, CO: Westview Press.

Triandis, H. C., Bontempo, R., Villareal, M. J., Asai, M., & Lucca, N. (1988). Individualism and collectivism: Cross-cultural perspectives on self-ingroup relationships. *Journal of Personality and Social Psychology, 54*, 323–338.

Triandis, H. C., Marin, G., Lisansky, J., & Betancourt, H. (1984). Simpatia as a cultural script of Hispanics. *Journal of Personality and Social Psychology, 47*, 1363–1374.

Tyler, T. R. (1989). The psychology of procedural justice: A test of the group value model. *Journal of Personality and Social Psychology, 57*, 333–344.

Tyler, T. R., & Smith, H. J. (1999). Justice, social identity, and group processes. In: T. R. Tyler & R. M. Kramer (Eds), *The psychology of the social self: Applied social research* (pp. 223–264). Mahwah, NJ: Lawrence Erlbaum.

Wilson, T. D. (2002). *Strangers to ourselves: Discovering the adaptive unconscious.* Cambridge, MA: Belknap Press.

Wilson, T. D., & Dunn, E. W. (2004). Self-knowledge: Its limits, value and potential for improvement. *Annual Review of Psychology, 55*, 493–518.

Witt, L. A., & Beorkrem, M. (1989). Climate for creative productivity as a predictor of research usefulness and organizational effectiveness in an R&D organization. *Creativity Research Journal, 2*, 230–240.

Yates, B. T., & Mischel, W. (1979). Young children's preferred attentional strategies for delaying gratification. *Journal of Personality and Social Psychology, 37*, 286–300.

Zhou, J. (1998). Feedback valence, feedback style, task autonomy, and achievement orientation: Interactive effects on creative performance. *Journal of Applied Psychology, 83*, 261–276.

Zuckerman, M., Porac, J., Lathin, D., Smith, R., & Deci, E. L. (1978). On the importance of self-determination for intrinsically motivated behavior. *Personality and Social Psychology Bulletin, 4*, 443–446.

IDEAS ARE BORN IN FIELDS OF PLAY: TOWARDS A THEORY OF PLAY AND CREATIVITY IN ORGANIZATIONAL SETTINGS

Charalampos Mainemelis and Sarah Ronson

ABSTRACT

Play is manifested in organizational behavior as a form of engagement with work tasks and as a form of diversion from them. In this paper we examine both manifestations of play as sources of creativity. We argue that when play is a form of engagement with an individual's organizational tasks it facilitates the cognitive, affective, and motivational dimensions of the creative process, while when play is a form of diversion from an individual's organizational tasks it fosters the peripheral social-relational dynamics that encourage creativity in the first place. We explore the personal and contextual conditions that influence the two manifestations of play and the relative balance between them in a work context. Drawing on our analysis and the extant creativity literature, we conceptualize play as the cradle of creativity in organizations. We suggest that by temporarily suspending ordinary conventions, structural obligations, and functional pressures, and by encouraging behaviors whose value may not be immediately evident, play stimulates, facilitates, and even rehearses creativity. We discuss the practical relevance of play for the

Research in Organizational Behavior: An Annual Series of Analytical Essays and Critical Reviews
Research in Organizational Behavior, Volume 27, 81–131
ISSN: 0191-3085/doi:10.1016/S0191-3085(06)27003-5

nature of work in creative industries and its larger intellectual importance for the study of human behavior in social systems.

INTRODUCTION

Play is a form of behavior that is readily and easily understood in experiential terms. We all know what play is and we all play, in work or in leisure, alone or with others, with objects, processes, or ideas. We recognize expressions of play in the world around us, and we are aware that play occupies social spaces of cultural and economic significance, such as theaters, cinemas, contests, sports, virtual games, games of chance, amusement parks, toys, hobbies, to name a few. While play as an experience is familiar to us, play as a topic of inquiry is among the least studied and least understood organizational behaviors. Despite its role in the economy, and despite the fact that other social sciences have long associated it with individual and social creative functioning, play usually appears in our literature only as an auxiliary or ill-defined construct. As a result, a number of important questions have not yet attracted systematic research attention. What is play in the context of an organization? What are its elements and manifestations? What are the consequences of play for organizational life? There is little published work on these issues and our field continues to lack conceptual frameworks and research agendas about the nature and roles of play in the world of work.

In this paper we suggest that play is a phenomenon that deserves systematic research attention because it is the cradle of an important organizational process, creativity. Although play could be discussed in relation to other organizational phenomena, its relationship with creativity is particularly important both in intellectual and practical terms. In intellectual terms, the relationship between play and creativity has found theoretical expression and empirical support in most other fields of social science. In their novel writings, Freud (1926), Vygotsky (1978), Huizinga (1955), Piaget (2001), Winnicott (2001), and Turner (1982) described play as a natural path to creativity. More recently, Russ (1999) and Dansky (1999) summarized empirical psychological studies which support that play fosters the creativity of children and adults alike. In two acclaimed biographical studies on exceptional professional creativity, Csikszentmihalyi (1997) and Gardner (1993) found that a common characteristic of their subjects was that they maintained a playful attitude toward their work throughout their careers. Research on play in other social sciences has led to a set of theoretical principles that appear to generalize in samples ranging from preschool children to Nobel laureates. These theoretical principles provide one useful starting point for thinking about the relationship between play and creativity in the world of work. Because work organizations are idiosyncratically complex social systems, however, it is important to develop theory and research about the manifestations and roles of play specifically in work contexts.

In practical terms, an investigation of the relationship between play and creativity is timely and overdue when considering the evolution of the work culture. Since the dawn of the Industrial Revolution play has been viewed as appropriate for children and poets but not for serious adults (Spariosu, 1989). The traditional administrative emphasis on rationality and consistency in human behavior has suppressed play (March, 1976), but it has not extinguished it (Sandelands, 1988). In 1927, Henri de Man observed that in the Tayloristic industrial system it was "psychologically impossible" to deprive employees from opportunities to satisfy "the instinct for play" (in Roy, 1959, p. 160). In the 1950s, two studies by Roy (1953, 1959) vividly illustrated that play occurs regularly even in inhospitable work environments. But much has changed since that time: work culture has started to slowly, but steadily, transform its assumptions about play.

A few organizations now institutionalize play times, fun times, and ceremonies (Dandridge, 1986; Locke, 1989, 1996). Some companies, like Southwest (Hallowell, 1996) and IDEO (Sutton & Hargadon, 1997), have elevated play to a central aspect of their cultures. The advent of the knowledge economy has also brought play into the core of certain productive activities. Some organizations now support "free times" in which people can play constructively with new ideas (Nemeth, 1997; Pinchot, 1985); others provide autonomy which allows employees to select and turn work tasks into play (Amabile, 1996; Starbuck & Webster, 1991); and those in the vast play industries even hire employees whose passions and hobbies are reflected in the work itself (Kelley & Littman, 2001). Some authors have noted that it is these firms that earn profits, attract market attention, shape their industries, and make it to the top of 'most-admired' company lists (O'Reilly & Rao, 1997). However, to date it is a relatively small number of firms that have recognized the value of play. Many organizations continue to see play as, at best, an occasionally affordable distraction from work that may boost employee morale but has little overall impact on their core business. A theory that guides empirical research to exploring play and its implications for creativity can help a wider group of organizations to understand that when play is woven into the deep fabric of organizational life it can transform the very nature of their products and work processes. Such a research stream will also strengthen the evolution of a more integrated work culture.

The importance of play for creativity has been recognized in our field, but has not received systematic attention. Thirty years ago, March (1976) suggested that play fosters creativity by legitimately freeing people from the requirement of behavioral consistency, and Weick (1979) argued that play fosters combinatorial flexibility, the novel recombination of the existing elements in one's behavioral repertoire. More recently, Amabile (1996) noted that a generous level of freedom encourages people to play constructively at their work by combining ideas in new ways that might not seem immediately useful in generating products or solutions. Other authors as well have proposed that play is important for creativity in the workplace (e.g., Barrett, 1998; Csikszentmihalyi & LeFevre, 1989; Glynn, 1994; Huy, 1999; Mainemelis, 2001). Although these articles offer a body of important insights, these insights have remained, to date, largely fragmented and dispersed across time and thematic areas. As a result, play has not yet claimed a significant role in organizational creativity research.

The knowledge and observations about play from other sciences, from our field, and from organizational practice are all pieces of the puzzle of play in organizational life. In this paper we arrange these pieces so as to advance the organizational literature in four ways.

First, previous articles have discussed play either without defining it (e.g., Roy, 1959) or by focusing only on one or two of its elements, be it means orientation (e.g., Glynn, 1994; Sandelands, 1988) or flexibility (e.g., Weick, 1979). This somewhat selective treatment has prevented the articulation of an encompassing definition of play as well as the development of a focused research stream to investigate play. In this paper we tackle the difficult but necessary step of defining the construct of play. We suggest that play is not a limited set of activities but a behavioral orientation to performing any type of activity. We define play as a behavioral orientation consisting of five interdependent and circularly interrelated elements: a threshold experience; boundaries in time and space; uncertainty-freedom-constraint; a loose and flexible association between means and ends; and positive affect. We describe in-depth the five elements of play, how they are interrelated, and how they differ, as a patterned behavioral orientation, from other forms of behavior.

Second, previous research has approached the organizational manifestations of play in a selective and perhaps dichotomous way. One part of the literature has focused on play as a diversion from work tasks (e.g., Elsbach & Hargadon, 2002; Jett & George, 2003; Roy, 1959), while the other part of the literature has discussed play as a way of engaging with work tasks (e.g., Amabile, 1996; Glynn, 1994; Mainemelis, 2001). In this paper we give equal attention to both manifestations of play, how they are interrelated, and under which conditions they interact to foster creativity. This dual focus allows us to create a more complete picture of the polymorphous nature and roles of play in organizational life.

Third, previous articles have explained the relationship between play and creativity mainly through cognitive (e.g., Glynn, 1994) and motivational (e.g., Amabile, 1996) mechanisms. Here we pay attention to the cognitive and motivational dimensions of this relationship, but we also give center stage to the role of affect as a link between play and creativity – a link which has largely been overlooked in the creativity literature, to date.

Finally, we address a question that has rarely been tackled, to date: how important exactly is play for creativity in organizations? We argue that play is very important because it is a context of behavior that can simultaneously encompass all the elements and processes identified by previous research as stimulants of creativity. Our argument is not that all play is creative but that, more often than not, creativity is born out of some form or moment of play. We suggest that play facilitates the full range of factors that enable individual creativity and that by nurturing play organizations can improve their creative output. When play is marginalized by being viewed as detrimental to work its benefits to creativity are also likely to be marginalized. We argue that the full benefits of play to creativity are more likely to be realized when play is accepted and encouraged as an integral part of organizational life.

We begin by defining play as a patterned behavioral orientation, which consists of five interrelated elements. We then discuss two manifestations of play in organizations, namely play as a form of engagement with work tasks and play as a form of diversion from them. Play as engagement is the fundamental and most important manifestation of play in relation to creativity. We suggest that play as engagement fosters creativity directly by facilitating the cognitive and affective dimensions of the creative process, as well as the motivational and skill conditions that support the creative process in the first place. In the following section we suggest that play as diversion fosters creativity as well, but in more peripheral, indirect ways. Play as diversion may include office celebrations, surfing the internet, joking with colleagues, and other activities that are not part of an individual's core work tasks. Although such activities are external to task performance, they are integral to the social context in which task performance takes place. Research has shown that the social context affects task performance (e.g., Amabile, Conti, Coon, Lazenby, & Herron, 1996). We argue here that, under certain conditions, play as diversion shapes the social context in a way that encourages and enhances creative task performance. In the following section, we discuss the conditions that facilitate play and influence the relationship between play as engagement and play as diversion. We suggest that the relative balance between the two manifestations of play depends upon and reflects the nature of work and the nature of creativity in organizational contexts. We also argue that the full benefits of play to creativity are realized when organizations embrace both play as engagement and play as diversion. Finally, in the last section we synthesize our arguments at a higher level of abstraction. We conceptualize play as an organizational space of creative potential and argue that, although on the surface the reality of play seems to contradict the very idea of work, play in fact creates new work for the future. We conclude by addressing limitations of our approach, remaining puzzles endemic to the nature of play, and future directions for organizational research.

ELEMENTS OF PLAY

Play is not a set of activities but a way of organizing behavior in relation to any activity (Miller, 1973). Designing and writing are play sometimes but not at other times; cooking and driving are play for some but not for others. The essence of play is that one does not "do" the activity in the ordinary sense; one, rather, "plays" it (Huizinga, 1955). Theories in anthropology (e.g., Huizinga, 1955; Miller, 1973; Turner, 1982), psychology (e.g., Bruner, 1972; Winnicott, 2001) and sociology (e.g., Caillois, 2001) describe play as a set of qualities that is superimposed upon an activity regardless of its content. Integrating and elaborating upon these insights, we define play as a behavioral orientation consisting of five elements: a threshold experience; boundaries in time and space; uncertainty-freedom-constraint; loose and flexible association between means and ends; and positive affect.

Threshold Experience

Play is accompanied by the awareness that it is distinct from ordinary life. To play is to stand at a threshold between what we normally perceive as two dichotomous states. Play is often a threshold between the true and the false, being itself neither true nor false (Sutton-Smith, 1997). In a playfight, a bite is both not a bite and not *not* a bite; in a game of cops-and-robbers, a robber is not a robber but also not *not* a robber, that is, she is not a real robber but she does behave as if she were one. Plays offer such thresholds between convention and illusion, the former involving the realization that what takes place is not true, the latter involving the enactment of those happenings as if they were true – the "willful suspension of disbelief" (Coleridge in Bailey & Ford, 1994, p. 385). Play, therefore, transforms the nature of an activity. The behaviors of a playfight are part of 'fighting', but much of the fear, risk, and objectives of a real fight are removed, so that the nature of the activity is not the same as fighting. Play transforms the nature of work tasks in the same way, so that the task involves work activity and may result in work products, but the task is not experienced and is not performed as work in the conventional sense of obligatory, instrumental, and efficiency-orientated activity (Glynn, 1994; Sandelands, 1988).

Play has also been described as a transitional space between inner and outer reality, an intermediate area of experiencing to which inner reality and external life both contribute (Winnicott, 2001). Simulations and role-plays offer such transitional microcosms in which managers can experiment with possible realities and identities (Schrage, 2000). Play may also be a threshold between stability and change, the process of leaving one thing without having fully left it, and of entering something else without yet being fully part of it (Ibarra, 2003; Levinson, 1981). This is known as liminality, a transitional phase which is distinct both from the old and from the new, it shares attributes of both, and encircles experimentation. Play, as a liminality context, temporarily suspends social conventions and rules, giving way to ambiguity, joy, frivolity, and exploration of alternative behaviors (Turner, 1982, 1987).

Between-and-betwixt the inner and the outer, the old and the new, or the true and the false, play has a threshold awareness that sets it apart from life as usual (Huizinga, 1955). For example, when salespeople stage comic acts that exaggeratedly mimic interactions with clients, they superimpose a symbolic reality upon ordinary life (Goffman, 1959), in the same way that toys and simulations serve as points of departure from a normal perceptual situation (Bruner, 1972), that is, as transitional spaces between the real and the imaginary.

Boundaries in Time and Space

Play is circumscribed within limits in time and space, be it material or ideal (Huizinga, 1955). Societies historically mark off a space and time for play. Sports, festivals, and spectacles are institutionalized forms of play that claim their own space, such as stages or playgrounds, and a "time out of time," an autonomous duration perceived not so much by clock time but by what internally happens within it from its beginning to its end (Falassi, 1987). These boundaries separate play from normal life, suspend normal rules, and legitimize undesirable, repressed, or unexpected social roles and behaviors (Turner, 1982). In an organizational celebration over the weekend, an employee can drink, eat, or joke more than usual, or she can be the leader of the basketball team in which her boss is a player. Falassi (1987, p. 3) notes that within the social boundaries of play,

> People do something they normally don't; they abstain from something they normally do; they carry to the extreme behaviors that are usually regulated by measure; they invert the patterns of daily social life. Reversal, intensification, trespassing, and abstinence are the four cardinal points of festive behavior.

Falassi's account applies not only to festive play, but also to play behaviors that take place within organizations and involve work tasks. Organizations like DuPont, Motorola, and Google permit people to spend up to 20 percent of their work time freely experimenting with new ideas they are intrinsically curious about (Battelle, 2005; Nemeth, 1997; Pinchot, 1985). Such practices institutionalize a legitimate space and time in which individuals feel safe to play with their work away from rigid structural requirements (Amabile, 1996) and social pressures for conformity (Nemeth, 1997) and behavioral consistency (March, 1976).

In a second sense, the boundaries of play are not institutionalized or conspicuously delineated. The same space may be a space for play at some times but not at other times. Locke (1989, 1996) found that informal social play usually takes places in the few moments before works starts, after work ends, or during breaks from work. The same space may also encircle play for some but not for other individuals. The boundaries of play in that case are not a property of the larger social system but are defined, instead, by the norms of a play community within it. This is evident in Roy's (1959) study of the informal social play of a group of machine operators. He notes that each day is marked by interruptions of work that are designated as ritualized "times" – 'banana time,' 'coffee time,' or 'peach time' – that delineate a play space of informal interactions that alleviate the monotony of manual work:

> If the daily series of interruption be likened to a clock, then the comparison might best be made with a special kind of cuckoo clock, one with a cuckoo which can provide variation in its announcements and can create such an interest in them that the intervening minutes become filled with intellectual content. The major significance of the interaction interruptions lay in such a carryover of interest. The physical interplay which momentarily halted work activity would initiate verbal exchanges and thought processes to occupy group members until the next interruption. The group interactions thus not only

marked off the time; they gave it content and hurried it along. (161–162) The 'beast of boredom' was gentled to the harmlessness of a kitten. (p. 164)

Finally, the limits of play may also be esoteric or reflect idiosyncratic motivations and work rhythms. Pinchot (1985) notes that failing to secure permission to work on a task they are passionate about, employees may stay late at work to play with new ideas or they may create their own 'hidden' space and time for play within the workday. Play may also involve states of flow (Csikszentmihalyi, 1990) and timelessness (Mainemelis, 2001), which command total affective, cognitive, and physical immersion in the task to the point that they collapse the distinction between self and activity and alter the perception of time and space (Mainemelis, Goldenberg, & Ranganathan, 2006). Intense forms of play involve such states of consciousness that separate them from the normal sociotemporal reality of the workplace.

Uncertainty-Freedom-Constraint

Play usually involves surprise, uncertainty, or unresolved possibility (Sandelands & Buckner, 1989). Play activities vary in terms of how much uncertainty they entail; for example, theater ranges from the highly scripted to the purely experimental (Turner, 1982). Most forms of play, however, tend to involve some uncertainty or unresolved possibility. One can internalize the rules of chess and master its strategies, but one can never tell how a game is going to unfold, for no two games of chess are ever alike. The uncertainty, or surprise, of play is linked, in turn, to both freedom and constraint. Play is relatively free from external constraints and allows participants a considerable degree of autonomy to manipulate processes and assume new, even unrealistic identities and roles (Caillois, 2001; Dansky, 1999). At the same time, play imposes its own internal constraints, which are determined or voluntarily accepted by the players themselves.

These elements are manifested in different ways across different forms of play. In competitive games, the constraints are fixed rules that do not determine the course of action or the outcome, but rather, enhance the uncertainty of the game. For example, sports have two elements that make them intrinsically rewarding: uncertain outcome, which stimulates surprise and excitement; and sanctioned display, which allows the demonstration of physical or intellectual dexterity within a set of rules (McPherson, Curtis, & Loy, 1989). Other play forms do not have fixed rules but are bounded by norms developed by the players. Informal social play is sustained by norms that stimulate novel interactions; evolve in time; and suspend play at once when they are violated (Roy, 1959). In improvisational play, constraints emerge from the interaction between players and events: constraints drive novel action, which creates new constraints for future action, in a mutually reinforcing process (Barrett, 1998; Nachmanovitch, 1990). Often, the players themselves introduce obstacles to make the activity more uncertain or more complicated than the situation demands (Piaget, 2001). Miller (1973) refers to this process as 'galumphing', the "patterned, voluntary elaboration or complication of process, where the pattern is not under the dominant control of goals" (p. 75).

Play allows the voluntary exercise of control systems in which the players can choose to some degree the arbitrariness of the constraints within which they will act or imagine (Sutton-Smith, 1997). Through the induction of constraints that introduce opportunities for further mastery or further chaos, play maintains its surprise and unpredictability and allows people to exert or to lose control in novel situations. Managerial simulations and role-plays provide such "contexts for experiments within which practitioners can suspend or control some of the everyday impediments to reflection-in-action" (Schon in Schrage, 2000, p. 33).

Loose and Flexible Association between Ends and Means

Play may be triggered spontaneously (e.g., fantasy); it may be undertaken deliberately but unfold arationally (e.g., improvisational play); or it may have goals that evolve over time (e.g., experimental play). Play may involve ends that defy reason (e.g., whirling around a circle) or ends that celebrate reason (e.g., chess). What defines play is not the presence or absence of goals but the fact that play is not motivated by the search for efficient means to satisfy a fixed goal in a reliable way (Glynn, 1994); not the degree of rationality it may or it may not have, but the flexible manner by which means and ends are handled (Dansky, 1999). "Play is not means without the end; it is a crooked line to the end; it circumnavigates obstacles put there by the player, or voluntarily acceded to by him" (Miller, 1973, p. 93). Bruner (1972, p. 689) refers to play as "that special form of violating fixity" where ends are often altered to meet the means at hand.

Positive Affect

Play involves positive affect that varies in its degree of intensity (from relaxation to frantic joy) and complexity (from simple feelings such as fun to complex feelings such as emotional relief). Play can be relaxing when one plays solitaire on the PC during a work break (D'Abate, 2004), or it can involve high arousal when a medical team celebrates with exuberant affect saving the life of a patient (Locke, 1996). While play is often thought of only as "fun," its affective structure is more complex and it often entails negative emotion.

The content of play may involve negative emotional themes. For example, children often act out angry, violent, or war-related themes (Russ & Kaugars, 2000–2001). Negative feelings are expressed through and even used in play, such as the channeling of aggression through sports. What is often positive in affective terms about play is that it offers a safe space for the expression and transformation of unpleasant or horrifying feelings, such as loss, pain, or death (Winnicott, 2001). Play allows people to cognitively work through and reconcile conflicting emotions, also enabling the relief of negative emotional states. Locke (1989, 1996) has used the term 'magical play' to describe the deliberate effort to draw into a moment of play someone in whom feelings such as doubt, anger, or despair are indicated. In her study in a pediatric clinic of seriously ill children, she observed this pattern in the interactions of medical teams who have just lost a patient and in the way physicians cope with the emotions of the parents of ill children. Play, therefore, involves positive and negative emotions, and cognitive and emotional elements, but it generally results in some form of positive affect, be it fun, relaxation, ecstatic joy, or emotional relief.

We have defined play as a behavioral orientation consisting of five elements: a threshold experience; boundaries in time and space; uncertainty-freedom-constraint; flexible and loose association between means and ends; and positive affect. These elements are not antecedents, consequences, or epiphenomena of something else that is play; rather, they are the very stuff play is made of. While not all five elements need to be present to transform an activity into a play, the more each of these elements is present, the more play-like the activity becomes. In its most intense forms, play involves a circular interaction among those elements. For example, the interaction between the relative freedom from external constraint and the imposition of internal constraints generates and sustains surprise and uncertainty.

While these elements can be manifested independently in other forms of behavior, in play they become coupled and take specific meaning. For example, the positive affect of play is not a general positive mood due to some largely unidentified reasons. Rather, it is positive affect tied to very specific reasons, such as involvement, surprise, uncertainty, and out-of-the-ordinary experience. Similarly, the joy experienced in play is not attached to attaining an effect; if it were, climbers would fly to the top of the mountain and tennis players would be happy to be declared winners without ever playing a match. But climbers climb and tennis players get thrills by hitting winners because they enjoy producing these effects and care about the activity, its rules, and its integrity (Glynn, 1994; Miller, 1973).

MANIFESTATIONS OF PLAY

As an organizational behavior, play is manifested in two general ways. First, play can be a form of diversion from work tasks. Designing is the core aspect of the work of an industrial designer; playing solitaire on the PC is not. We refer to the latter behavior as "diversionary play" to convey that such play behaviors occur daily when employees are not working on work tasks (Elsbach & Hargadon, 2002; Jett & George, 2003). We cite earlier a passage in which Roy (1959) suggests that diversionary play occurs daily at work and, often, it occurs with ritualistic precision. Play, in these terms, is not internal to work tasks but a part of the larger social context in which individuals perform them.

Second, play may also be internal to work tasks, that is, a way for engaging with one's work. Starbuck and Webster (1991, p. 87) write that, "Advertising agents, creative writers, designers, planners, and social theorists use fantasy and imagination. Athletes compete. Consultants and researchers explore. Mathematicians solve puzzles. Therapists may use therapeutic play. Such people cannot work without playing." In a study with 589 employees, Abramis (1990, p. 364) found that some experience their work as play; for example, an employee comments, "I can not believe that people pay me to do my hobby." Play as engagement refers to those occasions where employees do not halt or escape work to play but, rather, turn their work into play (Amabile, 1996; Beatty & Torbert, 2003). Play, in this sense, is a behavioral orientation to performing work, and as such, it has a direct functional relation to creativity. While play as diversion affects creativity indirectly, by shaping a favorable social-relational (Perry-Smith & Shalley, 2003) and affective (Elsbach & Hargadon, 2002) climate, play as engagement affects creativity directly because it is internal to an individual's work tasks in relation to which creativity is conceptualized and assessed. We analyze these relationships in the next sections.

PLAY AS ENGAGEMENT AND CREATIVITY

Creativity is the generation of ideas that are novel and potentially useful (Amabile, 1988; Woodman, Saywer, & Griffin, 1993). Psychological research has identified several cognitive (e.g., Guilford, 1968) and affective (e.g., Russ, 1993) processes that facilitate creativity. Organizational research has explored how creativity is influenced by motivation (e.g., Amabile, Hill, Hennessey, & Tighe, 1994); the work climate (e.g., Amabile et al., 1996); social-relational processes (e.g., Perry-Smith, in press); affect (e.g., Amabile, Barsade, Mueller, & Staw, 2005); finite states (e.g., Mainemelis et al., 2006); and the interaction between personal and contextual factors (e.g., Oldham & Cummings, 1996). This body of findings largely supports the componential theory of Amabile (1988), which suggests that the social context, motivation, domain-relevant skills, and creativity skills interact to facilitate creativity. Drawing on this extant knowledge, we propose below that play as engagement fosters the cognitive and affective dimensions of the creative process, as well as intrinsic motivation and the development of domain-relevant skills and creativity-relevant skills.

Play and Cognitive Processes

Play facilitates five creativity-relevant cognitive processes: *problem framing, divergent thinking, mental transformations, practice with alternative solutions,* and *evaluative ability.* Problem framing determines how the problem will be solved. When problems are posed in a unique way, their solutions are more likely to be novel. Problems can be presented or discovered, but in either case, framing the problem in a unique way is essential (Getzels & Csikszentmihalyi, 1976). Play provides ample room for redefinition of the situation. Its betwixt-and-between reality defamiliarizes the elements of even a familiar activity, increasing in that way the likelihood that the task will be framed in a unique way. Tasks are also more likely to be framed in unique ways when their constraints are internal to the task and under the control of the people performing them (Basadur, 1994; Runco & Sakamoto, 1999). The relative freedom of play from external constraint increases the likelihood that even familiar tasks will be reformulated in fresh ways. Furthermore, the loose and flexible association between means and ends in play encourages people to sense problems in the first place, that is, to avoid defining the task in the old and tried way that usually leads to already known rather than to novel solutions.

The novelty that is most important to creativity is primarily associated with two other cognitive processes, divergent thinking and mental transformations. Divergent thinking refers to the generation of information from given information where the emphasis is on variety of output from the same source (Guilford, 1968). It involves ideational fluency (numerous ideas), ideational flexibility (shifts in approach), and broad scanning (Torrance, 1995; Sternberg & O'Hara, 1999). Mental transformations entail the transformation of existing knowledge into new patterns of configurations (Guilford, 1968). They involve association, combination, or transformation of existing memory structures; metaphoric production; imagery; analogical thinking; and broad and flexible idea categorization (Ward, Finke, & Smith, 1999). Empirical psychological studies have shown that play involves a great deal of both divergent thinking and mental transformations (for reviews see Dansky, 1999; Runco, 1999; and Singer & Singer, 1990).

The boundaries and threshold reality of play stimulate novelty by encouraging experimentation with diverse ideas and possibilities that would not be tried under other circumstances. "Play decreases the risks commonly associated with experimentation and, thus, may produce more variance with its circuitous, organic, and galumphing responses" (Glynn, 1994, p. 43). The fluidity of play and its relative freedom from external constraint decrease the likelihood of functional fixedness and premature closure, and stimulate the generation of numerous and diverse ideas to the task at hand (Amabile, 1996). By liberating concepts, objects, and behaviors from their normal contexts, and by uncoupling means from ends, play also fosters unusual mental associations – the reconfiguration of the components of ideas, objects, or behaviors into new arrangements (Bruner, 1972). For example, in their long hours of play, two bicycle-store owners, the Wright brothers, combined their knowledge of bicycles with their observations of birds to invent the first flying airplane (Jacab, 1999).

Moreover, in play people step outside the familiar into the imagined and even into the contradictory (Bateson, 1955). This is facilitated by the nature of play as existing on the threshold between reality and unreality discussed above. The symbolic realities often enacted in play involve imagery, metaphors, and analogies, all of which facilitate creativity (Dansky & Silverman, 1973, 1975). Fein (1987) has observed that in play children not only enact alternative realities but also craft and manipulate within them elaborate symbol systems. In his seminal analysis of the creativity of Albert Einstein, Gardner (1993, p. 104) notes that Einstein found affective pleasure in creating imaginary worlds in which he developed and manipulated "his symbol systems of choice." Einstein himself wrote,

> The worlds of language, as they are written and spoken, do not seem to play any role in my mechanism of thought. The physical entities which seem to serve as elements in thought are certain signs and more or less clear images which can be "voluntarily" reproduced and combined ... From a psychological viewpoint this combinatory play seems to be the essential feature in productive thought. Conventional words or other signs

have to be sought for laboriously only in a secondary stage, when the mentioned associative play is sufficiently established and can be reproduced as well ... When I examine
myself and my methods of thought I come to the conclusion that the gift of fantasy has
meant more to me than my talent for absorbing positive knowledge ... Einstein obviously
enjoyed creating and exploring words with his own mind. (Gardner, 1993, p. 105)

The problems Einstein puzzled with did not have a known solution precisely
because he framed them in that way. In organizational contexts, however,
even when a task does not have a known solution, an ends orientation, in
which one is focused on the outcomes of the activity rather than its means,
usually leads managers to accept the first solution that is satisfactory enough
(Simon, 1997). More often than not, this is not the most creative solution.
Creativity requires exploring and practicing with alternative responses to the
task (Getzels & Csikszentmihalyi, 1976; Torrance, 1995). The fluidity and
flexibility of play decrease the likelihood of premature closure and stimulate
practicing with many alternative responses. By fostering the generation of
alternative responses, play also facilitates a better, more informed evaluation and selection of a solution (Singer & Singer, 1990), as well as the
generation of more creative solutions by possibly combining elements of
different solutions.

When individuals play, therefore, problem framing, divergent thinking,
mental transformations, practice with alternative solutions, and evaluative
ability are all facilitated. Put another way, creativity requires taking and
switching between different perspectives (Isen, 1999). Play facilitates exploring different perspectives, creating alternative worlds, assuming different
roles, enacting different identities, and also taking all these, and the players
themselves, out of the cognitive contexts in which they normally operate.

Play and Affective Processes

Affect achieves its impact on creativity by influencing cognitive functioning
(Amabile et al., 2005; Isen, 1999; Ward et al., 1999). Integrating several
studies, Russ (1993, 1999) has identified four specific affective processes that
influence the creative process: *affective pleasure in challenge, openness to
affective states, emotional modulation of affect, and access to affect-laden
thoughts*. In this section, we briefly discuss these four affective processes and
suggest that play is conducive to them.

Affective pleasure in challenge refers to the pleasure of identifying
the problem and the joy of seeking and achieving novel insights (Russ,
1993). Affective pleasure in challenge stimulates divergent thinking (Isen,
1999), decreases the likelihood of premature closure, and strengthens

persistence on the task (Csikszentmihalyi, 1990). Because the positive affect of play is not attached to attaining an effect but to producing it, affective pleasure in challenge, excitement attached to surprise or uncertainty, and the joy of "getting lost" in the task are all present in play (Russ, 1993). In fact, taking affective pleasure in challenge, tension, and uncertainty is the hallmark of play.

Openness to affective states refers to experiencing a wide range of emotions. Openness to affective states has been found to facilitate artistic (Getzels & Csikszentmihalyi, 1976), scientific (Feist, 1999a), architectural (Dudek, 1999), medical (Estrada, Young, & Isen, 1994), and managerial creativity (Amabile et al., 2005). The empirical literature suggests that positive affect fosters divergent thinking and mental transformations, while mild negative affect in the form of tension can motivate problem-finding (Feist, 1999b; Isen, 1999; Vosburg & Kaufmann, 1999). Creativity entails a wide range of emotions – joy, passion, excitement, anxiety, frustration, and disappointment (Amabile et al., 2005; Shaw, 1999). The emotional modulation of both positive and negative emotions facilitates divergent thinking and mental associations (Lieberman, 1977; Russ & Grossman-McKee, 1990). This process is affective as much as it is cognitive for it integrates affect within a cognitive context (Russ, 1993). Comfort with experiencing intense affect and tolerance of frustration and anxiety are some manifestations of this process.

Play permits the safe expression and modulation of a wide range of emotions (e.g., joy, passion, sadness, fear) because it allows the players to choose to some degree the limits within which they will act or imagine. Negative emotions are not excluded or suppressed in play; they are safely expressed up to a degree that does not destroy the overall positive affective quality of the experience (Fein, 1987). For example, in play children express as much aggression, fear, and primal "bloody themes" as they can tolerate while having fun (Russ, 2004). Similarly, a tennis player suggests (in Sutton-Smith, 1997) that the joy of play is often related to the release of aggression and the tension of its unpredictable twists:

> I think women's tennis is a ballet type of game. It's got beautiful movements and I think there is nothing else that combines the beauty of movement with the tremendously graceful spirit. But it really is also an assassin's game: if one person has won, the other one is dead. There is no compromise. I become quite aggressive on court. I get a thrill out of hitting a winner. (p. 88)

Research has shown that positive affect induced in a safe context stimulates divergent thinking and mental transformations, while positive affect induced in a threatening context leads to increased self-protection, risk-aversion, and concern with possible loss (Isen & Geva, 1987; Kahn & Isen, 1993). Play fosters creativity because it allows both the positive *and* safe experience and expression of emotion. Even when play entails negative affect, it results in an overall positive emotional experience, such as the channeling of aggression through sports. Furthermore, although play is not safe per se (things can and some times do go wrong in play), it is much safer than its morphological analogues in real life. Playing with a simulation of a market crash is more fun and safer than experiencing a real market crash (de Geus, 1996); playing with a prototype is safer than producing a product right away (Schrage, 2000). Also considering that jumping off a bridge with an attached cable is more fun and safer than jumping off without it, it seems that what people seek in play is not risk per se but variety; and it is variety, rather than risk per se, that stimulates divergent thinking and mental transformations (Isen, 1999).

Another process conducive to creativity is access to affect-laden thoughts (Russ, 1993). Affect-laden thoughts are concepts and images that contain emotional content. As such, they provide an associative bridge between cognitively remote concepts representing objects, persons, or events in memory (Getz & Lubart, 1999; Ortony, 1993). Concepts are stored in memory according to their cognitive components but an emotional component is also attached to them. When the affective tones of two concepts are shared, the two concepts might be perceived as more related than they would otherwise (Blaney, 1986; Isen, 1999). Concepts can resonate emotionally even when they seem unrelated in cognitive terms. This emotional link fosters associations between concepts stored in memory in distant mental categories. Affect-laden themes are especially conducive to imagery, metaphors, and analogies. They also help explain why accounts of even scientific, "technical" creativity are often associated with emotional recognition at the moment of key insights or discoveries (Feist, 1999b; Shaw, 1999).

Affect-laden themes may also be manifestations of primary-process thought, the process by which instinctual energy surfaces in the form of concrete images or ideas (Dudek, 1980). Unlike secondary-process (the abstract, logical mode of thought), primary-process is not subject to rules of logic or oriented to reality; it is affectively charged and guided by "a free flow of energy not bound by specific ideas or objects ... ideas are easily interchangeable and attention is flexibly and widely distributed" (Russ, 1993, p. 20). Access to affect-laden primary process themes has been found to facilitate creativity (Dudek, 1999; Feist, 1999b; Suler, 1980). Dreams are examples of primary process at sleep; fantasy play is the main gateway to primary-process while one is awake (Ederlyi, 1992; LeDoux, 1996; Russ, 1993).

Play offers access to affect-laden themes whether they are related to primary process or not. Getz and Lubart (1999) note that just because a link in memory resonates emotionally does not mean that it will be noticed and accessed consciously; in order to be detected, the emotional resonance has to pass a detection threshold beyond which the affective connection between two otherwise unrelated concepts is triggered. Positive affect appears to lower this threshold, allowing more affect-laden links to emerge in awareness, while negative affect appears to have the inverse effect (Isen, 1999). Like other positive affect states, play increases the likelihood that an affect-laden link will be consciously recognized. But unlike most other positive affect states, play lowers even further the point at which an emotional resonance is noticed, because it also lowers the threshold of rationality (LeDoux, 1996). Both experientially and structurally, play is fluid and not governed by strict rules of logic.

Moreover, like positive affect-laden themes, negative affect-laden themes can trigger mental associations that are useful to creativity (Russ, 1999). Because individuals can safely express emotion in play, they are more likely to access more and more diverse affect-laden material, including that with negative content. From theater (Turner, 1982) to simulations of air combat (Torrance, 1995), play fosters the symbolic enactment of even horrific situations because it allows people to experience to a mild degree the actual negative emotions attached to those situations in real life (e.g., fear, panic, death). This facilitates access to otherwise undesirable affect-laden material, fostering in that way associations between concepts or images stored in memory in very distant categories (Russ, 1993). By blending affect and cognition, the positive and the negative, and the true and the false, play provides individuals with access to more and more diverse material to work with in idea generation.

Therefore, play fosters affective pleasure in challenge, openness to affect states, and access to affect-laden thoughts. Play also aids the emotional modulation of affect states. Clearly, reciprocal effects between play, affect, and cognition occur in the creative process. Play stimulates affective pleasure in challenge, which stimulates divergent thinking, which may lead to surprising discoveries that reinforce affective pleasure in the task and play itself.

Play and Task Motivation

Besides its direct influences on the cognitive and affective dimensions of the creative process, play as engagement also achieves its impact on the creative process by facilitating three other factors: intrinsic motivation, domain-relevant skills, and creativity skills. Intrinsic motivation refers to engaging in the task for the inherent satisfaction one finds in it (e.g., interest, involvement, curiosity, positive challenge), while extrinsic motivation refers to engaging in the task in order to attain some outcome that is external to it (e.g., extrinsic rewards, expected evaluation, compliance with external directives; Amabile, 1996). Although extrinsic motivation is not necessarily detrimental to creativity, most studies have found that with little or no intrinsic motivation it is unlikely that individuals will be creative (for reviews see Amabile, 1996; Collins & Amabile, 1999; Shalley, Zhou, & Oldham, 2004).

Intrinsic motivation is not a necessary or sufficient condition for play. In other words, not all intrinsically motivated activities are play. Clearly, however, intrinsic motivation increases the likelihood of play for people are more likely to play with the activities they find intrinsically rewarding. The positive affect associated with playing these activities reinforces, in turn, one's intrinsic orientation toward them. Most importantly, however, play (with the specific task) facilitates intrinsic task motivation in those cases where the initial degree of intrinsic task motivation is low or tentative. Play is not a necessary condition of intrinsic task motivation but it is a sufficient one. We write earlier that play structures an activity in a way that stimulates and sustains surprise and affective pleasure. Controlling for the initial degree of intrinsic task motivation, empirical studies have found that play increases interest in, involvement with, and curiosity about the content of the task (Webster & Martocchio, 1992, 1993). This empirical finding resonates with our own experience in the classroom: play stimulates a great deal of interest regardless of the topic and students' initial attitudes toward it. Be it in a negotiation game or in a managerial role-play, the uncertainty, fluidity, and threshold reality of play itself usually stimulate excitement, tension, and fun.

Furthermore, play stimulates intrinsic task motivation even when it entails multiple personal and social goals (Starbuck & Webster, 1991). For example, athletes historically compete not only for the love of the sport, but also for glory, social status, and sponsorships; in the vast majority of cases, however, the structure of the game itself – its surprise and competition within a fixed set of rules – stimulates interest and the love of the sport (McPerson et al., 1989; Sutton-Smith, 1997). These intrinsic rewards increase, in turn, the likelihood that one will continue playing with the task in the long run. For example, Amabile (1996) notes that Michael Jordan played basketball for many external rewards but he also included in his contract a "love for the game clause" that he be free to play pick-up games any time he wished. Therefore, we suggest that there is a positive, two-way, reciprocal interaction between play and intrinsic task motivation, and we also clarify that play is a sufficient condition of intrinsic motivation while the inverse is not true.

Play and Domain-Relevant Skills

An individual's skill in a given task domain is another factor that underlies his or her ability to be creative in that domain (Amabile, 1988). Domain-relevant skills comprise the individual's knowledge and expertise in a domain, and provide a set of cognitive pathways for the individual to follow in approaching his or her work. For a chef, domain-relevant skills constitute his knowledge of flavors and ingredients, cuts and cooking techniques; for a lawyer, task skills include her understanding of laws and regulations, and her ability to be persuasive in the courtroom. Domain-relevant skills provide the initial set of elements (e.g., knowledge, talent, experience) that enter the "combinatorial game" of the creative process. Domain-relevant skills are determined by innate skills, formal education, and continuous practice (Amabile, 1996).

Play as engagement with work tasks allows individuals to improve their domain-relevant skills on the job. Play minimizes the potential for negative consequences of learning by providing a less risky situation (Bruner, 1972). This safety stimulates risk taking and learning from errors. In play, one is less afraid to make mistakes and less inclined to discard them as disturbing anomalies (Glynn, 1994). Errors are used in play as triggers of exploration and practice, allowing one to perfect his or her skill and to discover unnoticed variables or opportunities in some of the most troublesome or baffling parts of his or her work (Nachmanovitch, 1990; Schrage, 2000). In doing so, it provides the player with valuable information that enables her to refine her skill at the task and also broaden the repertoire of skills she has available to apply to the task.

Furthermore, skill development is facilitated when individuals are excited about the task, engage in it primarily in order to master it, and when the task involves an optimal level of challenge (not too difficult which leads to anxiety, not too easy which leads to boredom; Csikszentmihalyi & LeFevre, 1989; Deci & Ryan, 1985; Massimini & Delle Fave, 2000). By uncoupling means from ends, play fosters the exploration of task-related behaviors and variables which would be less likely to be tried in other situations, such as when one performs the task to attain an external outcome. Moreover, the voluntary exercise of control systems in play allows one not only to select an initial optimal balance between challenges and skills, but also to gradually adjust the level of optimal balance so as to continue practicing his or her skills at continuously higher levels of mastery (Csikszentmihalyi, 1990).

Play has, of course, drawbacks and is not a panacea to all forms of learning. Previous studies have shown that play is not the best way to learn when efficiency, reliability, and control of the learner are primary concerns (Glynn, 1994; Sandelands, 1988; Webster & Martocchio, 1992, 1993; see also Starbuck & Webster, 1991). However, the same studies have shown that play fosters involvement, exploration, experimentation, flexibility, and quality in learning, which, as the extant creativity and learning literature suggests, are particularly conducive to developing and refining domain-relevant skills (Csikszentmihalyi, 1990; Kolb, 1984; Nickerson, 1999).

Play and Creativity Skills

Research has shown that relatively stable individual characteristics influence creativity. Cognitive style, intelligence, and personality traits all play a role in determining creative potential (for reviews see Amabile, 1996; Feist, 1999a; Stenberg & O'Hara, 1999). At the same time, individuals can develop the main cognitive muscles of creativity – divergent thinking and transformation abilities (Feldman, 1999; Nickerson, 1999). Scratchley and Hakstian (2000–2001) controlled for the shared variance between divergent thinking and general intelligence (9%), and found that divergent thinking predicts managerial creativity but general intelligence does not. Divergent thinking can be developed (Basadur, Wakabayashi, & Graen, 1990), and play is a natural way for practicing it (Dansky, 1999; Kolb, 2000; Russ, Robins, & Christiano, 1999). Play calibrates a disposition for creativity by sharpening divergent thinking and combinatorial flexibility. When people play,

> They first of all may be mastering incidental skills. But, more important, they are using their capacity to combine pieces of behavior that would have no basis for juxtaposition in a utilitarian framework. They are creating novelty, however unimposing it might be, as is the dreamer whom Freud says "builds castles in the sky." It is the habit of occasionally creating novelty, rather than specific preparation, that makes us seem intelligent when, confronted with a new problem, or a new contingency in "reality," we have more than a random chance of marshalling the means at our disposal in a hitherto useless but now adaptive way. (Miller, 1973, p. 96)

There is no guarantee that what occurs in play is predictably isomorphic to future environmental demands. The transfer of specific responses from play to future situations occurs only occasionally. But what matters is the discipline of maintaining flexibility in behavior and plasticity in mental models, and play facilitates these processes. Play allows people to temporarily suspend their mental models and disbelief in favor of an immediate exploration of various possibilities (Kolb, 1996). This allows managers to modify their perceptual limits of the world by imagining and enacting them in different ways (Barrett, 1998). Of course, individuals can respond creatively to a novel problem without playing. However, the ability to respond creatively to novel problems does not seem to exist in a vacuum; rather, it requires some practice which play provides. Weick (1979) writes,

> Deliberate complication, if it gives the person experience in combining elements in novel ways, can be potentially adaptive for dealing with novel problems ... Play is important not because it teaches some new skill, but because it takes activities that are already in one's repertoire and gives one practice in recombining those into novel sets. What seems to be implied is a kind of second-order learning. It is not that one learns to recombine a single set of means into a clumsy but passable golf swing; what one may be learning, instead, is that it is possible to recombine the available repertoire of means in novel ways. A person gets repeated practice in doing this whenever he or she intentionally complicates a process. (p. 248)

Creativity is a generative adaptive process, and as such, it requires practicing the skills of creating novelty. Play contributes to an enduring disposition toward creativity by practicing the main cognitive skills of creativity. In play people practice framing problems in new ways, exploring alternative solutions, and evaluating different possibilities. In particular, play helps people to develop divergent thinking skills and transformation abilities (Dansky, 1999). These abilities turn out to be useful even in those situations that are not playful themselves. When people play, therefore, not only do they facilitate their creative process in the task at hand, but they also develop a more enduring disposition toward creativity. Although this is fostered to some extent by any type or form of play, play as engagement gives individuals the opportunity to practice and rehearse the creation of novelty specifically in the context of their work.

We have suggested so far that play as engagement facilitates the cognitive, affective, motivational, and skill dimensions of creativity. In the next section we argue that play as diversion influences creativity more indirectly by shaping a favorable social climate.

PLAY AS DIVERSION AND CREATIVITY

Much of our time at work is spent not engaging in work activities, and sometimes specifically disengaging from work activities. People perform a variety of personal tasks and leisure activities during the workday, such as playing computer games or participating in office betting pools (D'Abate, 2004). Traditionally, organizational scholars are tempted to view these play activities as an inefficiency that diverts attention and effort away from the core work of the organization. However, these activities form the context in which people work, and as such, they can influence creativity in an indirect, peripheral way. Specifically, diversionary play can facilitate creativity by influencing people's psychological processes and also by creating a social-relational and cultural context that is conducive to creativity.

Play and Psychological Adjustment

Diversionary play helps people to adjust psychologically to their work by facilitating *restoratory* and *compensatory* functions. In jobs that involve physical effort diversionary play can facilitate physical relaxation, and in jobs that involve cognitive effort diversionary play can facilitate cognitive restoration. Roy (1959) has found that the diversionary play of manual workers offers physical relaxation for "tired legs and sore feet" (p. 160), while Jett and George (2003) and Elsbach and Hargadon (2002) suggest that diversionary play alleviates the cognitive exhaustion associated with the otherwise relentlessly mindful jobs of knowledge workers. In knowledge-intensive jobs, diversionary play provides periods of mental breaks, which are important for incubation (Elsbach & Hargadon, 2002), the stage of the creative process that involves much unconscious processing and free re-combination of ideas.

Play has many forms that offer many possibilities for restoration, which can help people to return refreshed to the same task or to make a transition to a new task. In the fast-paced and multi-task modern corporate environments, employees have to make frequent transitions between different work tasks. To make transitions effectively, people need to shift cognitive gear and to prevent the transfer of anxiety, worries, and frustration from one task to another (Asforth, Kreiner, & Fugate, 2000). Peripheral play offers a between-and-betwixt context which can facilitate the transition between tasks by inducing positive affect and by absorbing one's attention from the existing task to the play task which makes easier, in turn, the redirection of attention to the next core work task (Mainemelis, 2001).

Isen (1999) has summarized several empirical studies which show that the positive affect induced in play on an unrelated task generalizes on subsequent core tasks with positive effects on cognitive flexibility, associative fluency, and idea categorization, all of which facilitate creativity. When play is a diversion from work, it may be a welcome relief or a spontaneous surprise, and may therefore promote an even greater sense of positive affect. Social psychological studies usually induce positive affect through play; this testifies to the fact that play may be the most direct and perhaps the most natural way for people to find a moment of fun or positive surprise in their workplace and elsewhere.

Of course, whether or not the positive affect induced in diversionary play increases the likelihood of creativity on the subsequent core work task depends on whether the subsequent work task provides some opportunity for creativity in the first place. Returning to a less-than-interesting task after a fun moment of play not only fails to make people more creative (cf. Roy, 1959) but it may also lead to feelings of resentment that 'playtime' is over and therefore create negative affect (Filipowicz, 2003). An important implication of this is that attempting to externally manipulate positive affect in the workplace through play, for example through parties or other "fun times," may actually backfire when people return to a core task that is less than playful, less than autonomous, and less than creative (Filipowicz, 2003). In contrast, when people return to a core task that provides opportunities for play as engagement, the risk of this is much less. We suggest later that it is therefore important to consider the organizational context in which play as diversion occurs.

Diversionary play also serves compensatory functions. It is a context which, bounded-off from the execution of core work tasks, allows the fulfilment of psychological needs that work cannot satisfy or that work itself creates. Roy's (1959) study shows that while work in his group was routine and required little cognitive effort, diversionary play satisfied needs for fun and excitement and filled their days with intellectual content and imagination. On the other hand, the diversionary play of Locke's (1996, 1989) sample of highly educated physicians in a clinic of seriously ill children was not primarily focused on intellectual themes. It revolved more around themes of bonding, intimacy, and optimism, which helped the medical practitioners and their patients to adjust psychologically to their daily contact with fear, pain, and death. While in Roy's study diversionary play compensated for needs related to an environment of low-task significance, low-task variety, and low-task complexity, in Locke's studies diversionary play compensated for needs associated with highly challenging, highly meaningful, and highly complex work. As we suggest later on, job complexity is a critical factor in understanding the relationship between play as engagement and play as a diversion in organizations.

Play and the Social Context

The social context in which an individual works influences creativity (Amabile, 1988; Madjar, Oldham, & Pratt, 2002; Perry-Smith & Shalley, 2003). Diversionary play forms part of this larger work context and influences the nature of social relations within the organization. By creating social bonds between members of the organization, diversionary play makes individuals more willing to engage in the creative process, and more able to gain useful inputs into the creative process from others. Diversionary play achieves these effects by strengthening psychological safety, by countering cultural resistance to creativity, and by increasing the flow of diverse information through social networks.

Play and Psychological Safety
Diversionary play often blurs the lines of hierarchical relationships by freeing people from the normal roles and expected behaviors of the workplace (Falassi, 1987; Locke, 1989; Tuner, 1982), and giving them an opportunity to relate personally to one another in a time and space that is free from the pressure of work. For example, when organizational members play together on the corporate softball team, a secretary may be the team manager, while the boss is a player, allowing them to transcend their working relationship and develop an informal social bond. By altering the nature of relationships and enabling people to relate personally to one another, play helps organizational members to feel comfortable with and trust one another. Informal social play helps people connect to a broader entity – such as their work group, their department, or the organization at large – that provides them with a sense of belonging (Dandridge, 1986; Dutton, Dukerich, & Harquail, 1994; Marotto, Statler, Victor, & Roos, 2003). Inclusion in informal social play lets group members know that they are part of the group (Duncan, Smeltzer, & Leap, 1990; Roy, 1959), preventing them in that way from feeling alienated (Boland & Hoffman, 1983).

The result is that play superimposes organic personal relationships upon mechanistic work relationships (Locke, 1989). The benefit for creativity is increased psychological safety for experimenting with diverse ideas and processes. Psychological safety is the belief that one is free from evaluation, and that one will be accepted unconditionally, regardless of how he behaves in a given situation (Rogers, 1954). Psychological safety reduces the anxiety and fear of negative evaluation for risky interpersonal behaviors, such as experimenting, asking questions, and suggesting new ideas (Edmondson,

1999; Rogers, 1954), which are necessarily involved in the creative process. Diversionary play makes people more willing to engage in creative behavior by helping them to build trusting relationships with colleagues. Although diversionary play is not the only way to create such bonds in the workplace, it is one of the most common and perhaps most important ways for people to create informal personal bonds in organizations and in other contexts of social life (Sandelands, 2003).

Play and Organizational Culture
Diversionary play is a central aspect of organizational culture. The values and beliefs of an organization are exhibited through organizational myths or legends that are passed on to new members about the organization's leader (Deal & Kennedy, 1982) or through ceremonies celebrating specific values like excellence or speed (Dandridge, 1986; Pfeffer, 1981). Play demonstrates values in a way that is more vivid and concrete, and therefore more persuasive and memorable, than the direct communication of mission statements or corporate releases (Meyer, 1982; Wilkins, 1983). Socially relating these myths or stories to one another may become a form of diversionary social play, particularly as stories become embellished or even mocked. Highly formalized, sequential socialization processes (Van Maanen, 1978) that aim to communicate corporate information in a sober and prescribed way may become the subject of ridicule or teasing in informal interactions, which may undermine their message. This creates an alternative that resists the existing order of the social system and provides an opportunity for creative action.

Social play allows organizational members to safely express conflicts and tensions that may otherwise disrupt their relationships (Anand & Watson, 2004; Dandridge, 1986; Deal & Kennedy, 1982). Because it is inherently ambiguous and subjective, play also enables the experimentation with multiple frames of interpretation, thereby allowing the culture to simultaneously value the conflicting ideals that are pervasive in organizational life (Boland & Hoffman, 1983; Pondy, 1983). These contradictory attributes of play allow organizational members to develop a sense of the organizational culture that is personally meaningful, because it is both clear and subjective. A great deal of creative action in organizations can spark from such play contexts that question the dominant organizational mindsets.

Diversionary play facilitates the formation of sub-cultures that may offer an impetus for cultural change. In work contexts with excessive social pressures for conformity (Nemeth, 1997), social play is often the only channel available to employees for voicing disagreement, doubt, and even frustration. Locke (1989) writes that employees find in informal social play an illicit voice for criticism, dissent, and autonomy, and an impudent voice that crosses hierarchical lines, "breaks the social restraints on expressive content" and verbalizes "those sentiments inappropriate to their role identities" (pp. 116–117). Although the expression of such feelings through play does not guarantee creativity, it provides an impetus for creativity. Creativity is next to unthinkable unless one is willing to entertain alternative perspectives to the dominant interpretations of organizational realities and to express these views to others (Nemeth, 1997; Staw, 1995). In highly cohesive organizations, where social pressures for conformity and behavioral consistency rule, diversionary play can foster creativity by nurturing an informal social space that supports the creation and expression of alternative interpretations to the dominant organizational realities, mindsets, and processes.

At the other end of spectrum, firms with a commitment to creativity often embrace and legitimize diversionary play in explicit ways. Isaksen, Lauer, Ekvall, and Britz (2000–2001) found that organizations that embrace diversionary play tend to be more creative than those that do not. By encouraging diversionary play, such organizations encourage in fact the free expression and exchange of diverse ideas and varied perspectives to the dynamics of the workplace. A useful reminder here is that creativity has historically reached its peak in eras and cultures that embraced play and perceived it as anything but frivolous or useless (Barron, Montuori, & Barron, 1997; Csikszentmihalyi, 1997; Gardner, 1993; Mainemelis, 2002). For example, the social, intellectual, and scientific breakthroughs of classical Athens or of Italy in the Renaissance took place in social contexts where theater, sports, and other forms of social play flourished and were perceived not as trivial pastimes but as key cultural institutions that gave expression to the ideals, norms, and conflicts of the social system. From this point of view, playful organizational cultures do not appear to be idiosyncratic historical exceptions. Rather, across cultures and eras, there appears to be a link between a social system's willingness to nurture play and its ability to be creative. An organizational culture that supports diversionary play appears to be serving this function in modern organizations.

Play and Social Networks
Diversionary play facilitates the creation and maintenance of weak social network ties to other members of the organization as well as to colleagues outside the organization. Playful interactions, social gatherings, and hobbies among colleagues are the rule rather than the exception of professional life.

Furthermore, play can help one to initiate informal social contact with strangers he or she encounters in the daily course of work, especially when the situation would otherwise be stressful or uncomfortable. For example, doctors use playful, humorous interactions to introduce themselves to critically ill children, who are likely to be filled with anxiety (Locke, 1989).

Play can also help organizational members who rarely interact to create and maintain a social bond by increasing the number of interactions between them. These weak network ties enhance creativity by giving people access to more remote information and more diverse perspectives, without promoting the type of conformity that may occur in closer groups (Burt, 2004; Granovetter, 1973; Perry-Smith & Shalley, 2003). Diversionary play also breaks down the barriers between isolated functional areas (Kelley & Litman, 2001), providing a forum for individuals who normally would have no reason to come into contact with each other to meet, and in doing so, provides an opportunity to initiate learning from those outside one's main functional area. Once people have made these contacts, they may incorporate them into work routines, particularly on ambiguous creative tasks that can benefit from diverse information and resources (Starbuck & Webster, 1991). Thus, diversionary play loosely connects organizational members to one another in a way that gives them access to diverse perspectives, diverse information, and other important creative inputs.

One boundary condition on the relationships we have examined so far is that the nature of diversionary play must be social. Solitary diversionary play, such as playing a computer game on one's work PC, may have other benefits for individuals in an organization – for example, providing them with a break from cognitively demanding work (Elsbach & Hargadon, 2002) – but will have limited effect on the social processes of the work environment. However, social interactions provide broad scope for diversionary social play and occur frequently in organizations (Sandelands, 2003).

CONDITIONS OF PLAY

Given that play is not a set of activities but a behavioral orientation to any activity, what conditions influence the likelihood that individuals will employ the play orientation to perform an activity in the workplace? In this section we suggest that job complexity, environmental threat, a legitimate organizational time and space for play, and individual differences are four important factors that influence the likelihood of play in a work setting.

Job Complexity

The nature of the job itself is an important factor that influences the likelihood of play as engagement in organizations. Jobs with higher levels of autonomy, greater complexity, and skill variety (Hackman & Oldham, 1980) will encourage play as engagement. Individuals with a high degree of autonomy have the discretion to choose strategies for accomplishing tasks and to schedule work without supervisory restriction, and therefore a greater opportunity to engage in play. These elements should allow them to experience higher levels of affective pleasure while performing tasks. Task complexity and skill variety enhance these effects. Because complex tasks have high informational requirements and lack clear means-end relationships (Campbell, 1988), they are inherently ambiguous and require flexibility, experimentation, and cognitive processing. These sorts of tasks leave open the possibility for creative engagement and play, as one searches for the best approach to the task (Amabile, 1988; Shalley et al., 2004).

Recall that uncertainty, fluidity, and relative freedom from external constraint are key elements of play. When a job is rigidly structured, efficiently standardized, and clearly streamlined in advance, play as engagement is much less likely. Roy (1959) found that people tried to play even with routine tasks but that did not make them more creative. We view job complexity as an antecedent rather than a moderator of play because, as Roy's (1959) study has also shown, routine and monotonous tasks cannot sustain play beyond a few hours or a few days. In his study, people quickly took their play elsewhere – to their interactions during work breaks (diversionary play). Therefore, we view job complexity both as an antecedent of play as engagement and as an important factor in explaining the relative balance between play as engagement and play as diversion in an organizational setting. In work environments characterized by routine and monotonous work, we expect people to engage primarily in diversionary play. In low job complexity work environments diversionary play compensates for what work cannot provide (e.g., fun, challenge, intellectual stimulation). In such environments, however, we expect diversionary play to have little or no direct effect on people's creativity on their work tasks, because the work tasks themselves do not require or allow creative thinking.[1] On the other hand, high job complexity environments increase the likelihood of play as engagement, which increases, in turn, the likelihood of people's creativity on their work tasks through the cognitive, affective, motivational, and skill conditions we have discussed in an earlier section.

For highly autonomous professionals in cognitively complex jobs the boundaries between play as diversion and play as engagement may become blurred. A social scientist who on a Saturday evening visits the opera, a theater, or a sports game, may obtain a wealth of information and inspiration for his or her research on the role of emotions in work group interactions; a dinner party at a restaurant may provide an interior designer with ideas and insights about designing restaurants. These examples illustrate that the creative mind does not stop working at the end of the workday but, rather, transcends and blurs the boundaries between "work" and "nonwork." As a result, it may also blur the distinctions between play as engagement and play as diversion. In a series of interviews with creative individuals, Csikszentmihalyi (1997) found that the most rewarding aspect of their jobs was that their work was also their passion and hobby, and vice versa. Similarly, in a study with 589 employees, Abramis (1990) found that many reported that their work provides them with a salary for exercising their hobbies. Kelley and Littman (2001) also discuss the tendency of some sport retailers to hire sales employees who have a personal passion for playing sports.

While in these cases play as diversion and play as engagement may actually become blurred, our formal distinction between the two is anything but arbitrary. For many people in organizations what is work, what is not work, and where they can find play is a clear rather than an ambiguous question. Furthermore, the distinction between play as diversion and play as engagement is important in theoretical terms because play as engagement and play as diversion affect creativity in different ways, as discussed earlier.

Environmental Threat

Play rarely occurs under conditions of external threat (Bruner, 1972). Humans and animals alike rarely play when their survival is at stake. In organizations, changes in the environment lead to changes in strategies and procedures as managers interpret environmental events and translate them into action (Dutton & Jackson, 1987). Environmental threats are negative situations that cannot be easily controlled and that contain the potential for loss, such as threat in the competitive environment, decreases in market size, or scarcity of resources (Staw, Sandelands, & Dutton, 1981). Organizations respond to macro-environmental threat with rigid cognitive and behavioral responses (Staw et. al., 1981). They tend to rely on previously learned knowledge and have a reduced ability to process new and ambiguous information. Under threat, organizations also tend to increase their degree of control by formalizing procedures, by centralizing authority, and by trying to conserve their resources.

These changes limit the opportunities individuals have to play with their work. Under threat, organizations will eliminate slack both in terms of time and other resources, so that work must be accomplished more efficiently and on budget. There will be no time available for experimentation, and no budgetary slack to support "wanderings" or uncertain tests. These changes will also decrease the likelihood of play as engagement by making it less safe in psychological terms. Changes such as reducing individual autonomy as authority becomes centralized, reining in individual budgets, and reducing expenditures through, for example, downsizing, will create an environment of anxiety and even fear with employees (Amabile & Conti, 1999). When individuals experience high levels of stress and anxiety, they tend to stick to previously learned behaviors and become less flexible in their responses to problems (Luchins, 1942; Staw et al., 1981). Thus, individuals in organizations under threat will likely feel that it is not safe to play with their work tasks. Although some diversionary play may be entertained during periods of crisis and threat, play as engagement is highly likely to suffer.

Time and Space for Play

Societies historically institutionalize play by providing a space and time that legitimizes the expression of behaviors that society normally discourages or forbids. For example, while hypocrisy is normally seen as an immoral and deviant behavior in society, it is encouraged and colorfully celebrated within the space and time of the theater (Turner, 1982). Organizations can nurture play in the same way. Companies like Google and DuPont permit their employees to use up to 20% of their work time to freely explore ideas they are curious about. Such practices legitimize play as engagement and make it safe and sustainable over relatively long periods of time. A work behavior that is normally discouraged, for example working on an idea that is not a part of one's job description or not linked to any obvious organizational strategy, is now encouraged and supported within the protected and clearly delineated space and time of play. Although practices like the 20% "free-time" rule are not synonymous with play (for individuals must be willing to play as well), they certainly encourage and protect it.

Other practices can provide a space and time for play. Schrage (2000) describes simulations as "transitional theaters" where the suspension of disbelief turns ends into means, and Abramis (1990) writes about the president of a company who used to convert strategic planning sessions into a game in which top managers played their own roles, as well as the roles of their competitors and regulatory agencies. While such practices may take different forms (e.g., free-time, simulations, scenarios, role-plays), they can all stimulate play as engagement, as long as they temporarily suspend normal organizational rules (March, 1976) and other pressures for consistency and efficiency (Nemeth, 1997).

Several of the benefits of play emanate from the fact that play is not efficient, predictable, or streamlined but, rather, flexible, uncertain, and often erratic. Because these qualities of play have organizational costs, an important function of a legitimate space and time is that it contains to some extent these risks and costs associated with play behavior. Organizational members are less likely to play when they perceive that their managers will punish them for potential accidents or errors associated with play behavior. Organizational members are more likely to engage in play within a clear delineated time and space that temporarily suspends normal rules and encourages them to play without worrying about consequences. Managers, on their part, are less likely to encourage play when they are concerned about the inefficiency and potential errors associated with play behavior. Managers are more likely to encourage play when they feel confident that the potential costs of play behavior are bounded within a legitimate time and space that does not interfere with the ability of the organization to pursue fixed goals in an efficient and streamlined way. A legitimate time and space therefore makes play safe, or safer, both for the organization and its members. March (1976) writes,

> Playfulness is the deliberate, temporary relaxation of rules in order to explore the possibilities of alternative rules. When we are playful, we challenge the necessity of consistency. In effect, we announce – in advance – our rejection of the usual objections to behavior that does not fit the standard model of intelligence. Playfulness allows experimentation. At the same time, it acknowledges reason. It accepts an obligation that at some point either the playful behavior will be stopped or it will be integrated into the structure of intelligence in some way that it makes sense. The suspension of the rules is temporary (p. 77). We encourage organizational play by permitting (and insisting on) some temporary relief from control, coordination, and communication (p. 81).

Organizations can also provide a time and space for diversionary play. Providing a time and space for play to be a diversion from work will promote a culture in which play and creativity can flourish, as long as the job itself requires and invites creativity. This time and space can be both physical and psychological. Many companies provide physical space and time for diversionary play by having corporate off-sites, office birthday parties, or in-house gyms or relaxation rooms. More importantly, however, people must psychologically feel safe to take advantage of these, or to make their own time and space for playful diversions. This safety is created when the organization develops a culture that recognizes and values play. For example, by decorating its workspace with foam cubes and other artifacts (Kelley & Littman, 2001), IDEO stimulates and encourages play by sending a clear message to employees that taking a break to play is allowed. Thus, by providing a physical space for play, IDEO also enables employees to create their own psychological space for play.

Individual Differences

Individual differences is another factor that influences play behavior in organizations. The term *playfulness* refers to the predisposition to engage in an activity as play. Jackson (1984) measured playfulness with the Personality Research Form (RPF) as a stable individual-difference *motivational trait*. Costa and McRae (1988) found small positive correlations between the playfulness scale of the RPF and the scales of the NEO inventory that assess the *personality traits* of fantasy, positive emotions, experimental actions, liberal values, gregariousness, and warmth. They also found that playfulness has a small negative correlation with age, is not associated with education, and that females are more playful than males. Glynn and Webster (1992) developed the Adult Playfulness Scale (APS) and found that it is positively related to cognitive spontaneity, creativity, positive task evaluations, involvement, and quality of performance, and negatively related to a quantitative functional orientation. Clerical employees scored higher on playfulness than staff employees, and no consistent differences were found in terms of age and gender.

While these instruments are useful toward exploring individual differences in the degree to which people are predisposed to play, they entail some narrow or conflicting assumptions. The RPF views playfulness as 'logical' and 'rational,' but play can be irrational or arational. The APS views playfulness as the opposite of reason, but playing chess does not seem to be the opposite of reason. While in the APS playfulness involves a preference for social interaction rather than for solitary activity, acclaimed studies have shown that individuals often engage in solitary play (e.g., Csikszentmihalyi, 1997). Our view is that play is polymorphous, which implies that individuals may vary also in terms of how they like to play and at what level of social interaction. While there is little research in this area, this hypothesis is reasonable. Is the chemist who shuts herself in the lab to play alone with ideas also predisposed to play socially in 'fun times'? Is a propensity for fantasy higher in those who frequent casinos? Are the people who play games that stress individual differences (e.g., sports, chess) more likely to play games that stress chance (e.g., lottery)? Perhaps *how* people are predisposed to play is equally, if not more, important than *how much*. Individual differences, therefore, influence not only the overall degree to which people play, but also the form of play and the level of social interaction at which people prefer to play.

DISCUSSION

In the previous sections we employed a highly analytical approach. We have first disentangled the basic elements of play and the basic elements of creativity, and then we compared the two classes of elements so as to articulate the cognitive, affective, motivational, and social-relational mechanisms through which play affects creativity. In this section we synthesize our arguments at a higher level of abstraction, and in relation to two additional discussion anchors. First, given that play is a behavioral orientation to any activity, what are some other behavioral orientations and how do they compare with play in terms of creativity? Second, given that our model operates primarily at the micro level, what would the nexus of our arguments look like at the larger organizational level?

With regard to the first question, play is antithetical to four other behavioral orientations: apathy; consummatory behavior; instrumental action leading detectably to consummatory behavior, or to a detectable goal that is extrinsic to the behavior itself; and socially prescribed behavior when the behavior occurs in a context in which the prescription is socially sanctioned and enforced (Klinger, 1971). It would hardly be controversial to state that 60 years after the inauguration of creativity research (Guilford, 1950) there is no evidence that apathy, consummatory, or socially prescribed forms of behavior facilitate creativity. On the contrary, the extant literature suggests that creativity requires affective pleasure and involvement, resisting immediate gratification and premature closure, and psychological safety to deviate from socially prescribed behaviors and ordinary conventions. Instrumental action does not necessarily hurt creativity, but as we write earlier, in and of itself it is not particularly useful either (Amabile, 1996).

The problem is that, since the dawn of the Industrial Revolution, the juxtaposition of instrumental action, socially prescribed and enforced behavior, and often apathy, has left a strong imprint upon the very idea of work in organizations. Efficient, standardized, and routinized work, enforced by social controls, and performed with dreadful boredom is exactly what Roy (1959) described 50 years ago. In his study, there was a clear and sharp line dividing play and work. The same line divided work and creativity for the latter was not even possible for his subjects. But creativity is the requirement of many types of work today; and this is where play becomes important, not as the point at which work stops, but as the point in which work originates.

Our literature describes play and work not as two sets of activities but as two antithetical behavioral orientations distinguished in terms of how the means and ends of any activity are handled (e.g., Glynn, 1994; Sandelands, 1988). Play is characterized by uncertainty-freedom-constraint and the loose and flexible association between means and ends; in fact, Webster's (1998) dictionary defines play as "*to move lightly, rapidly, or erratically; ... to amuse oneself; ... to move freely within limits.*" Work, on the other hand, is an instrumental orientation where the means are used to efficiently accommodate ends fixed in advance (March, 1976; Miller, 1973). That being the case, we may ask if at any given moment in time an activity in the workplace is either play or work (Glynn, 1994; Sandelands, 1988). It is unreasonable, however, to assume that the months or years of "moments" invested in discovering a treatment for cancer or in developing an advertising campaign are only play or only work. The very definition of work as an ends-orientated activity implies that the ends are known in advance. In creative industries, however, the ends are often so vague that one cannot know and pursue them without exploring "freely and erratically within limits." To work, one must have a purpose; to do creative work, one must move freely and erratically so as to discover and understand what is the purpose. From this point of view, the very purpose of work is often invented in play.

Roy's (1959) subjects did not play with their tasks because their tasks were fixed and efficiently streamlined in advance. But in creative industries the ends are only occasionally fixed in advance, and even when the ends are fixed in advance either the means are unclear and/or efficiency is rarely the major requirement. For example, if the task were to advertise a new car, the most efficient and streamlined orientation to the task would be to copy the existing campaign of an older car. This is hardly what you call work in advertising. When creativity is a requirement, the imperative is often to match means and ends not in an efficient or known way but in a surprising and unexpected way; which is to say, to intentionally complicate the activity – to play with the various possible configurations between means and ends.

In our "closet" research we have observed animation professionals in a broadcasting corporation whose job was to create fictional stories for children's television. Occasionally, they took flights of fancy, laughed, and fantasized ludicrously about seven-legged creatures, green zebras, and sharks flying in space shuttles. Is this play or work? It is play that creates work. It is a fluid between-and-betwixt world that generates a rich variety of characters, imagery, plots, and symbolism, some of which will later become the building blocks of work products in such organizational contexts.

During the last two decades, organizational research has focused on identifying personal, contextual, and situational determinants of creativity. An interesting question is what contexts of behaviors can simultaneously encompass all these diverse factors. In previous sections we have analyzed these factors and compared them with the elements of play to suggest that play may be in fact the only context of behavior that serves this function. In other words, we believe that, more often than not, creativity is born out of play. This statement may seem surprising when considering that play has historically been seen as a useless or even dangerous behavior in the workplace. However, a useful reminder here is that creativity itself has become important for organizations only in recent years. In fact, prior to the publication of Amabile's (1988) componential theory there was very little organizational research about creativity. Although today we know a lot about creativity, and although the modern work culture vividly celebrates the notions of "creativity" and "innovation" in general, it appears that actually nurturing creativity in practice is a difficult puzzle for most organizations, especially large, established firms (Dougherty & Heller, 1994; Staw, 1995). We believe that nurturing play in the workplace is an aspect of the same puzzle.

The very idea of a social organization implies order (Weick, 1998), which requires to some extent the control of behavior according to social prescriptions and rules. Organizations also have to balance immediate proliferation (by efficiently meeting instrumental ends) with future adaptation, which requires them to cultivate creativity and the ability to adapt flexibly to change (March, 1991). It would be instructive to consider how societies, as larger scale social systems, historically tackle this puzzle. Turner (1982) and Sutton-Smith (1997) have proposed that cultures historically balance these competing demands by maintaining two different social structures: a *normative structure*, a working equilibrium of roles, norms, rules, and structural obligations; and a *proto-structure*, a play-space of latent potential from which novelty can arise. Play temporarily dissolves the normative structure, frees people from structural obligations, and fosters novelty by defamiliarizing the elements of the familiar (Turner, 1982). Play gives birth to new ideas, which, once rehearsed, may become part of the normative structure and lose their playful character. Play itself, however, maintains its capacity to produce novelty.

Huizinga (1955) traced the roots of most western institutions to the world of play. He notes, for instance, that the idea of *fair play* – the pursuit of mastery and excellence within a set of fixed and equal rules – first appeared in the Olympic Games two centuries before it became a principle of a new political system, democracy; and that the idea of betting on future potentialities of non-economic nature, including life and death, was first played in the Middle Ages as an infamous and even illegal game many centuries before it was transformed to a legitimate new business, life insurance. Entire industries, like aerospace engineering (Jacab, 1999), and companies, like Harley-Davidson, were born by the play of their founders rather than by planned instrumental activity: "One could say that the whole of Silicon Valley stems from gangs of young men who carried on playing together beyond their college years" (Nicholson, 2000, p. 179).

Work organizations as well can, and some times do, maintain such proto-structures. March (1976) argues that organizations are built upon three interrelated assumptions: the pre-existence of purpose, the primacy of consistency, and the primacy of rationality in human behavior. These three assumptions have improved the ability of organizations and their members to act purposively, consistently, and rationally, but the side effect is that they may lead to rigidity and adaptive failure in the long run. These assumptions strengthen the ability of the organization to flourish in the present but comprise its ability to create variability so as to adapt flexibly to change (March, 1991). It seems rational to consistently reproduce successful behaviors but this reduces variability because it results in a bias against alternatives that initially may appear to be worse than they actually are (Audia, Locke, & Smith, 2000; Denrell & March, 2001). A behavior that is successful in adaptive terms today may actually be ineffective or even dangerous tomorrow when the environment changes.

Organizations can prevent such problems by giving license to people to play with their work, temporarily freed from the rules of consistency, command, and control. The role of play is not to abolish purpose, consistency, and rationality from organizational life; rather, the role of play is to help organizations maintain more flexible and more sophisticated forms of consistency by encouraging their members to occasionally experiment with possible realities, behaviors, or identities (Barrett, 1998; March, 1976; Weick, 1979).

We view the normative organizational structure as consisting of rules, norms, and pressures for behavioral consistency; functional pressures; structural obligations; and a bias toward pursuing a pre-existing purpose by rationally accommodating means to ends. We have suggested that organizations can maintain a proto-structure and nurture play in two ways. First, delineating a space and time that legitimately, if temporarily, dissolves the normative structure is the most direct way for an organization to stimulate play; it is also the organizational structural analogue to what cultures have been doing throughout the course of civilization. Second, by providing freedom and stimulating work, which allow individuals to create their own play spaces within their workday. The boundaries of play in this case are not conspicuously institutionalized but are determined at individuals' discretion. Of course, individuals can also take the initiative and play, for example, by taking work home or by staying late at work, even when their organization does not support play (Pinchot, 1985). Similarly, diversionary play can occur spontaneously among colleagues be it within or out of the regular word day. These ways of enabling play are not mutually exclusive but may coexist.

In addition, we have argued that play facilitates creativity in three general ways. First, we have suggested that play as engagement with work tasks increases the likelihood of creativity in relation to the problem or task at hand via cognitive, affective, and motivational mechanisms. Play may generate new ideas for products or processes, which may then enter the normative structure and lose their playful character. For example, an industrial designer may generate in play a new idea for a toy or a mobile phone, but once this idea enters the normative organizational structure it will likely be manufactured in a streamlined, efficient, standardized, and routinized way. Play itself, however, maintains its capacity to produce novelty, that is, industrial designers can generate through play more new ideas for products. Second, we have suggested that play as engagement also develops an enduring disposition toward creativity. Play allows organizational members to practice the cognitive muscles of creativity, and by doing so, to strengthen their ability to respond creatively to future environmental demands. Play achieves this effect by providing a context in which people can practice the free recombination of their skills, experiences, and very perceptions of reality. Finally, we have argued that, by increasing psychological safety, by strengthening a culture's tolerance for new ideas, by offering to employees a channel for expressing disagreement and dissent, and by increasing the flow of diverse information through social networks, play as diversion contributes to the creation of a social context that is conducive to creativity.

Furthermore, play also generates many ideas that are inapplicable. These ideas may reenter the play world for further refinement or they may stay in the play world forever. This is sheer inefficiency, however, it is the type of inefficiency that creativity requires: to discover one idea that is original and useful, one has to generate variance – several ideas that are original but not useful or applicable. We cite earlier a passage in which Albert Einstein suggests that creativity is a "combinatorial play" where the existing elements of thought are freely combined to produce a large number of associations. Creativity depends on novelty, and novelty depends on such cognitive variation: the more and the more diverse cognitive elements are combined to solve a problem, the more original the solution will be (Simonton, 1999). We suggest earlier that, through both cognitive and affective mechanisms, play increases both the number and the diversity of cognitive elements that enter the creative process. Play is powerful precisely because in it people suspend disbelief and explore ideas that may seem at first unrealistic or improbable. The fact that many of them turn out to indeed be unrealistic or improbable should be viewed as a necessity, not a problem. While the cost of play is inefficiency, errors, or dead ends, the cost of not playing may actually be even more severe to organizations whose survival and prosperity depend on creative ability. By constraining play, such organizations may actually be constraining the creative process itself.

New ideas usually encounter resistance or rejection in the workplace (Dougherty & Heller, 1994; see also Amabile et al., 2005). Organizational resistance may be directed at constraining exploration in the first place or at questioning the commercial viability of a new idea once exploration is over. While the latter form of resistance is true and inevitable to some extent for the majority of new ideas in the stock market of organizational creativity, the former is disastrous for creativity because it blocks creativity before it can even begin. An important implication of this is that, although the ideas that emerge from the time and space of play may not be embraced by the organization for a while, or they may not be embraced at all, encouraging play allows the organization to cultivate a pool of numerous and diverse ideas for new products, processes, or solutions.

Fundamentally, the inefficiency and novelty of play raise a question of balance – a balance that is difficult to find when considering how easily the standard assumptions of rationality, consistency, and fixed purpose can drive out play from an organizational setting (Benner & Tushman, 2003; March, 1993). From this point of view, the tendency of some organizations to legitimize a time and space for play is not surprising. By developing rules about play (such as demanding that people spend 10 or 20% of their time experimenting), organizations can control the degree of inefficiency. A legitimate space and time serves this dual function: it contains to some extent the negative consequences of play while, at the same time, it nurtures and protects play from the functional pressures, structural obligations, and social pressures of the workplace. We also reiterate that such practices in and of themselves do not constitute play for individuals must be willing to play with their work as well.

Illustrative Examples

Pinchot (1985) has discussed several examples where a legitimate organizational time and space for play has led directly to creative ideas for new products, including the invention of the fiber Kevlar, one of the most successful and profitable innovations in DuPont over the years. Kevlar was invented when a team explored the idea in "free-time" for six months. During this period, no one else knew anything about the project. When asked why she kept the project secret, the chief chemist replied, "It was my job to spend some of my time exploring new ideas on my own. I did not need anyone's permission" (Pinchot, 1985, p. 212). Engineers at Google as well are expected to spend 20% of their time on non-core projects. They are encouraged to explore new products without allowing profitability or marketability to hinder their product-development efforts. Google CEO Eric Schmidt claims that most of the company's new products are not part of a strategic vision for the organization but result from these side projects (Batelle, 2005). O'Reilly and Rao (1997) mention Pfizer as an example of an organization that encourages play by pressing researchers not to fall into the common trap of concentrating in areas where they are familiar and comfortable but to stretch, instead, into new areas and approaches.

Deutschman (2004) has described the invention of the Elixir guitar strings at Gore. In one of Gore's medical products plants, an engineer took advantage of "free-time" to improve the gears of his mountain bike, inventing in that way Gore's "Ride-On" line of bike cables. Then he used that idea to develop cables that control the movement of oversized puppets in such places as Disney World, using guitar strings to control the movements. When he noticed that the guitar strings easily broke, he asked how he could develop less-brittle guitar strings. He teamed-up with a colleague who was an amateur musician and another colleague who helped develop Gore's non-breakable "Glide" dental floss. They played together for five years, in Gore's "free-time" and in their own free time, without "asking for anyone's permission or being subjected to any kind of oversight" (p. 61). According to Deutschman (2004), today Gore controls 35% of the acoustic guitar strings market, although Gore had absolutely nothing to do with the music market prior to this invention.

These cases of creativity are next to inconceivable from the point of view of rationality, consistency, and fixed purpose that have long dominated management thinking. In the modern corporate contexts where time pressures and fixed ends rule, how can firms support the five-year-long exploration of a new product when the product itself is not known or when the idea behind the product keeps on changing all the time? How do you invent a non-breakable guitar string when your original purpose was to improve bike gears? When guitar strings, bike gears, and your own bike are not part of the activities at a medical products plant? How do you become the leader in the guitar strings market when you are not in that market and have not even considered entering it? When there is nothing in the identity, strategy, vision, or competence of the organization that actually points to that direction?

In our view, the answer to these questions is "by playing." By temporarily suspending functional pressures, structural obligations, and pressures for conformity and consistency, play delineates a transitional space, a between-and-betwixt world, in which organizational members explore and experiment with new variables, behaviors, or identities which may not seem immediately useful in generating products or solutions. By generating such variety in ideas and products, play leads to a more diverse set of options from which some get selected into our organizations and society (Campbell, 1960; Simonton, 1999). This play space thus functions as the cradle of creativity by allowing individuals to rehearse the production of novelty, to build a reservoir of adaptive responses that may turn out to be quite useful in the future, and also to generate creative ideas – new work for the future.

REMAINING PUZZLES

In this paper, we have defined play as an orientation consisting of five elements: a threshold experience; boundaries in time and space; uncertainty-freedom-constraint; a loose and flexible association between means and end; and positive affect. We have drawn a distinction between two organizational manifestations of play, play as engagement and play as diversion. We have argued that play as engagement facilitates the cognitive, affective, motivational, and skill dimensions of the creative processes, while play as diversion fosters a psychological and social-relational climate that is conducive to creativity. We have discussed four conditions that facilitate or inhibit play, namely, job complexity, environmental threat, a legitimate organizational time and space for play, and individual differences, as well as the relationship between play as engagement and play as diversion. Finally, we have synthesized our arguments to conceptualize play as an organizational space of novelty potential. There are limitations, omissions, as well as contributions in our approach.

First, we have not addressed the epistemological debates surrounding the definition of play (cf. Sutton-Smith, 1997). However, previous organizational authors have discussed play without defining it (e.g., Amabile, 1996; Roy, 1959) or by focusing only on one or two of its elements (e.g., Glynn, 1994; Sandelands, 1988; Weick, 1979). While we reiterate that play is elusive, complex, and continues to defy a concise and broadly accepted definition, we have developed here a detailed definition of play that is well-anchored in influential works from diverse social science literatures.

Second, play can be defined not only at the behavioral but also at the evolutionary and cultural levels. Play is a fundamental human function whose manifestation is not limited to any gender, race, age, culture, or era (Huizinga, 1955). Play is at first a kind of biological, pre-linguistic enactment that places its own demands on human existence across cultures and eras (Sutton-Smith, 1997). Before it becomes a hobby or a game, play is a natural impulse – an evolutionary endowment to humans that lasts from childhood to senility (Sandelands, 1988). Furthermore, while the play impulse is a gift of nature, the expression of play itself is a cultural phenomenon. Even solitary forms of play are cultural phenomena for, historically, not all children have played with Barbie dolls and not all societies have played monopoly. Play is an indispensable element of culture – it shapes and it is shaped, in turn, by it (Huizinga, 1955). The performances, contests, and festivals of play, expressed in rich and highly varied stylizations, have been at the core of social and cultural life from the story-telling gatherings of the primitive caves to the modern city sports, theaters, and festivals (Sandelands, 2003; Turner, 1982). Portrayals of play as an evolutionary mechanism for enforcing organismic adaptive variability (Sutton-Smith, 1997) and as a social protoplasmic element in which culture originates (Huizinga, 1955), are well in line with and could further enhance our arguments. Given the complex nature of play, however, we had to make some choices in this paper in order to explore it as an organizational behavior.

Third, our analysis lacks some precision in the sense that play is polymorphous and manifested in varied forms (e.g., simulations, role-plays, fantasy, rule-bound games). While there are differences between these forms, we view our discussion of the elements of play as generally applying well enough across all forms of play. Furthermore, while previous articles have largely focused on either play as diversion or play as engagement, we have maintained here a dual focus that allows a more complete picture of play to emerge. That said, our understanding of play can and should be advanced by exploring in greater detail its diverse forms. For example, fantasy may be more important to affect-laden thoughts (LeDoux, 1996), while group simulations may be more important to developing collective adaptive variability (de Geus, 1996). Future research can shed light on these issues and explore in greater detail various manifestations, forms, and "moments" of play in organizational life.

Fourth, we have not discussed the effects of play on group-level creativity. Our literature on play has been so limited, to date, that we had to introduce several concepts at the individual level of analysis. For example, examining how "affect-laden thoughts" appear at the group level would require us to write a paper only about group play. Furthermore, key creativity variables, such as the creative process, have not been adequately theorized at the group level, to date. We hope that our arguments about play and creativity at the individual level will be further developed by future research to include group processes. Moreover, although our analysis has focused on the micro level, we have also explored several macro-level issues, such as the relationship between play and organizational culture, and the ways by which organizations can nurture and benefit from play.

Last but not least, while our focus was on the relationship between play and creativity, we emphasize that play offers several other opportunities for novel theory development and empirical research. Play appears to be a factor in other phenomena that, like creativity, are at the heart of organizational life. In recent years, our field has started to explore the role of play in other fruitful areas of organizational research, including work identity (e.g., Ibarra, 1999, 2003), collective identity (e.g., Marotto et al., 2003; Sandelands, 2003), psychological adjustment to the realities of the workplace (e.g., Elsbach & Hargadon, 2002; Jett & George, 2003), and organizational culture (e.g., Deal & Kennedy, 1982; Sutton-Smith, 1997). When these dimensions of organizational life are also taken into account, play appears to be an important phenomenon embedded in the deep texture of organizational life.

To wonder about play is to puzzle with questions that are at the heart of our discipline. For example, why have centuries of attempts at rationalizing work behavior failed to extinguish play from organizations? Perhaps play can help us reexamine what is timeless and what is ephemeral in human behavior.

Why have play institutions, like the theater, stood the test of time? Perhaps play can help us to understand why our modern organizations often live and die too fast. Why is the passion and devotion with which people pursue their play activities at home often only a dream for many employing organizations? Perhaps play can teach us a lot about human motivation. The fact that the idea of free competition within a set of equal rules was born in play should remind us of how our economic markets got started. In an era where our "serious" economies are troubled by corruption and scandals, play in its undiluted forms can educate us about competition that is serious indeed.

In 1788 Goethe (1987, p. 30) observed that while in the classical era people could enjoy theater a few weeks of the year, "at present there is at least one play-house [in Rome] open in summer and autumn as well as winter." Goethe would be surprised if he knew that today there is a plethora of theaters, playhouses, operas, and sports arenas in our cities. Although the nature of these institutions and the nature of play itself have been transformed over the centuries, there is something that appears to have not changed at all: people continue to find some of the fullest and most rewarding experiences in their lives in such play spaces. In an era biased toward "real" and "true" information, why do people find meaning and joy in creating and enacting "false," symbolic worlds? Perhaps because there is something more fundamental in human nature than the image of the "sober," rational agent. In probably the most important treatise on play of all times, Huizinga (1955) wrote that, alongside the original world of nature, humans create through play a poetic world of fiction, contest, and imagination in which all culture and novelty originate. If a fraction of Huizinga's argument were true, several dimensions of organizational behavior – and the very idea of behavior in organizations – could be revisited in novel, fresh ways. The field of play, and the field for play, remains for us an inviting, puzzling, and exciting territory of organizational behavior.

NOTES

1. Taking too much time away from monotonous tasks to play computer games or play with other colleagues can have important economic costs for organizations. This is, in fact, the reason that diversionary play is often seen as a waste of time. Note, however, that what triggers work disengagement in this case is not play itself but the very nature of the work. Considering the psychological costs associated with monotonous, boring, and alienating organizational work, diversionary play seems to be more of an alleviation of the problem and less of the problem itself. We do not explore this issue further here because it is associated with organizational contexts where creativity is usually not a requirement or even a possibility of the job.

ACKNOWLEDGMENTS

We thank Charlan Nemeth, Nigel Nicholson, Randall Peterson, and Barry Staw for their comments on previous drafts of the manuscript, and Chris Early, Rob Goffee, Alice Kolb, and David Kolb for their suggestions in the early phases of our research.

REFERENCES

Abramis, D. J. (1990). Play in work: Childish hedonism or adult enthusiasm? *American Behavioral Scientist, 33*, 353–373.

Amabile, T. M. (1988). A model of creativity and innovation in organizations. In: B. M. Staw & L. L. Cummings (Eds), *Research in organizational behavior*, (Vol. 10, pp. 123–167). Greenwich, CT: JAI.

Amabile, T. M. (1996). *Creativity in context*. Boulder, CO: Westview Press.

Amabile, T. M., Barsade, S. G., Mueller, J. S., & Staw, B. M. (2005). Affect and creativity at work. *Administrative Science Quarterly, 50*, 367–403.

Amabile, T. M., & Conti, R. (1999). Changes in the work environment during downsizing. *Academy of Management Journal, 42*, 630–640.

Amabile, T. M., Conti, R., Coon, H., Lazenby, J., & Herron, M. (1996). Assessing the work environment for creativity. *Academy of Management Journal, 39*, 1154–1184.

Amabile, T. M., Hill, K. G., Hennessey, B. A., & Tighe, E. (1994). The work preference inventory: Assessing intrinsic and extrinsic motivational orientations. *Journal of Personality and Social Psychology, 66*, 950–967.

Anand, N., & Watson, M. R. (2004). Tournament rituals in the evolution of fields: The case of the Grammy awards. *Academy of Management Journal, 47*, 59–80.

Asforth, B. E., Kreiner, G. E., & Fugate, M. (2000). All in a day's work: Boundaries and micro role transitions. *Academy of Management Review, 25*, 472–491.

Audia, P. G., Locke, E. A., & Smith, K. G. (2000). The paradox of success: An archival and a laboratory study of strategic persistence following radical environmental change. *Academy of Management Journal, 43*, 837–853.

Bailey, J. R., & Ford, C. M. (1994). Of methods and metaphors: Theatre and self-exploration in the laboratory. *Journal of Applied Behavioral Science, 30*, 381–396.

Barrett, F. J. (1998). Creativity and improvisation in jazz and organizations: Implications for organizational learning. *Organization Science, 9*, 605–622.

Barron, F., Montuori, A., & Barron, A. (1997). *Creators on creating*. New York: Tarcher/Putnam.

Basadur, M. (1994). Managing the creative process in organizations. In: M. A. Runco (Ed.), *Problem solving, problem finding, and creativity* (pp. 237–268). Norwood, NJ: Ablex.

Basadur, M., Wakabayashi, M., & Graen, G. B. (1990). Individual problem-solving styles and attitudes toward divergent thinking before and after training. *Creativity Research Journal, 3*, 22–32.

Bateson, G. (1955). A theory of play and fantasy. *Psychiatric Research Reports, 2*, 39–51.

Battelle, J. (2005). The 70 percent solution. *Business 2.0, 6*, 134–136.

Beatty, J. E., & Torbert, W. R. (2003). The false duality of work and leisure. *Journal of Management Inquiry, 12*, 239–252.

Benner, M. J., & Tushman, M. L. (2003). Exploitation, exploration, and process management: The productivity dilemma revisited. *Academy of Management Review, 28*, 238–256.

Blaney, P. H. (1986). Affect and memory: A review. *Psychological Bulletin, 99*, 229–246.

Boland, R. J., & Hoffman, R. (1983). Humor in a machine shop: An interpretation of symbolic action. In: L. R. Pondy, P. J. Frost, G. Morgan, & T. C. Dandridge (Eds), *Organizational symbolism* (pp. 187–198). Monographs in Organizational Behavior and Industrial Relations. Greenwich, CT: JAI.

Bruner, J. S. (1972). Nature and uses of immaturity. *American Psychologist, 27*, 687–708.

Burt, R. S. (2004). Structural holes and good ideas. *American Journal of Sociology, 110*, 349–399.

Caillois, R. (2001). Man, play, and games. In: M. Barash (Trans.). New York: Free Press.

Campbell, D. J. (1988). Task complexity: A review and analysis. *Academy of Management Review, 13*, 40–53.

Campbell, D. T. (1960). Blind variation and selective retention in creative thought as in other knowledge processes. *Psychological Review, 67*, 380–400.

Collins, M. A., & Amabile, T. M. (1999). Motivation and creativity. In: R. Sternberg (Ed.), *Handbook of creativity* (pp. 297–312). Cambridge, MA: Cambridge University Press.

Costa, T. P., & McCrae, R. R. (1988). From catalog to classification: Murray's needs and the five-factor model. *Journal of Personality and Social Psychology, 55*, 258–265.

Csikszentmihalyi, M. (1990). *Flow: The psychology of optimal experience.* New York, NY: Harper & Row.

Csikszentmihalyi, M. (1997). *Creativity: Flow and the psychology of discovery and invention.* New York: HarperPerennial.

Csikszentmihalyi, M., & LeFevre, J. (1989). Optimal experience in work and leisure. *Journal of Personality and Social Psychology, 56*, 815–822.

D'Abate, C. P. (2004). *All in a day's work: Personal business on the job and the factors behind nonwork engagement.* Paper presented at the annual meeting of the Academy of Management, New Orleans, LA.

Dandridge, T. C. (1986). Ceremony as an integration of work and play. *Organization Studies, 7*, 159–170.

Dansky, J. L. (1999). Play. In: M. A. Runco & S. R. Pritzker (Eds), *Encyclopedia of creativity*, (Vol. 2, pp. 393–408). San Diego, CA: Academic Press.

Dansky, J. L., & Silverman, I. W. (1973). Effects of play on associative fluency in pre-school aged children. *Developmental Psychology, 9*, 38–43.

Dansky, J. L., & Silverman, I. W. (1975). Play: A general facilitator of associative fluency. *Developmental Psychology, 11*, 104.

de Geus, A. P. (1996). Planning as learning. In: K. Starkey (Ed.), *How organizations learn* (pp. 92–99). London, UK: International Thomson Business Press.

Deal, T. E., & Kennedy, A. A. (1982). *Corporate cultures: The rites and rituals of corporate life.* Reading, MA: Addison-Wesley.

Deci, E. L., & Ryan, R. M. (1985). *Intrinsic motivation and self-determination in human behavior.* New York: Plenum.

Denrell, J., & March, J. G. (2001). Adaptation as information restriction: The hot stove effect. *Organization Science, 12*, 523–538.

Deutschman, A. (2004). The fabric of creativity. *Fast Company*, (89) 54–62.

Dougherty, D., & Heller, T. (1994). The illegitimacy of successful product innovations in established firms. *Organization Science*, (5), 200–218.

Dudek, S. Z. (1980). Primary process ideation. In: Woody, R.H. (Ed.), *Encyclopedia of Clinical Assessment* (Vol. 1, pp. 520–539). San Francisco: Jossey-Bass.

Dudek, S. Z. (1999). Affect in artists and architects. In: S. W. Russ (Ed.), *Affect, creative experience, and psychological adjustment* (pp. 109–127). Philadelphia, PA: Brunner/Mazel.

Duncan, W. J., Smeltzer, L. R., & Leap, T. L. (1990). Humor and work: Applications of joking behavior to management. *Journal of Management, 16*, 255–278.

Dutton, J. E., Dukerich, J. M., & Harquail, C. V. (1994). Organizational images and member identification. *Administrative Science Quarterly, 39*, 239–263.

Dutton, J. E., & Jackson, S. E. (1987). Categorizing strategic issues: Links to organizational actions. *Academy of Management Review, 12*, 76–90.

Ederlyi, M. H. (1992). Psychodynamics and the unconscious. *American Psychologist, 47*, 784–787.

Edmondson, A. (1999). Psychological safety and learning behavior in work teams. *Administrative Science Quarterly, 44*, 350–383.

Elsbach, K.D., & Hargadon, A.B. (2002). *Enhancing creativity through "mind-less" work: An expanded model of managerial job-enrinchment.* Paper presented at the annual meeting of the Academy of Management, Denver, CO.

Estrada, C., Young, M., & Isen, A. M. (1994). Positive affect influences creative problem solving and reported source of practice satisfaction in physicians. *Motivation and Emotion, 18*, 285–299.

Falassi, A. (1987). Festival: Definition and morphology. In: A. Falassi (Ed.), *Time out of time* (pp. 1–10). Albuquerue: University of New Mexico Press.

Fein, G. (1987). Pretend play: Creativity and consciousness. In: P. Golritz & J. Wohlwill (Eds), *Curiosity, imagination, and play* (pp. 281–304). Hillsdale, NJ: Lawrence Erlbaum.

Feist, G. J. (1999a). The influence of personality on artistic and scientific creativity. In: R. J. Sternberg (Ed.), *Handbook of creativity* (pp. 273–296). New York: Cambridge University Press.

Feist, G. J. (1999b). Affect in artistic and scientific creativity. In: S. W. Russ (Ed.), *Affect, creative experience, and psychological adjustment* (pp. 93–108). Philadelphia, PA: Brunner/Mazel.

Feldman, D. H. (1999). The development of creativity. In: R. J. Sternberg (Ed.), *Handbook of creativity* (pp. 169–186). New York, NY: Cambridge University Press.

Filipowicz, A. (2003). Playtime is over: The influence of positive affect on subsequent interaction tasks. Paper presented at the annual meeting of the Academy of Management, Seattle, WA.

Freud, S. (1926). Creative writers and daydreaming. In: P. E. Vernon (Ed.), *Creativity* (pp. 126–136). New York: Penguin.

Gardner, H. (1993). *Creating minds.* New York: Basic Books.

Getz, I., & Lubart, T. I. (1999). The emotional resonance model of creativity: Theoretical and practical extensions. In: S. W. Russ (Ed.), *Affect, creative experience, and psychological adjustment* (pp. 41–56). Philadelphia, PA: Brunner/Mazel.

Getzels, S., & Csikszentmihalyi, M. (1976). *The creative vision: A longitudinal study of problem-finding in art.* New York: Wiley.

Glynn, M. A. (1994). Effects of work task cues and play task cues on information processing, judgment, and motivation. *Journal of Applied Psychology, 79*, 34–45.

Glynn, M. A., & Webster, J. (1992). The adult playfulness scale: An initial assessment. *Psychological Reports, 71*, 83–103.

Goethe, von J. W. (1987). The Roman carnival. In: A. Falassi (Ed.), *Time out of time* (pp. 13–34). Albuquerue: University of New Mexico Press. (Originally published 1789.)

Goffman, E. (1959). *The presentation of self in everyday life*. New York: Anchor.
Granovetter, M. S. (1973). The strength of weak ties. *American Jounal of Sociology, 78*, 1360–1380.
Guilford, J. P. (1950). Creativity. *American Psychologist, 5*, 444–454.
Guilford, J. P. (1968). *Intelligence, creativity, and their educational implications*. San Diego: Knapp.
Hackman, J. R., & Oldham, G. R. (1980). *Work redesign*. Reading, MA: Addison-Wesley.
Hallowell, R. (1996). Southwest Airlines: A case study linking employee needs satisfaction and organizational capabilities to competitive advantage. *Human Resource Management, 35*, 513–534.
Huizinga, J. (1955). *Homo ludens: A study of the play element in culture*. Boston, MA: Beacon Press.
Huy, Q. N. (1999). Emotional capability, emotional intelligence, and radical change. *Academy of Management Review, 24*, 245–325.
Ibarra, H. (1999). Provisional selves: Experimenting with image and identity in professional adaptation. *Administrative Science Quarterly, 44*, 764–791.
Ibarra, H. (2003). *Identity play/identities in play: Transition, experimentation, and the process of career change*. Paper presented at the annual meeting of the Academy of Management, Seattle, WA.
Isaksen, S. G., Lauer, K. J., Ekvall, G., & Britz, A. (2000–2001). Perceptions of the best and worst climates for creativity: Preliminary validation evidence for the situational outlook questionnaire. *Creativity Research Journal, 13*, 171–284.
Isen, A. M. (1999). On the relationship between affect and creative problem solving. In: S. W. Russ (Ed.), *Affect, creative experience, and psychological adjustment* (pp. 3–17). Philadelphia, PA: Brunner/Mazel.
Isen, A. M., & Geva, N. (1987). The influence of positive affect on acceptable level of risk: The person with a large canoe has a large worry. *Organizational Behavior and Human Decision Processes, 39*, 145–154.
Jacab, P. L. (1999). Wilbur and Orville Wright. In: M. A. Runco & S. R. Pritzker (Eds), *Encyclopedia of creativity* (Vol. 2, pp. 721–726). San Diego, CA: Academic Press.
Jackson, D. N. (1984). *Personality research form manual*. Port Huron, MI: Research Psychologists Press.
Jett, Q. R., & George, J. M. (2003). Work interrupted: A closer look at the role of interruptions in organizational life. *Academy of Management Review, 28*, 494–507.
Kahn, B., & Isen, A. M. (1993). The influence of positive affect on variety-seeking among safe, enjoyable products. *Journal of Consumer Research, 20*, 257–270.
Kelley, T., & Littman, J. (2001). *The art of innovation*. London, UK: Harper Collins.
Klinger, E. (1971). *Structure and functions of fantasy*. New York: Wiley.
Kolb, A. Y. (2000). *Play: An interdisciplinary integration of research*. Doctoral dissertation, Case Western Reserve University, Cleveland, OH.
Kolb, D. A. (1984). *Experiential learning: Experience as the source of learning of development*. Englewood Cliffs, NJ: Prentice-Hall.
Kolb, D. A. (1996). Management and the learning process. In: K. Starkey (Ed.), *How organizations learn* (pp. 270–287). London, UK: International Thomson Business Press.
LeDoux, D. J. (1996). *The emotional brain*. New York: Touchstone.
Levinson, D. J. (1981). *The Season's of a man's life*. New York: Ballantine Books.
Lieberman, J. N. (1977). *Playfulness: Its relation to imagination and creativity*. San Diego, CA: Academic Press.

Locke, K. D. (1989). Social play in daily interactions at the workplace: An ethnographic description of social play and its relationship to social solidarity in a medical setting. Doctoral dissertation, Case Western Reserve University, Cleveland, OH.

Locke, K. D. (1996). A funny thing happened! The management of consumer emotions in service encounters. *Organization Science, 7,* 40–59.

Luchins, A. S. (1942). Mechanization in problem solving. *Psychological Monographs, 54*(248), 1–95.

Madjar, N. G., Oldham, G. R., & Pratt, M. G. (2002). There's no place like home? The contributions of work and nonwork support to employees' creative performance. *Academy of Management Journal, 45,* 757–767.

Mainemelis, C. (2001). When the muse takes it all: A model for the experience of timelessness in organizations. *Academy of Management Review, 26,* 548–565.

Mainemelis, C. (2002). Time and timelessness: Creativity in (and out of) the temporal dimension. *Creativity Research Journal, 14,* 227–238.

Mainemelis, C., Goldenberg, V., & Ranganathan, R. (2006). *Inside the black box of total involvement: Immersion, joy, and creativity at work.* Working paper. London Business School.

March, J. G. (1976). The technology of foolishness. In: J. G. March & J. Olsen (Eds), *Ambiguity and choice in organizations* (pp. 69–81). Bergen, Norway: Universitetsforlaget.

March, J. G. (1991). Exploration and exploitation in organizational learning. *Organization Science, 2,* 71–87.

Marotto, M., Statler, M., Victor, B., & Roos, J. (2003). *Creating collective virtuosity through serious play.* Paper presented at the annual meeting of the Academy of Management, Seattle, WA.

Massimini, F., & Delle Fave, A. (2000). Individual development in a bio-cultural perspective. *American Psychologist, 55,* 24–33.

McPherson, B. D., Curtis, J. E., & Loy, J. W. (1989). *The social significance of sport.* Champaign, IL: Human Kinetics Press.

Meyer, A. D. (1982). How ideologies supplant formal structures and shape responses to environment. *Journal of Management Studies, 19,* 45–61.

Miller, S. (1973). Ends, means, and galumphing: Some leitmotifs of play. *American Anthropologist, 75,* 87–98.

Nachmanovitch, S. (1990). *Free play.* New York: Tarcher/Perigee.

Nemeth, C. J. (1997). Managing innovation: When less is more. *California Management Review, 40,* 59–74.

Nicholson, N. (2000). *Managing the human animal.* London: Texere.

Nickerson, R. S. (1999). Enhancing creativity. In: R. J. Sternberg (Ed.), *Handbook of creativity* (pp. 392–430). New York: Cambridge University Press.

Oldham, G. R., & Cummings, A. (1996). Employee creativity: Personal and contextual factors at work. *Academy of Management Journal, 39,* 607–634.

Ortony, A. (1993). Metaphor, language, and thought. In: A. Ortony (Ed.), *Metaphor and thought* (2nd ed.). New York: Cambridge University Press.

O'Reilly, B., & Rao, R. M. (1997). New products new ideas. *Fortune, 135,* 60–65.

Perry-Smith, J. E. (2006). Social yet creative: The role of social relationships in facilitating individual creativity. *Academy of Management Journal, 49,* 85–101.

Perry-Smith, J. E., & Shalley, C. E. (2003). The social side of creativity: A static and dynamic social network perspective. *Academy of Management Review, 28,* 89–106.

Pfeffer, J. (1981). Management as symbolic action: The creation and maintenance of organizational paradigms. *Research in Organizational Behavior, 3,* 1–52.

Piaget, J. (2001). *Play, dreams, and imitation in childhood.* London, UK: Routledge (Original work published 1951.)

Pinchot, G. (1985). *Intrapreneuring.* New York: Harper & Row.

Pondy, L. R. (1983). The role of metaphors and myths in organization and in the facilitation of change. In: L. R. Pondy, P. J. Frost, G. Morgan & T. C. Dandridge (Eds), *Organizational symbolism. Monographs in organizational behavior and industrial relations* (pp. 81–92). Greenwich, CT: JAI.

Rogers, C. (1954). Towards a theory of creativity. In: M. A. Runco & R. S. Albert (Eds), *Theories of creativity* (pp. 234–249). Newbury Park, CA: Sage Publications.

Roy, D. F. (1953). Work satisfaction and social reward in quota achievement: An analysis of piecework incentive. *American Sociological Review, 18,* 507–514.

Roy, D. F. (1959). "Banana time." Job satisfaction and informal interaction. *Human Organization, 18,* 158–168.

Runco, M. A. (1999). Divergent thinking. In: M. A. Runco & S. R. Pritzker (Eds), *Encyclopedia of creativity* (Vol. 1, pp. 577–582). San Diego, CA: Academic Press.

Runco, M. A., & Sakamoto, S. O. (1999). Experimental studies of creativity. In: R. J. Sternberg (Ed.), *Handbook of creativity* (pp. 62–92). New York: Cambridge University Press.

Russ, S. W. (1993). *Affect and creativity: The role of affect and play in the creative process.* Hillsdale, NJ: Lawrence Erlbaum.

Russ, S.W. (Ed.). (1999). Play, affect, and creativity: Theory and researcht. In: *Affect, creative experience, and psychological adjustment* (pp. 57–75). Philadelphia, PA: Brunner/Mazel.

Russ, S. W. (2004). *Play in child development and psychotherapy: Toward empirically supported practice.* Mahwah, NJ: Lawrence Erlbaum.

Russ, S. W., & Grossman-McKee, A. (1990). Affective expression in children's fantasy, primary process thinking on the Rorschach, and divergent thinking. *Journal of Personality Assessment, 54,* 756–771.

Russ, S. W., & Kaugars, A. S. (2000–2001). Emotion in children's play and creative problem solving. *Creativity Research Journal, 13,* 211–219.

Russ, S. W., Robins, A. L., & Christiano, B. A. (1999). Pretend play: Longitudinal prediction of creativity from affect in fantasy in children. *Creativity Research Journal, 12,* 129–139.

Sandelands, L. E. (1988). Effects of work and play signals on task evaluation. *Journal of Applied Social Psychology, 18,* 1032–1048.

Sandelands, L. E. (2003). *Thinking about social life.* Lanham, MD: University Press of America.

Sandelands, L. E., & Buckner, G. C. (1989). Of art and work: Aesthetic experience and the psychology of work feelings. In: L. L. Cummings, & B. M. Staw (Eds), *Research in Organizational Behavior,* 11, 105–131.

Schrage, M. (2000). *Serious play.* Cambridge, MA: Harvard Business School Press.

Scratchley, S. S., & Hakstian, A. R. (2000–2001). The measurement and prediction of managerial creativity. *Creativity Research Journal, 13,* 367–384.

Shalley, C. E., Zhou, J., & Oldham, G. R. (2004). The effects of personal and contextual characteristics on creativity: Where should we go from here? *Journal of Management, 30,* 933–958.

Shaw, M. P. (1999). On the role of affect in scientific discovery. In: S. W. Russ (Ed.), *Affect, creative experience, and psychological adjustment* (pp. 57–75). Philadelphia, PA: Brunner/Mazel.

Simon, H. A. (1997). *Administrative behavior.* New York: Free Press (First published 1945).

Simonton, D. K. (1999). Creativity as blind variation and selective retention: Is the creative process Darwinian? *Psychological Inquiry, 10,* 309–328.

Singer, D. G., & Singer, J. L. (1990). *The house of make-believe.* Cambridge, MA: Harvard University Press.

Spariosu, M. I. (1989). *Dionysus reborn: Play and the aesthetic dimension in modern philosophical and scientific discourse.* Ithaca, NY: Cornell University Press.

Starbuck, W. H., & Webster, J. (1991). When is play productive? *Accounting, Management, & Information Technology, 1,* 71–90.

Staw, B. M. (1995). Why no one really wants creativity. In: C. M. Ford & D. A. Gioia (Eds), *Creative action in organizations: Ivory tower visions and real world voices* (pp. 161–166). Thousand Oaks, CA: Sage.

Staw, B. M., Sandelands, L. E., & Dutton, J. E. (1981). Threat-rigidity effects in organizational behavior: A multilevel analysis. *Administrative Science Quarterly, 26,* 501–525.

Sternberg, R. J., & O'Hara, L. A. (1999). Creativity and intelligence. In: R. J. Sternberg (Ed.), *Handbook of creativity* (pp. 251–272). New York: Cambridge University Press.

Suler, J. R. (1980). Primary process thinking and creativity. *Psychological Bulletin, 88,* 144–165.

Sutton, R. I., & Hargadon, A. (1997). Brainstorming groups in context: Effectiveness in a product design firm. *Administrative Science Quarterly, 42,* 685–718.

Sutton-Smith, B. (1997). *The ambiguity of play.* Cambridge, MA: Harvard University Press.

Torrance, E. P. (1995). The nature of creativity as manifest in its testing. In: R. J. Sternberg (Ed.), *The nature of creativity* (pp. 43–75). New York: Cambridge University Press.

Turner, V. (1982). *From ritual to theatre: The human seriousness of play.* New York: PAJ.

Turner, V. (1987). Carnival, ritual, and play in Rio de Janeiro. In: A. Falassi (Ed.), *Time out of time* (pp. 74–90). Albuquerue: University of New Mexico Press.

Van Maanen, J. (1978). People processing: Strategies of organizational socialization. *Organizational Dynamics, 7,* 18–36.

Vosburg, S., & Kaufmann, G. (1999). Mood and creativity research: The view from the conceptual organizing perspective. In: S. W. Russ (Ed.), *Affect, creative experience, and psychological adjustment* (pp. 19–39). Philadelphia, PA: Brunner/Mazel.

Vygotsky, L. S. (1978). *Mind in society.* Cambridge, MA: Harvard University Press.

Ward, T. B., Smith, S. M., & Finke, R. A. (1999). Creative cognition. In: R. J. Sternberg (Ed.), *Handbook of creativity* (pp. 189–212). New York: Cambridge University Press.

Webster, J. (1998). *Webster's new world dictionary and thesaurus.* Renton, WA: Topics Entertainment.

Webster, J., & Martocchio, J. J. (1992). Microcomputer playfulness: Development of a measure with workplace implications. *MIS Quarterly,* (16), 201–226.

Webster, J., & Martocchio, J. J. (1993). Turning work into play: Implications for microcomputer software training. *Journal of Management, 19,* 127–146.

Weick, K. E. (1979). *The social psychology of organizing.* Reading, MA: Addison-Wesley.

Weick, K. E. (1998). Improvisation as a mindset for organizational analysis. *Organization Science, 9,* 543–555.

Wilkins, A. L. (1983). Organizational stories as symbols which control the organization. In: L. R. Pondy, P. J. Frost, G. Morgan & T. C. Dandridge (Eds), *Organizational symbolism. Monographs in organizational behavior and industrial relations* (pp. 81–92). Greenwich, CT: JAI.

Winnicott, D. W. (2001). *Playing and reality.* London, UK: Brunner-Rutledge (first published 1971).

Woodman, R. W., Sawyer, J. E., & Griffin, R. W. (1993). Toward a theory of organizational creativity. *Academy of Management Review, 18,* 293–321.

"HOW MUCH IS IT WORTH TO YOU? SUBJECTIVE EVALUATIONS OF HELP IN ORGANIZATIONS"

Francis J. Flynn

ABSTRACT

Helping behavior is a fundamental aspect of life in organizations, but subjective evaluations of giving and receiving help often diverge. What one employee believes is a generous act might seem insignificant to another. Such disparity in evaluations of helpful acts can negatively affect interpersonal cooperation among peer employees. In this article, I review research on the topic of subjective evaluation in social exchange, present a preliminary model of how members of organizations construct evaluations of help, and explain how these evaluations may shape their work experiences. I conclude by discussing the implications of this framework for research on employee exchange and outline some directions for future research.

Cooperation is a fundamental aspect of organizational life that has become increasingly important. Whereas early organizations depended on division of labor and clearly delineated job roles to ensure the swift execution of tasks, many modern organizations tend to be more complex. Interdependent job roles are more common, organizational structures are less

Research in Organizational Behavior: An Annual Series of Analytical Essays and Critical Reviews
Research in Organizational Behavior, Volume 27, 133–174
Copyright © 2006 by Elsevier Ltd.
ISSN: 0191-3085/doi:10.1016/S0191-3085(06)27004-7

hierarchical, and managerial practices based on employee involvement (e.g., self-managing work teams) are more popular. Indeed, for most members of organizations, cooperation with fellow coworkers (that which goes beyond their formal job description) is a routine exercise. These acts of cooperation are not just pervasive, but essential to organizational functioning. Various forms of interpersonal cooperation represent a critical means by which employees, and the organizations they represent, can accomplish their goals (e.g., Blau, 1963; Flynn, 2003b). As a topic of scholarly interest, then, cooperation stands poised to occupy a highly prominent position in the field of organizational behavior.

Regarding employee cooperation, the question that concerns organizational scholars is the same question that concerns leaders of organizations – how can organizational members be encouraged to cooperate with one another? Organizations depend on resource sharing among their members to ensure strong performance, but peer employees often are reluctant to help one another. Such reluctance is understandable because cooperation can be risky, particularly for more generous employees (Katz & Kahn, 1978; Blau, 1963). On the one hand, more generous employees will develop a better reputation than those who are less generous. On the other hand, if generous employees are frequently performing favors for others in lieu of performing their own duties, their generosity may hinder their job performance. Thus, cooperation becomes a problem in the sense that it is easy to encourage, but difficult to achieve.

To better understand this "cooperation problem," organizational scholars have developed various theoretical perspectives. Some scholars have focused on identity as a primary determinant of cooperative behavior (Chatman & Flynn, 2001; Tyler & Blader, 2001; Flynn, 2005a), arguing that cooperation is more likely to occur when employees share membership in a common group and value that group membership highly. Others suggest that cooperation depends on how employees construe their work roles – those who construe their roles more broadly will be willing to sacrifice their self-interest for the benefit of others (Organ, 1990; Morrison, 1994; Van Dyne, Cummings, & McLean Parks, 1995). Finally, some contend that cooperation stems from individual dispositions, either a concern with impression management (e.g., Bolino, 1999) or a concern with others' needs (Penner, Dovidio, Piliavin, & Schroeder, 2005). Although these views seem disparate, one common thread weaving among them is a keen interest in increasing the incidence of employee cooperation.

Increasing the incidence of cooperation is certainly a noble objective. However, it might not be effective in developing healthy patterns of cooperation, at least not in some cases. For example, Flynn (2005b) recently found that favors performed by women were not valued as highly as favors performed by men. Instead, employees who received favors from female coworkers assumed that these women were altruistic by nature and therefore felt less obligated to offer reciprocation. Moreover, help from women was requested more frequently because it was less painful and awkward for coworkers to impose on female colleagues whom they assumed were more willing to offer assistance. This led to an asymmetric pattern of exchange in which women were continually sought out for help, but such help did not elicit full reciprocation. In this case, female employees may have been cooperating more frequently, but this increased incidence of cooperation might also lead them to develop feelings of frustration and enmity.

The norm of reciprocity avers that "people should help those who have helped them" (Gouldner, 1960, p. 171). But how much help is one entitled to receive in return for a specific helpful action? The answer is unclear for two reasons. First, the norm of reciprocity does not specify how much help someone should request or provide in reciprocation. Rather, it is up to each actor to determine privately what amount of reciprocation might be appropriate. Second, it is difficult for people to evaluate the worth of a helpful action. Reciprocal favors often involve fundamentally different resources that cannot be easily evaluated and compared with a common metric. Further, explicitly discussing our impressions of favor value is strictly a taboo, particularly among friends and coworkers. Given these significant constraints, a balance pattern of reciprocal exchange may be difficult to ensure.

Past research on interpersonal cooperation in organizations has always taken the matter of agreement in evaluating help as a given. While this work has been useful in highlighting the reciprocal, long-term nature of employee cooperation, it fails to appreciate the psychology involved in a single episode of helping behavior. Rather, it assumes that people have similar impressions of the same episode when, in fact, people can construe episodes of cooperation in different ways depending on their perspective and on the characteristics of the situation. What seems like valuable help to one employee might seem worthless to another. Such disparity, if consistently biased against a focal employee, can lead to a decreased willingness to cooperate in the future. Therefore, subjective construal and evaluation of helping behavior represents a phenomenon of fundamental interest to researchers interested in employee cooperation.

In this article, I attempt to explain how evaluations of employee helping behavior are constructed, often in ways that are clearly biased. I begin by reviewing research on the topic of subjective evaluation in social exchange, drawing from research across several disciplines. Next, I present a preliminary model of how people evaluate helping behavior, arguing that the value of help is ambiguous and that personal and situational cues may anchor these evaluations. In particular, the model suggests that employees' evaluations of helping episodes are influenced by (1) an egocentric bias, (2) characteristics of the exchange relation, (3) individual differences, (4) the conditions in which requests for help are made, and (5) the language used during the exchange. In outlining the model, I focus on the episodic level of analysis and then explain how these episodic evaluations, in aggregate form, can shape our experiences in organizations. I conclude by discussing the implications of this framework for research on employee exchange and outline some directions for future research.

SUBJECTIVE EVALUATION IN EPISODES OF INTERPERSONAL COOPERATION

Research on subjective evaluation in episodes of interpersonal cooperation has its deepest roots in three academic disciplines: organizational behavior, social psychology, and sociology. In organizational behavior research, two theories have focused heavily on the issue of subjective evaluation. Equity theory (Adams, 1965), which draws heavily from social comparison theory (Festinger, 1954), assumes that employees calibrate their level of motivation according to their perception of the relationship between outcomes (what they get from the job), and inputs (what they contribute). To anchor their perceptions of equity, employees compare their outcome/input ratio to a referent's ratio. When inequity is perceived (e.g., my referent has a more favorable outcome/input ratio than my own), satisfaction decreases and workers are motivated to restore equity. Equity theory assumes that the perception of outcomes and inputs is biased, so that most people believe they are insufficiently compensated for their contributions (Walster, Walster, & Berscheid, 1978).

Psychological contracts theory is akin to equity theory in that it considers the individual's perception of reciprocal contributions between her and her employer (Rousseau, 1995). However, the psychological contracts framework also assumes that employees have pre-existing notions of what their employer has promised and use this as a means to evaluate their satisfaction with their job and with the organization. Employees can develop different impressions of what the employer has promised to them, even when efforts have been made to convey similar promises (e.g., safe work environment).

Like equity theory, the psychological contract framework assumes that the evaluation of reciprocal contributions is subjective in nature and therefore may be biased, particularly in a self-enhancing manner (Rousseau & McLean Parks, 1993; Rousseau, 1995).

Both equity theory and psychological contracts theory have attempted to understand how the subjective evaluation process is influenced by multiple factors, including internal predispositions (e.g., cognitive styles, self-schemas) and the external influences that operate in the work setting (e.g., human resource practices, social cues). Whereas these paradigms have highlighted several sources of bias in forming subjective evaluations, these biases are primarily related to how an individual construes their exchanges with an organization. In these frameworks (and in related paradigms, such as research on organizational citizenship behavior), the exchanges an employee has with other employees, matters only to the extent that they inform the focal employee's impression of the organization. In general, the manner in which employees form subjective evaluations about their exchange relations with others, particularly peer employees (see leader-member exchange theory for a discussion of subjective evaluation in supervisor-subordinate exchange, e.g., Dansereau, Graen, & Haga, 1975), has been understudied in the organizational behavior literature.

Social psychology research has focused more attention than organizational behavior on the process of helping behavior among peers (for a review, see Batson, 1998). For example, studies of bystander intervention (Latane & Darley, 1970) and the arousal cost-reward model (Pilliavin, Dovidio, Gaertner, & Clark, 1981) offer insight on why people are motivated to help others and how their decisions to offer help are biased depending on the nature of the request and on the circumstances surrounding it. However, the relevance of these theoretical perspectives to individual behavior in organizations is limited because they primarily focus on emergency circumstances. When will we feel compelled to provide assistance to someone else in a crisis and when will we shrink from this responsibility? While the answers to these research questions bear obvious importance to society, their application to everyday behavior in organizations is narrower.

For scholars interested in interpersonal cooperation among members of organizations, a more relevant literature in social psychology may be the social influence paradigm, which attempts to identify factors that lead to greater compliance in episodes of helping behavior (e.g., Cialdini, 1988). Hundreds of studies, which are primarily experimental, have revealed a set of fundamental principles that people rely on when deciding whether to say "yes" to a request for help. These insights have found their way into many business school classes and practitioner-oriented books. Despite their popularity, we know little about the relevance of these principles in long-term relationships because experimental social psychology research is generally restricted to one-shot trials. In organizations, where exchange relations are more lasting, getting someone to say "yes" may not be the only outcome of concern when making a request for help. Rather, employees may be equally concerned about reciprocating help they have given in the past and ensuring they can still obtain help in the future when they need it.

Perhaps the most direct study of subjective evaluation and interpersonal cooperation in social psychology comes from Thibaut and Kelley (1959), whose model of social interaction is akin to theories of rational choice and social exchange. Thibaut and Kelley argue that people attempt to predict the outcome of an interaction before it takes place. They further argue that people consider several possible behaviors and select the alternative that yields the most significant value for the focal individual. Their model assumes that our impressions of value in judging each alternative are accurate and follow the "minimax" principle – choosing the alternative that maximizes rewards, while minimizing costs for the focal actor. Unfortunately, Thibaut and Kelley's rigorous approach to understanding social interaction has not received much empirical attention, except for adherents to social penetration theory (Altman & Taylor, 1973), whose work focuses on self-disclosure tendencies in relationships.

Thibaut and Kelley's theoretical framework is quite similar to that of sociologists who study the dynamics of social exchange. More than social psychologists, sociological exchange theorists have paid attention to the concept of value in interpersonal cooperation (e.g., Homans, 1958; Blau, 1964; Emerson, 1987; Molm & Cook, 1995). Like Thibaut & Kelley's (1959) model of social interaction, social exchange theory assumes that people can accurately predict the benefits of their actions and make sensible choices based on these predictions. However, unlike social psychologists who study interpersonal cooperation, social exchange theorists focus on the structure of the exchange relation as the basic unit of analysis (e.g., Kollock, 1994; Molm, Takahashi, & Peterson, 2000). They pay less attention to how individuals construe a single episode of exchange and instead concentrate on the pattern of exchange that develops over multiple episodes (cf. Lawler & Yoon, 1993).

Social exchange theorists suggest that subjective evaluations of helping behavior are based on our perceptions of the costs and benefits involved in an episode of exchange (Greenberg, 1980; Greenberg, Block, & Silverman, 1971). They assume that the perception of costs and benefits in social exchange are generally accurate, or at least agreed on by both actors

(Greenberg, 1980; Emerson, 1987). However, the extent to which people's perceptions of costs and benefits are aligned may be greater in some forms of exchange than in others. In particular, negotiated exchange differs from other exchange forms in that the terms of the exchange are openly discussed and the giving and receiving of reciprocal benefits is often simultaneous (Molm et al., 2000; Malhotra & Murnighan, 2002). Because the terms of the exchange are explicit in negotiated exchange, it is more likely that two parties will be consistent in their perceptions of costs and benefits and will come to a mutual agreement about the values of goods exchanged.

Helping behavior among peer employees is more akin to reciprocal exchange than negotiated exchange (Blau, 1963, 1964). In reciprocal exchange, unilateral contributions are made in separate, rather than simultaneous, episodes (Emerson, 1976). For example, an employee who needs technical advice may ask a colleague with more expertise for assistance (Blau, 1963). If the colleague provides assistance in accordance with the rules of reciprocal exchange, she will be expected to wait before soliciting any reciprocation. In addition, bargaining in reciprocal exchange is taboo; helpers are not permitted to say, "I'll do X for you, so long as you agree to do Y for me in the future." Rather than openly discuss the terms of the exchange, the expectation of reciprocity is left implicit – one actor begins the process without knowing for certain if and when she can expect reciprocation (Heath, 1976).

Compared with the actors involved in an episode of negotiated exchange, the actors involved in an episode of reciprocal exchange are less likely to reach agreement about their perceptions of costs and benefits because their evaluations are privately constructed and tacitly held. People may sometimes state their assessments of a favor's magnitude (e.g., "thanks, that was a big help."), but these statements tend to be vague. Blau (1994) identified this criterion as the critical difference between economic exchange and social exchange, arguing that "social exchange engenders diffuse obligations, whereas those in economic exchange are specified" (pp. 152–156). Given the diffuse quality of these evaluations, disagreement about the costs and benefits involved in an episode of helping behavior (and the magnitude of reciprocation expected) may be common. Although such disagreement can occur frequently, its presence may be difficult to detect because both parties' private evaluations are undisclosed.

Social exchange theorists concede that two actors' perceptions of the costs and benefits involved in an episode of helping behavior can differ, particularly in reciprocal exchange (see Greenberg, 1980, for some discussion). However, they have not examined these differences in any systematic fashion. Instead, much of the research on perceived utility and value in social exchange theory is derived from game theory. Although rigorous, this experimental work is not particularly useful in understanding evaluative processes in social exchange because it tends to simplify the exchange process, causing us to overlook the ambiguous nature of subjective evaluations (Davis, 1970; Guiasu & Malitza, 1980). In a review of social exchange theory, Emerson (1987) lamented this problem, noting that exchange theorists may have misunderstood how people calculate utility in their exchange relations. He concluded that "What social exchange theory now needs is a *theory of value* based upon empirical psychology" (Emerson, 1987, p. 13).

Emerson's request for a theory of value in social exchange has gone unfulfilled in the field of sociology (Molm & Cook, 1995). Likewise, organizational scholars remain in need of a theoretical perspective on the topic of subjective evaluation and interpersonal cooperation – one that can describe how members of organizations construe episodes of helping behavior. The main thesis of this article is that understanding the longevity of interpersonal cooperation requires first understanding the manner in which individual episodes of exchange are viewed. Whether these views of a single helpful act diverge or coalesce may impact the development of employee exchange relations in profound ways.

Summary. Several academic disciplines are concerned with the processes of subjective evaluation and interpersonal cooperation, but none have considered these issues simultaneously. In organizational behavior, researchers have primarily examined how the process of subjective evaluation affects the employee–employer relationship, rather than dyadic exchange relations. Social psychologists who are interested in prosocial behavior have studied interpersonal exchange dynamics, but they are more concerned with compliance rather than subjective evaluations. Social exchange theorists may be the closest to developing a theory of value in interpersonal cooperation. Yet, their theory relies heavily on models of rational behavior when, in reality, the evaluation of interpersonal cooperation is fraught with error and subjectivity. It seems apparent, then, that a better understanding of subjective evaluation in episodes of employee cooperation is needed. The best place to begin to develop this understanding is by exploring the evaluation process in interpersonal relations.

EVALUATING EPISODES OF HELPING BEHAVIOR

A model of subjective evaluations of helping behavior begins with the concept of reciprocity. According to Gouldner (1960), reciprocity is a moral norm that maintains equality in interpersonal exchange by mobilizing "egoistic motivations in the service of social system stability" (p. 173). Reciprocal exchange is enforced, in part, by implicit threats of ostracism and the withholding of future benefits (Mauss, 1925 [1967]). However, the norm of reciprocity primarily operates, not by threatening punishment, but by engendering a sense of indebtedness in those who receive social benefits. Psychologists have described this feeling of indebtedness as an aversive mental state with motivational properties, so that the greater its magnitude, the greater the resultant arousal and discomfort and the stronger the ensuing attempts to reduce it by providing reciprocation (Cialdini, et al., 1975; Greenberg, 1980).

The value of a helpful action is equivalent to the amount of reciprocation it elicits in return (i.e., more valuable favors are those that elicit more substantial forms of reciprocation), which is based on each party's perceptions of the costs and benefits involved (Greenberg, 1980; Thibaut & Kelley, 1959). Benefits may be judged by the magnitude of the receiver's need and the extent to which the giver's effort fulfills the receiver's request for help. Conversely, perceptions of cost are based on what each party believes the giver has sacrificed in the exchange (Emerson, 1987, p. 13). As both parties' perceptions of benefit provided to the receiver and/or cost incurred by the giver increase, their evaluation of a helpful action will increase (i.e., their expectations of reciprocation will increase).

Expectations of reciprocation might also be based on the influence of social norms that govern episodes of helping behavior (Grice, 1975). In particular, norms of politeness can directly influence the evaluation of favor requests because such requests are threatening to the face needs of the giver and the receiver (Brown & Levinson, 1987). However, the influence of politeness norms may vary. For example, givers and receivers may respond to different politeness norms because they have different rights and duties as participants in the exchange (Gouldner, 1960). Further, politeness norms can become more salient under certain circumstances, so that the obligation to be polite in requesting or performing a favor may vary from one situation to the next even if the same favor was provided in each case.

The notion that norms of politeness can affect people's evaluations of helping behavior contradicts a core assumption of social exchange theory, which is the principle of rational action. This idea implies that people are not only interested in maximizing the rewards they obtain and minimizing the costs they incur in episodes of exchange, but that they are accurate in perceiving these costs and benefits. The implicit assumption is that we are all, in effect, folk social exchange theorists and that we make well-informed cost-benefit calculations in evaluating episodes of exchange. In reality, our evaluations are likely biased by situational norms that color our perspective in the interaction. In the following section, I explain how norms of politeness can act as one source of bias in evaluating episodes of helping behavior. These norms can affect both givers' and receivers' impressions of favor value, sometimes in similar ways, but often in ways that lead to conflicting evaluations of the same episode.

Norms of Politeness and Evaluating Helping Behavior

Asking for help can be awkward for multiple reasons. First, the requester, or receiver, must identify a personal shortcoming and impose on someone else for assistance (Goffman, 1971). Second, because he exposes himself to the risk of rejection, the receiver assumes a vulnerable position, one that is uncomfortable and potentially embarrassing. Therefore, in posing a request for help, the receiver is motivated to be polite by expressing gratitude to the giver (Green, 1975). Gratitude can be expressed in several different ways, such as apologizing (e.g., "I'm sorry to impose, but ..."), offering polite nonverbal signals (e.g., smiling), or communicating felt appreciation (e.g., "thank you"). Expressing gratitude will help the receiver minimize the likelihood of rejection and might even increase her attractiveness in the eyes of the giver (Brown & Levinson, 1987). By conforming to norms of politeness, receivers hope to reaffirm the giver's altruistic inclinations ("you're too kind"), which, in turn, may benefit the receiver in future episodes of exchange (Greenberg & Frisch, 1972).

Whereas receivers must express gratitude in an episode of helping behavior, givers are obligated to maintain a generous image. A request for help presents an imposition to the giver (Goldschmidt, 1998), but rather than react with displays of annoyance and frustration, givers are expected to "save" the embarrassing situation (Goffman, 1955). If the request is reasonable, the giver is expected to offer compliance in a generous or magnanimous manner (Goffman, 1971). Further, the giver must downplay the imposition by responding courteously, offering compliance with alacrity, and making statements that diminish the significance of the favor (e.g., "it was nothing," "no trouble at all," or "no big deal"). The giver is motivated to maintain a generous image so that she establishes a reputation as a generous exchange partner in the eyes of the receiver and others who might witness the interaction (Blau, 1964).

This need for the giver to maintain a generous image and for the receiver to maintain a grateful image, which has been referred to as "the modesty bias" (e.g., McGuire, 2003), may indirectly shape evaluations of helping behavior (e.g., Flynn, 2003a). According to self-perception theory, when people are faced with ambiguous criteria, they form evaluations of objects and events "by inferring them from observations of their own overt behavior and/or the circumstances in which this behavior occurs" (Bem, 1972, p. 2). Having conflicting obligations to maintain a generous image or a grateful image may lead givers and receivers to construct differing evaluations of the same favor, based on their differing behavior. Consistent with this idea, research has found that givers tended to form relatively lower evaluations of help than receivers immediately following an episode of helping behavior (e.g., Flynn, 2003a; McGuire, 2003).

The impact of the modesty bias may be particularly strong in the workplace. Given their common membership in a group (e.g., a team, a department, an organization), peer employees are expected to cooperate with one another even in cases where it is not necessarily required (Organ, 1990). However, downplaying one's contributions in the workplace can also be damaging to one's reputation and productivity (Flynn, 2005b). Thus, an employee may be motivated to maximize coworkers' evaluations of her helpful acts while adhering to the modesty bias. For example, an employee might let the fact that she stayed late at the office to perform a favor slip out during conversation ("... while I was putting together the document you needed last night at the office, I came across another ..."). According to Cialdini (forthcoming), employees may be able to subtly manipulate language in order to set expectations of reciprocation. Instead of saying "don't worry about; it's no big deal," one might also say "don't worry about it; I know you'd do the same for me." The latter statement allows the giver to maintain a generous image ("don't worry about it"), while reinforcing the expectation of reciprocation ("I know you'd do the same for me.").

The need to maintain a generous or grateful image may change depending on the situation and the perspective of those involved. Below, I identify five domains that can affect subjective evaluations of helping behavior by influencing either the perceived magnitude of costs and benefits and/or the obligation to maintain a generous or grateful image. First, our evaluations of past behavior often are affected by an egocentric bias – our tendency to believe we have been more generous with others than an outside observer would. Second, certain characteristics of the exchange relation (e.g., relative status) might lead both parties to view the costs and benefits involved differently. Third, some individual differences can influence how people perceive their own generosity and that of others. Fourth, the conditions in which the favor is performed might increase or decrease the perceived magnitude of costs and benefits. Finally, the way in which both parties use language to "frame" an episode of helping behavior can direct their attention to certain aspects of the exchange that may alter their evaluations of favor magnitude (Goldschmidt, 1998; Grice, 1975). These five domains, and the factors identified within them, are not meant to be exhaustive, but rather illustrative. That is, what follows is merely a preliminary look at the variables that might influence subjective evaluations of helping behavior.

Egocentric Bias

The egocentric bias is a tendency to make self-serving assessments in judging personal characteristics and behavior (Goethals, 1986). In the context of helping behavior, people tend to believe they are more charitable, on average, than their peers. They believe they are more likely than the average person to cooperate in a prisoner's dilemma game, give up their seat on a bus to a pregnant woman, and donate blood (Bierbrauer, 1976; Goethals, Messick, & Allison, 1991; Goethals, 1986). These specific self-serving judgments translate into more general self-serving accounts of helping behavior in exchange relations. For example, members of organizations will report they have contributed more to a joint product than has anyone else on their team and offered more help to their coworkers than has the average employee (Ross & Sicoly, 1979; Robinson, Kraatz, & Rousseau, 1994; Flynn, 2003b).

Theory and research on egocentric biases offer both cognitive and motivational accounts. As a cognitive explanation, Ross and Sicoly (1979) suggest that previous help given by a focal person is more available (i.e., more frequently and easily recalled) than help given by someone else. Other researchers point to the need for self-enhancement to explain the presence of egocentric biases (Greenwald, 1980). People are motivated to present themselves as having better qualities than the average individual. This might lead them to overestimate the value of their contributions in order to present themselves as being more generous than others (Sprecher, 1988). Both cognitive and motivational drivers of egocentric biases would appear to produce the same result – that people evaluate helping behavior in ways that flatter the self, leading them to believe they have given relatively more than they have received in their exchange relations with others.

Some variables might influence the strength of egocentric biases in evaluations of helping behavior. For example, Savitsky, Van Boven, Epley, and Wight (in press) demonstrated that self-serving judgments in evaluating contributions to a work group are much less pronounced when the perceiver must "unpack" each member's contributions (i.e., evaluate them individually, rather than collectively). Further, Flynn (2003a) demonstrated that egocentric biases can strengthen over time. Givers initially value favors less than receivers do, but givers eventually increase their evaluations while receivers decrease their evaluations. These changes may reflect the waning of normative pressures to maintain a generous or grateful image and the intensifying of cognitive and motivational drivers underlying egocentric biases.

Characteristics of the Exchange Relation

Aside from egocentric biases, there are many characteristics of the exchange relation that can influence perceptions of generosity and feelings of indebtedness. Relative status, frequency of exchange, and pre-existing indebtedness can each alter whether givers feel obligated to discount their acts of kindness in order to maintain a generous image. Further, they may affect whether receivers feel obligated to express gratitude that may, in turn, inflate their evaluation of a request for help. Although other characteristics of the exchange relation are undoubtedly important, I will focus on these three for illustrative purposes.

Relative Status

Evaluations of helping behavior can be influenced by the relative status of the giver and receiver. Status differences correspond to asymmetric feelings of respect and esteem among group members (Anderson, John, Keltner, & Kring, 2001). Those who have higher status command more respect from their peers than those who have lower status. Behaviors performed by members of lower and higher status groups are interpreted differently according to common beliefs that "attach differential social worthiness and competence to states of characteristics on which people are perceived to differ" (Ridgeway, 1997, p. 138). As such, favors performed by an individual with higher status than the receiver may be appraised differently from favors performed by an individual with lower status than the receiver (e.g., Blau, 1963; Romer, Bontemps, Flynn, & McGuire, 1977). A favor performed by a higher-status individual for a lower-status individual will, likely, carry greater value than will the same favor performed by a lower-status person for a higher-status person.

The impact of status on evaluations of helping behavior in exchange relations is reminiscent of Malinowski's (1922 [1961]) ethnography of exchanges in the Kula Ring, which revealed that the tribe's chief tended to receive greater benefits in his exchanges with commoners, although both parties strongly believed that such exchanges were fair. Similarly, previous research on dyadic exchange behavior in organizations found that employees perceived their exchange relations with colleagues to be reciprocal, but these same employees believed they over benefited in exchange relations with their direct supervisors (e.g., Buunk, Doosje, Jans, & Hopstaken, 1993; Blau, 1963). What might be contributing to this phenomenon are different values ascribed to favors based on perceived status differences. Norms of politeness may change when the people involved in a dyadic interaction possess unequal status (Brown & Levinson, 1987). People may feel less compelled to maintain a generous image in the eyes of lower-status individuals than in the eyes of higher-status individuals, and, by the same token, may feel more compelled to express gratitude for receiving a favor from a higher-status person than from a lower-status person.

Different values ascribed to favors based on status differences might lead to an unhealthy pattern of cooperation. According to expectation states theory, group members immediately assess each other's ability to perform tasks that require them to work together. Status is conferred on those who are believed to be the most talented and therefore most likely to help the group to achieve success. To fulfill their expectations of high-status members' performance, low-status group members contribute resources to high-status group members (e.g., Berger, Fisek, Norman, & Zelditch, 1977). Since high-status group members draw critical resources away from low-status colleagues, the presence of a high-status group member may impair a low-status member's performance (Berger, Conner, & Fisek, 1974). If, as suggested here, low-status group members are inclined to inflate their evaluation of the contributions made by high-status group members, they may be content with this unbalanced exchange dynamic (i.e., "X is deserving of more reciprocation than I am because they are higher status") despite the fact that it unfairly hinders their own success and their ability to claim higher status.

Frequency of Exchange

Frequency of exchange might also affect the magnitude of givers' and receivers' respective favor evaluations by altering normative expectations of generosity and gratitude. Past research has found that favors performed among close friends and family members tend to be viewed by both the giver and the receiver as less significant and less deserving of reciprocation (e.g., Pryor & Graburn, 1980). This devaluation may be driven, in part, by the fact that relationships with close friends and family members tend to emphasize a more frequent pattern of exchange (e.g., Sahlins, 1972). As more frequent exchange strengthens person-to-person bonds, exchange partners are expected to demonstrate more generosity in future episodes (e.g., Lawler & Yoon, 1993; Sahlins, 1972). Thus, a giver who exchanges favors with a receiver more frequently may feel more obligated to demonstrate generosity than a giver who exchanges favors with a receiver less frequently (e.g., Goldschmidt, 1998; Goffman, 1971).

Conversely, expressions of gratitude may be less emphasized in episodes of helping behavior between frequent exchange partners (Goffman, 1971). As the frequency of exchange increases, favors tend to be viewed as routine, rather than exceptional, acts of generosity (Blau, 1964). Therefore, a receiver who exchanges favors with a giver frequently may feel less obligated to convey gratitude than will a stranger. Indeed, politeness theory suggests that receivers frame their communication in a more polite fashion when requesting favors from strangers than from familiar others (Brown & Levinson, 1987). This may be problematic for an employee who interacts with both familiar and unfamiliar exchange partners. He may feel more compelled to express more generosity with a stranger than with a close colleague. However, a close colleague who observes this pattern may feel put off by this apparent devaluing of their assistance. The strength of their exchange relation may decrease accordingly.

Perceived Indebtedness

The norm of maintaining a generous or grateful image during episodes of helping behavior may be further influenced by perceptions of receiver-indebtedness. As perceived receiver-indebtedness increases, givers may feel less motivated to maintain a generous image because they have already demonstrated generosity in the past by performing favors that have not yet been reciprocated (e.g., Greenberg, 1980; Blau, 1964; Cotterell, Eisenberger, & Speicher, 1992). In the mind of the giver, the receiver's request for additional help without first providing reciprocation may seem like a violation of the norm of reciprocity. As a result, givers might evaluate a favor request more highly and expect more in return if receivers are more, rather than less, indebted to them.

Receivers may be similarly concerned about requesting favors from givers to whom they are already indebted. As the magnitude of perceived indebtedness increases, feelings of arousal and discomfort will increase in intensity and the prospect of making a request for help may appear more daunting (Greenberg, 1980). To cope with aversive feelings of indebtedness, people tend to treat their creditors with greater deference (e.g., Blau, 1963) and are more polite in framing favor requests (Brown & Levinson, 1987). The greater the perceived imposition of the favor, the more polite the receiver needs to be in the exchange (Goffman, 1971, p. 186). For receivers who are more indebted, this intense feeling and demonstration of gratitude might lead them to increase their evaluations of the magnitude of the request and their willingness to provide reciprocation.

On the other hand, the egocentric bias implies that givers and receivers will develop different perceptions of receiver-indebtedness (e.g., Flynn, 2003a). Specifically, receivers will believe they have received less from the giver in the past than the giver assumes they have contributed. Indeed, in a study of engineers in a telecommunications firm, Flynn (2003b) found that employees tended to report they were more generous with each of their colleagues in their exchange relations than their colleagues had been with them. This suggests that an increase in perceived indebtedness may cause problems in an employee exchange relation. If the giver naturally holds a higher evaluation of the receiver's indebtedness than the receiver holds, the giver may be more inclined to reject the receiver's request for assistance than the receiver feels is justified.

Individual Differences

The evaluation of helping behavior might also depend on the characteristics of the helper and those being helped. The same helpful action can appear more valuable when it is provided to one coworker rather than another, even if both recipients occupy the same position, have the same level of familiarity with the focal party, and have experienced the same history of exchange with that person. What are some personal characteristics that might influence how generous we feel we have been to others or how generous we feel others have been with us? Below, I describe two individual differences – demographic characteristics and personality traits – that may play a role in the evaluation process.

Demographic Characteristics

The evaluation of helping behavior can be influenced by the demographic characteristics of the helper and the stereotypes those demographic characteristics invoke (Siem & Spence, 1986). As mentioned earlier in this chapter, help provided by a woman often is viewed by the recipient as less significant than the same helpful action provided by a man (Heilman & Chen, 2005). Part of this discounting effect may be driven by the persistent gender stereotype that women are less competent than men (Swim, Borgida, Maruyama, & Myers, 1989). People tend to believe that male colleagues provide advice that is sounder, political assistance that is more effective, and resources that are more valuable. Discounting might also be driven by the assumption that women are altruistic by nature. If women are believed to be predisposed to perform altruistic acts, others may feel that imposing on them for help is "no big deal" (Heilman & Chen, 2005). That is, people may be less inclined to provide reciprocation when the helper is a woman because she is perceived to be more amenable to offer help.

Other demographic traits might also affect our evaluations of how generous we have been with our colleagues or how generous they have been with us. People tend to believe it will take longer to help a member of a minority group or an elderly person solve a complicated problem because the target lacks sufficient intelligence or a common understanding of the issue at hand, either of which would facilitate helping (Batson, 1991). In general, the costs of helping someone with the same demographic background may be seen as less significant than the costs of helping someone with a different demographic background. In short, demographic characteristics can increase or decrease the perceived value of a favor depending on the demographic profiles of the employees involved and the stereotypes associated with their characteristics.

Personality Traits

Some personality traits might lead people to judge help from one person as less valuable than the same help from another person. For example, the personality construct of agreeableness incorporates traits such as warm, pleasant, friendly, and trusting. More agreeable people are more "cooperative (trusting of others and caring), as well as likeable (good-natured, cheerful, and gentle)" (Judge, Higgins, Thoresen, & Barrick, 1999). Agreeable people tend toward acquiescence in groups, toward being accommodating, and toward modesty (John, 1990). More agreeable people perform more prosocial behaviors, such as helping strangers in distress or donating to charity (McCrae & Costa, 1987). Whereas this selfless orientation may suit their goal in interpersonal interactions – attaining intimacy and solidarity with others, particularly those who provide emotional rewards – it may be problematic to demonstrate too much modesty in performing such acts of kindness.

Agreeableness can exacerbate the "modesty bias" (Flynn, 2003a; McGuire, 2003). More agreeable people tend to be more generous than less agreeable people, but they are also more modest and motivated to make others feel comfortable (John, 1990). Such modesty and interest in facilitating awkward situations (e.g., favor requests) might lead those who are more agreeable to publicly downplay the value of their helpful actions ("it was nothing"), which may, in turn, invite others to impose on them more frequently. Consistent with this idea, Flynn and Brockner (2003) found that when givers were more agreeable in complying with favor requests (e.g., performing the favor quickly, treating the other party with dignity and respect), receivers were more inclined to ask for additional help. One of the reasons for this increased willingness to impose on the helper again may be that the previous imposition did not seem significant to the receiver.

Other personality traits, besides agreeableness, might affect the evaluation of helping behavior. For example, a helpful employee's predisposition to express positive emotion might lead others to discount the value of her help (or at least feel less obligated to provide reciprocation) because the employee would appear "happy to help." Narcissistic people, who tend to inflate their perceptions of self-worth and importance, might be more likely than others to show evidence of an egocentric bias in evaluating their own helpful acts. A narcissist may assume his advice is worth more than anyone else's, even if it is no different in quality or content. On the other hand, those with low self-esteem would be less likely to show evidence of an egocentric bias in evaluating their previous contributions and instead would be more likely to discount the value of their contributions.

Features of the Request for Help

Aside from relational characteristics and individual differences, subjective evaluations of helping behavior might be affected by the conditions surrounding a request for help. One request for help is not necessarily like another. Instead, several features of the request might increase or decrease its evaluation, including (1) whether the request is considered in-role or extra-role, (2) the extent to which the request conveys some urgency or perceived need on the part of the receiver, and (3) the relative level of resources held by the giver and the receiver.

Extra-Role/In-Role Differences

Employees may change their evaluations of helping behavior depending on how they construe the in-role/extra-role boundaries of their job responsibilities (Kiesler, 1966). In organizations, extra-role helping behaviors are defined as "unrequired and unenforceable" (Vey & Campbell, 2004). Although performing such acts of help can be beneficial to the organization (and those requesting help), they can also distract the helper from the performance of her regular duties, and, in some cases, may lead to a loss of extrinsic rewards (Organ, 1990; Flynn, 2003b). This added cost incurred by employees who agree to perform extra-role behaviors, along with the lack of relevance to their formal role, might lead some employees to view such favor requests as being less legitimate.

A request for help asks "for something outside of the [helper's] daily routine" (Goldschmidt, 1998, p. 131). To the extent this imposition seems legitimate, or justified, (e.g., the requester is in need of help that the giver is expected to provide), the giver is obligated to maintain a generous image by downplaying the magnitude of the favor. If the imposition seems less legitimate, or unjustified, (e.g., the requester is in need of help that the giver is not expected to provide), the giver is less obligated to downplay the helpful act (Grice, 1975). Instead, the giver may increase her evaluation of the magnitude of the request and expect more in return for help that required her to go out of her way. This suggests that givers would provide higher evaluations of extra-role behaviors than in-role behaviors.

Research on organizational citizenship behavior has found variance in what people consider to be in-role or extra-role requests for assistance (Konovsky & Organ, 1996; Morrison, 1994). For example, Morrison (1994) showed that employees who were more highly committed to their employer were more likely to consider a helpful act to be in-role rather than extra-role. These highly committed employees (who thought their help was in-role) probably did not consider their assistance to be deserving of as much reciprocation as did a less committed employee (who thought their help was extra-role). This would suggest that, in general, while most employees consider extra-role help to be more deserving of assistance than in-role help, some employees may be more likely to consider their helpful acts *to be extra-role* and therefore more deserving of assistance. If two employees do not implicitly agree on whether the favors they exchange or in-role or extra-role, they may be less likely to develop a healthy pattern of cooperation.

Perceived Urgency

A critical aspect of the decision to provide help is whether the target appears to be in need and whether such need for assistance is urgent. For example, Latane and Darley's (1970) model of bystander intervention predicted that people would be more likely to help in emergency situations if they could perceive the urgency with which their help was needed. In the empathy-altruism model of helping behavior (see Batson, 1991, for a review), the decision to help depends on empathic feeling – people are more inclined to provide help when they can feel the needs of the other party on an emotional level and can sense the urgent nature of these needs. In both of these models, the outcome of concern following an episode of helping behavior is compliance, or whether the giver decided to help. However, aside from increasing or decreasing the likelihood of compliance, the perceived urgency of a request for help might also affect an individual's expectations of future reciprocation.

If a receiver has a critical need for assistance, which is satisfied by someone else, the receiver would likely to feel more grateful, and more willing to provide reciprocation, than if the request had been less urgent. For example, consider an employee who is trying to finalize an important client presentation that she must deliver in a few minutes. She attempts to print out her presentation, but it will not print. She asks for some assistance from a more technically savvy coworker, who obliges and then manages to resolve the problem quickly. The focal employee would certainly feel indebted to her coworker for this timely assistance, perhaps more so because her need for assistance was pressing. Her strong feelings of appreciation would correspond to her willingness to provide reciprocation. Indeed, helping recipients may be willing to provide more in reciprocation as the urgency of their perceived need intensifies.

While help recipients' willingness to provide reciprocation may increase as the perceived urgency of their requests increases, the helper may not hold similar expectations of reciprocation. Instead, according to the empathy-altruism model of helping behavior (e.g., Batson & Coke, 1981), the helper who vicariously experiences the distress of the help recipient will feel a positive sense of relief at having provided assistance. To the extent that the recipient's need was judged to be urgent, the help will be considered by the giver to be appropriate, rather than extraordinary, and therefore the giver will feel less entitled to reciprocation for his assistance. In fact, the giver may even obtain some psychological benefit from helping a person in distress (see Maner et al., 2002). If the giver's expectations of reciprocation are less substantial than the receiver's willingness to provide reciprocation, this may strengthen their exchange relation. Even if the giver requests reciprocation that she believes is equivalent to the assistance she provided, the receiver may still feel indebted to the giver and willing to provide future assistance.

Relative Levels of Resources
Subjective evaluations of helping behavior may also depend on the relative levels of resources held by the giver and the receiver. Past research has found that donors who gave from smaller resources tended to receive more help in return than donors who gave from larger resources (e.g., Pruitt, 1968;

Gergen, Ellsworth, Maslach, & Seipel, 1975; Tesser, Gatewood, & Driver, 1968). Presumably, a contribution from a less affluent donor was more impressive than the same contribution given by a more affluent donor because the former represented a larger portion of available resources than did the latter. Along the same vein, receivers may feel less indebted and givers may expect less in return for favors given from relatively larger resources because the cost incurred is relatively less. Both parties may subsequently decrease their perceptions of favor magnitude, and, in turn, their expectations of reciprocation, because the giver's level of generosity will appear less significant, at least in relative terms.

In organizations, one example of a resource that can affect subjective evaluations of helping behavior is time. Some employees make requests for help because they lack the time to perform a desired task on their own. They may be relatively busier because they are unfairly overburdened with tasks or have suddenly experienced an increase in their workload due to unforeseen circumstances. These busier employees may be viewed as more deserving of help, so long as others do not believe that such busyness stems from incompetence. If the receiver's busyness is not driven by incompetence, both the giver and the receiver may decrease their expectations of reciprocation because the request for assistance is considered more legitimate (and the help given is therefore considered more appropriate) than if the receiver was simply idle. However, agreement in judgments of busyness may be rare. The actor–observer effect suggests that the giver will perceive the receiver is less busy (and that their request for assistance is less legitimate) than the receiver believes she is. This discrepancy in judgments of busyness may lead to disparity in both parties' subsequent expectations of reciprocation.

Language and Subjective Evaluations

The final domain I will consider is the language used to frame episodes of helping behavior. Language can play a key role in influencing people's impressions of how much help was given and how much help is expected in return. For example, givers and receivers base their impressions of costs and benefits, in part, on information gathered from the other party (Goffman, 1971). In many cases, however, the other party is in a position to convey information about the cost or benefit in a way that alters its perceived magnitude and either increase or decrease expectations of reciprocation (e.g., Ames, Flynn, & Weber, 2004). Below, I focus on three examples of manipulating perceptions of favor magnitude and expectations of reciprocation through language: (1) framing the magnitude of the request,

(2) clarifying the magnitude of the costs and benefits involved, and (3) emphasizing the legitimacy of the request.

Framing the Magnitude of a Request
Favor asking belongs to the directive form of speech acts, in which the manipulation of language attempts to accomplish a goal through another person's action (Goldschmidt, 1998). There are many ways that favor requests can be used to elicit compliance. For example, the common question "Can you do me a favor" elicits precommitment to provide an unspecified service or resource (Goldschmidt, 1998). Givers are inclined to respond affirmatively to this question, despite its vagueness, because it is consistent with their benevolent self-images (Grice, 1975). Once the giver agrees to the initial question, he is more likely to comply with the subsequent request for help to remain consistent with his previous commitment (Freedman & Fraser, 1966). This script can also be used to subtly define the magnitude of the request. "Can you do me a tiny favor?" may anchor the giver on an impression that the favor request is negligible, whereas "Can you do me a huge favor?" would have the opposite effect. It may be more difficult for the giver to refuse the first request because a refusal would be inconsistent with the norm of maintaining a generous image (Goffman, 1971).

To establish and maintain a positive reputation as an exchange partner, employees must adhere to norms of politeness in framing their requests for help. At the same time, the manner in which they pose a request for help can effectively downplay the magnitude of the cost incurred or the benefit provided (Goffman, 1971). For example, in posing a request for help, the receiver may apologize for inconveniencing the giver on "such a trivial matter" or for taking "just a few minutes out of their schedule." These phrases can frame the request as being negligible while still adhering to norms of politeness. In addition, receivers might ask probing questions of another employee ("Hey, are you busy right now?") in order to establish whether the employee will construe the favor request as being significant.

Conversely, when informing the receiver that a favor has been performed, the giver might pass along a light-hearted message about the expectation of future reciprocation ("Don't worry about it; you can get me back some other time"). In addition, they may attempt to clarify the magnitude of a future request for reciprocation by saying things such as "you owe me a big one" (e.g., Goldschmidt, 1998). Although scripts such as these are subtle and easily overlooked, they can have a significant impact on our evaluations of an episode of cooperation and our expectations of reciprocation (Langer, Blank, & Chanowitz, 1978; Flynn & Bohns, 2005). They provide a means by which receivers can downplay the magnitude of the benefit provided, while maintaining a grateful image or by which givers can play up the magnitude of the cost incurred while maintaining a generous image.

Clarifying the Magnitude of the Costs and Benefits Involved

Episodes of interpersonal cooperation often are characterized by information asymmetry – receivers are less aware of the cost incurred than the benefit provided, whereas givers have the opposite viewpoint. Because favors are not necessarily performed in the presence of the receiver (Goldschmidt, 1998), the receiver may be unaware of (1) sacrifices the giver made to comply with the receiver's request or (2) difficulties the giver may have encountered in performing the favor. Conversely, the giver may be unaware of the full set of benefits the receiver obtained from the giver's helpful gesture.

By having more or less access to information about the cost incurred and benefit received in the exchange, the giver and the receiver may form conflicting evaluations of favor magnitude. While the giver may prefer to be forthright in conveying to the receiver full information about the cost incurred in performing the favor, the receiver may prefer to downplay the benefit he obtained. If effective, the extent to which either party is candid can shift the expectation of reciprocation in her favor. It may be considered inappropriate, however, for the receiver to downplay the benefit provided or for the giver to clarify the cost incurred in performing a favor. If detected by the other party, this behavior might elicit a backlash. In this case, the critical factor for both parties may be whether they can manage information asymmetry while adhering to norm of politeness.

Emphasizing the Legitimacy of the Request

The legitimacy of a request for help can affect our willingness to provide assistance. In a classic study by Langer and Abelson (1972), participants were significantly more likely to help someone deliver a package when the requester explained that she was "late for a train" rather than "trying to do some shopping." Targets regarded the need to continue shopping as a less justified basis for imposing on them than the need to catch a train, even though the reason that the requester was late for the train was not provided. Of course, many participants in Langer and Abelson's (1972) study still provided help when the "shopping" excuse was given. However, even if these participants complied, they may still have considered the request for help to be illegitimate. Thus, they may have agreed to help, but their evaluation of what they expect in return might also have been greater. In exchanges such as these, there is a less intense need for the giver to maintain a generous image by downplaying the magnitude of the favor and therefore they may increase their expectations of reciprocation.

In another study, Langer and her colleagues (Langer et al., 1978) demonstrated that people are not always mindful in processing requests for help. The researchers shut down all but one of the copiers in a library, which resulted in a long queue. A confederate then approached the person at the front of the queue and made a request to "cut" in line in one of three ways. In the control condition, the subject asked, "Excuse me. May I use the Xerox machine?" In another condition they continued to say "... because I am late for class" and in a third condition "... because I have to make copies." Compliance rates in the second and third conditions were not significantly different from one another, but they were much higher than in the control condition. According to the researchers, sometimes people are not mindful in processing requests for help – they attend only to the form of the request (request + reason) rather than whether the request is legitimate.

In organizations, people may be similarly "mindless" when it comes to processing requests for assistance. That is, employees may use heuristics to judge the legitimacy of a request for help rather than seriously consider the nature of the request in order to determine its true legitimacy. For example, requests for help are sometimes posed on behalf of one's coworkers ("it's not for me; it's for the team"). These requests may be considered more legitimate than a request for personal assistance because organizations tend to emphasize norms of selfless behavior. Thus, the giver may feel more inclined to agree to requests for help that benefit the group to which they belong because they automatically assume these requests for help are more legitimate. In addition, since these requests for help will be viewed as more legitimate, they may also elicit lower expectations of reciprocation. However, the "mindful" or "mindless" processing of these requests for help is unclear. Perhaps they induce "mindless" processing when used sparingly, but "mindful" processing when used regularly, in which case they may elicit higher expectations of reciprocation.

Summary. Past theory and research on helping behavior has tended to focus on factors that increase the likelihood of compliance, while little attention has been given to variables that might influence subjective evaluations and expectations of reciprocation. The strength of the norm of reciprocity may vary, however, so that the willingness to request and reciprocate a favor changes from one episode of exchange to the next (Gouldner, 1960). Even if a favor performed in one dyad is identical to a favor performed in another, several features, such as the relational characteristics of the parties involved, the conditions under which the request is made, and the language used can lead to evaluative differences across the two episodes. Assuming that perceptions of favor magnitude correspond with expectations of reciprocation, our understanding of this evaluative process can help us understand why employees sometimes develop unhealthy patterns of cooperation and why they may be unwilling to cooperate with their coworkers.

EVALUATIONS OF HELPING BEHAVIOR AND EMPLOYEE OUTCOMES

Research on helping behavior among peer employees has tended to focus on how helping behavior can impact an organization (Van Dyne et al., 1995). Although the effect of helping behavior on the success of the functioning of organizations is clearly important, understanding how helping behavior can affect the individual is no less important. In this section, I describe how subjective evaluations of helping behavior can influence a number of employee outcomes, including (1) power, (2) performance, (3) status, (4) commitment, and (5) interpersonal conflict.

Power

Helping behavior can be an important source of power for members of organizations (Blau, 1963; Flynn, 2003b). According to Coleman (1988), a helpful act is like a "credit slip" that an employee can "call in if necessary." For example, if an employee is having difficulty accomplishing a task, she may enlist the support of coworkers who have received favors from her in the past. If these coworkers have not yet reciprocated, then they are obligated to provide help in return. Power is therefore derived from the expectation to provide reciprocation. Such acts of reciprocation can be enforced by the withholding of future favors, although the need for any punishment is rare because adherence to the norm of reciprocity is difficult to resist (e.g., Cialdini, 1988). Instead, employees tend to reciprocate favors they receive from others, or at least report they do so in retrospective accounts of their exchange relations (e.g., Ross & Sicoly, 1979; Flynn, 2003b).

According to social exchange theorists, the balance of power in any exchange relation can be determined by accounting for previous acts of generosity (Thibaut & Kelley, 1959; Blau, 1964; Emerson, 1976). Following each episode of exchange, the giver increases her power over the receiver (or decreases the receiver's power over her if the receiver has been relatively more generous in the past). The extent to which power is accrued (or decreased) by performing a favor depends on the magnitude of both parties' respective evaluations. As the receiver's evaluation of favor magnitude increases, her sense of indebtedness and willingness to reciprocate also increase, which suggests that the giver can request more in return for larger favors and expect a higher likelihood of compliance. It also suggests that an employee's level of power is based, at least in part, on others' perceptions of how generous she has been in the past.

The amount of power gained from an episode of helping behavior depends on both the giver and the receiver's evaluations of the amount of help given. For example, a favor-giver may feel that the help she provided was substantial, while the receiver might have considered it to be negligible. Unfortunately, for the giver, the amount of power derived from such an episode would not be "substantial." Instead, it would be "negligible" because the recipient would only be willing to credit the giver a negligible amount in their mental accounting of "IOUs." Put differently, in order to derive a substantial amount of power from an episode of helping behavior, both the giver and the receiver must evaluate the favor as being substantial. A giver who believes a favor was valuable will fail to increase her power unless the receiver implicitly agrees with the giver's evaluation.

This "accounting" approach to assessing power derived from episodes of helping behavior is straightforward, but also lacking sophistication. For any employee exchange relation, shifts in the balance of power can be complicated by other factors. For example, an employee might feel a favor she received provided little value to her, but she might appreciate the giver's good intentions in trying to provide assistance. Such noble gestures, even if they are futile, can still be effective in eliciting future reciprocation (e.g., Greenberg & Frisch, 1972). In addition, the frequency with which requests for help are made might play a role. Consider one employee who has requested a small number of large favors and another employee who has requested a large number of small favors, each from the same generous coworker (an equal amount, in each case). Is the coworker's subjective evaluation of the help given to each employee equivalent or would more frequent, smaller requests be more salient and therefore considered more substantial than less frequent, larger requests? These and other related questions may be worth exploring, particularly for scholars interested in the dynamics of power and exchange.

Performance

Regardless of whether they are line staff or upper-level managers, employees often need to ask for assistance from coworkers who control critical resources, have access to important people, or occupy a position of authority (Pfeffer, 1981). Such assistance may go a long way toward helping employees accomplish their assigned tasks. However, requests for help are also denied in many cases. One reason for noncompliance is that employees do not feel obligated to provide assistance to their coworkers, particularly those who are only loosely connected to them. To improve their performance through helping behavior, then, members of organizations must increase their level of interpersonal power by performing favors for other employees who, upon request, will feel obligated to reciprocate. As an employee's level of interpersonal power increases, she can request more favors from coworkers that will be useful in performing important tasks.

Having power derived from helping behavior will not necessarily improve performance (Flynn, 2003b). Instead, employees must request reciprocation in order to reap the rewards of previous generosity. Further, they must request it on a regular basis. Otherwise, if their exchange relations with their coworkers become unbalanced (i.e., the focal employee is owed a significant amount), others will become less willing to request favors from the focal employee because of their aversion to increased dependence (Emerson, 1962; Gergen, et al., 1975). In addition, subjective evaluations of helping behavior made by receivers depreciate over time (Flynn, 2003a). This implies that any delay in asking for reciprocation can result in a less substantial return on an individual's previous generosity. Employees may therefore wish to maintain a minimal balance of power in their exchange relations in order to maximize their performance (Flynn, 2003b).

The subjective evaluation of helping behavior can also affect employee performance in more indirect ways. Employees who provide valuable assistance in the form of services or advice can use these interactions to convey their competence and expertise (see Blau, 1963, for a lengthy discussion). This public display of competence, in turn, may help the generous employee develop a reputation as an outstanding performer. As a young congressional aide, Lyndon Johnson possessed a singular ability to secure hotel rooms in Washington, DC where hotel rooms were always scarce (Caro, 1990). Many out-of-town visitors sought Johnson's assistance, which he happily provided by going to great lengths to find available space in the city's few hotels. Johnson was careful, however, in framing his compliance. Rather than lament how much work was required to perform the helpful gesture, he suggested that securing a room would be "no problem" at all. Reports of Johnson's "amazing" and "magical" talents spread through the Congressional network. Although Johnson may have secured a greater amount of reciprocation by clarifying the costs involved, he boosted his reputation as a strong performer by downplaying these costs.

As this example suggests, helping behavior, or social exchange, can play an important role not only in increasing actual productivity but also in shaping employees' subjective impressions of one another's performance. In many professions, social exchange has become so critical that the evaluation of an employee's performance and the evaluation of his exchange behavior may be inextricably linked. For example, Heidi Roizen is a partner at Mobius, a venture capital firm in Silicon Valley. Her value as a partner in the firm is derived from her ability to "leverage her vast personal and professional network" in order to request and obtain valuable resources for the firm (McGinn, 2000). Roizen has been able to manage the dynamics of giving and receiving favors so effectively that she has been elevated to the upper ranks of her profession. Of course, this example is not unique. People in organizations often draw impressions of their colleagues' fundamental traits (e.g., competence, cooperativeness) by evaluating their performance in episodes of helping behavior. They can use this information to help predict the focal employee's future performance in other domains.

Social Status

Another outcome of employee helping behavior is social status. Status is conferred on people based on their possession of personal attributes or instrumental skills regarded as ideal by other members of their social group (Berger, et al., 1977; Bourdieu, 1984; Sorokin, 1927; Anderson et al., 2001; Blau, 1964; see Wegener, 1992, for a review). An individual's ability to elicit status conferrals is facilitated by others' belief that the focal individual possesses something that is not only highly valued, but considered critical to the group's success (Crozier, 1964). Helping behavior among peer employees can therefore serve as a fundamental source of status conferrals because it contributes to the success of the organization, or a group therein.

Blau (1963) proposed that status can be conferred as a sign of deference and acknowledgement for favors received, but not yet reciprocated. In his study of advice exchanges, Blau noted that less competent employees became indebted to "experts" for their advice and that this sense of indebtedness operated as a "basic source of the informally generated status differences in the group" (Blau, 1963, p. 140). In support of this idea, Flynn (2003b) found that people who gave more help than they received were conferred higher social status by their colleagues, controlling for other factors, such as access to resources. The status implications of helping behavior seem clear – those who tend to seek help from others will be viewed as lower-status and those who tend to be the object of help seeking will be viewed as higher-status. This relationship between status and helping behavior is likely linear, so that the debtor's willingness to confer status to his creditor will increase as the perceived magnitude of the debt increases. To the extent that employees' helpful gestures are viewed as being more substantial, they will be considered of higher status by their colleagues.

Commitment

Subjective evaluations of helping behavior might also explain feelings of psychological attachment (e.g., Konovsky & Pugh, 1994). Previous studies on the relationship between helping and commitment have focused on direct exchanges between individuals and organizations (e.g., Dansereau et al., 1975; Konovsky & Pugh, 1994) and not surprisingly, a lack of perceived organizational support led to lower levels of organizational commitment (e.g., Settoon, Bennett, & Liden, 1996) and higher levels of burnout (e.g., VanHorn, Schaufeli, & Enzmann, 1999). Although not previously considered, subjective evaluations of helping behavior in employee exchange relations might also have an indirect effect on organizational commitment (cf. Rodwell, Kienzle, & Shadur, 1998) and a direct effect on feelings of attachment to other employees.

In social exchange, feelings of commitment to another individual can come from two types of subjective evaluations – (1) how much the focal individual believes she has contributed in the past and (2) how much the focal individual believes the other party has reciprocated. Regarding the first evaluation, performing favors can engender in givers a sense of commitment to receivers through a process of self-perception (Bem, 1972). Past research suggests that if we perform a favor for someone, we are inclined to justify this action by convincing ourselves the receiver is an attractive, likable, and deserving person (e.g., Jecker & Landy, 1969). Assuming that employees' feelings of commitment can be driven by the self-perception process, it follows that the strength of their commitment to their coworkers will depend on the amount of benefit they believe they have provided to each other.

Employees' feelings of commitment may also be influenced by how much they believe they have received in return for their previous contributions.

When employees perceive their generosity with coworkers has been reciprocated, feelings of commitment are likely to increase. Social exchange theory relies on the principle of operant conditioning – that people learn to
establish exchange relations with others when they believe the reciprocal
exchange of valued benefits can occur (Molm & Cook, 1995). Successful
episodes of exchange, which involve the reciprocation of helping behavior,
make people feel good, whereas failure makes them feel bad (Willer,
Lovaglia, & Markovsky, 1997). The concept of relational cohesion suggests
that these positive emotions will be attributed to the other party in the
exchange (Lawler, Thye, & Yoon, 2000, p. 623). As the perceived amount of
reciprocation increases, employees will experience higher levels of positive
affect, which, in turn, would increase their commitment to their exchange
partners and, perhaps, to the organization.

Interpersonal Conflict

Given the constraints, limitations, and ambiguity involved in evaluating
episodes of helping behavior, disparity in employees' perceptions of
generosity may be pervasive. Such disparity can lead to episodes of interpersonal conflict if one employee believes he has contributed more
than others believe he has contributed (e.g., Flynn, 2003b). In other words,
interpersonal conflict is more likely when one party believes she has been
shortchanged or "taken advantage of" by the other (Emerson, 1976). These
feelings of resentment are intensified by episodes of noncompliance. Deny-
ing a favor request can irritate the requester if she believes the other party is
indebted for previous favors rendered (Greenberg, 1980). However, the
other party may not believe he is indebted and therefore feels no obligation
to comply.

When people fail to adhere to the universal norm of reciprocity, others
feel entitled, and in some cases compelled, to offer a rebuke (Mauss (1925
[1967]); Lande, 1977). Indeed, Mauss (1925 [1967]) referred to a failure to
reciprocate as being akin to an "act of war" in some cultures. Most scholars
recognize that a violation of the norm of reciprocity occurs when a unilateral act of helping goes unreciprocated. However, this may not be the
only case that represents a violation of the norm of reciprocity. Reciprocation might be granted, but there may still be disagreement about whether
the reciprocating favor was sufficient. Just as employees may become upset
when they feel that their annual bonus is not commensurate with their
annual toils, they may also bear a grudge to those colleagues who fail to

reciprocate their helping behavior *fully*. Again, this indicates that the problem with employee cooperation may not be that employees are unwilling to cooperate with one another, but that they cannot agree on the value of their cooperative efforts. One employee may view her helping behavior as constituting full reciprocation whereas others view the same helping behavior as woefully inadequate.

Summary. The impact of helping behavior on individual employee outcomes is based largely on subjective evaluations, which are recorded in loose mental accounts. Although these accounts are not precise, they likely take note of whether the pattern of giving and receiving in an exchange relation is balanced or unbalanced. These judgments of inequity may derive from evaluations of helping episodes that, in aggregate form, shape our experiences in organizations and our relationships with others at work. The predictions made here are based on the individual's personal accounting. However, other employees likely maintain corresponding accounts of helping behavior (e.g., Flynn, 2003b). Given the ambiguity involved in the evaluation process, symmetry across these accounts is likely to be the exception to the rule. Nevertheless, both sets of accounts (the focal individual's and their coworkers') may play a key role in determining the impact of helping behavior on employee outcomes.

DISCUSSION

Developing healthy patterns of employee cooperation is a primary concern for managers in organizations – one that presents a difficult problem. Many employee exchange relations are characterized by nonreciprocal patterns of helping, in which one employee has consistently given more help to another than he or she has received in return (e.g., Flynn, 2003b). Further, employees' perceptions of generosity often conflict, so that one employee believes she has been very generous in the past, but her colleagues disagree (Flynn, 2003b). What factors contribute to this disparity? Further, how might such disparity affect an individual's experience at work? While previous research on dyadic exchange has proved quite useful in explaining patterns of cooperation in organizations, it is time to delve deeper into the psychology of the exchange process. Specifically, it is necessary to understand how employees construe and appraise episodes of cooperation in order to understand how successful patterns of employee cooperation can be developed.

The ideas advanced here are grounded in theory and research on norms of interpersonal interaction (e.g., Goffman, 1959, 1971; Brown & Levinson,

1987; Pryor & Graburn, 1980). People are motivated to project positive images of self during episodes of social exchange. Specifically, givers are motivated to convey generosity whereas receivers are motivated to convey gratitude. These normative demands may directly influence employees' subjective evaluations of helping behavior (e.g., Bem, 1972). Further, the normative pressures to maintain a generous or grateful image may be influenced by egocentric bias, characteristics of the exchange relation, individual differences, conditions under which the request is made, and language used to frame the request. As these factors influence the need to convey generosity and gratitude, employees' evaluations of others' helping behavior and their willingness to cooperate in future of exchange may change accordingly.

This unique perspective on image maintenance and normative pressures in episodes of employee exchange can be useful in understanding various individual outcomes. Given the intense strain toward normative behavior in organizational settings (e.g., Nemeth & Staw, 1989), employees may monitor how well others adhere to norms of politeness when seeking or considering requests for help. Their impressions may go a long way toward forming reputations (e.g., Flynn, 2003b), exchange relations (e.g., Flynn & Brockner, 2003), and attitudes toward an organization (Eisenberger et al., 2001). Negative outcomes will likely develop when an employee believes others have not adequately reciprocated her contributions (Rousseau, 1995). For individual employees, the ability to achieve instrumental benefits from episodes of cooperation may partly depend on how well they diagnose and respond to normative pressures that affect others' subjective evaluations of the help they have given in the past.

The implications of this perspective on helping behavior are not limited to employee outcomes. Indeed, for many firms, success depends on developing healthy patterns of interpersonal cooperation. Given the high level of interdependence in most modern organizations, the need for high levels of employee helping behavior may be stronger now than ever before. Noting this, macro organizational scholars interested in firm productivity may take account of the balance of employee-exchange relations. According to the arguments presented here, firm productivity will likely increase when the balance of employee-exchange relations becomes more symmetrical (or at least is perceived to be symmetrical by the employees involved). To the extent that such symmetry exists, employees will feel motivated to cooperate with their coworkers because they are encouraged by evidence of a reciprocal pattern of exchange.

Interventions that facilitate the development of healthy patterns of cooperation may be introduced at the organization level. For example, developing norms of interpersonal cooperation that guide the process of subjective evaluation might help reconcile employees' discrepant views. Such norms, if widely shared and strongly held, could help clarify that helping behaviors are considered "routine," or part of the job role, and which are considered "extraordinary," or beyond the expectations of an assigned role. At the same time, this theoretical perspective on subjective evaluations of helping behavior highlights several points of tension between what is best for the individual employee and what is best for the firm. In particular, while it might be beneficial for a focal employee to inflate others' perceptions of his or her generosity (she would benefit by accruing higher levels of status and power), such inflated evaluations might work against a firm-wide system of employee exchange that depends on the accurate appraisal of cooperative acts.

Advantages of Adopting an Episodic Approach

One of the primary contributions of this discussion of helping behavior is its focus on the episode rather than the exchange relation. Previous research has examined retrospective accounts of employee exchange, but this retrospective view can obscure differences at the episodic level. For example, help performed by low-status members of an organization (e.g., women, minorities) may be considered less valuable or worthy of reciprocation than help performed by high-status members. This difference may be apparent when evaluating a single episode of exchange, but perhaps not in a retrospective account of several episodes (see Flynn, 2005b). Instead, status may appear to have no effect on perceptions of generosity in retrospective accounts of "who helped whom" relatively more because favors will be requested more frequently from low-status employees (the psychological costs of indebtedness are not as significant). This discrepancy in the frequency of requesting help may mask any difference in employees' long-term evaluations of helping behavior. In order to avoid this concern, researchers interested in understanding patterns of employee cooperation should focus more attention on evaluations of helping behavior at the episodic level.

Another advantage of the episodic model is that it can provide a prospective view of the process of helping behavior. For example, prior to making a request for help, an employee must consider the magnitude of the request. Is it large enough that it might be considered unreasonable and either result in rejection or damage to her reputation? Employees may be biased in evaluating these potential requests for help just as they are biased in evaluating previous episodes of helping behavior. Before an employee solicits a favor, the need to have the favor performed and the awkwardness of imposing on another employee is most salient in her mind, but after receiving the favor, these factors are removed. Such anxiety might lead employees to inflate their impressions of favor magnitude before making a request, which would, in turn, decrease their willingness to ask for help when it is needed.

A recent study by Flynn and Bohns (2005) supports the notion that people inflate their evaluations of a potential favor request. Fifty undergraduate students were instructed to approach people on campus and ask them to complete a brief questionnaire. To complete their task, each student needed to get five people to complete the questionnaire. Prior to making any requests, half the students estimated the number of people they would need to ask before five agreed. They estimated that it would require 21 people, on average, to get five to agree. In fact, they needed to approach only nine (this outcome was not significantly different from those who made no estimates in advance). These findings suggest that people may be very poor judges of whether others are willing to agree to provide help, or whether they will consider the magnitude of the request to be too unreasonable. One of the dangers of miscalibrating perceptions of favor magnitude in this way is that it might lead to miscalibrating others' willingness to cooperate. This is a significant problem if we assume that organizations are interested in increasing the incidence of cooperation among their employees.

Finally, this paper has centered on understanding successful episodes of cooperation, or requests for help that are fulfilled. However, requests for help in organizations often are refused. How do employees evaluate these episodes of noncompliance and how do their subjective evaluations affect their future behavior? Many of the factors identified here may once again come into play in episodes of noncompliance. For example, the egocentric bias would suggest that people make favorable evaluations when judging episodes of noncompliance. To justify their refusal to cooperate and somehow maintain a generous image, givers will likely inflate their evaluations of favor magnitude ("I would have been happy to help, but he was just asking for too much"). For receivers the opposite may be true – they downplay the magnitude of their requests to align their behavior with norms of politeness ("I don't know why they wouldn't provide help. It wasn't a very big request at all"). The extent to which both parties construe the episode with an egocentric bias might increase the intensity of any ensuing interpersonal conflict.

Strategic Implications

There are many opportunities for research that builds on the ideas presented here. In particular, one possible extension of these ideas is to test their strategic implications. For example, if favors are initially valued more by receivers than by givers, it is only a small step to suggest that receivers may be willing to reciprocate more in return for the favors they receive. However, if receivers' evaluations of favor worth depreciate over time, the extent to which they are willing to offer reciprocation may diminish as well (e.g., Burger et al., 1997; Flynn, 2003a). Employees who are interested in maximizing value in their exchange relations may wish to request reciprocation *sooner rather than later*. Otherwise, the receiver's continually diminishing evaluation will result in diminishing returns to the giver for their helpful gesture.

The strategic implications of subjective evaluations of helping behavior may also apply to the selection of an exchange partner. Employees may be relatively better off performing favors for those who highly value their help, but this strategy may also backfire. For example, favors performed by relatively higher-status employees may be valued more than favors performed by relatively lower-status employees, which implies that people can gain more power by helping those who have lower status. This advice, however, assumes that lower-status employees have the resources to provide reciprocation. It also seems to contradict previous research on status, which suggests that association with higher-status actors increases status and influence and association with lower-status actors decreases status and influence (e.g., Benjamin & Podolny, 1999). Indeed, there may be tradeoffs between the gain of associating with higher-status employees by performing favors for them and the loss of power in having these favors discounted. Future research might tease apart tradeoffs such as these in trying to understand how employees can be strategic in their selection of exchange partners.

Finally, it is important to consider not only whether strategic implications of evaluating helping behavior exist, but whether employees are aware that they exist. Increasing one's level of power by taking advantage of subjective evaluations of helping behavior requires taking account of one's own mind and the minds of others. Some employees may be especially adept at the process of detecting evaluative differences. High self-monitors, for example, demonstrate greater awareness of social situations, in general, and greater accuracy in judging others' thoughts and feelings, in particular (Ickes, Stinson, Bissonette, & Garcia, 1990; Funder & Harris, 1986; Mill, 1984).

Their heightened awareness of others' minds might prove to be advantageous in managing employee exchange relations and could explain some of the successful outcomes that correspond to higher levels of self-monitoring (e.g., Kilduff & Day, 1994; Mehra, Kilduff, & Brass, 2001). Individual differences in detecting and acting on evaluative asymmetry in employee helping behavior may prove to be fertile ground for future research on the determinants of social power in employee exchange relations.

CONCLUSION

This article suggests that favors performed by one employee for another are not "real" currencies, easily traded with fixed prices and enforceable rules of exchange. Rather, an episode of helping behavior is a subjective experience – different people can perceive the same favor in different ways that affect their respective evaluations. Role requirements outlined by norms of interpersonal interaction can have a different or, in some cases, similar impact on evaluations of helping behavior that lead people to believe others have been more or less cooperative in the past. By outlining how people construct subjective evaluations of helping behavior, the framework presented here may be useful in helping us understand how successful patterns of interpersonal cooperation can be developed in organizations.

REFERENCES

Adams, J. S. (1965). Inequity in social exchange. In: L. Berkowitz (Ed.), *Advances in experimental social psychology*, (Vol. 2, pp. 267–299). New York: Academic Press.

Altman, I., & Taylor, D. (1973). *Social penetration: The development of interpersonal relationships*. NewYork: Holt, Rinehart and Winston.

Ames, D., Flynn, F. J., & Weber, E. (2004). It's the thought that counts: On perceiving how favor-givers decide to help. *Personality and Social Psychology Bulletin, 30*(4), 461–474.

Anderson, C. P., John, O. J., Keltner, D., & Kring, A. M. (2001). The origins of status within face-to-face social groups. *Journal of Personality and Social Psychology, 81*, 116–132.

Batson, C. D. (1991). *The altruism question: Toward a social psychological answer*. Hillsdale, NJ: Lawrence Erlbaum.

Batson, C. D. (1998). Altruism and prosocial behavior. In: D. T. Gilbert, S. T. Fiske & G. Lindzey (Eds), *The handbook of social psychology*, (Vol. 2, pp. 282–316). Boston: McGraw-Hill.

Batson, C. D., & Coke, J. S. (1981). Empathy: A source of altruistic motivation for helping? In: J. P. Rushton & R. M. Sorrentino (Eds), *Altruism and helping behavior: Social, personality, and developmental perspectives.* Hillsdale, NJ: Lawrence Erlbaum Associates.

Bem, D. J. (1972). Self-perception theory. In: L. Berkowitz (Ed.), *Advances in experimental social psychology* (pp. 1–62). New York: Academic Press.

Benjamin, B., & Podolny, J. (1999). Status, quality, and social order in the California wine industry. *Administrative Science Quarterly, 44,* 563–589.

Berger, J., Conner, T. L., & Fisek, M. H. (1974). *Expectation states theory: A theoretical research program.* Cambridge, MA: Winthrop.

Berger, J., Fisek, M. H., Norman, R. Z., & Zelditch, M., Jr. (1977). *Status characteristics and social interaction: An expectation states approach.* New York: Elsevier.

Bierbrauer, G. (1976). Why did he do it? Attribution of obedience and the phenomenon of dispositional bias. *European Journal of Social Psychology, 9,* 67–84.

Blau, P. M. (1963). *The dynamics of bureaucracy: A study of interpersonal exchange in two government agencies.* Chicago: University of Chicago Press.

Blau, P. M. (1964). *Exchange and power in social life.* New York: Wiley.

Blau, P. M. (1994). *Structural contexts of opportunities.* Chicago: University of Chicago Press.

Bolino, M. C. (1999). Citizenship and impression management: Good soldiers or good actors? *Academy of Management Review, 24,* 82–98.

Bourdieu, P. (1984). *Distinction: A social critique of the judgment of taste.* Cambridge: Harvard University Press.

Brown, P., & Levinson, S. (1987). *Politeness: Some universals in language usage.* Cambridge: Cambridge University Press.

Burger, J. M., Horita, M., Kinoshita, L., Roberts, K., & Vera, C. (1997). Effects of time on the norm of reciprocity. *Basic and Applied Social Psychology, 19*(1), 91–100.

Buunk, B. P., Doosje, B. J., Jans, L. G., & Hopstaken, L. E. (1993). Perceived reciprocity, social support, and stress at work: The role of exchange and communal orientation. *Journal of Personality and Social Psychology, 65*(4), 801–811.

Caro, R. (1990). *The path to power.* New York: Vintage Books.

Chatman, J. A., & Flynn, F. J. (2001). The influence of demographic composition on the emergence and consequences of cooperative norms in work teams. *Academy of Management Journal, 44*(5), 956–974.

Cialdini, R. B. (1988). *Influence: Science and practice* (2nd ed.). Glenview, IL: Scott, Foresman.

Cialdini, R. B., Vincent, J. E., Lewis, S. K., Catalan, J., Wheeler, D., & Darby, B. L. (1975). Reciprocal concessions procedure for inducing compliance: The door-in-the-face technique. *Journal of Personality and Social Psychology, 31,* 206–215.

Coleman, J. (1988). Social capital in the creation of human capital. *American Journal of Sociology, 94,* S95–S120.

Cotterell, N., Eisenberger, R., & Speicher, H. (1992). Inhibiting effects of reciprocation wariness on interpersonal relationships. *Journal of Personality and Social Psychology, 62*(4), 658–668.

Crozier, M. (1964). *The bureaucratic phenomenon.* Chicago: University of Chicago Press.

Dansereau, F., Graen, G., & Haga, W. J. (1975). A vertical dyad linkage approach to leadership within formal organizations. *Organizational Behavior and Human Performance, 13,* 46–78.

Davis, M. D. (1970). *Game theory: A nontechnical introduction.* New York: Basic Books.

Eisenberger, R., Armeli, S., Rexwinkel, B., Lynch, P. D., & Rhoades, L. (2001). Reciprocation of perceived organizational support. *Journal of Applied Psychology, 86,* 42–51.

Emerson, R. (1962). Power-dependence relations. *American Sociological Review, 27,* 31–41.

Emerson, R. (1976). Social exchange theory. *Annual Review of Sociology, 2,* 335–362.

Emerson, R. (1987). Toward a theory of value in social exchange. In: K. Cook (Ed.), *Social exchange theory* (pp. 11–46). Beverly Hills, CA: Sage.

Festinger, L. (1954). A theory of social comparison processes. *Human Relations, 7,* 117–140.

Flynn, F. J. (2003a). What have you done for me lately? Temporal changes in subjective favor evaluations. *Organizational Behavior and Human Decision Processes, 91*(1), 38–50.

Flynn, F. J. (2003b). How much should I help and how often? The effects of generosity and frequency of favor exchange on social status and productivity. *Academy of Management Journal, 46*(5), 539–553.

Flynn, F. J. (2005a). Identity orientations and forms of social exchange in organizations. *Academy of Management Review, 30,* 737–750.

Flynn, F. J. (2005b). *Thanks for nothing: The influence of sex and agreeableness on evaluations of help in organizations.* Working paper. Columbia University.

Flynn, F. J., & Bohns, V. (2005). *Need help, just ask: How people underestimate the likelihood of compliance in favor exchange.* Working paper. Columbia University.

Flynn, F. J., & Brockner, J. (2003). It's different to give than to receive: Asymmetric reactions of givers and receivers to favor exchange. *Journal of Applied Psychology, 88*(6), 1–13.

Freedman, J. L., & Fraser, S. C. (1966). Compliance without pressure: The foot-in-the-door technique. *Journal of Personality and Social Psychology, 4,* 195–203.

Funder, D. C., & Harris, M. J. (1986). On the several facets of personality assessment: The case of social acuity. *Journal of Personality, 54,* 528–550.

Gergen, K. J., Ellsworth, P., Maslach, C., & Seipel, M. (1975). Obligation, donor resources, and reactions to aid in three cultures. *Journal of Personality and Social Psychology, 31,* 395–400.

Goethals, G. R. (1986). Fabricating and ignoring social reality: Self-serving estimates of consensus. In: J. M. Olson, C. P. Herman & M. P. Zanna (Eds), *Social comparison and relative deprivation: The Ontario symposium,* (Vol. 4, pp. 135–157). Hillsdale, NJ: Erlbaum.

Goethals, G. R., Messick, D. M., & Allison, S. T. (1991). The uniqueness bias: Studies of constructive social comparison. In: J. Suls & T. A. Wills (Eds), *Social comparison: Contemporary theory and research* (pp. 149–176). Hillsdale, NJ: Erlbaum.

Goffman, E. (1955). On face-work. *Psychiatry, XVII,* 213–231.

Goffman, E. (1959). *The presentation of self in everyday life.* New York: Doubleday.

Goffman, E. (1971). *Relations in public.* Harmondsworth: Penguin.

Goldschmidt, M. M. (1998). Do me a favor: A descriptive analysis of favor asking sequences in American English. *Journal of Pragmatics, 29,* 129–153.

Gouldner, A. W. (1960). The norm of reciprocity: A preliminary statement. *American Sociological Review, 25,* 161–178.

Green, G. M. (1975). How to get people to do things with words: The whimperative question. In: P. Cole, & J. Morgan (Eds), *Syntax and semantics* (Vol. 3: Speech acts, pp. 107–141). New York: Academic Press.

Greenberg, M. S. (1980). A theory of indebtedness. In: K. Gergen, M. Greenberg & R. Willis (Eds), *Social exchange: Advances in theory and research,* (pp. 3–26). New York: Plenum.

Greenberg, M. S., Block, M. W., & Silverman, M. A. (1971). Determinants of helping behavior: Person's rewards versus other's cost. *Journal of Personality, 39*(1), 79–93.

Greenberg, M. S., & Frisch, D. M. (1972). Effect of intentionality on willingness to reciprocate a favor. *Journal of Experimental Social Psychology, 8*, 99–111.

Greenwald, A. G. (1980). The totalitarian ego: Fabrication and revision of personal history. *American Psychologist, 35*(7), 603–618.

Grice, H. P. (1975). Logic and conversation. In: P. Cole, & J. Morgan (Eds), *Syntax and semantics* (Vol. 3: Speech acts, pp. 41–58). New York: Academic Press.

Guiasu, S., & Malitza, M. (1980). *Coalition and connection in games.* New York: Pergamon Press.

Heath, A. (1976). *Rational choice and social exchange: A critique of exchange theory.* Cambridge: Cambridge University Press.

Heilman, M. E., & Chen, J. J. (2005). Same behavior, different consequences: Reactions to men's and women's altruistic citizenship behavior. *Journal of Applied Psychology, 90*(3), 431–441.

Homans, G. C. (1958). Social behavior as exchange. *American Journal of Sociology, 63*, 597–606.

Ickes, W., Stinson, L., Bissonette, V., & Garcia, S. (1990). Naturalistic social cognition: Empathic accuracy in mixed-sex dyads. *Journal of Personality and Social Psychology, 59*, 730–742.

Jecker, J., & Landy, D. (1969). Liking a person as a function of doing him a favor. *Human Relations, 22*, 371–378.

John, O. P. (1990). The 'Big Five' factor taxonomy: Dimensions of personality in the natural language and in questionnaires. In: L. A. Pervin (Ed.), *Handbook of personality: Theory and practice* (pp. 66–96). New York: Guilford Press.

Judge, T. A., Higgins, C. A., Thoresen, C. J., & Barrick, M. R. (1999). A five-factor theory of personality. In: L. A. Pervin & O. P. John (Eds), *Handbook of personality: Theory and research.* NY: Guilford.

Katz, D., & Kahn, R. L. (1978). *The social psychology of organizations* (2nd ed.). New York, NY: Wiley.

Kiesler, S. B. (1966). The effect of perceived role requirements on reactions to favor-doing. *Journal of Experimental Social Psychology, 2*, 198–210.

Kilduff, M., & Day, D. (1994). Do chameleons get ahead: The effects of self-monitoring on managerial careers. *Academy of Management Journal, 37*, 1047–1060.

Kollock, P. (1994). The emergence of exchange structures: An experimental study of uncertainty, commitment, and trust. *American Journal of Sociology, 100*, 315–345.

Konovsky, M. A., & Organ, D. W. (1996). Dispositional and contextual determinants of organizational citizenship behavior. *Journal of Organizational Behavior, 17*(3), 253–266.

Konovsky, M. A., & Pugh, S. D. (1994). Citizenship behavior and social exchange. *Academy of Management Journal, 37*, 656–669.

Lande, C. H. (1977). The dyadic basis of clientelism. In: S. Schmidt, J. Scott, C. Lande & L. Guasti (Eds), *Friends, followers, and factions: A reader in political clientelism* (pp. xiii–xxxvii). Berkeley: University of California Press.

Langer, E. J., & Abelson, R. P. (1972). The semantics of asking for a favor: How to succeed in getting help without really dying. *Journal of Personality and Social Psychology, 24*, 26–32.

Langer, E., Blank, A., & Chanowitz, B. (1978). The mindlessness of ostensibly thoughtful action: The role of "placebic" information in interpersonal interaction. *Journal of Personality and Social Psychology, 36*, 635–642.

Latane, B., & Darley, J. M. (1970). *The unresponsive bystander: Why doesn't he help?* New York: Appleton-Century-Crofts.

Lawler, E., & Yoon, J. (1993). Power and the emergence of commitment behavior in negotiated exchange. *American Sociological Review, 58*, 465–481.

Lawler, E., Thye, S., & Yoon, J. (2000). Emotion and group cohesion in productive exchange. *American Journal of Sociology, 106*(3), 616–657.

Malhotra, D., & Murnighan, K. (2002). The effects of contracts on interpersonal trust. *Administrative Science Quarterly, 47*(3), 534–559.

Malinowski, B. (1922 [1961]). *Argonauts of the Western Pacific: An account of native enterprise and adventure in the archipelagos of Melanesian New Guinea.* New York: E.P. Dutton.

Maner, J., Luce, C., Neuberg, S., Cialdini, R., Brown, S., & Sagarin, B. (2002). The effects of perspective taking on motivations for helping: Still no evidence for altruism. *Personality and Social Psychology Bulletin, 28*, 1601–1610.

Mauss, M. (1925 [1967]). *The gift: Forms and functions of exchange in archaic societies. (Translated by I. Cunnison).* New York: W. W. Norton.

McCrae, R. R., & Costa,, P. T., Jr. (1987). Validation of the five-factor model of personality across instruments and observers. *Journal of Personality and Social Psychology, 52*, 81–90.

McGinn, K. (2000). *Heidi Roizen. Harvard business school case #9-800-228.* Cambridge, MA: Harvard Business School Publishing.

McGuire, A. (2003). It was nothing – extending evolutionary models of altruism by two social cognitive biases in judgments of the costs and benefits of helping. *Social Cognition, 21*, 363–394.

Mehra, A., Kilduff, M., & Brass, D. (2001). The social networks of high and low self-monitors: Implications for workplace performance. *Administrative Science Quarterly, 46*, 121–146.

Mill, J. (1984). High and low self-monitoring individuals: Their decoding skills and emphatic expression. *Journal of Personality, 52*, 372–388.

Molm, L., & Cook, K. (1995). Social exchange and exchange networks. In: K. Cook, G. Fine & J. House (Eds), *Sociological perspectives on social psychology* (pp. 209–235). Boston: Allyn and Bacon.

Molm, L., Takahashi, N., & Peterson, G. (2000). Risk and trust in social exchange: An experimental test of a classic proposition. *American Journal of Sociology, 105*, 1396–1427.

Morrison, E. W. (1994). Role definitions and organizational citizenship behavior: The importance of the employee's perspective. *Academy of Management Journal, 37*(6), 1543–1567.

Nemeth, C. J., & Staw, B. M. (1989). The tradeoffs of social control and innovation in groups and organizations. In: L. Berkowitz (Ed.), *Advances in experimental social psychology* (pp. 175–210). San Diego, CA: Academic Press.

Organ, D. W. (1990). The motivational basis of organizational citizenship behavior. In: B. Staw & L. Cummings (Eds), *Research in Organizational Behavior* (pp. 43–72). Greenwich, CT: JAI Press.

Penner, L., Dovidio, J., Piliavin, J., & Schroeder, D. (2005). Prosocial behavior: Multilevel perspectives. *Annual Review of Psychology, 56*, 365–392.

Pfeffer, J. (1981). *Power in organizations.* Boston, MA: Pittman.

Pilliavin, J. A., Dovidio, J. F., Gaertner, S. L., & Clark, R. D. (1981). *Emergency intervention.* New York: Academic Press.

Pruitt, D. G. (1968). Reciprocity and credit building in a laboratory dyad. *Journal of Personality and Social Psychology, 8,* 143–147.

Pryor, F. L., & Graburn, N. H. (1980). The myth of reciprocity. In: K. Gergen, M. Greenberg & R. Willis (Eds), *Social exchange: Advances in theory and research* (pp. 215–237). New York: Plenum Press.

Ridgeway, C. L. (1997). Where do status beliefs come from? In: J. Szmatka, J. Skvoretz & L. Berger (Eds), *Status, network, and structure* (pp. 137–158). Stanford, CA: Stanford University Press.

Robinson, S., Kraatz, M., & Rousseau, D. (1994). Changing obligations and the psychological contract: A longitudinal study. *Academy of Management Journal, 37*(1), 137–152.

Rodwell, J. J., Kienzle, R., & Shadur, M. A. (1998). The relationships among work-related perceptions, employee attitudes, and employee performance: The integral role of communication. *Human Resource Management, 37*(Fall/Winter), 277–293.

Romer, D., Bontemps, M., Flynn, M., & McGuire, T. (1977). The effects of status similarity and expectation of reciprocation upon altruistic behavior. *Personality and Social Psychology Bulletin, 3,* 103–106.

Ross, M., & Sicoly, F. (1979). Egocentric biases in availability and attribution. *Journal of Personality & Social Psychology, 37*(3), 322–336.

Rousseau, D. M. (1995). *Psychological contracts in organizations: Understanding written and unwritten agreements.* Thousand Oaks, CA: Sage.

Rousseau, D. M., & McLean Parks, J. M. (1993). The contracts of individuals and organizations. In: B. Staw & L. Cummings (Eds), *Research in Organizational Behavior,* (Vol. 15, pp. 1–43). Greenwich, CT: JAI Press.

Sahlins, M. D. (1972). *Stone age economics.* Chicago, IL: Aldine-Atherton.

Savitsky, K. K., Van Boven, L., Epley, N., & Wight, W. (2005). The unpacking effect in allocations of responsibility for group tasks. *Journal of Experimental Social Psychology, 41,* 447–457.

Settoon, R. P., Bennett, N., & Liden, R. C. (1996). Social exchange in organizations: Perceived organizational support, leader-member exchange, and employee reciprocity. *Journal of Applied Psychology, 81*(3), 219–227.

Siem, F. M., & Spence, J. T. (1986). Gender-related traits and helping behaviors. *Journal of Personality & Social Psychology, 51*(3), 615–621.

Sorokin (1927). *Social mobility.* New York: Harper & Row.

Sprecher, S. (1988). Investment model, equity, and social support determinants of relationship commitment. *Social Psychology Quarterly, 51*(4), 318–328.

Swim, J., Borgida, E., Maruyama, G., & Myers, D. G. (1989). Joan McKay versus John McKay: Do gender stereotypes bias evaluations? *Psychological Bulletin, 105,* 405–429.

Tesser, A., Gatewood, R., & Driver, M. (1968). Some determinants of gratitude. *Journal of Personality and Social Psychology, 9,* 233–236.

Thibaut, J. W., & Kelley, H. H. (1959). *The social psychology of groups.* New York: Wiley.

Tyler, T. R., & Blader, S. L. (2001). Identity and prosocial behavior in groups. *Group Processes and Intergroup Relations, 4*(3), 207–226.

Van Dyne, L., Cummings, L., & McLean Parks, J. (1995). Extra-role behaviors: In pursuit of construct and definitional clarity (A bridge over muddied waters.). In: L. Cummings & B. Staw (Eds), *Research in organizational behavior,* (Vol. 17, pp. 215–285). Greenwich, CT: JAI Press.

VanHorn, J. E., Schaufeli, W. B., & Enzmann, D. (1999). Teacher burnout and lack of rec-
    iprocity. *Journal of Applied Social Psychology*, *29*(1), 91–108.
Vey, M., & Campbell, J. (2004). In-role or extra-role organizational citizenship behavior: Which
    are we measuring? *Human Performance*, *17*, 119–135.
Walster, E., Walster, W., & Berscheid, E. (1978). *Equity: Theory and research*. Boston: Allyn &
    Bacon.
Wegener, B. (1992). Concepts and measurement of prestige. *Annual Review of Sociology*, *18*,
    253–280.
Willer, D., Lovaglia, M., & Markovsky, B. (1997). Power and influence: A theoretical bridge.
    Social Forces, *76*(2), 571–603.

HOW, WHEN, AND WHY BAD APPLES SPOIL THE BARREL: NEGATIVE GROUP MEMBERS AND DYSFUNCTIONAL GROUPS

Will Felps, Terence R. Mitchell and Eliza Byington

ABSTRACT

This paper presents a review and integrative model of how, when, and why the behaviors of one negative group member can have powerful, detrimental influence on teammates and groups. We define the negative group member as someone who persistently exhibits one or more of the following behaviors: withholding effort from the group, expressing negative affect, or violating important interpersonal norms. We then detail how these behaviors elicit psychological states in teammates (e.g. perceptions of inequity, negative feelings, reduced trust), how those psychological states lead to defensive behavioral reactions (e.g. outbursts, mood maintenance, withdrawal), and finally, how these various manifestations of defensiveness influence important group processes and dynamics (e.g. cooperation, creativity). Key mechanisms and moderators are discussed as well as actions that might reduce the impact of the bad apple. Implications for both practice and research are discussed.

Research in Organizational Behavior: An Annual Series of Analytical Essays and Critical Reviews
Research in Organizational Behavior, Volume 27, 175–222
ISSN: 0191-3085/doi:10.1016/S0191-3085(06)27005-9

Organizations are increasingly relying on the work team model to capture efficiencies and create value, with estimates predicting that as much as half of the U.S. workforce will be working in teams by the year 2010 (Stewart, Manz, & Sims, 1999). Indeed, most models of the "organization of the future", such as networked, clustered or horizontal forms, are implicitly or explicitly based on teams as the central organizing unit. As groups have become more common, so has the importance of scholarly efforts to understand their potentialities and limitations (see for reviews Cohen & Bailey, 1997; Hackman, 1987; Ilgen, 1999; Ilgen, Hollenbeck, Johnson, & Jundt, 2005; Kozlowski & Bell, 2003). However, all teams are not equal, and as the literature continues to evolve, we are beginning to understand how and why these differences emerge.

In this vein, researchers have noted that, while some teams achieve cohesion between members, a mutually supportive ethos, and high collective efficacy, other groups exhibit divisiveness, conflict, as well as the tendency to "burn themselves up" (Kozlowski & Bell, 2003). As noted by Hackman (2002) "Some project groups do turn out to be more frustrating that fulfilling, more a source of angst than of learning ... . Teams can stress their members, alienate them from one another, and undermine their confidence in their own abilities" (p. 29). Many groups fail, but our understanding of how and why this occurs is limited.

To date, the academic literature tends to highlight group-level phenomena (Kozlowski & Bell, 2003) such as group paranoia (Kramer, 2001), group think (Janis, 1982; Moorhead, Neck, & West, 1998) and low group efficacy (Gully, Incalcaterra, Joshi, & Beaubien, 2002) as the culpable forces behind ineffective teams. While these group-level variables are surely important, this paper argues that, in some cases, a single, toxic team member may be the catalyst for group-level dysfunction. This is a perspective echoed in Keyton's (1999) review of dysfunctional teams, which states that in most models of group process or performance "group members are [treated as] equal or interchangeable" and that there is a paucity of "attention to difficult group members" (p. 492). He goes on to claim that "[s]ometimes the source of the dysfunction is one individual" (p. 493).

Upon first blush, Keyton's statement seems obvious. Indeed, the common idiom "a bad apple spoils the barrel" captures the core idea of negative individuals having an asymmetric and deleterious effect on others. In a Harvard Business Review article, Wetlaufer (1994) talks about "team destroyers", taking for granted that persistent negative behavior can have huge repercussions on group functioning. In an HR Magazine cover story on "hard-core offenders", Andrews (2004) describes how "egregious employee behavior can ... cripple employee morale" (p. 43). Similarly, in an article on training, Tyler (2004) urges, "[b]efore the whole bunch spoils, train managers to deal with poor performers" and says these "bad apples" are "like a cancer that spreads throughout the entire workplace" (p. 77). But despite this provocative rhetoric, the truth is that we currently know very little about how, when, or why a negative member might have an asymmetric effect on teammates, group processes, or group outcomes.

Moreover, academic theory is almost totally silent about these issues. Indeed, given current accounts, it is unclear exactly how a negative individual would persist in a group, or have powerful effects if they did. For example, in his influential work on how groups influence individuals, Hackman (1976) suggested that members co-regulate each other's behavior through ambient and discretionary stimuli to effectively produce uniformity among members (p. 1473). Recently, Lepine and Van Dyne (2001) suggested four potential peer responses to low performers: training, compensation, motivation, or rejection. In both of these seminal and recent models, the roseate conclusion seems to be that difficult teammates will be rehabilitated, ousted, or teammates will compensate for them.

In contrast, we are interested in the instances when constructive responses are not available or utilized and when negative behavior persists day after day with little recourse. These scenarios may result when the harmful person has seniority, political connections, task expertise, or when teammates choose ineffective response strategies. We believe these scenarios describe the circumstances under which the "bad apple spoils the barrel", through a profound and harmful effect on the group. In other words, the focus of this paper are those situations where the group functions poorly, and may alternately fail or disband as a result of one member's actions. By integrating and extending prior work, we detail which negative behaviors are a threat to effective group functioning, the conditions under which groups are able to deal with negative behavior; how negative members influence the thoughts, feelings, and behaviors of teammates; and the mechanisms by which these "bad apples" can provoke dysfunctional group dynamics. We conclude with a discussion of what can be done to alleviate these negative effects and, perhaps, "save the barrel".

EXTANT EVIDENCE OF BAD APPLE EFFECTS

The central goal of this paper is to explain how, when, and why negative group members might have a powerful, asymmetric effect on the group. But first, it is important to firmly establish that this effect occurs at all. To date, the primary evidence relevant to the "bad apple" phenomenon has been the linkage between member personality and group outcomes. And indeed, the evidence here is remarkably robust even if the causal explanations are sparse or non-existent. This personality-based research has found that how low the lowest teammate is on the variables of conscientiousness, agreeableness, and emotional stability is usually a strong predictor of group-level variables. The ostensible implication is that the "worst" group member can have important effects. We briefly review the relevant studies below.

Across several companies, Barrick, Stewart, Neubert, and Mount (1998) researched how members' personalities affected group outcomes in 51 manufacturing-related work teams. They were surprised to find that the lowest team member's score for conscientiousness, agreeableness, and emotional stability was a good predictor of social cohesion ($r = 0.14$, 0.38, 0.34 respectively), communication ($r = 0.29$, 0.50, 0.50), team conflict ($r = -0.39$, -0.51, -0.40), and perceptions of equitable workload sharing ($r = 0.30$, 0.62, 0.33). Moreover, across these group process variables and across the three personality dimensions, these worst member correlations were substantially stronger predictors than the team's mean personality scores or the highest (e.g. "best") person's score. For the outcome variable of task performance, the scores for the least conscientious and agreeable member predicted team performance fairly well ($r = 0.34$ and 0.32 respectively).

The findings of Barrick et al. (1998) are not isolates. Indeed, an increasingly common practice is to actually operationalize "group personality" as the lowest member's score. Theoretically, this is predicated on Steiner's (1972) argument that the weakest link is particularly important in conjunctive tasks. In the laboratory study of Lepine, Hollenbeck, Ilgen and Hedlund (1997), using the Team Interactive Decision Exercise (TIDE), they test the role of the personality variable of conscientiousness on group performance, and find that the lowest member's score is an important predictor ($r = 0.18$), but that the mean score is not. They use this as evidence that the task is a conjunctive one. Similarly, Neuman and Wright (1999) conducted a study of teams of human resource professionals, and found that the lowest member's score for conscientiousness and agreeableness predict group performance ($r = 0.36$ and 0.27 respectively), and to do so over and above cognitive ability. Chatman and Barsade operationalized collectivism as agreeableness and found that less agreeable members depressed the cooperativeness of more agreeable members, but that the reverse did not hold true. Again, this indicates an asymmetric effect of negative teammates, as defined by their personality. Finally, in one of the few studies linking emotional stability to group performance, Camacho and Paulus (1995) compared the creativity of groups with different combinations of member social anxiety. Teams composed of all socially anxious (e.g. emotionally unstable) members came up with relatively few ideas ($M = 45.8$); while teams composed of all socially calm members were much more creative ($M = 85.5$); but most interesting and relevant to our purposes, teams composes of two anxious and two stable members performed about as badly ($M = 53.2$) as the group with all socially anxious members – again indicating an asymmetric effect of negative individuals.

However, while these results are interesting, and provide broad support for the "bad apple" phenomenon, they are not adequate. First, they are theoretically inadequate in that most were post hoc findings that were not central to the original questions under investigation. Second and more importantly, the personality approach to understanding the bad apple phenomenon is inherently problematic. There are many situational variables which inhibit or enable the behavioral expression of personality in the workplace (Tett & Burnett, 2003). For example, in many cases, a person with low conscientiousness can force themselves to act thoughtfully and carefully, at least for a while (Tett & Burnett, 2003). But it is the behavioral expressions of negativity, not personalities, that upsets others and blocks key group processes. A direct focus on the asymmetric influence hypothesis requires moving away from distal personality measures to more proximal causal variables of actual negative behaviors and dysfunctional group processes. A recent review of the relationship between personality and group outcomes says it better than we can:

> "Future research ... should focus on refining our understanding of how personality traits are related to the task and interpersonal behaviors in group processes ... . The inattention to mediating mechanisms is exacerbated in the literature by the tendency to focus on desirable behaviors (e.g. helping, cooperation). For the most part, undesirable behaviors such as malingering, social loafing, dishonesty, and sabotage have been ignored ... . We suspect, in short, that many of the process theories need to explicate the negative individual behaviors that cause poor group performance" (Moynihan & Peterson, 2001, p. 340).

After briefly discussing the boundary conditions of this paper, we return to this challenge of Moynihan and Peterson's, and attempt to specify precisely which negative behaviors cause which dysfunctional reactions, group processes, and group outcomes.

BOUNDARY CONDITIONS

McGrath (1984) defines a group as "an entity that interacts, is interdependent, mutually aware, with a past and an anticipated future" (p. 6). We are employing this definition and narrowing the scope of our analysis to small groups for several related reasons. First, we believe that destructive behavior will be particularly impactful in small groups, which are often characterized by a high degree of interaction and interdependence (Wageman, 2000), two factors that are predicted to make dysfunctional behavior both more salient and disruptive. Second, and as a consequence of their interdependence, small groups tend to be less tolerant of negative behaviors than independent individuals (Liden et al., 1999). Members of small groups have a greater motivation to identify and address behavior, which threatens the group. The third reason for focusing on a small group context is that these groups have properties that facilitate responses to negative group member behavior. Small groups build a consensual social reality that is negotiated through reoccurring interaction and discussion (Hardin & Higgins, 1996), which in turn facilitates other members responding as a coordinated coalition (Lyons, Mickelson, Sullivan, & Coyne, 1998). In sum, we delimit our focus to the small group simply because it is "where the action is" – where a negative group member will have an increased impact, but also where the group will have stricter standards, social norms about appropriate behavior, and the potential to build coalitions. While chronically dysfunctional people may have impacts in many settings, small groups are a particularly appropriate venue for investigating their effects.

We also limit our focus to a subset of the behaviors, which might be considered "negative". A dysfunctional member's behavior inhibits essential group functions, processes, and goals. As such, we chose a pan-group definition of a bad apple member as *individuals who chronically display behavior which asymmetrically impairs group functioning*. Three parts of this definition bear noting. First, for the purpose of this analysis, who counts as a bad apple is defined by their pattern of behaviors in a particular group setting. These negative behaviors might variously be a function of dysfunctional roles, dispositions, negative life events, substance abuse, some combination of these, or something else entirely. By defining negative team members in terms of clearly observable behavior – rather than these varied and more distal contributors – much more specific predictions can be made. Second, for the purposes of this paper, a group member is considered negative only to the extent that their behavior violates norms that are empirically supported as necessary for effective group functioning. Specifically, we are investigating group members who violate norms of equity, positive affect, and appropriate social functioning. We will elaborate on the support and relevancy of these categories in our discussion on types of negative group members. Finally, we would assert that this definition is not tautological despite the fact that bad apple behaviors are defined as a function of their effects on group performance. Tautologies are redundant statements that do not add understanding and which are true by virtue of their logical form alone. In contrast, our definition of what would constitute bad apples is open to revision and disconfirmation and, as we will see, includes fairly elaborate predictions of unfolding effects and underlying processes. More-over, we would argue that our definition is completely consistent with other prevalent theories. For example, work on organizational citizenship be-havior is defined as a function of the contextual behaviors that contribute to organizational functioning, and even more broadly, personality (defined as tendencies to express behavior) is often empirically linked to expressions of behavior.

BAD APPLE TEAM MEMBERS

Types of Bad Apple Team Members

In researching dysfunctional group dynamics, we identified three categories of difficult team member behavior, which are especially likely to "spoil the barrel" if left unchecked: withholding of effort, being affectively negative, and violating important interpersonal norms. These categories emerged from an analysis of the major categories of behavior that are needed for a group to be successful. First, and most simply, members must contribute adequate effort by working towards group goals with intensity and persist-ence (Mitchell, 1997). Second, group members must perform "emotional labor" by regulating their expressions of feelings to facilitate comfortable and positive interpersonal interactions within the group (Hochschild, 1983; Morris & Feldman, 1996). Finally, members must perform "contextually", by not violating or detracting from the organizational, social, and psycho-logical environment, which they inhabit (Motowidlo, Borman, & Schmit, 1997). Contextual performance is accomplished through expressions of interpersonal respect and adherence to interpersonal norms (Tyler & Blader, 2001). Our paper reviews evidence, which suggests that under cer-tain circumstances, group members who persistently and consistently under-perform these three types of behavior can have a severe impact on group functioning.

Withholders of effort intentionally dodge their responsibilities to the group and free ride off the efforts of others. Behavioral examples of withholding effort consist largely of not doing something – of not completing tasks or contributing adequate time, not taking on risks or responsibilities, or not disclosing aptitudes in the hope that others will compensate. While these behaviors have alternately been labeled *shirking* (by economists), *free riding* (by sociologists), and *social loafing* (by psychologists), Kidwell and Bennett (1993) convincingly argue that these terms just describe different reasons and contexts in which people withhold effort from the collective. We agree and refer to all three literatures when discussing withholders of effort.

Second, a person may continually express a negative mood or attitude. We call this kind of member *affectively negative*, employing the broad usage of *affect* to encompass the triumvirate of emotion, mood, and attitude (c.f. Brief, 1998). To assess this construct, Furr and Funder (1998) combined measures of depression, happiness, satisfaction, and self-esteem. Then, from an analysis of a series of dyadic interactions, Furr and Funder constructed behavioral profiles of this sort of individual, who they call personally negative. They found that "personally negative" individuals were more likely to exhibit an awkward interpersonal style and to more frequently express pessimism, anxiety, insecurity, and irritation. Diverging from Furr and Funder, we are interested in those individuals who are especially high in these dimensions. Moreover, as noted previously, the focus is behaviors rather than the personality variables that underlie those behaviors, since it is behavioral expressions rather than internal states that will impact other group members.

Finally, those that detract from the group's contextual environment by violating interpersonal norms of respect are called *interpersonal deviants* (Robinson & Bennett, 1995; Bennett & Robinson, 2000). Bennett and Robinson have conducted a series of studies to try to understand which workplace behaviors are consistently considered deviant. They have found seven common behaviors which are reliably assessed as deviant: making fun of someone, saying something hurtful, making an inappropriate ethnic or religious remark, cursing at someone, playing mean pranks, acting rudely, and publicly embarrassing someone. For our purposes, these seven behaviors define the category of interpersonal deviance.

Note that these three categories are not all encompassing – not everyone considered an "undesirable" group member is eligible for "negative member" status. For example, many characteristics like shyness, lacking a sense of humor, or being unpredictable do not enter into our definition because they are unlikely to seriously disrupt important group processes. Instead, the focus is on negative interpersonal behaviors, whose persistence would have important harmful effects on the dynamics, processes, and team outcomes. Other harmful behaviors like theft, cheating, sabotage, or vandalism are excluded since they affect the organization rather than teammates (c.f. Robinson & Bennett, 1995). Similarly, we do not include group members with distinctive demographic backgrounds or those who have divergent opinions about the best way to accomplish group goals (O'Leary-Kelly, 2005). Although some group members may consider these characteristics difficult to deal with, both demographic diversity and divergent opinions may improve group functioning, and are consequently of a qualitatively different variety than our three destructive behaviors (e.g. Nemeth & Kwan, 1987). Further, we omit individuals who are motivated to achieve group goals but do not have the requisite ability. While poor performance can certainly diminish group performance, this low performance does not depend on negative interpersonal reactions for its effect, and indeed tends to evoke sympathy and compensation from teammates (Jackson & Lepine, 2003; Taggar & Neubert, 2004). Moreover, to the extent that these individuals have negative effects, they are likely to be additive rather than asymmetric. Finally, given the focus on "spoiled barrels", there is little reference to whistleblowers, positive deviants, change leaders, or exceptional individuals who carry the group (c.f. Warren, 2003).

At this point, we can display Fig. 1, which depicts the organization of this paper. We have described above the three categories of behavior that define what we call a bad apple group member. Initially, when these behaviors surface or are noticed they might be described as episodic (box 1). Our next section described how the group will try to change the behavior or perhaps oust the negative member. If that does no't work, we are left with a more persistent and chronic problem (box 2). It is at this point where negative psychological reactions become more apparent (box 3) and we will discuss the factors that may make this situation better or worse (the moderators in box 4). The negative psychological states will lead to defensive behaviors by group members (box 5) and through the mechanisms of aggregation, spillover, and sensemaking, these behaviors will come to influence group processes (box 6) and group outcomes (box 7).

Note again that the underlying message and contribution of this paper is *not* that one bad group member can cause groups to fail or disband. We already know that a bad apple can sometimes spoil the barrel (see Barrick et al, 1998; Chen & Bachrach, 2003; Camacho & Paulus, 1995; Dunlop &

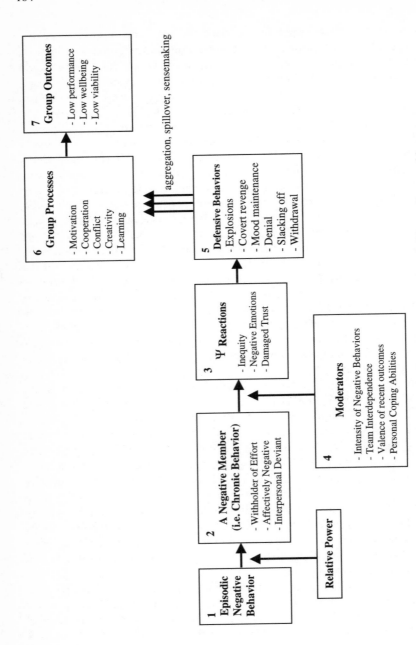

Fig. 1.   The Bad Apple Phenomenon Aggregation, Spillover, Sensemaking.

Lee, 2004; Haythorn, 1953; Neuman & Wright, 1999). Instead, our analysis shows how this process evolves over time, how individual reactions become group dysfunction, and describes the major steps involved. It confronts the questions of why, when, and how this happens. And in the process we will discover some research areas where our knowledge is solid and some other areas where more work needs to be done. These are the focus and contribution of the paper.

Responses to Negative Members

Several research efforts have investigated initial responses to the sort of people we designate as withholders of effort, affectively negative, and interpersonal deviants. The following section concerns itself with a description of these responses.

Across disparate literatures, the same reactions to negative behavior crop up again and again under different labels. We believe that these reactions can be parsimoniously collapsed into three classes of teammate response – motivational intervention, rejection, and defensiveness. Each of these three responses have a common foundation; the desire to improve an aversive experience. However, where these responses differ is in their aims – e.g. towards either changing the negative person's behavior (motivational intervention), removing negative people (rejection), or protecting one's own self (defensiveness). If either the motivation intervention or rejection is successful, the negative member never becomes a bad apple or spoils the barrel. But it is still important to review these three responses in greater detail.

We define the motivational intervention as *those acts of teammates which intend to change negative behavior though the application of influence tactics* (Orcutt, 1973). The literature provides evidence that the motivating response is a common reaction to both withholders of effort (Jackson & Lepine, 2003) and interpersonal deviants (Taggar & Neubert, 2004; Schachter, 1951), but is used less frequently with affectively negative individuals. It seems as though teammates lack efficacy in boosting a teammate's negative moods, and so tend to reject affectively negative individuals rather than attempt to motivate them (Helweg-Larsen, Sadeghian, & Webb, 2002). This is an example of the broader finding from the attributional research literature that motivating responses are particularly likely when the focal person's behavior is ascribed to controllable causes (Jackson & Lepine, 2003; Green & Mitchell, 1979; Sampson & Brandon, 1964; Taggar & Neubert, 2004; Weiner, 1993).

In any case, when team members do believe change is possible, motivating actions may include the withholding of praise, respect, or resources until behavior changes (Hackman, 1976), subtle and not so subtle confrontations (Lepine & Van Dyne, 2001; Lubit, 2004), formal administration of punishments (Liden et al., 1999; Hackman, 1976), or demands of apology and compensation (Bies, Tripp, & Kramer, 1997). A classic example of teammates motivating a negative member can be found in the Hawthorne studies (Homans, 1950). When a person was not working hard enough (what the men at the plant called a "chiseler") co-workers would "bing" the man on the upper arm and criticize his laziness. This was remarkably effective, more so than managerial supervision or incentives. In another early ethnography, Rosabeth Moss Kanter (1972) reviews how the Oneida community used "public criticism" as a formal mechanism to ensure that those who deviated from the norm were provided "enlightening" feedback. Of course, these formal and informal punishments might be coupled with positive reinforcement for more desirable behaviors. Whether explicit or implicit, punishments or rewards, a motivational response means that teammates will try to bring negative members back into the fold by changing their behavior.

Multiple taxonomies also identify *rejection* as a common response to negative members, especially after motivational attempts fail (Orcutt, 1973). For our purposes, rejection can be defined as *those acts which intend to minimize or eliminate interaction with the negative member*. There is evidence that rejection is a common response for withholders of effort (Lepine et al., 1997), for affectively negative individuals (Coyne, 1976; Furr & Funder, 1998; Helweg-Larsen et al., 2002), and for interpersonal deviants (Taggar & Neubert, 2004; Schachter, 1951). Like motivational responses, research on attributions has been instrumental in predicting when rejection will occur – namely when negative behavior is ascribed to stable and uncontrollable causes (Jackson & Lepine, 2003; Green & Mitchell, 1979; Sampson & Brandon, 1964; Schachter, 1951; Taggar & Neubert, 2004; Weiner, 1993).

The most prototypical example of rejection would involve ejecting a negative individual from the group. Lacking this option, members of groups with a fixed constituency will change the "psychological composition" (Festinger, 1950) of the group by ostracizing negative members, reducing social interaction, talking at rather than with, exclusion from decisions, or removing responsibilities that require them to interact with others (Hackman, 1976; Lepine et al., 1997). Alternately, when ostracism is unfeasible due to organizational constraints such as seniority or formal role sets, the difficult person may be "rejected" in more subtle ways. Teammates can restructure work to decrease task interdependence, or segment responsibilities so that goals and rewards are less interdependent. As a concrete example, faculty at a university might decide to forego an integrated curriculum in order to avoid having to interact with a frustrating individual. In summary, this response type entails rejecting the negative individuals through expulsion, psychological distancing, or altering task interdependence to reduce the impact of the negative behavior.

If they work, both motivational interventions and rejection are fairly constructive responses to a negative individual. They represent what is probably a minor distraction from task performance; a bump in the group's unfolding path towards goal attainment. It could even be argued that these two responses might serve as mastery experiences (Bandura, 1986) that could strengthen members' efficacy in dealing with difficult social situations, and reaffirm the group's normative order (Dentler & Erickson, 1959). While little empirical evidence exists about the net effect of motivating or rejecting a negative individual, we would suggest that the ultimate consequence will be modest, either way. However, more severe effects can be expected if motivation or rejection isn't possible – that is if the social context is constrained in such a way that group members are powerless to motivate or reject.

Accordingly, the final category of response is defensiveness. For our purposes, defensiveness is defined as *those acts which intend to protect and repair one's own sense of autonomy, status, self-esteem, or wellbeing*. Manifestations of defensiveness can include lashing out, revenge, unrealistic appraisals, distraction, various attempts at mood maintenance, and withdrawal. When motivation and rejection fail, groups are faced with the dilemma of a negative member who they cannot change or get rid of, the primary condition under which a "bad apple" might "spoil the barrel". As such, defensiveness will be a major focus of our analysis and is discussed in much greater detail as we proceed.

Antecedents to Defensiveness

As mentioned above, a motivation intervention or rejection requires that teammates have some power. When unempowered, teammates become frustrated and defensive. According to Janis and Mann's (1977) model of decision-making, members of groups become defensive when all decision alternatives have low probabilities for success. In the case of the bad apple, frustration is caused by an individual who behaves in dysfunctional ways, has a negative impact on personal well-being, impedes performance – and yet, due to organizational constraints on acceptable social action – cannot be easily reformed or rejected. When there's no viable way to deal with a harmful person, but members are still strongly influenced by them, the only recourse is defensive self protection.

The inclusion of defensiveness as a reaction to a negative member recognizes that peoples' reactions to difficult circumstances (especially if attempts to change the situation fail or cannot be tried) are often less than rational. Moreover, in contrast to responses like rejection or motivation, defensiveness does not resolve the negative member problem; rather, it can intensify the problem as teammates either withdraw or lash out in emotionally motivated attempts to protect themselves. In the following section, we discuss the two key factors that promote defensiveness: a lack of power and the basic psychological tendency to react strongly to negative behavior. In conjunction, these two answer the question of *why* bad apples can have asymmetric negative effects on others.

Low Power Situations

Group members can be relatively powerless either because the negative member has power or because the group member in question does not. The negative member's power may originate from social resources, such as personal connections to higher ups, prestigious degrees, or knowledge of "where the skeletons are buried" (Morrill, 1995). Power could also originate from structural characteristics, such as instances when others are highly dependant on the negative individual for unique knowledge or skills (Robinson & O'Leary-Kelly, 1998), or when the negative individual is placed at a critical juncture in workflow (i.e. a secretary or facilitator) (Doerr, Mitchell, Schriesheim, Freed, & Zhou, 2002). Finally, power can be formal, such as whenever the negative individual has direct control over the allocation of rewards and punishments. Whether leaders are more or less likely to be bad apples is an unanswered empirical question. Organizations will probably attempt to avoid hiring or promoting difficult individuals for leadership positions, but research suggests that dysfunctional people do hold leadership positions with some frequency (Ashforth, 1994; Pearson, Andersson, & Porath, 2000).

Finally, teammates themselves may not have the power needed to respond to a negative member. In many cases group members may look to their leader to punish a deviant group member (Butterfield, Trevino, & Ball, 1996). Poor leadership may allow a negative person to persist in their destructive activity. Relatedly, the group members may lack the resources or empowerment to enact change. Kirkman and Rosen (1999) suggest that members of the groups with low empowerment will not have the decision-making authority, responsibility, adequate experience, or confidence to take decisive action. Thus, powerlessness constrains the available response behaviors. But paradoxically, this powerlessness in the face of threat is also extremely frustrating and is actually likely to intensify psychological reactions to bad apple behavior.

Bad is Stronger than Good

As reviewed by Baumeister, Bratslavsky, Finkenauer, and Vohs (2001), "bad is stronger than good" in many areas of human psychology. Negative cognitions, feelings, and events will usually produce larger, more consistent, and long-lasting effects as compared to equivalent positive thoughts, feelings, and events. Manifested in varied and subtle ways, this pervasive phenomenon holds across information interpretation, impression formation, relationship maintenance, experiencing emotions, memory, learning, and health (Baumeister et al, 2001; Lewicka, Czapinski, & Peeters, 1992; Rozin & Royzman, 2001; Taylor, 1991). Lewicka et al. (1992) and Skowronski and Carlston (1989) have found that the strength of bad over good also holds in social environments, where negative interpersonal interactions elicit uncertainty, anxiety or fear, such that processing these events becomes a high priority.

Adaptability is the rationale underlying Baumeister's arguments for the relative salience and influence of negativity. Generally, negative events have greater survival implications and denote more information than positive events about the environment. According to Baumeister et al., the strength and salience of bad over good "may in fact, be a general principle or law of psychological phenomena possibly reflecting the innate predispositions of the psyche or at least the almost inevitable adaptation of each individual to the exigencies of life" (p. 323).

The "bad is stronger than good" effect is especially noticeable in the social realm. Studying romantic relationships, Gottman and coworkers (Gottman & Krokoff, 1989; Levenson & Gottman, 1985) found that the frequency, intensity, and reciprocity of negative interactions are much more predictive of marital satisfaction and divorce than are positive interactions. Gottman's (1994) rule of thumb is that positive interactions must outnumber negative ones by a ratio of 5:1 if the relationship is to have a good chance of success. Additionally, Baumeister et al. (2001) review nine studies which compare the effects of social support and social undermining across diverse populations. They summarize their findings by saying that "[t]aken together, these studies suggest that helpful aspects of one's social network bear little or no relation to depression, well-being, and social support satisfaction, while upsetting or unhelpful aspects do ... . Bad interactions have stronger, more pervasive, and longer lasting effects" (p. 340).

Recent research in organizations has also explored the topic of negative relationships and behavior, confirming that bad is often stronger than good in this setting. Gersick, Bartunek, and Dutton (2000) conducted numerous interviews with academics about relationships that influenced their careers. While positive relationships were more frequent according to the academics' self-reports, the negative ones were reported to be very important with a substantial impact on career success. A recent paper by Labianca and Brass (in press) finds that while negative relationships may be rare (constituting between 1–8% of ties), they have greater impact on job satisfaction and organizational commitment than do positive or neutral associations. These scholars also find that negative effects are most pronounced in high density, high interdependence situations (e.g. teams). Finally, in a study of fast food restaurants, Dunlop and Lee (2004) compared the effects of organizational citizenship behaviors and deviant workplace behaviors. They found that deviant behaviors explained considerably more of the variance in subjective and objective work group outcomes than did the citizenship behaviors.

A lack of power is what prevents reform or rejection, and the "bad is stronger than good phenomenon" is what allows negative team members to have an asymmetrically strong effect on others. By extension, this asymmetric effect explains why dysfunctional individuals are an important concern for groups. In interdependent teams where people depend on each other, these intense psychological reactions are more likely to spillover beyond dyadic interactions to influence the broader social environment. As noted by Baumeister et al. (2001), "in order for a system to function effectively, each component of the system must do its part." At the level of the individual's relation to the group, bad is undeniably stronger than good; any individual part can prevent the system from functioning; but no individual part can by itself cause the system to succeed. This is especially true of social groups ... marked by a division of labor" (p. 358). In summary, the conjoint of intense psychological reactions at the individual level, and spillover effects onto group dynamics underlies the assertion that a "bad apple can spoil the barrel".

NEGATIVE PSYCHOLOGICAL STATES

In this case, we are confronted with a situation where a member's behavior is persistently and consistently negative. The bad behavior is noticed and influential in its effects on group members who do not have the power or wherewithal to enact change. What happens now? We will review the likely psychological states that emerge in response to each of the three negative member behavioral categories.

The Withholder of Effort. A bad apple who withholds effort from the collective triggers some undesired cognitions. If free riding persists, teammates face the challenge of correcting equity imbalances in input to outcome ratios relative to others (Adams, 1963). Research finds that the most common referent that people look to for social comparison (the "other" in the equity formulation) are the peers one works with every day (Kulik & Ambrose, 1992). It follows that social loafing by a teammate can be a major source of distress, as it violates effort norms and takes advantage of other members' good-faith contributions. It is also important to note that being under-rewarded, as is the case here, produces stronger psychological effects than being over-rewarded (e.g. Bloom, 1999) – another example of "bad being stronger than good". As such, perceptions of inequity will arise when group members compare their own contributions to those of a withholder of effort in their team, and will result in a desire to restore equity by reducing contributions (Jackson & Harkins, 1985; Schroeder, Steel, Woodell, & Bembenek, 2003). However, due to task interdependence, this scenario creates a dilemma for contributing group members in which they are motivated to avoid being a "sucker" and decrease their own contributions to the group – but in doing so they risk rupturing relations with other members and compromising group outcomes themselves. Thus, withholders of effort produce feelings of inequity with no easy resolution in a team environment.

The Affectively Negative Individual. Affectively negative individuals influence their teammates' affect (including attitudes, moods and emotions). Empirical work has shown that simply observing another person's expressions of affect can generate those feelings in others. Hatfield, Cacioppo, and Rapson's (1994) book Emotional Contagion describe how the diffusion of affect is "unintentional, uncontrollable and largely inaccessible to awareness" (p. 5), picked up unconsciously through facial expressions, vocalizations (e.g. tone, intensity, volume), postures, and movement. Using a confederate trained to display positive and negative affect, Barsade (2002) found that subjects working together on a task partially adopted the confederate's mood. Even more simply, subjects observing angry facial expressions quickly become angry themselves (Dimberg & Ohman, 1996). The negative emotions engendered by bad apple behavior may also be long lasting. Whereas a positive emotion (i.e. compassion) wears off relatively quickly, researchers find that when they give someone a negative feeling (i.e. anger) to concentrate on, the physiological effects last over 5 h (Rein, McCraty, & Atkinson, 1995). An extension of the negativity bias would suggest that individuals will pay more attention to negative others and are therefore prone to use negative others as a referent for social comparisons, give negative emotional information more credibility, experience negative emotions for a longer period, and ruminate more on negative events (Baumeister et al., 2001; Rozin & Royzman, 2001). However, this hypothesis is tempered by the lack of support for Barsade's (2002) hypothesis that negative affect would spread more completely through the group than positive affect. Clearly, more research is needed to understand if and when negative affect will have an asymmetric effect.

The Interpersonal Deviant. As described earlier, the interpersonal deviance category is defined by seven behaviors (e.g. making fun of a teammate, acting rudely, saying something hurtful, etc). It is therefore somewhat broader than the withholding effort and affectively negative categories. Despite that breadth, we believe that these behaviors have similar goals and mort importantly, similar consequences. More specifically, the main effect of an interpersonal deviant is to undermine trust in that individual. In teams, this can be problematic, since members depend on each other to take advantage of division of labor efficiencies or develop transactive memory models (Wageman, 2000). Conversely, distrust in a group member requires increased monitoring of the interpersonal deviant, and can distract from task performance. Like inequity and negative emotions, trust is also asymmetric, easier to damage than it is to build (Lewicki & Bunker, 1995).

More Complex Psychological Effects of Negative Teammates

The above discussion suggests some simple, direct effects of each type of negative behavior – namely that withholding effort produces perceptions of inequity, affective negativity spreads contagiously to teammates, and interpersonal deviance engenders distrust. However, beyond direct effects, each of these states can also have a secondary impact on the other two. With respect to inequity, although Adams' original focus was on cognition, other research has clearly demonstrated that inequity also produces strong emotional reactions (Goodman, 1977), and one can expect trust in a difficult team member to deteriorate. With respect to emotions, negative feelings trigger the search for mood-congruent cues (Meyer, Dayle, Meeham, & Harman, 1990), and ambiguous social information is more likely to be interpreted as inequitable or signaling untrustworthiness. Finally, since trustworthy behavior is generally expected, a secondary consequence of distrust is negative feelings such as anger, anxiety, and fear (Kramer & Wei, 1999). The "collateral damage" is potentially extensive.

Moreover, to fully consider the effect of any one specific negative member requires other considerations. For example, imagine a person who is severely depressed. They are highly likely to be affectively negative, but they might also be unmotivated to put forth much energy into tasks – e.g. withholding effort from the group. Or consider the interpersonal deviant who yells and bullies at the slightest provocation while concomitantly expressing pessimistic attitudes. A benefit of understanding the primary and secondary effects of each class of bad apple behavior is that these combinations can be addressed. At the current time, little evidence exists to guide predictions of how these behaviors might interrelate. However, at least three theoretical possibilities exist. One alternative is that multiple behaviors will be largely independent (i.e. be additive) such that someone who displays two categories of behaviors will have double the impact of a member who engages in only one. Another possibility is that there is a limit to how upsetting one individual can be, with multiple types of negative behavior drawing from the same reservoir of defensiveness. A third option is that different types of negative behavior will interact to reinforce and compound each other, resulting in ultimately larger impacts on teammates.

Finally, it seems to us that while negative affect can definitely cause unconstructive outcomes, the withholding of effort and particularly interpersonal deviance can cause even more acute negative effects. The interpersonal deviant directly and powerfully threatens other members and challenges the normative integrity of the group as a whole. Given the interdependence of groups, the sense of inequity produced by a withholder of effort will likely also be quite distressing. In contrast, affective negativity may have a smaller effect size since it operates through the less direct (and arguably less powerful) mechanism of contagion. But again, these are conjectures for future research. To the best of our knowledge, no studies have compared the effect sizes of these negative behaviors against each other. Next, the discussion elaborates on the consequences of teammate psychological states on behaviors.

Defensive Behavioral Reactions

Generally, defensive responses are self-protective efforts to cope with a negative internal state. This negative state might arise from threats to autonomy (Ashforth, 1989), identity (Aquino & Douglas, 2003), self-esteem

(Baumeister, Dale, & Sommer, 1998) or general well-being (Berkowitz, 1989). Persistent and consistent harmful behavior by a negative member challenges these core concerns and leads to ongoing perceptions of threat. These threats can be countered in two ways – externally or internally. Externally directed responses include acting against the negative member to restore feelings of autonomy, identity, self-esteem, and well-being. Internally directed responses involve taking steps to change one's own moods, emotions, or appraisals. Our subsequent discussion will include external forms of defensiveness, such as emotional explosions or revenge, as well as more internally focused efforts, such as mood maintenance, distraction, denial, and withdrawal from the group. However, while different, both types of defensiveness are caused by the same psychological states, and both lead to dysfunctional group processes and outcomes.

When experiencing aversive events, people often react emotionally (Berkowitz, 1989). Following Bies et al. (1997), we call this defensive response "exploding". Exploding is a direct and intense release of negative feelings, and is usually motivated by the desire to dominate or attack a frustrating person (Aquino, Galperin, & Bennett, 2004). However, explosions often lead to retaliation from those who are the target of these emotional releases. As such, they can sometimes result in an escalating tit-for-tat spiral of retaliation (Andersson & Pearson, 1999).

Additionally, rather than emotionally exploding, a person can defend themselves through the more controlled act of *revenge*. Revenge is motivated by a desire to restore perceptions of equity and justice. As noted by Bies et al. (1997) "Any perceived inequities on the job or violations of fairness norms can motivate revenge" (p. 21). Using their extensive interviews, they go on to note what kinds of things provoke revenge and uncover precisely what we would call bad apple behaviors. "Violations include bosses or co-workers who shirk their job responsibilities, take undue credit for a team's performance, or outright steal ideas" (p. 21). Morrill's (1995) ethnography, The Executive Way documents that managers are often loath to confront each other directly, but are still ingenious in the ways they sabotage those who frustrate them. For example, Morrill tells of coworkers who enact revenge by giving the "perpetrator" wrong information, distorted files, or sending them on "wild goose chases". However, experiments in the lab point out an inherent difficulty of revenge in the team settings. Using a social dilemma framework, Chen and Bachrach (2003) found that when a single individual free rides across experimental trials it led to an asymmetric and precipitous decline in teammate contributions. One interpretation of this finding is that offended members wanted to restore equity perceptions, but could not get even without also harming themselves and their group. This prevented the group as a whole from provisioning the social good and meant that all members were worse off. Chen and Bachrach's study underscores that in interdependent teams, confining the effect of revenge acts is often difficult. Next, we turn to internal manifestations of defensiveness.

When feeling emotionally negative, people often take action to improve their mood. *Mood maintenance* behaviors are efforts to improve one's affect and can be either consciously or unconsciously motivated (Baumeister, Heatherton, & Tice, 1994; Thayer, 1996). For group members, examples may include the seeking out of positive social interactions – i.e. lunch outings, happy hour, etc. – or more individual mood elevators like taking breaks, eating, or smoking. While perfectly functional for the individual, mood maintenance may have an adverse affect on the group. Indeed, a laboratory study by Tice, Bratslavsky, and Baumeister (2001) found that repairing negative emotions takes precedent to considerations of task performance when people are emotionally depleted. As such, people at their wits end might socialize with others, eat a treat, or surf the internet, but tend to direct attention away from the task performance.

Said another way, a negative member can be a *distraction*. In an article by Andrews (2004), one interviewee stated: "If you've ever been in a situation where you feel offended by the behavior of a coworker – you know that you can't bring your best effort to work. Emotionally, intellectually and behaviorally, you're just not going to be all there" (p. 45). Supporting this assertion, field work by Pearson et al. (2000) found that over one half of those who experienced incivility at work reported that they lost time worrying about the uncivil incident and its future consequences. Other research on affect also confirms that feelings of anxiety, anger, or sadness tend to distract and demotivate (George & Brief, 1996).

A fourth form of defensiveness is *denial*, a strategy by which an individual avoids dealing with negative events by behaving as if group problems are not occurring, significant, or the result of the negative member. Denial has been evocatively described as "a primitive and desperate method of coping with otherwise intolerable conflict, anxiety, and emotional distress or pain" (Laughlin (1970, p. 57), originally cited in Brown (1997)). However, the interdependence of group work and the persistence of negative behavior conspire to make denial at best only a temporary stop-gap to the negative group member problem. One can only override genuine emotions for so long before becoming emotionally depleted (e.g. Baumeister et al., 1994) and suffering the explosive effects mentioned above.

The final defensive response we will explore is *withdrawal* from the group. Social interactions are often stressful, and are likely to be more so in the presence of a negative teammate. As such, a particularly easy, and hence probable, response is to *withdraw* into oneself by not fully engaging in the group (Bergman & Volkema, 1989; Bies et al., 1997). Pearson and Porath (2005) document that 20% of the workers they interviewed report that they reduced their rate of work as a result of incivility and 10% said they deliberately cut back the amount of time they spent at work. Pearson et al. (2000) find that over 25% of individual who were targets of incivility acknowledged withdrawing from work situations. They summarize their findings by noting,

> Through all phases of our study, people told us that after being targets they ceased voluntary efforts. Some stopped helping newcomers; others stopped offering assistance to colleagues. Additionally, targets reduced their contributions to the organization as a whole, whether by pulling themselves off task forces and committees, or by reducing efforts to generate or inspire innovation (p. 130).

More extremely, teammates might even exit the group to escape the negative thoughts and feelings induced by a negative member. Pearson et al.'s data is instructive, finding that half of the individuals interviewed contemplated leaving their jobs after being the target of incivility, and a full 12% reported actually quitting.

We have reached a point in our discussion where the negative members' behaviors have undermined perceptions of equity, mood, and trust. Members may respond defensively to these psychological states via explosions, revenge, mood maintenance, distraction, denial, and withdrawal. In sum, withholding effort, affective negativity, and interpersonal deviance can each trigger defensive thoughts and behaviors with powerful consequences.

MODERATORS OF THE BAD APPLE EFFECT

Thus far, we have reviewed the factors that motivate members of teams to respond defensively to a difficult individual. However, this response is moderated by several factors, which influence *when* bad behavior will impact the psychological reactions and subsequent actions of teammates. Specifically, four variables emerge from the literature that seem especially important in determining perceived impact severity – (1) intensity of the negative behaviors exhibited, (2) the group's interdependence,

(3) whether outcomes are successes or failures, (4) and the teammates' coping abilities.

Intensity of Negative Behaviors. The potency and frequency of negative behavior will determine its perceived intensity. First, of the three classes of behavior that have been identified as likely to elicit a group response (e.g. withholding effort, affective negativity, and interpersonal deviance), each has a range of severity. One affectively negative individual might be extremely pessimistic, while another might be only mildly depressed. Indeed, the widely employed "circumplex" model of emotion is based on an intensity dimension (Larsen & Diener, 1992), as is Ajzen's (2001) conceptualization of attitude. Similarly, the withholder of effort might slack off a little or do next to nothing. The literature on social loafing recognizes this and measures free riding as a continuous variable (Karau & Williams, 1993). Further, the interpersonal deviant might purposefully sabotage other's efforts or display the milder behavior of mean-spirited criticism. Robinson and Bennett's (1995) inductive typology of interpersonal deviance is supportive, finding that people naturally categorize deviance from mild to severe. In sum, potency is a central part of theories of effort, affect, and deviance. Second, in addition to the behaviors exhibited, the frequency of those actions is likely to play a role in perceptions of intensity. In an interesting analogy, Cunningham, Barbee, and Druen (1997) suggest that aversive behaviors can be thought of as "social allergens", where increased exposure leads to increased sensitivity. However, this fascinating hypothesis has yet to be tested. Regardless, more potent and frequent negative member behaviors will have a greater impact on teammates.

Interdependence. If the group is highly interdependent, then dysfunctional behavior is of more consequence. Groups can be interdependent to varying degrees in terms of tasks, goals, feedback, or rewards (Wageman, 2000). Highly interdependent groups have more interaction and the content of that interaction is more central to accomplishing the work task. As such, high interdependence means there are more opportunities for affect to contagiously spread to others and a greater chance for interpersonal attacks. In addition, the inequity caused by shirking is more noticeable and meaningful when members are interdependent and receive rewards based mainly on group accomplishment. Whereas a group that is not interdependent allows members to "do their own thing", a highly interdependent group provides less opportunity for avoidance. The experience of threat is ever-present, and so is the chance of acrimonious interpersonal conflict. This is especially problematic since interdependent tasks necessitate that a group maintains higher quality social relationships in order to effectively coordinate their activities (Gittell, 2003).

Outcomes. Work team outcomes can exert a powerful influence on the perceived severity of negative member behavior. After a team failure occurs, the negative member behaviors are more salient, and thus more influential. According to attribution theory (Weiner, 1980, 1995), failure triggers the process of determining causal factors, and relatively innocuous behavior can be reclassified as a significant threat to team functioning. If unchangeable, this newly salient dysfunction provokes the defensive reactions we have detailed. In addition the severity of the outcome can influence the response. This assertion is supported by Mitchell and Wood's (1980; Mitchell, Green, & Wood, 1981) research, which gave nurse managers scenarios of offenses that nurses had actually committed. In one condition, the nurse had left down a bed rail and the patient fell out and broke a hip, while in another the nurse had made the same mistake, but the patient did not fall. The punishments that managers recommended in the first condition were quite severe, including dismissal and probation. The punishments were much milder in the second condition, with the most common response being a verbal reminder of hospital procedure. Accordingly, reactions by group members to negative behavior will be more extreme when the behavior results in failure outcomes, and when those failure outcomes are more consequential.

Coping Skills. Finally, individuals are also likely to differ in their personal coping skills. A high locus of control would lead to beliefs that life events and reactions to life events are controlled internally. If teammates have high self-esteem, they know that their essential needs will be met. If they have high generalized self-efficacy, then they are likely to have confidence that either the negative member or the situation can be changed. Further, if they are calm (low neuroticism), then their reactions will be extreme. Notably, the work by Judge and his coworkers on core self-evaluations integrates and aggregates these four classic psychological variables – providing compelling reasons and evidence for conceptualizing and measuring a single underlying construct (Erez & Judge, 2001; Judge, Locke, Durham, & Kluger, 1998; Judge, Van Vianen, & De Pater, 2004). These self-attributes are useful because they change the meaning of threatening situations. For example, someone with a highly positive core self-evaluation might interpret interpersonally deviant behavior as merely a nuisance rather than a substantial threat. Or they might find a silver lining to the situation, such as a chance to learn conflict management skills. Using such mental techniques, those with high core self-evaluations are likely to be motivated and able to reconstruct the meaning of the bad apple's behaviors to be less negative. In summary, if a teammate has extensive coping resources then negative behaviors will have less intense psychological impact.

GROUP TRANSITION MECHANISMS

Thus far, we have defined the behaviors that make someone a negative group member and described how chronic display of those behaviors can subsequently influence other individuals to feel and act defensively. So far, this description has been initially unidirectional, then dyadic. However, we mentioned at the beginning of this paper that most of the research on team effectiveness has focused on how team attributes and processes result in effective team performance. At this point in our analysis, we will explore how individual states and actions transition to group constructs and behavior, and move from one conceptual level to the next.

One of the major shifts in team research documented by Ilgen et al. (2005) is that more emphasis is being placed on multilevel theoretical and analytical contributions. Ilgen elaborates on the fact that organizations are multilevel and that many of the variables central to understanding teams appear at the group level as well as the individual level. He also points out that there are many parallel constructs, ones that have both an individual and team counterpart. For example, motivational constructs such as efficacy and emotional constructs like mood can be construed at both these levels. Theoretically, these collective constructs are usually assembled from individual interactions. When A talks to B, and B responds in some way, we have what Weick (1979) calls a "double interact". It is the structure and function of these double interacts that are the building blocks of collective constructs. These "[c]ollective structures emerge, are transmitted, and persist through the actions of members of the collective" (Morgeson & Hofmann, 1999, p. 53). We support Morgeson and Hofmann's notion that "[i]ntegrating across levels may provide a more veridical account of organizational phenomena" (p. 249). The question for the moment is how these individual interactions, which we have described are translated into group constructs and then into group action. We describe three mechanisms below: addition, spillover, and sensemaking.

Additive Defensiveness. The simplest and most obvious transition occurs using an additive mechanism. Obviously, the more types of negative behavior, and the more interactions with team members, the more negative psychological states and defensive behaviors will accrue. Brass, Butterfield, and Skaggs (1998) discuss how the impact of a negative member on a team depends on the ratio of contacts the person has with group vs. non-group members. Duffy, Ganster, and Pagon (2002) summarize their discussion of social undermining behaviors by commenting that "their efforts add up over time" (p. 233).

Spillover Effects. A different mechanism for moving from dyadic ex-change to group level constructs is caused by what we call a *spillover effect*. The subtle and automatic form of spillover occurs through the process of modeling behaviors. Seeing others act antisocially makes those behaviors more mentally accessible and lowers inhibitions about behaving in a similar fashion. Bandura's famous "Bobo the Clown" studies demonstrate that even strangers can be influential models of antisocial behavior (Bandura, Ross, & Ross, 1963). These social learning effects are likely to be even stronger in groups. Indeed, a paper entitled "Monkey See, Monkey Do" by Robinson and O'Leary-Kelly (1998) found precisely that; the more in-terdependent the social context, the greater the effects of social learning. Keaton (1999) even suggests that these other team members can become "secondary provokers" or negative members themselves. In short, through mimicry and modeling, spillover effects of negative thoughts, feelings, and actions can move from individual to group level characteristics.

Spillover can also be seen in the phenomenon of displaced aggression. While we are often able to use regulatory skills to control frustration in the moment, as those resources are expended, group members become more likely to lash out at others (Muraven & Baumeister, 2000). Sometimes those others are entirely removed from the situations and people who are the source of frustration (Marcus-Newhall, Pederson, Carlson, & Miller, 2000). Research shows that provoked participants readily displace aggression onto blameless individuals (e.g. Worchel, Hardy, & Hurley, 1976), especially when social and status hierarchies constrain direct expression of aggression – e.g. in comparatively low power situations (Marcus-Newhall et al., 2000). Folger and Skarlicki (1998) describe this sort of spillover as a "popcorn model" of aggression, where aggression or violence can ricochet throughout a group; setting off one individual after another and lowering everyone's inhibitions.

Just as contagion serves as a mechanism for spreading mood from A to B, it can also spread from B to C, C to D and so on; spillover occurs when team members' individual responses to the bad apple start to have an impact on other team members, an "interaction breeds similarity" effect (Brass et al., 1998, p. 25). In one of the more definitive pieces of evidence to date, Barsade's (2002) article on the "ripple effect" found that a confederate displaying physical manifestations of negative affect (e.g. posture, manner-isms, facial expressions) was able to engender negative moods in groups, and multi-level modeling techniques (HLM) affirmed that these effects perme-ated the group above and beyond dyadic contagion. Bartel and Saavedra (2000, p. 197) describe this effect in their research, stating that "Group members come to develop mutually shared moods and emotion". Evidence of these affective spillover effects has accumulated in recent years (Bakker & Schaufeli, 2000; George, 1990; Totterdell, Kellett, Teuchmann, & Briner, 1998). The transfer of affect is largely automatic and subconscious, occurring through mimicry and psychological feedback (Hatfield et al, 1994).

Sensemaking Effects. More conscious processes can occur as well. In many cases a negative member may act out in a public context (e.g. bully a teammate, refuse to contribute in a social problem solving context) or behave so egregiously that it requires sensemaking by one or more team members (Weick, 1995). The recipient of an attack, or an observer of one, may seek out the advice and interpretation of other team members or even outsiders. Social communication can be an important part of individual sensemaking (Hardin & Higgins, 1996). Pearson and Porath found that over 90% of people who were treated badly (i.e. uncivilly) say they sought the counsel of someone else. Moreover, research by Rime, Finkenauer, Luminet, Zech, and Philippot, (1998) describes the process of "secondary social sharing" where those who have heard about frustrating interactions themselves share it with others. Rime's research indicates that this secondary social sharing occurs with surprising frequency – around two thirds of the time negative events are shared a second time. Finally, their studies show that such sharing is especially likely to happen when the event is intense or negative (Christophe & Rime, 1997; Luminet, Bouts, Delie, Manstead, & Rime, 2000).

An obvious outcome of this sensemaking process is that people agree that the negative member is different and dysfunctional and the group tries to change or reject this person. However, it is also possible that neither response is viable (described earlier), and under these circumstances the negative effects are likely to have a wider and more substantial impact on the team. Lacking power to enact change prompts group member sensemaking about one's own relationship to the group. When a group has lost its instrumental ability to effectively enforce norms, elicit cooperation and achieve goals, members may no longer recognize the team as a desirable entity with which to be associated. When members loose faith in the groups of which they are a part, it is called de-identification (Dutton, Dukerich, & Harquail, 1994). One of the major drives behind identifying with a collective is the desire to be part of something positive that enhances one's own self concept (Dutton et al., 1994). As the group loses its positive ethos, members de-identify from the collective and categorize themselves more as an individual and less as a part of the group. As members physically and psychologically disengage, the character of the group is marked by decreasing commitment to group goals and dissatisfaction with team membership (Ouwerkerk, Ellemers, & de Gilder, 1999). In closing, it is sufficient to say that the individual actions of a negative member can spread in various ways to the group – through aggregation, spillover, and sensemaking – and that it is through these transformational mechanisms that dyadic effects come to be a group level phenomenon – i.e. a spoiled barrel.

GROUP CONSTRUCTS

We have argued that the individual and dyadic effects of the negative member can be transmuted into group constructs – what Cohen and Bailey (1997) call group psychosocial traits – through the mechanisms off aggregation, spillover, and sensemaking. In the abstract, group constructs are mental heuristics to think about qualities of a collective (Morgeson & Hofmann, 1999). However, when recognized and internalized by group members, group psychosocial traits come to have a life of their own and exist apart from individuals. As Weick and Roberts (1993) point out, people "construct their actions while envisaging a social system of joint action" (p. 363). In short, we act as if social groups have a character of their own, and so, in a way, it comes to be true.

NEGATIVE MEMBER'S EFFECTS ON GROUP PROCESSES AND OUTCOMES

Effective groups have two meta-skills – their members produce as individuals, and together as a group they effectively coordinate and integrate individual action into a coherent whole constituting a group output (Hackman, 1987). This first skill, the ability to produce, depends on having a team that is motivated, capable, and able to learn and change. These are the basic building blocks for performance, without which there would be little to integrate. The second skill, group integrative actions, includes the group processes of productive conflict and cooperation (Smith et al., 1994). Having a bad apple in a group will have a negative impact on the group production related processes of motivation, creativity, and learning and on the integrative processes of cooperation and conflict. Without these processes in place, groups fail.

Motivation. Motivation to perform is central to work behavior (Mitchell, 1997). We have already discussed how motivation at the individual level could suffer and, in addition, influence collective motivational constructs such as group efficacy (Gully et al., 2000). Teams with lower efficacy exert less effort, set lower goals, and perform less well than group with higher efficacy (Gully et al., 2000). Beyond efficacy, a negative group affective tone also has a deleterious affect on group performance (George, 1990). Negative moods and emotions engendered by the negative member will distract other team members from focusing on the task. This distraction might take the form of ruminating on the negative interactions or gossiping about them with others (Burt & Knez, 1995; Rimes et al., 1998). This assertion is consistent with the findings of Grawitch, Munz, and Kramer (2003) that negative group moods focus attention on interpersonal issues and away from task concerns. Lastly, recent work by van Knippenberg (2000; van Knippenberg & van Schie, 2000) suggests that since the prototype of a "good" employee is usually a motivated employee, group members who categorize themselves as part of a healthy group will conform to that identity by displaying more task motivation. Thus, if a destructive group member causes de-identification, there is likely to be a decrease in task effort and persistence as the team members deviate from the "good worker" prototype (see also Hogg, 2000 and Shamir, 1990). In summary, having a negative member in the group will decrease motivation through the processes of lowered efficacy, distraction (e.g. gossiping, affective rumination, and mood maintenance), and de-identification.

Creativity and Learning. Creative problem solving is seen to be increasingly important in groups (Paulus, 2000). In a recent article (Amabile, Barsade, Mueller, & Staw, 2005) shows that positive affect facilitates cognitive variation and yields new associations, thereby enhancing creativity in a linear fashion. But creativity also depends on several fragile conditions, including the free exchange of ideas, confidence that innovation is possible, and the motivation to create (West, 2002). Further, the creative process of coming up with new ideas is intimately related to the group's ability to learn. The same safe and motivated environment that allows groups to come up with new ideas also allows them to learn and remember effective methods of action (West, 2002). While learning and creativity are not synonymous, both involve an intellectual openness to new possibilities, and are consequently coupled together here.

The negative member's behavior can have a major effect on the creative and learning processes in groups. In inequitable situations, such as with a withholder of effort, teammates are unlikely to be motivated to contribute to the collective pool of ideas or to teach and learn from others (West, 2002). In addition, numerous empirical studies have found that negative feelings have a chilling effect on creativity for individuals (see for a review Isen, 2000) and on groups (Grawitch et al., 2003). Specifically, research exploring the contagion of the negative emotion of social anxiety has discovered that the worst (i.e. most socially anxious) group member exerts a powerful asymmetric effect on team creativity (Camacho & Paulus, 1995). Similar to our affectively negative individual, the most socially anxious person paralyzed other members' ability to creatively perform. Finally, threat generally hinders inventiveness by restricting one's behavior to well-established patterns (West, 2002; Staw, Sandelands, & Dutton, 1981). A similar logic holds true for learning in groups. A perception of threat triggers defensive reactions aimed towards self-protection (Aquino & Douglas, 2003). Groups composed of self-protective members will not feel safe, and so will be reluctant to do things like admit a knowledge deficit or ask for help in developing competencies (Edmondson, 1999, 2002), which will impede learning. Finally, given that knowledge can be a source of power, those who do not identify with the group are more likely to hoard information and ideas for political purposes (Jones & George, 1998). If, by engendering a hostile atmosphere, a negative member may cause the group to be mute about problem areas and engage in political use of knowledge. Again, group learning is likely to suffer. In sum, equity perceptions, group affective tone, feelings of safety, and identification each play an important role in prompting creativity and learning but will be undermined by the behaviors of a negative group member.

We now shift our attention to the ways that a negative member may influence the integrative processes necessary to coordinate various members' efforts. These integrative processes may be especially compromised as team members rush meetings to hasten their escape from negative interactions, and succumb to the common bias of coordination neglect (Heath & Staudenmayer, 2000).

Cooperation. Cooperation is perhaps the most quintessentially "integrative" component of group work. One way bad apples inhibit cooperation is by undermining what has been called "depersonalized trust" or the "positive expectation or presumption that interpersonal risks can be assumed with a reasonable degree of confidence that others [in the group] will not betray or violate the trust" (Kramer & Wei, 1999, p. 146). A central facet of depersonalized trust is the knowledge that others will abide by norms of civil behavior. When a negative member steals credit or spreads negative gossip, other employees' begin to lose confidence (i.e. decrease their expectations) that cooperation will result in mutually beneficial outcomes. Kramer and Wei note that a violation "may create problems that undermine the smooth exchanges, disclosures, affirmations, and validations associated with group-based trust (p. 147). According to rational models of human behavior, as expectancies worsen, so will the motivation to cooperate (Bommer, Miles, & Grover, 2003). Identity theory makes similar predictions along less ca-lculative premises of human behavior. Lind and Tyler's (1988) group value model of behavior argues that cooperation is an expressive sign of feeling respected and respecting others. When people identify with the group, they feel a moral duty to cooperate (Kramer & Goldman, 1995) and sometimes do so even when it is not in their best interest (Brann & Foddy, 1988; Dawes, van de Kragt, & Orbell, 1990). On the other hand, when people categorize themselves as individuals rather than as members of a group, they withdraw from collective life by thinking and acting more selfishly (Kramer, Brewer, & Hanna, 1996). In sum, decreased perceptions of depersonalized trust provide an instrumental rationale for avoiding cooperation; and de-identification produces expressive reasons for eschewing cooperation.

Conflict. Group conflict was once considered anathema (Robbins, 1974). However, recent thinking and research indicates that under certain circum-stances, conflict can benefit groups. Specifically, a distinction is drawn be-tween relational conflict (i.e. about the person) and task conflict (i.e. about how to work). While relational conflict indeed detracts and distracts, task conflict can actually serve to reinforce social responsibilities, enhance de-cision quality by checking assumptions, and clarify group members' mental models (Jehn, 1995; Tjosvold, 1998). It seems likely that the interpersonal deviant and the withholder of effort are likely to provoke both immediate and sustained relational conflict by breaking important norms such as mu-tual respect and parity of effort. Evidence suggests that even the affectively negative individual may prompt conflict by causing reactions of irritation, condescension, and humorlessness (Furr & Funder, 1998). And as other group members rebuke or retaliate against this member, relational tensions will escalate (Andersson & Pearson, 1999). Moreover, some of the resulting hostility is likely to be "displaced" towards other group members (Marcus-Newhall et al., 2000), increasing overall relational conflict. Finally, by cre-ating a threatening psychological environment, a negative member could also cause people to retreat inwards, resulting in hesitance to engage in constructive task conflict, since it may result in unpleasant acrimony. As such, the groups with a negative member might experience relatively more interpersonal conflict along with relatively less task conflict – a doubly counter productive state of affairs. However, this is a place where our knowledge is somewhat speculative and more empirical evidence would be useful.

In conclusion, through various individual cognitions (e.g. inequity, negative mood, and distrust) and group level constructs (e.g. lower mood, potency, safety, and group-based trust), the key processes that make groups effective (e.g. motivation, creativity, learning, cooperation, and task conflict) will be undermined.

Group Outcomes. These individual and group effects mean that the ultimate outcomes for the group include poor performance, low viability (e.g. a weakened social structure), and an unhappy team. Group performance will suffer as measured in terms of quantity, quality, and timeliness. The link between group processes and group outcomes is a rich and well-researched topic (see Cohen & Bailey, 1997; Campion, Medsker, & Higgs, 1993; McGrath, 1984). So as not to reinvent the wheel, we will merely reiterate that group behavioral variables such as motivation, creativity, cooperation, and conflict are central mediators between inputs such as group member's abilities and the key outcomes of performance, worker well-being, and group viability. However, one interesting long-term consequence of the negative member invites further elaboration. Since members of dysfunctional groups are likely to be dissatisfied and to de-identify, we would expect increased absenteeism and turnover (Pelled & Xin, 1999), each of which have significant negative impacts on group functioning (Mitchell & Lee, 2001). In fact, the desire to avoid a negative member may even explain additional variance in turnover that would not surface in traditional predictors like job satisfaction. For example, Mitchell and Lee (2001) note that events like fights with a coworker may act as a "shock" that precipitates leaving. Moreover, since the best employees have greater job mobility, they are often the most likely to leave (Mitchell & Lee, 2001). As the best group members jump ship, one can imagine a downward spiral in group performance, unfolding over time.

DISCUSSION

Over the last half century, a clearer understanding has emerged about the power of collectives to reconstruct the goals, behaviors, and perceptions of the individual to serve the needs of the group. However, it is often overlooked that people conform and converge largely because they want to; they want to belong and have clear expectations about normatively appropriate behavior (Baumeister & Leary, 1995; Salancik & Pfeffer, 1978; Sherif, 1935). Sometimes individuals behave in ways that do not benefit the group; sometimes individuals are negative, refuse to contribute effort or break important group norms. This behavior presents a challenge at both practical and theoretical levels. Practically, chronic expressions of harmful behaviors allow these people to become a figurative thorn in the groups' side – clearly a distraction and possibly a "destroyer" of the group itself (Wetlaufer, 1994). Theoretically, these negative behaviors threaten our standard assumptions about groups as homogeneous structures capable of cohesive action (e.g. Hackman, 1976). And yet, despite the importance of the topic, the field has yet to find the theoretical traction that would allow for a complete and coherent understanding of the key issues implicated by these negative group members.

Our analysis and review attempts to fill that gap. We present an unfolding model that describes the prototypical process by which one individual behaving badly might have a profoundly negative impact on the group. We suggest that the three most salient and important behaviors of a negative member are the withholding of effort, the demonstration of negative affect, and the violation of important interpersonal norms. At the beginning of this process, team members will react by trying to change this negative behavior. If that fails, the attribution becomes that the person's behavior is stable and intractable. Next, members will look to reject the person. But when this is not possible due to social constraints, more defensive psychological reactions and behaviors are likely to occur. Defensiveness is an especially intense experience due to two factors – the aversiveness of not having the control over the environment (i.e. low power), and due to the psychological principle that bad experiences are hard to ignore, require attention and sensemaking, and consume large amounts of time and energy (i.e. bad is stronger than good). The direct reactions to this persistent and unchangeable negative member are the feeling of inequity when confronted with someone withholding effort, the spreading of negative affect to other members through contagion, and the loss of confidence and trust in an interpersonal deviant. These negative states lead to defensive behaviors.

Defensiveness is associated with dysfunctional behaviors such as explosions, revenge, mood maintenance, distraction, denial, and withdrawal. These reactions are especially likely to occur when the negative behaviors of the negative member are intense, when the group is interdependent or experiences bad outcomes, and when group members lack the coping skills to deal with the situation. Moving forward in this unfolding process, it is through additive, spillover and sensemaking mechanisms that these behaviors come to influence group psychosocial constructs such as group mood, group potency, and psychological safety. As a result, group activities such as motivated effort, cooperation, coordination, creativity, learning, and helpful conflicts are decreased and diminished, eventually resulting in poor group performance, lower well-being, and possibly team collapse.

It is important to note, however, that the negative member phenomenon does not explain every instance of group dysfunction. Other factors such as lack of organizational support, work-family issues, inadequate member competencies, or unclear directions provide a host of alternative causes. In other words, there is reason to be cautious in applying a bad apple label to a particular member when confronted with a dysfunctional group. The fundamental attribution error (Ross, Amabile, & Steinmetz, 1977) and the sinister attribution error (Kramer & Wei, 1999) both argue that people have a penchant for pinning ambiguous problems on an individual group member, particularly those that are disliked (Naquin & Tynan, 2003). By doing so, groups might incorrectly label someone a bad apple and blame them for negative outcomes. Moreover, a group may succumb to the cognitive "performance-cue" bias, where outcome success unduly influences judgment and recollection of the event (Staw, 1975). For example, if a group's project is unsatisfactory to members, they are likely to look backwards and judge ambiguous or marginal behavior as dysfunctional. Moreover, cognitive psychology research finds that when someone is in a negative frame of mind, negative behaviors will be more easily and clearly recalled (Meyer et al., 1990). Finally, in these same situations, there is a motivational bias to blame someone for bad outcomes. In order to protect the image of the group and the member's self-esteem, the least proto-typical member is often used as a scapegoat for what was really a collective failure (Eagle & Newton, 1981; Marques, Abrams, & Serodio, 2001).

This presents a troubling methodological conundrum – people who are "positive deviants" or "devil's advocates" will likely be resented for not conforming, and thus will be scapegoated and derided, particularly when negative outcomes have recently occurred. That is, dissent will likely lead to a negative halo which may increase reportage of the person as expressing bad apple behaviors of withholding effort, negative affectivity, and interpersonal deviance. This would seem to present a threat to the validity of survey measures of the effects of bad apples. So, how is a researcher to know if bad apples caused negative outcomes or if negative outcomes caused someone to be labeled a bad apple? One admittedly imperfect resolution would be to assess factors we already know to be associated with scapegoating – such as opinion deviance and recent negative feedback – and show that bad apple behaviors explain incremental variance. Another approach is to have a confederate display bad apple behaviors in a laboratory context and to show asymmetric effects in a context where the performance-cue bias in not operable. We should also add that while opinion deviance may lead to some bad apple labeling, it is unlikely that such behavior will have the same extreme effects. First, opinion deviance may in fact lead to positive outcomes (Nemeth & Staw, 1989). Second, it is less likely to be taken personally and result in the same negativity caused by bad apple actions. But clearly, the relative effect of opinion deviants and bad apples is an issue needing more research.

Our initial examination of the frequency of spoiled barrels suggested that while negative members who persist over time and eventually produce dysfunctional groups are probably not ubiquitous,[1] their effects are substantial. Teams may identify negative members and their destructive behaviors – but organizational constraints may limit the group's ability to remedy the situation. We have suggested that the negativity bias and various processes of social interaction operate to make the negative member behaviors disproportionately recognized, informative and influential.

But what explains why theorists have overlooked this fundamental dynamic about responses to negative individuals? One reason seems to be that scholars have considered it "beyond the scope" of their own works. Mitchell's research looks at *leader's* responses to poor performing workers, and consequently did not need to contend with situations of low empowerment (Mitchell et al., 1981; Mitchell & O'Reilly, 1983; Mitchell & Wood, 1980). In addition, that research focused on individuals, not teams. Lepine and Van Dyne (2001) are more overt, explicitly assuming that "the peer who notices the low-performing coworker is competent and capable ... is committed to the group and the group's goals ... and that situational factors do not overly constrain peer responses" (p. 69). In short, they assume away the problem that we are interested in – e.g. when "bad apples might spoil the barrel". We relax those assumptions, and propose that there are hosts of situations when teammates are not powerful, competent, capable, committed, or unconstrained – in short, situations where teammates are unempowered.

A second reason is that most researchers have only examined parts of our overall picture and have captured just a small portion of what unfolds over time. The typical study may look at only two or three variables such as how negative affect can spread through a group (Barsade, 2002) or how a coworker who withholds effort causes other team members to have feelings of inequity (Jackson & Harkins, 1985). In addition, some authors focus on immediate individual reactions (the front end of our analyses) like motivational and isolation attempts by coworkers (Lepine & Van Dyne, 2001) while others focus on the relationships between group psychosocial traits like low-efficacy and outcomes like group motivation or performance

(Gully et al., 2002); relationships that are the last step in our analysis. Still others look at how personality variables (e.g. low conscientiousness or low agreeableness) affect the very distal dependant variable of team performance (Barrick et al., 1998; Haythorn, 1953), but confess ignorance when it comes to explaining *why* negative individuals have such a large asymmetric effect on the group.

In looking over the totality of our presentation we know that we have introduced a number of "sets" of states and behaviors at the individual and group level. Some things are included, some excluded. We have tried to be precise about what is in or out, partly through our definition of what constitutes a negative member (e.g. withholding effort, negative affectivity, and interpersonal deviance). These three sets of behavior drive much of what follows in terms of states and actions. However, it is also important to recognize that our guide for inclusion or exclusion was the research literature itself. We focused on phenomena that people have written about and empirically researched. Obviously, some things were omitted due to these judgment calls but we are fairly confident that we have not overlooked any *major* components for our review.

FUTURE RESEARCH

We have presented a model that captures how the effects of the behaviors of a negative group member unfold over time and across conceptual levels. While many of the pairwise relationships that adjoin neighboring stages of our analysis (see Fig. 1) are well documented; it is the distal and mediating aspects of our approach that need more work. In addition, we have little idea about the combinational properties of our states and behaviors at both the individual and group level. Which states are most important or when are they important? How do they combine: additively, multiplicatively? Are there thresholds which must be surpassed for effects to occur and if so what are they? In addition, we present our analysis in a lock step fashion over time. In reality both individual and group psychological actions and reactions may occur simultaneously and interact over time. Some stages may take longer, others shorter. There is lots of research left to be done.

However, there are major problems with conducting such research. Because we are describing offensive behaviors and intense reactions, field research would seem to be most appropriate. Also, the dynamic nature and extended time frame point to field investigation. Extreme behaviors and lengthy periods of interaction are hard to capture in the laboratory. However, the chances of actually observing a bad apple spoil the barrel is low since such events are infrequent and organizations are not particularly likely to encourage or support such invasive research. Moreover, questionnaires are also problematic, given the retrospective biases discussed above. And, as we have suggested, the process is complex, especially with respect to identification of causal and mediating mechanisms. A more refined and detailed analysis would usually be most easily accomplished with laboratory research. However, the use of ad hoc groups, the lack of real world outcomes and the ethical problems with creating real negative experiences all mitigate against choosing to conduct this research solely in the lab. What is left?

We would suggest a combination of traditional research strategies along with some less frequently used methods. First, laboratory studies could be used to confirm some of the less emotionally charged and less temporally extended links depicted in Fig. 1. For example, we could demonstrate through manipulation (e.g. using a confederate) that certain bad apple behaviors cause negative psychological reactions and defensive behaviors. We could, for example, have one confederate embarrass or be rude to another confederate and observe the consequences for other team members in terms of perceived trust and defensive behaviors such as mood maintenance. We could also use scenarios or scripted film clips to obtain similar responses. Second, in the field, we could have employees respond to questionnaires describing bad apple experiences and how the person and their group responded.

Beyond these traditional strategies, we would suggest two other research techniques that could contribute to our understanding. We could use qualitative techniques to investigate groups struggling with a bad apple. In particular, a mainstay of the recent spate of reality TV shows (e.g. The Apprentice, Real World, Survivor, etc.) is the inclusion of a "bad apple" member with whom others are required to interact. These videos constitute a rich archive of real people coping with bad apples over time in interdependent circumstances. Finally, we should add that the bad apple phenomenon takes place at two levels – the individual and the group. Any research that attempts to encompass both parts of the process will require both measurement and the use of analytic techniques that are appropriate for these multiple levels. For example, one promising alternative is the use agent-based computer simulations, which allow for a better understanding of the dynamic and multi-level relations that occur in groups. Variables such as group size, empowerment, and negative relations could all be modeled in this context (Kitts, Macy, & Flache, 1999). In short, conducting bad apple research, because of the negative behaviors and emotions, extended time dimension, and multiple levels presents a number of challenges. However, the problem is real, its effects can be dramatic, and it is worthy of study.

Our analysis also underscores the importance of practical responses to the bad apple phenomenon, such as selection, placement, and training. For example, it seems clear that to the extent management can identify people who deleteriously influence others with negative affective attributes and a damaging disregard for group norms (such as mutual respect and equality of effort), such people should not be hired, or at least not placed in groups. Letters of recommendation, psychological tests, and work group simulations can all help assess these attributes. Once the person is hired and placed in a group, then ways to attenuate a destructive group member's effects include structuring the task to minimize interdependence or, more plausibly, limiting the negative member's power by not selecting them as a leader or facilitator. In addition, groups can be trained in ways to handle destructive behaviors when they occur. Management may also work to minimize dysfunctional behaviors – for example by monitoring and punishing group members who consistently flout group norms or withhold effort. To do this requires expanding what is included in performance appraisals beyond task performance to including measures of the frequency and potency of negative behaviors.

Whether in organizations or other types of groups, our dynamic and unfolding perspective implicates two key leverage points for dealing with negative members. First, empowerment is critical to effective resolution of the difficult member dilemma (e.g. rejection or motivation). Groups can empower themselves by building coalitions or by reinforcing relationships threatened by spillover effects. Additionally, leaders with structural authority (i.e. a team coach or therapist) can intervene to motivate or expel a negative member, or they can provide tools to empower the team (e.g. Hackman, 2002). For example, a select group of progressive firms are using what is called 360-degree feedback, where peers formally comment on each other's behavior. However, at this point, we know very little about the effectiveness, or relative effectiveness, of selection, group training, interventions, placement, firing, or team empowerment, in resolving the bad apple problem.

Second, this model highlights how important it is to quickly mobilize a response. Rather than members remaining in a psychological state of defensiveness, a quick response minimizes the individual and group level effects of a negative member. Moreover, as we have touched on, there is some speculation that there may be some vicious cycles instigated by a negative member. Nipping this harmful behavior in the bud, so to speak, would avoid these downward spirals.

CONCLUSION

Over the last 20 years, the field of organizational research has seen a dramatic increase in the study of negative behavior at work. Some of these actions violate internal rules and external laws – e.g. discrimination, sexual harassment, violence, stealing, and dishonest reporting. Our focus is different. It is on legal, but negative, interpersonal behaviors within a team context. Almost all of us have either had the personal experience of working with someone who displayed bad apple behaviors or had a friend, coworker, or spouse who has shared such stories with us. When this process starts to unfold at work, it consumes inordinate amounts of time, psychological resources, and emotional energy. We believe that our personal and indirect experience with such circumstances underlie many people's reluctance to fully commit to teams, despite the enthusiasm of psychologists and proclamations of popular management authors.

We have presented an analysis of when, how, and why such reactions occur. We notice the behaviors, they offend us, reduce our enthusiasm, change our mood and may ultimately lead us to personally de-identify or leave the group, with a high likelihood that the group itself will perform poorly, fail, or disband. Hopefully, our description of this process can clarify our thinking, initiate research that confirms or disconfirms the relationships proposed, and eventually lead to strategies that decrease bad apple effects. In conclusion, we believe that the bad apple phenomenon is real and important, and that its inclusion in future organizational research will help us to understand and improve dysfunctional groups.

NOTES

1. While not ubiquitous, that does not mean bad apples are a rarity in groups. The reason is simple arithmetic. Since groups contain several people (for sake of example, let us say seven), even a small number of bad apples (say 2% of individuals) could produce a significant percentage of groups containing at least one bad apple (e.g. $7 \times 2\% = 14\%$).

ACKNOWLEDGMENT

The authors would like to thank Anne O'Leary-Kelly for her insightful comments on an earlier draft of this paper.

REFERENCES

Adams, J. S. (1963). Toward an understanding of inequity. *Journal of Abnormal and Social Psychology, 67,* 422–436.

Ajzen, I. (2001). Nature and operation of attitudes. *Annual Review of Psychology, 52,* 27–58.

Amabile, T. M., Barsade, S. G., Mueller, J. S., & Staw, B. M. (2005). Affect and creativity at work. *Administrative Science Quarterly, 50*(3), 367–403.

Andersson, L. M., & Pearson, C. M. (1999). Tit for tat? The spiraling effect of workplace incivility. *Academy of Management Review, 24,* 452–471.

Andrews, L. W. (2004). Hard-Core Offenders. HR Magazine, 49 (12), 45–55.

Aquino, K., & Douglas, S. (2003). Identity threat and antisocial behavior in organizations: The moderating effects of individual differences, aggressive modeling, and hierarchical status. *Organizational Behavior and Human Decision Processes, 90*(1), 195–208.

Aquino, K., Galperin, B. L., & Bennett, R. J. (2004). Social status and aggressiveness as moderators of the relationship between interactional justice and workplace deviance. *Journal of Applied Social Psychology, 34*(5), 1001–1029.

Ashforth, B. E. (1989). The experience of powerlessness in organizations. *Organizational Behavior and Human Decision Processes, 43,* 207–242.

Ashforth, B. E. (1994). Petty tyranny in organizations. *Human Relations, 47,* 755–778.

Bakker, A. B., & Schaufeli, W. B. (2000). Burnout contagion processes among teachers. *Journal of Applied Social Psychology, 30,* 2289–2308.

Bandura, A. (1986). *Social foundations of thought and action: A social cognitive theory.* Englewood Cliffs, NJ: Prentice-Hall.

Bandura, A., Ross, D., & Ross, S. A. (1963). Imitation of film-mediated aggressive models. *Journal of Abnormal & Social Psychology, 66*(1), 3–11.

Barrick, M. R., Stewart, G. L., Neubert, M. J., & Mount, M. K. (1998). Relating member ability and personality to work-team processes and team effectiveness. *Journal of Applied Psychology, 83*(3), 377–391.

Barsade, S. G. (2002). The ripple effect: Emotional contagion and its influence on group behavior. *Administrative Science Quarterly, 47,* 644–675.

Bartel, C. A., & Saavedra, R. (2000). The collective construction of workgroup moods. *Administrative Science Quarterly, 45,* 197–231.

Baumeister, R. F., Bratslavsky, E., Finkenauer, C., & Vohs, K. D. (2001). Bad is stronger than good. *Review of General Psychology, 5,* 323–370.

Baumeister, R. F., Dale, K., & Sommer, K. L. (1998). Freudian defense mechanisms and empirical findings in modern social psychology: Reaction formation, projection, displacement, undoing, isolation, sublimation, and denial. *Journal of Personality, 66,* 1081–1124.

Baumeister, R. F., Heatherton, T. F., & Tice, D. M. (1994). *Losing control: How and why people fail at self-regulation.* San Diego, CA: Academic Press.

Baumeister, R. F., & Leary, M. R. (1995). The need to belong – desire for interpersonal attachments as a fundamental human-motivation. *Psychological Bulletin, 117*(3), 497–529.

Bennett, R. J., & Robinson, S. L. (2000). Development of a measure of workplace deviance. *Journal of Applied Psychology, 85,* 349–360.

Bergman, T. J., & Volkema, R. J. (1989). Understanding and managing interpersonal conflict at work: Issues, interactive processes, and consequences. In: M. Rahim (Ed.), *Managing conflict: An interdisciplinary approach* (pp. 7–19). New York: Praeger.

Berkowitz, L. (1989). Frustration–aggression hypothesis: Examination and reformulation. *Psychological Bulletin, 106*, 59–73.

Bies, R. J., Tripp, T. M., & Kramer, R. M. (1997). At the breaking point: Cognitive and social dynamics of revenge in organizations. In: J. Greenberg & R. Giacalone (Eds), *Anti-social behavior in organizations* (pp. 18–36). Thousand Oaks, CA: Sage.

Bloom, M. (1999). The performance effects of pay dispersion on individuals and organizations. *Academy of Management Journal, 42*, 25–40.

Bommer, W. H., Miles, E. W., & Grover, S. L. (2003). Does one good turn deserve another? Coworker influences on employee citizenship. *Journal of Organizational Behavior, 24*, 181–196.

Brann, P., & Foddy, M. (1988). Trust and the consumption of a deteriorating resource. *Journal of Conflict Resolution, 31*, 615–630.

Brass, D. J., Butterfield, K. D., & Skaggs, B. C. (1998). Relationships and unethical behavior: A social network perspective. *Academy of Management Review, 23*(1), 14–31.

Brief, A. P. (1998). *Attitudes in and around organizations.* Thousand Oaks, CA: Sage.

Brown, A. D. (1997). Narcissism, identity, and legitimacy. *Academy of Management Review, 22*(3), 643–686.

Burt, R. S., & Knez, M. (1995). Kinds of 3rd-party effects on trust. *Rationality and Society, 7*(3), 255–292.

Butterfield, K. D., Trevino, L. K., & Ball, G. A. (1996). Punishment from the manager's perspective: A grounded investigation and inductive model. *Academy of Management Journal, 39*(6), 1479–1512.

Camacho, M. L., & Paulus, P. B. (1995). The role of social anxiousness in group brainstorming. *Journal of Personality and Social Psychology, 68*(6), 1071–1080.

Campion, M. A., Medsker, G. J., & Higgs, A. C. (1993). Relations between work group characteristics and effectiveness – implications for designing effective work groups. *Personnel Psychology, 46*(4), 823–850.

Chen, X. P., & Bachrach, D. G. (2003). Tolerance of free-riding: The effects of defection size, defection pattern, and social orientation in a repeated public goods dilemma. *Organizational Behavior and Human Decision Processes, 90*(1), 139–147.

Christophe, V., & Rime, B. (1997). Exposure to the social sharing of emotion: Emotional impact, listener responses and secondary social sharing. *European Journal of Social Psychology, 27*(1), 37–54.

Cohen, S. G., & Bailey, D. E. (1997). What makes teams work: Group effectiveness research from the shop floor to the executive suite. *Journal of Management, 23*(3), 239–290.

Coyne, J. C. (1976). Depression and response of others. *Journal of Abnormal Psychology, 85*(2), 186–193.

Cunningham, M. R., Barbee, A. P., & Drues, P. B. (1997). Social allergens and the reactions that they produce. In: R. M. Kowalski (Ed.), *Aversive interpersonal behaviors* (pp. 133–165). New York: Plenum Press.

Dawes, R. M., van de Kragt, A. J. C., & Orbell, J. M. (1990). Cooperation for the benefit of us – not me, or my conscience. In: J. Mansbridge (Ed.), *Beyond self-interest* (pp. 16–55). Chicago: University of Chicago Press.

Dentler, R. A., & Erikson, K. T. (1959). The function of deviance in groups. *Social Problems, 7*, 98–107.

Dimberg, U., & Ohman, A. (1996). Behold the wrath: Psychophysiological responses to facial stimuli. *Motivation and Emotion, 20*, 149–182.

Doerr, K. H., Mitchell, T. R., Schriesheim, C. A., Freed, T., & Zhou, X. H. (2002). Heterogeneity and variability in the context of flow lines. *Academy of Management Review*, *27*(4), 594–607.

Duffy, M. K., Ganster, D. C., & Pagon, M. (2002). Social undermining in the workplace. *Academy of Management Journal*, *45*(2), 331–351.

Dunlop, P. D., & Lee, K. (2004). Workplace deviance, organizational citizenship behavior, and business unit performance: The bad apples really do spoil the whole barrel. *Journal of Organizational Behavior*, *25*, 67–80.

Dutton, J. E., Dukerich, J. M., & Harquail, C. V. (1994). Organizational images and member identification. *Administrative Science Quarterly*, *39*(2), 239–263.

Eagle, J., & Newton, R. (1981). Scapegoating in small groups: An organizational approach. *Human Relations*, *34*, 283–301.

Edmondson, A. (1999). Psychological safety and learning behavior in work teams. *Administrative Science Quarterly*, *44*(2), 350–383.

Edmondson, A. C. (2002). The local and variegated nature of learning in organizations: A group-level perspective. *Organization Science*, *13*(2), 128–146.

Erez, A., & Judge, T. A. (2001). Relationship of core self-evaluations to goal setting, motivation, and performance. *Journal of Applied Psychology*, *86*(6), 1270–1279.

Festinger, L. (1950). Informal social communication. *Psychological Review*, *57*, 271–282.

Folger, R., & Skarlicki, D. P. (1998). A popcorn metaphor for workplace violence. In: R. W. Griffin, A. O'Leary-Kelly & J. Collins (Eds), *Dysfunctional behavior in organizations: Violent and deviant behavior*, (Vol. 23, pp. 43–81). Greenwich: JAI Press Monographs in organizational behavior and relations.

Furr, R. M., & Funder, D. C. (1998). A multimodal analysis of personal negativity. *Journal of Personality and Social Psychology*, *74*, 1580–1591.

George, J. M. (1990). Personality, affect and behavior in groups. *Journal of Applied Psychology*, *75*, 107–116.

George, J. M., & Brief, A. P. (1996). Motivational agendas in the workplace: The effects of feelings on focus of attention and work motivation. In: B. M. Staw & L. L. Cummings (Eds), *Research in Organizational Behavior* (Vol. 18, pp. 75–109). Greenwich, CT: JAI Press.

Gersick, C. J. G., Bartunek, J. M., & Dutton, J. E. (2000). Learning from academia: The importance of relationships in professional life. *Academy of Management Journal*, *43*(6), 1026–1044.

Gittell, J. H. (2003). A theory of relational coordination. In: K. S. Cameron, J. E. Dutton & R. E. Quinn (Eds), *Positive organizational scholarship: Foundations of a new discipline*. San Francisco, CA: Berrett-Koehler Publishing.

Goodman, P. S. (1977). Social comparison processes in organizations. In: B. M. Staw & G. R. Salancik (Eds), *New directions in organizational behavior* (pp. 97–132). Chicago: St. Clair Press.

Gottman, J. M. (1994). *Why marriages succeed or fail*. New York: Simon & Schuster.

Gottman, J. M., & Krokoff, L. J. (1989). Marital interaction and satisfaction: A longitudinal view. *Journal of Consulting and Clinical Psychology*, *57*, 47–52.

Grawitch, M. J., Munz, D. C., & Kramer, T. J. (2003). Effects of member mood states on creative performance in temporary workgroups. *Group Dynamics – Theory Research and Practice*, *7*(1), 41–54.

Green, S. G., & Mitchell, T. R. (1979). Attributional processes in leader–member interactions. *Organizational Behavior and Human Performance, 23*, 429–458.

Gully, S. M., Incalcaterra, K. A., Joshi, A., & Beaubien, J. M. (2002). A meta-analysis of team-efficacy, potency, and performance: Interdependence and level of analysis as moderators of observed relationships. *Journal of Applied Psychology, 87*(5), 819–832.

Hackman, J. R. (1976). Group influences on individuals. In: M. D. Dunnette (Ed.), *Handbook of industrial and organizational psychology* (pp. 1455–1552). Palo Alto, CA: Consulting Psychologists Press.

Hackman, J. R. (1987). The design of work teams. In: J. Lorsch (Ed.), *Handbook of organizational behavior* (pp. 315–342). Englewood Cliffs, NJ: Prentice-Hall.

Hackman, J. R. (2002). *Leading teams: Setting the stage for great performances.* Cambridge, MA: Harvard University Press.

Hardin, C. D., & Higgins, E. T. (1996). Shared reality: How social verification makes the subjective objective. In: R. M. Sorrentino & E. T. Higgins (Eds), *Handbook of motivation and cognition: The interpersonal context* (Vol. 3, pp. 28–84). New York: Guilford Press.

Hatfield, E., Cacioppo, J., & Rapson, R. L. (1994). *Emotional contagion.* New York: Cambridge University Press.

Haythorn, W. (1953). The influence of individual members on the characteristics of small groups. *Journal of Abnormal and Social Psychology, 48*(2), 276–284.

Heath, C., & Staudenmayer, N. (2000). Coordination neglect: How lay theories of organizing complicate coordination in organizations. In: B. M. Staw & R. I. Sutton (Eds.), *Research in Organizational Behavior* (Vol. 22, pp. 153–191). Greenwich, CT: JAI Press.

Helweg-Larsen, M., Sadeghian, P., & Webb, M. S. (2002). The stigma of being pessimistically biased. *Journal of Social and Clinical Psychology, 21*(1), 92–107.

Hochschild, A. R. (1983). *The managed heart.* Berkeley, CA: University of California Press.

Hogg, M. A. (2000). Self-categorization and subjective uncertainty resolutions: Cognitive and motivational facets of social identity and group membership. In: J. P. Forgas, K. D. Williams & L. Wheeler (Eds), *The social mind: Cognitive and motivational aspects of interpersonal behavior* (pp. 323–349). New York: Cambridge University Press.

Homans, G. C. (1950). *The human group.* New York: Harcourt, World, and Brace Inc.

Ilgen, D. R. (1999). Teams embedded in organizations: Some implications. *American Psychologist, 54*, 129–139.

Ilgen, D. R., Hollenbeck, J. R., Johnson, M., & Jundt, D. (2005). Teams in organizations: From input-process-output models to IMOI models. *Annual Review of Psychology, 56*, 517–543.

Isen, A. M. (2000). Positive affect and decision making. In: M. Lewis & J. M. Haviland-Jones (Eds.), *Handbook of emotions* (2nd ed., pp. 417–435). New York: Guilford Press.

Jackson, J. M., & Harkins, S. G. (1985). Equity in effort: An exploration of the social loafing effect. *Journal of Personality and Social Psychology, 49*, 1199–1206.

Jackson, C. L., & Lepine, J. A. (2003). Peer responses to a team's weakest link: A test and extension of Lepine and van Dyne's model. *Journal of Applied Psychology, 88*(3), 459–475.

Janis, I. (1982). *Groupthink* (2nd ed.). Boston: Houghton-Mifflin.

Janis, I. L., & Mann, L. (1977). *Decision making: A psychological analysis of conflict, choice, and commitment.* New York: The Free Press.

Jehn, K. A. (1995). A multi-method examination of the benefits and detriments of intragroup conflict. *Administrative Science Quarterly, 40*(2), 256–282.

Jones, G. R., & George, J. M. (1998). The experience and evolution of trust: Implications for cooperation and teamwork. *Academy of Management Review, 23*(3), 531–546.

Judge, T. A., Locke, E. A., Durham, C. C., & Kluger, A. N. (1998). Dispositional effects on job and life satisfaction: The role of core evaluations. *Journal of Applied Psychology, 83*(1), 17–34.

Judge, T. A., Van Vianen, A. E. M., & De Pater, I. E. (2004). Emotional stability, core self-evaluations, and job outcomes: A review of the evidence and an agenda for future research. *Human Performance, 17*(3), 325–346.

Kanter, R. M. (1972). *Commitment and community: Communes and Utopias in sociological perspective*. Cambridge, MA: Harvard University Press.

Karau, S. J., & Williams, K. D. (1993). Social loafing: A meta-analytic review and theoretical integration. *Journal of Personality and Social Psychology, 65*(4), 681–706.

Keyton, J. (1999). Analyzing interaction patterns in dysfunctional teams. *Small Group Research, 30*(4), 491–518.

Kidwell, R. E., & Bennett, N. (1993). Employee propensity to withhold effort – a conceptual model to intersect 3 avenues of research. *Academy of Management Review, 18*(3), 429–456.

Kirkman, B. L., & Rosen, B. (1999). Beyond self-management: Antecedents and consequences of team empowerment. *Academy of Management Journal, 42*(1), 58–74.

Kitts, J. A., Macy, M. W., & Flache, A. (1999). Structural learning: Attraction and conformity in task-oriented groups. *Computational & Mathematical Organization Theory, 5*(2), 129–145.

Kozlowski, S. W. L., & Bell, B. S. (2003). Work groups and teams in organizations. In: W. C. Borman, D. R. Ilgen & R. J. Klimoski (Eds), *Handbook of psychology: Industrial and organizational psychology*, (Vol. 12, pp. 333–375). London: Wiley.

Kramer, R. M. (2001). Organizational paranoia: Origins and dynamics. *Research in Organizational Behavior, 23*, 1–42.

Kramer, R. M., Brewer, M. B., & Hanna, B. A. (1996). Collective trust and collective action: The decision to trust as a social decision. In: R. M. Kramer & T. R. Tyler (Eds), *Trust in organizations: Frontiers of theory and research* (pp. 357–389). Thousand Oaks, CA: Sage.

Kramer, R. M., & Goldman, L. (1995). Helping the group or helping yourself? Social motives and group identity in resource dilemmas. In: D. A. Schroeder (Ed.), *Social dilemmas*. New York: Praeger.

Kramer, R. M., & Wei, J. C. (1999). Social uncertainty and the problem of trust in social groups: The social self in doubt. In: T. R. Tyler, R. M. Kramer & P. J. Oliver (Eds), *The psychology of the social self*. Mahwah, NJ: Erlbaum.

Kulik, C. T., & Ambrose, M. L. (1992). Personal and situational determinants of referent choice. *Academy of Management Review, 41*, 55–67.

Labianca, G., & Brass, D. J. (In Press). Extending the social ledger: Correlates and outcomes of negative relationships in workplace social networks. *Administrative Science Quarterly*.

Larsen, R. J., & Diener, E. (1992). Problems and promises with the circumplex model of emotion. *Review of Personality and Social Psychology, 13*, 25–59.

Laughlin, H. P. (1970). *The ego and its defenses*. New York: Appleton-Century-Crofts.

Liden, R. C., Wayne, S. J., Judge, T. A., Sparrowe, R. T., Kraimer, M. L., & Franz, T. M. (1999). Management of poor performance: A comparison of manager, group member, and group disciplinary decisions. *Journal of Applied Psychology, 84*(6), 835–850.

Lind, A. E., & Tyler, T. R. (1988). *The social psychology of procedural justice.* New York: Plenum Press.

Lepine, J. A., Hollenbeck, J. R., Ilgen, D. R., & Hedlund, J. (1997). Effects of individual differences on the performance of hierarchical decision-making teams: Much more than g. *Journal of Applied Psychology, 82*(5), 803–811.

Lepine, J. A., & Van Dyne, L. (2001). Peer responses to low performers: An attributional model of helping in the context of groups. *Academy of Management Review, 26*(1), 67–84.

Levenson, R. W., & Gottman, J. M. (1985). Physiological and affective predictors of change in relationship satisfaction. *Journal of Personality and Social Psychology, 45*, 587–597.

Lewicki, R. J., & Bunker, B. B. (1995). Trust in relationships: A model of trust development and decline. In: B. B. Bunker & J. Z. Rubin (Eds), *Conflict, cooperation, and justice.* San Francisco: Jossey-Bass.

Lewicka, M., Czapinski, J., & Peeters, G. (1992). Positive–negative asymmetry or 'When the heart needs a reason'. *European Journal of Social Psychology, 22*, 425–434.

Lubit, R. H. (2004). *Coping with toxic managers, subordinates, and other difficult people.* Upper Saddle River, NJ: Prentice-Hall.

Luminet, O., Bouts, P., Delie, F., Manstead, A. S. R., & Rime, B. (2000). Social sharing of emotion following exposure to a negatively valenced situation. *Cognition and Emotion, 14*(5), 661–688.

Lyons, R. F., Mickelson, K. D., Sullivan, M. J. L., & Coyne, J. C. (1998). Coping as a communal process. *Journal of Social and Personal Relationships, 15*(5), 579–605.

Marcus-Newhall, A., Pederson, W. C., Carlson, M., & Miller, N. (2000). Displaced aggression is alive and well: A meta-analytic review. *Journal of Personality and Social Psychology, 78*, 670–689.

Marques, J. M., Abrams, D., & Serodio, R. G. (2001). Being better by being right: Subjective group dynamics and derogation of in-group deviants when generic norms are undermined. *Journal of Personality and Social Psychology, 81*(3), 436–447.

McGrath, J. E. (1984). *Groups: Interaction and performance.* Englewood Cliffs, NJ: Prentice-Hall.

Meyer, J. D., Dayle, M., Meeham, M. E., & Harman, A. K. (1990). Toward a better specification of the mood-congruency effect in recall. *Journal of Experimental Psychology, 26*, 465–480.

Mitchell, T. R. (1997). Matching motivational strategies with organizational contexts. In: L. L. Cummings & B. M. Staw (Eds.), *Research in Organizational Behavior* (Vol. 19, pp. 57–149). Greenwich, CT: JAI Press.

Mitchell, T. R., Green, S. G., & Wood, R. E. (1981). An attributional model of leadership and the poor performing subordinate: Development and validation. In: L. L. Cummings & B. M. Staw (Eds.), *Research in Organizational Behavior* (Vol. 3, pp. 197–234). Greenwich, CT: JAI Press.

Mitchell, T. R., & Lee, T. W. (2001). The unfolding model of voluntary turnover and job embeddedness: Foundations for a comprehensive theory of attachment. In: B. M. Staw & R. I. Sutton (Eds.), *Research in Organizational Behavior* (Vol. 23, pp. 189–246). Greenwich, CT: JAI Press.

Mitchell, T. R., & O'Reilly, C. A. (1983). Managing poor performance and productivity in organizations. *Research in Personnel and Human Resources Management, 1*, 201–234.

Mitchell, T. R., & Wood, R. E. (1980). Supervisor's responses to subordinate poor performance: A test of an attributional model. *Organizational Behavior and Human Performance, 25*, 123–138.

Moorhead, G., Neck, C. P., & West, M. S. (1998). The tendency toward defective decision making within self-managing teams: The relevance of groupthink for the 21st century. *Organizational Behavior and Human Decision Processes, 73*(2–3), 327–351.

Morgeson, F. P., & Hofmann, D. A. (1999). The structure and function of collective constructs: Implications for multilevel research and theory development. *Academy of Management Review, 24*(2), 249–265.

Morrill, C. (1995). *The executive way: Conflict management in corporations.* Chicago: University of Chicago Press.

Morris, J. A., & Feldman, D. C. (1996). The dimensions, antecedents, and consequences of emotional labor. *Academy of Management Review, 21*, 986–1000.

Motowidlo, S. J., Borman, W. C., & Schmit, M. J. (1997). A theory of individual differences in task and contextual performance. *Human Performance, 10*, 71–83.

Moynihan, L. M., & Peterson, R. S. (2001). A contingent configuration approach to understanding the role of personality in organizational groups. In: B. M. Staw & R. I. Sutton (Eds.), *Research in Organizational Behavior* (Vol. 23, pp. 327–378). Greenwich, CT: JAI Press.

Muraven, M., & Baumeister, R. F. (2000). Self-regulation and depletion of limited resources: Does self-control resemble a muscle? *Psychological Bulletin, 126*(2), 247–259.

Naquin, C. E., & Tynan, R. O. (2003). The team halo effect: Why teams are not blamed for their failures. *Journal of Applied Psychology, 88*(2), 332–340.

Nemeth, C. J., & Kwan, J. L. (1987). Minority influence, divergent thinking and detection of correct solutions. *Journal of Applied Social Psychology, 17*(9), 788–799.

Nemeth, C. J., & Staw, B. M. (1989). The tradeoffs of social control and innovation within groups and organizations. In: L. Berkowitz (Ed.), *Advances in experimental social psychology,* (Vol. 22, pp. 175–210). New York: Academic Press.

Neuman, G. A., & Wright, J. (1999). Team effectiveness: Beyond skills and cognitive ability. *Journal of Applied Psychology, 84*(3), 376–389.

O'Leary-Kelly, A. M. (2005). A stranger among us: How do groups react to deviant members? Paper presented at AOM meetings in Honolulu, Hawaii.

Orcutt, J. D. (1973). Societal reaction and the response to deviation in small groups. *Social Forces, 52*, 259–267.

Ouwerkerk, J. W., Ellemers, N., & de Gilder, D. (1999). Social identification, affective commitment and individual effort on behalf of the group. In: N. Ellemers, R. Spears & B. J. Doosje (Eds), *Social identity: Context, commitment, and content* (pp. 184–204). Oxford: Blackwell.

Paulus, P. B. (2000). Groups, teams, and creativity: The creative potential of idea-generating groups. *Applied Psychology – An International Review, 49*(2), 237–262.

Pearson, C. M., Andersson, L. M., & Porath, C. L. (2000). Assessing and attacking workplace incivility. *Organizational Dynamics, 29*(2), 123–137.

Pearson, C. M., & Porath, C. L. (2005). On the nature, consequences and remedies of workplace incivility: No time for "nice"? Think again. *Academy of Management Executive, 19*(1), 7–18.

Pelled, L. H., & Xin, K. R. (1999). Down and out: An investigation of the relationship between mood and employee withdrawal behavior. *Journal of Management, 25*(6), 875–895.

Rein, G., McCraty, R., & Atkinson, M. (1995). The physiological and psychological effect of compassion and anger. *Journal of Advancement in Medicine, 8*(2), 87–105.

Rime, B., Finkenauer, C., Luminet, O., Zech, E., & Philippot, P. (1998). Social sharing of emotion: New evidence and new questions. In: W. Stroebe & M. Hewstone (Eds), *European Review of Social Psychology* (Vol. 9, pp. 145–189). Chichester, UK: Wiley.

Robbins, S. P. (1974). *Managing organizational conflict: A nontraditional approach.* Upper Saddle River, NJ: Prentice-Hall.

Robinson, S. L., & Bennett, R. J. (1995). A typology of deviant workplace behaviors: A multidimensional scaling study. *Academy of Management Journal, 38,* 555–572.

Robinson, S. L., & O'Leary-Kelly, A. M. (1998). Monkey see, monkey do: The influence of work groups on the antisocial behavior of employees. *Academy of Management Journal, 41*(6), 658–672.

Ross, L., Amabile, T. M., & Steinmetz, J. L. (1977). Social roles, social control, and biases on social-perception processes. *Journal of Personality and Social Psychology, 35,* 485–494.

Rozin, P., & Royzman, E. B. (2001). Negativity Bias, negativity dominance, and contagion. *Personality and Social Psychology Review, 5,* 296–320.

Sampson, E. E., & Brandon, A. C. (1964). The effect of role and opinion deviation on small group behavior. *Sociometry, 27,* 261–281.

Salancik, G. R., & Pfeffer, J. (1978). Social information-processing approach to job attitudes and task design. *Administrative Science Quarterly, 23*(2), 224–253.

Schachter, S. (1951). Deviation, rejection, and communication. *Journal of Abnormal and Social Psychology, 46,* 190–207.

Schroeder, D. A., Steel, J. E., Woodell, A. J., & Bembenek, A. F. (2003). Justice within social dilemmas. *Personality and Social Psychology Review, 7*(4), 374–387.

Shamir, B. (1990). Calculations, values, and identities: The sources of collectivistic work motivation. *Human Relations, 43,* 313–332.

Sherif, M. (1935). A study of some social factors in perception. *Archives of psychology, 27*(187), 1–60.

Skowronski, J. J., & Carlston, D. E. (1989). Negativity and extremity biases in impression formation – a review of explanations. *Psychological Bulletin, 105*(1), 131–142.

Smith, K. G., Smith, K. A., Olian, J. D., Sims, H. P., Jr., O'Bannon, D. P., & Skully, J. (1994). Top management team demography and process: The role of social integration and communication. *Administrative Science Quarterly, 39,* 412–438.

Staw, B. M. (1975). Attribution of causes of performance – general alternative interpretation of cross-sectional research on organizations. *Organizational Behavior and Human Performance, 13*(3), 414–432.

Staw, B. M., Sandelands, L. E., & Dutton, J. E. (1981). Threat-rigidity effects in organizational behavior: A multi-level analysis. *Administrative Science Quarterly, 26,* 501–524.

Steiner, I. D. (1972). *Group process and productivity.* New York: Academic Press.

Stewart, G. L., Manz, C. C., & Sims, H. P., Jr. (1999). *Team work and group dynamics.* New York: Wiley.

Taggar, S., & Neubert, M. (2004). The impact of poor performers on team outcomes: An empirical examination of attribution theory. *Personnel Psychology, 57*(4), 935–968.

Taylor, S. E. (1991). Asymmetrical effects of positive and negative events: The mobilization-minimization hypothesis. *Psychological Bulletin, 110,* 67–85.

Tett, R. P., & Burnett, D. D. (2003). A personality trait-based interactionist model of job performance. *Journal of Applied Psychology, 88*(3), 500–517.

Thayer, R. E. (1996). *The origin of everyday moods: Managing energy, tension, and stress.* New York: Oxford University Press.

Tice, D. M., Bratslavsky, E., & Baumeister, R. F. (2001). Emotional distress regulation takes precedence over impulse control: If you feel bad, do it!. *Journal of Personality and Social Psychology, 80*(1), 53–67.

Tjosvold, D. (1998). Co-operative and competitive approaches to conflict: Accomplishments and challenges. *Applied Psychology: An International Review, 47*, 285–342.

Totterdell, P., Kellett, S., Teuchmann, K., & Briner, R. B. (1998). Evidence of mood linkage in work groups. *Journal of Personality and Social Psychology, 74*(6), 1504–1515.

Tyler, K. (2004). One bad apple: Before the whole bunch spoils, train managers to deal with poor performers. *HR Magazine,* 49n(12), 77–86.

Tyler, T. R., & Blader, S. L. (2001). Identity and prosocial behavior in groups. *Group processes and intergroup relations, 4*(3), 207–226.

van Knippenberg, D. (2000). Group norms, prototypicality, and persuasion. In: D. J. Terry & M. A. Hogg (Eds), *Attitudes, behavior, and social context: The role of norms and group membership* (pp. 157–170). Mahwah, NJ: Lawrence Erlbaum.

van Knippenberg, D., & van Schie, E. C. M. (2000). Foci and correlates of organizational identification. *Journal of Occupational and Organizational Psychology, 73*(2), 137–147.

Wageman, R. (2000). The meaning of interdependence. In: M. E. Turner (Ed.), *Groups at work: Advances in theory and research.* Hillsdale, NJ: Erlbaum.

Warren, D. E. (2003). Constructive and destructive deviance in organizations. *Academy of Management Review, 28*(4), 622–632.

Weick, K. E. (1979). *The social psychology of organizing* (2nd ed.). Reading, MA: Addison-Wesley.

Weick, K. E. (1995). *Sensemaking in organizations.* Thousand Oaks, CA: Sage.

Weick, K. E., & Roberts, K. H. (1993). Collective mind and organizational reliability: The case of flight operations on an aircraft carrier deck. *Administrative Science Quarterly, 38*, 357–381.

Weiner, B. (1980). A cognitive (attribution)-emotion-action model of motivated behavior: An analysis of judgments of help-giving. *Journal of Personality and Social Psychology, 39*, 186–200.

Weiner, B. (1993). On sin versus sickness: A theory of perceived responsibility and social motivation. *American Psychologists, 48*(9), 957–965.

Weiner, B. (1995). *Judgments of responsibility: A foundation for a theory of social conduct.* New York: Guilford.

West, M. A. (2002). Sparkling fountains or stagnant ponds: An integrative model of creativity and innovation implementation in work groups. *Applied Psychology – An International Review, 51*(3), 355–387.

Wetlaufer, S. (1994). The team that wasn't. *Harvard Business Review, 72*(6), 22–38.

Worchel, S., Hardy, T. W., & Hurley, R. (1976). The effects of commercial interruption of violent and non-violent films on viewer's subsequent aggressiveness. *Journal of Experimental Social Psychology, 12*(2), 220–232.

TOWARD A SYSTEMS THEORY
OF MOTIVATED BEHAVIOR
IN WORK TEAMS

Gilad Chen and Ruth Kanfer

ABSTRACT

Work motivation theories and research have tended to focus either on individual motivation, ignoring contextual influences of team processes on individuals, or on team motivation, ignoring individual differences within the team. Redressing these limited, single-level views of motivation, we delineate a theoretical multilevel model of motivated behavior in teams. First, we conceptualize motivational processes at both the individual and team levels, highlighting the functional similarities in these processes across levels of analysis. We then delineate a set of theoretical propositions regarding the cross-level interplay between individual and team motivation, and antecedents and outcomes of individual and team motivation. Finally, we discuss the implications of our theoretical model for future research and managerial practices.

In developed countries, the shift from an industrial to a post-industrial economy has increased the use of work teams to accomplish a variety of organizational tasks, including management, special projects, production,

Research in Organizational Behavior: An Annual Series of Analytical Essays and Critical Reviews
Research in Organizational Behavior, Volume 27, 223–267
Copyright © 2006 by Elsevier Ltd.
All rights of reproduction in any form reserved
ISSN: 0191-3085/doi:10.1016/S0191-3085(06)27006-0

and service (Sundstrom, 1999). Cohen and Bailey (1997), for example, es-
timate that over 80 percent of organizations worldwide currently utilize some
form of work teams, broadly defined as "a distinguishable set of two or more
people who interact, dynamically, interdependently, and adaptively toward a
common and valued goal/objective/mission, who have each been assigned
specific roles or functions to perform, and who have a limited life-span of
membership" (Salas, Dickinson, Converse, & Tannenbaum, 1992, p. 4).[1]

The trend toward team-based work has, in turn, generated a plethora of
new questions and challenges for work motivation researchers, and has
also prompted a host of new management issues. From a theoretical perspective, relatively little is known about the determinants, mechanisms, and
consequences of team-level motivation processes. For example, although
the importance of leadership, cohesion, and communication for collective
behavior and performance is well-known (e.g., Chen & Bliese, 2002; Gully,
Devine, & Whitney, 1995; Hoffman & Jones, 2005; Marks, Mathieu, &
Zaccaro, 2001), we know much less about specific team-level and individual-
level motivational processes that are affected by these factors. From a
practical perspective, understanding how team and individual motivation
processes interact has important implications for how best to lead and
manage teams and the individuals that comprise them. Accordingly, the
primary purpose of this chapter is to address this gap in the work motivation literature and to consider the implications of a multilevel systems
approach for leadership, human resource management, and work design.

Although organizational scholars have long recognized the importance of
teams (as one element of work design) and the socio-technical context for
understanding work motivation (see, e.g., Lewin, 1951; Parker & Wall,
2001), surprisingly few contemporary work motivation theories directly address the dynamic and reciprocal influences of the individual-team level
interface. Dominant theories of work motivation, such as expectancy
and goal setting theories, typically assume that team-level processes affect
individual-level motivation indirectly, through their effects on individual-
level attitudinal and affective determinants of goal choice, goal commitment, and/or goal striving (cf. Kanfer, 1990). Some social-psychological
theories, such as groupthink (Janis, 1972), propose that team-level processes
affect both individual- and team-level motivation through their effects on
specific team-level variables, such as group cohesion and group norms. Still
other group-oriented theories, such as group information processing (e.g.,
Hinsz, Tindale, & Vollrath, 1997), focus primarily on the influence of team-
level constructs and processes, and largely neglect the impact of individual
differences among team members in affect, cognitions, and behaviors on

collective actions. These various perspectives, with their exclusive and separate emphases on different aspects of the individual, team, and the individual-team interface, have led Kozlowski and Bell (2003) to conclude that, "relatively little work has directly considered the issue of motivation in teams … [and] there are no well-developed theories that explicitly incorporate the team level (p. 360)."

Following recent advances in the multilevel literature (e.g., Chan, 1998; Chen, Bliese, & Mathieu, 2005a; Chen, Mathieu, & Bliese, 2004; Kozlowski & Klein, 2000; Morgeson & Hofmann, 1999), we propose three requirements for developing a true multilevel conceptualization of motivated behavior in teams. First, it is important to identify parallel, or functionally similar, constructs and relationships that underlie motivation processes at both the individual and team levels. Identifying parallelism in the content and function of the motivation process across levels can help generalize motivation theory from one level to another, as well as provide a basis for explicitly comparing similarities and differences in the determinants and outcomes of motivation across levels. Second, we need to consider cross-level influences between individual and team motivation. In particular, we need to consider both *top-down effects* of team characteristics and processes on individual cognition and behavior as well as *bottom-up effects* of individual cognition and behavior on team processes. Finally, we need to examine antecedents and outcomes of motivation at both the individual and team levels. Indeed, it is possible that unique and complimentary means are required to promote individual and team motivation (e.g., Chen & Bliese, 2002; Chen, Kirkman, Kanfer, Allen, & Rosen, in press), and that considering both individual and team motivation would help to better explain differences in individual and team performance outcomes. Thus, a multilevel approach would advance our understanding of the interplay between team and individual motivation, resulting in better explanation of both team member and team effectiveness.

Accordingly, in this chapter we build upon prior findings and emerging theoretical perspectives to develop a broad, *multilevel* formulation of work motivation that takes into account the dynamic, mutual influences of the individual and the team context on individual and team motivation and motivation outcomes. The model we delineate considers motivational processes that: (a) occur simultaneously at the individual and team levels (i.e., *multilevel processes*), and which involve parallel direct and indirect relationships constituting individual and team motivation, as well as (b) transverse between the individual and team levels (i.e., *cross-level processes*), and which include top-down contextual influences of team motivation on

individual motivation and bottom-up emergent effects of individual motivation on team motivation. Specifically, we seek to extend past work by
mapping the interconnections between individual and team motivation
processes over the course of naturally occurring performance episodes. Although we recognize that factors other than motivation (e.g., members'
ability, situational constraints) also contribute to individual and team
effectiveness, our focus in this chapter is primarily on the interplay
between individual and team motivation, and on the multilevel motivational
processes that can explain performance in and of teams.

The organization of this chapter, and the associated development of our
systems model of work motivation, follows what Stokes (1989) refers to as a
use-inspired research approach. Accordingly, we begin by posing two closely
related scientific problems of practical value – namely, how to understand
and predict: (1) collective motivation and its outcomes, and (2) individual
motivation and its outcomes in the context of teams. We address these open-
ended questions by focusing on three critical issues, organized into five
main sections. The first issue, addressed in the first section, deals with the
problem of specifying a tractable conceptualization of team-level, collective
motivation processes. Despite extensive theory and research on motives for
group action and process-oriented models of team-level motivation (e.g.,
Hackman, 1987; Marks et al., 2001), we still know little about the content,
meaning, and processes involved in team-level motivation. Following a brief
review of relevant individual- and team-level research, we propose parallel
individual- and team-level process models based on evidence that supports
the notions of isomorphism and homology (i.e., similarity or parallels)
between individual- and team-level motivational constructs and processes.

Having tentatively identified basic individual- and team-level mechanisms,
the next two sections (sections two and three) address the second problem
confronting the development of a systems or multilevel motivation model –
namely, how best to delineate the interconnections between individual- and
team-level motivational processes. The key questions we address in the second section include: (1) what makes an individual's motivation in the team
context different from motivation in the individualistic context; and (2) how
do individual differences in team member motivation and the social context
affect team motivation? Again, although there is some evidence showing
cross-level influences on motivation processes and outcomes, much of this
research appears in disparate literatures. What is needed is an organizing
heuristic for delineating the possible structure of cross-level relations. Toward
this objective, in the third section we provide the conceptual foundation for
proposed cross-level influences from general systems theories. Specifically, we

introduce key features of the general systems paradigm that have import for the architecture of individual–team interconnections by considering examples of how the paradigm has been used in the biological sciences to understand object recognition and group activities, such as ant raids, termite nest building, and locomotion in schools of fish.

After considering the key components of individual and team motivation, and the unique aspects and complexities involved in their interconnectedness, in the fourth section we delineate an explicit multilevel model of motivation in and of teams. Specifically, we propose a set of cross-level pathways and discuss their expected effects on individual- and team-level work motivation processes and outcomes. The fifth and final section then focuses on the potential advantages and disadvantages of our conceptualization for science and practice; that is, addressing the classic "so what" question. In this section we discuss implications of the proposed model for research and practice from three perspectives. First, we discuss implications of the model for predicting the impact of common antecedent inputs, such as leadership, staffing, and work design. Second, we use the proposed framework to identify salient levers through which managers can enhance individual and team motivation. Finally, we use the model to develop a forward-looking research agenda for the study of work motivation in and of teams.

TOWARD A PROCESS MODEL OF MOTIVATION *IN* AND *OF* TEAMS

The popular literature is replete with stories about the importance of team-level motivation – that is, team success attributable to the motivation of the collective rather than to each team member (see, e.g., Hackman, 2002). In many stories, particularly stories associated with positive team outcomes, coaches, leaders, and team members describe a motivational process in which the team espouses a lofty performance goal (e.g., winning the division playoff), and collectively sets about accomplishing the goal (e.g., tireless practice of offensive plays). Although intuitively appealing, such anecdotal stories raise a fundamental and as yet unanswered question about team-level motivation – namely, whether basic motivation processes, traditionally examined at the individual level, might apply to collective social systems, and in particular teams. In other words, what are the processes and mechanisms by which teams are motivated to perform? Before considering how motivation operates at the team level, we first briefly summarize the evidence on how work motivation processes operate at the individual level.

Individual-Level Motivation Processes

Over 80 years of research on the topic of employee work motivation has yielded substantial progress in the identification of major motivation constructs and the processes by which they affect job attitudes, behaviors, and performance (see, e.g., Campbell & Pritchard, 1976; Katzell & Austin, 1992; Staw, 1984). Although many diverse theories of work motivation have been promulgated, most current approaches depict work motivation as a multifaceted, intra-psychic process that governs the direction, intensity, and persistence of attention, energy (or effort), and behavior (Kanfer, 1990). In this perspective, perceptions of the environment, motives, attitudes, cognitions, and affective states are posited to contribute to motivation through their influences on both what an individual chooses to do (i.e., goal choice) and the strategies by which the individual seeks to accomplish cognized goals (i.e., goal striving). The relative influence of these factors on goal choice and goal striving represents the major distinction among extant theories of motivation, and has long served to organize motivational formulations into groupings that place greater emphasis on either the person (e.g., expectancy theories) or the situation (e.g., job design, behavioral theories) (see for reviews Ambrose & Kulik, 1999; Kanfer, 1990, 1992; Latham & Pinder, 2005; Mitchell, 1997).

The conceptualization of human motivation as comprised of two distinct, but inter-related systems represents one of the most important theoretical advances in the field during the late 20th century (cf. Latham & Pinder, 2005). In the organizational sciences, the distinction between these portions of the motivational system has been frequently described in terms of goal choice and goal striving (Kanfer & Ackerman, 1989; Kanfer & Kanfer, 1991). In the goal choice portion of the motivational system, individuals engage in two distinct, but related types of actions; namely, deliberative activities undertaken for the purpose of evaluating and selecting among goal options, and planning activities undertaken for the purpose of providing a template or model by which to accomplish chosen goals (Locke & Latham, 1990). That is, individuals consider which goal to select and how the goal will be accomplished. For the remainder of this chapter, we use to the term *goal generation*, rather than goal choice, to provide a more complete depiction of the constituent elements (e.g., goal choice, strategy formulation, and planning) that comprise the "pre-action" phases of motivational processing (cf. Gollwitzer, 1990).

In the *goal striving*, or self-regulatory/action portion of the motivational system, an individual's goal and strategies for accomplishing the goal set the stage for cognitive and affective activities that support behaviors leading to goal attainment (Kanfer & Erez, 1983). In the work setting, for example, goal generation processes may lead a sales associate to commit to a sales goal of $1 million dollars total over a 12-month period, as well as a set of specific strategies and plans for achieving this goal. Goal striving, in turn, pertains to the ongoing self processes by which the salesperson regulates her affect, cognitions, actions, and the environment for the purpose of accomplishing this goal by the end of the 12-month period.

In theories of individual motivation, goal generation and goal striving processes have long been assumed to be closely related, such that goal generation sets the stage and affects the initiation, direction, intensity, and persistence of goal striving. Conversely, obstacles in goal accomplishment during goal striving may influence goal commitment and subsequent goal generation. There is a voluminous body of research on the determinants and consequences of goal generation and goal striving, as well as their interrelations (see, for example, Carver & Scheier, 1981; Locke & Latham, 1990; Naylor, Pritchard, & Ilgen, 1980). For example, research on the cognitive architecture by which individuals accomplish complex, long-term goals, such as obtaining a medical degree or becoming a chief financial officer, indicates a hierarchical organization of goals such that broad goals condition the content and range of specific goal choices that the individual faces in daily work (Austin & Vancouver, 1996). Individuals who establish a goal of creating a new product may generate a host of subordinate task and social goals and plans, such as gathering materials and enlisting the aid of others, that are perceived to be necessary for goal accomplishment. Obstacles to the attainment of subordinate goals that cannot be overcome through greater allocations of effort may, in turn, instigate revision or abandonment of broad goals. That is, what and how individuals choose to do in their work (i.e., goal generation) helps to guide, direct, and sustain their actual effort on work tasks (i.e., goal striving), which in turn may lead them to alter their chosen goals, or to generate alternative goals and courses of actions altogether.

A second line of research that demonstrates the closely related nature of goal generation and goal striving processes stems from social-cognitive and goal theorizing by Bandura (1986, 1997), Dweck (1986), Higgins (1997) and others (e.g., Thomas & Velthouse, 1990). In contrast to cybernetic approaches that emphasize feedback functions, these approaches focus on the critical influence of *proximal motivational states*, such as task self-efficacy, goal orientation, sense of empowerment, and regulatory focus on both goal generation and striving. Specifically, these formulations suggest that a host of environmental variables as well as stable individual differences in cognitive and non-ability traits influence these proximal motivational states. These states, in turn, are posited to affect both the goal generation process and the differential use of self-regulatory strategies during the goal striving process. In the organizational behavior domain, research findings by VandeWalle, Cron, and Slocum (2001) on goal orientation, for example, show that individuals with a learning goal orientation employ different goal striving strategies and modify goals in response to performance feedback differently than individuals with a performance goal orientation. Likewise, self-efficacy has been shown to be positively associated with choice of more difficult goals and the allocation of greater effort towards accomplishing one's goals, as well as to mediate the influence of ability and non-ability traits on such outcomes (e.g., Chen, Gully, Whiteman, & Kilcullen, 2000; also see for a review Bandura, 1997).

In summary, modern individual-level theories of work motivation posit a temporal ordering of micro-analytic processes organized around goal generation and goal striving. Empirical findings across a range of theoretical perspectives provide convergent support for this representation of motivational processing at the individual level of analysis. Findings associated with social-cognitive and goal theories also provide broad support for the notion that proximal motivational states are an important conditioning influence on motivational processing. In the context of building a team-level model of motivation processing, motivational findings at the individual level suggest that two interrelated motivational systems may be involved; namely, team processes directed toward generation and commitment to a collective goal, and team processes directed toward collective actions that support accomplishment of the team goal. Consistent with recent goal and cybernetic theories and research we further expect that: (a) proximal motivational states influence the operation of these motivational subsystems, and (b) goal generation and goal striving to be linked through a hierarchical and recursive structure. As such, we anticipate team-level motivation to be affected by emergent motivational states as well as positive and negative feedback associated with individual and collective outcomes.

Team-Level Motivation Processes

A fundamental question for understanding motivation of teams is whether the goal generation and goal striving subsystems traditionally studied at the individual level have similar meaning and provide a good representation of motivational processes at the team level. Over the past two decades, a growing body of theory and research has emerged to suggest that team-level motivational phenomena may indeed be understood by generalizing individual-level theories through the use of isomorphic analogues of basic motivation constructs.

Team-Level Goal Generation and Goal Striving Processes

Comparable to individuals, many work teams also generate task goals and work towards accomplishing their goals. At the team level, however, the identification of the operational goals and the processes by which the team accomplishes those goals typically occurs through the collective and coordinated actions of team members. Retail store sales teams, hospital in-service teams, and marketing teams, to name just a few, often engage in multiparty deliberations to establish team-level goals and strategies, and then work in a coordinated manner with respect to the direction and intensity of effort in order to accomplish their goals. Similarly, action teams (e.g., flight, search and rescue, or combat teams) in military settings often generate goals and plans during pre-mission briefings, and then collectively strive to accomplish team goals during the mission. Indeed, research on goal setting has shown that goal-related processes, such as goal setting, task strategy selection, and effort allocations for goal accomplishment are very similar at the individual and team levels (see Locke & Latham, 1990). In one study (Weingart, 1992), groups who were assigned a difficult performance goal outperformed those assigned an easy performance goal, at least partially because they exerted a higher level of collective effort directed at accomplishing their goal. Moreover, a meta-analysis study by O'Leary-Kelly, Martocchio, and Frink (1994) suggests that the effect of group goals on group performance is positive and of similar magnitude to that obtained in individual-level studies. Taken together, these results suggest that team- and individual-level goal-related processes are similar, which lends support to the notion that motivation is a phenomenon that generalizes to teams.

Additional evidence for the similarity between individual- and team-level motivational processing stems from recent theorizing and research focused exclusively on team-level processes. Following a review of the team literature, Marks et al. (2001) suggested that team processes may be best described as interdependent team member activities that "direct, align, and monitor taskwork" (p. 357). This definition of processes complements individual-level motivation formulations that emphasize motivation as a force for the direction and regulation of behavior. Marks et al. (2001) further proposed that the various processes studied by team researchers could be classified into three broad clusters (transition, action, and interpersonal), two of which – transition and action – appear to correspond well to the individual-level goal generation and goal striving processes, respectively.

Specifically, Marks et al. (2001) suggested a functional correspondence between team-level transition processes and individual-level goal generation activities. Similar to individual-level activities involved in goal generation, team-level transition processes yield collective goals that are arrived at following deliberative activities that take into account collective desired outcomes, alternative outcomes, and some consideration of how goals may be accomplished. At the team level, such processes may include analysis of the team's mission, specifying and prioritizing goals, and formulating plans for accomplishing team goals. For instance, a combat flight team may need to collectively consider the location of enemy forces and their targets, and the terrain of alternative flight routes, when generating various plans for accomplishing their goals of hitting certain enemy targets. Comparable to individual-level goal generation, transition processes usually take place prior to or in-between task engagements (i.e., between performance episodes), when team members decide how and where to allocate their collective effort (Marks et al., 2001). Thus, there is a clear parallel between what Marks et al. (2001) refer to as team transition processes and the goal generation processes delineated in the individual-level work motivation. The functional similarity of these team- and individual-level processes provides initial conceptual support for the notion of generalizability of this aspect of the motivation system across levels of analysis.

Marks et al. (2001) distinguished further between team transition processes and team action processes, which include the monitoring of goal progress, monitoring of external conditions that could affect goal accomplishment, backing-up team members who need assistance, and coordination of interdependent tasks among members. We suggest that this set of team action processes are functionally similar to the goal striving process described in the work motivation literature, in that they involve the collective regulation of team activities during goal pursuit. Comparable to individual-level goal striving, team-level action processes typically occur during task engagement, when team members work towards accomplishing their project or mission objectives (Marks et al., 2001). For instance, combat flight teams likely engage in collective, team goal striving processes when executing their flight missions. Likewise, a project team of product developers may engage in team goal striving processes such as backing up members or coordination when briefing managers in their client organization regarding the advantages of the new web-application system they have developed for their clients.

In sum, we propose that motivation processes are functionally similar at the individual and team levels of analysis, in that they both involve *goal generation* (i.e., deciding where and via which strategies to allocate either individual or team effort) and *goal striving* (i.e., regulating and sustaining individual or team effort toward goal accomplishment). This is perhaps not surprising given that both individuals and teams can be conceptualized as goal-driven living systems. However, team motivation is built on shared or at least common interactions among team members. Specifically, goal generation can only be meaningful at the team level when team members come to consensus regarding what objectives the collective pursues, and, likewise, goal striving at the team level requires that team members coordinate their collective effort towards accomplishing common goals. Hence, building on definitions of individual motivation, we define team motivation as *the collective system by which team members coordinate the direction, intensity, and persistence of their efforts.*

Team-Level Motivational States

There is also a large body of research attempting to generalize individual motivational states to the team level. At the team-level, motivational states reflect a shared belief among members regarding various aspects of their capabilities and tasks. Such shared states emerge from both individual states and beliefs and from mutual interactions among members, and thus have been dubbed "team emergent states" (Marks et al., 2001). The two team emergent motivational states that have received the most attention in the literature are team (or collective) efficacy and team empowerment. Researchers have suggested that collective or team efficacy is a team-level analogue of self-efficacy, which captures the shared belief among members of a team that their team can accomplish certain tasks (Bandura, 1997). For instance, members of an R&D project team may share the belief they can collectively develop unique patents, or that they can collectively develop new drugs to battle cancer. Likewise, team empowerment has been defined as an isomorphic construct to individual empowerment, capturing the extent to which teams share the multidimensional belief they have the autonomy and capability to perform meaningful tasks that have the potential to make a difference in or beyond their organization (Kirkman & Rosen, 1999).

In addition to the correspondence in conceptual definitions of individual- and team-level motivational state constructs, a number of studies provide evidence for correspondence in the relations of these variables to performance and goal generation and goal striving processes at individual and team levels of analysis. In the domain of efficacy, for example, meta-analytic findings obtained by Stajkovic and Luthans (1998) on the self-efficacy – individual performance relation (estimated true score $r = 0.38$) and meta-analytic findings obtained by Gully, Incalcaterra, Joshi, and Beaubien (2002) on the team efficacy – team performance relation (estimated true score $r = 0.39$) show a positive relationship of similar magnitude. Moreover, a study by Chen et al. (2002) directly compared the individual- and team-level efficacy–performance relationship in two different samples of action teams (simulated flight teams and basketball teams), and found these relationships to be very similar across levels. Likewise, Chen et al. (in press) and Kirkman and Rosen (1999) found correspondence in empowerment – performance relations at the individual and team levels. Findings obtained by DeShon, Kozlowski, Schmidt, Milner, and Weichmann (2004) and Chen, Thomas, and Wallace (2005b) also show similar patterns of association among motivational states, goal generation, and goal striving at the individual and team levels of analysis. DeShon et al. found that, at both the individual and team levels, motivational states (e.g., efficacy beliefs) were positively related to performance through strategy and effort. Chen et al. found that, in addition to the correspondence in relations among efficacy beliefs, goal generation, and goal striving at the individual and team levels of analysis, motivational processes mediated the relationships between efficacy beliefs and task performance at both the individual and team levels.

Summary
The research summarized above provides initial empirical support for the basic "building blocks" of our proposed model, shown in Fig. 1. As shown in the figure, we propose that individual- and team-level motivation is similarly comprised of three key components – motivational states, goal generation, and goal striving – and that the relations among these system processes are similar across levels of analysis. Consistent with empirical findings to date, we also propose that motivational states, such as efficacy and empowerment, operate as a proximal influence on team-level motivational processes in a manner similar to that observed at the individual level.

Nonetheless, it is important to recognize that motivation, while functionally similar across levels, manifests differently at the individual and team levels. The individual-level variables (i.e., those at the lower portion of the model) and team-level variables (i.e., those at the upper portion of the model) differ in that the individual-level variables reflect individual differences among team members, whereas team-level variables reflect collective activities or beliefs that are shared among, or common to, all members. That is, individual variables focus on the individual "parts" within the team,

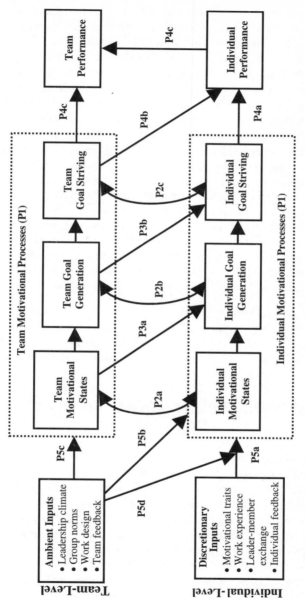

Fig. 1. An Integrative Theoretical Model of Individual and Team Motivation; *Note:* **P** = Proposition.

whereas team variables reflect the team as a "whole." For instance, individual goal generation reflects individual activities that support the generation of individual and team goals and plans, and individual goal striving reflect how hard each member of the team works towards accomplishing individual and team goals. In contrast, team goal generation and goal striving reflect the *collective* effort of the team directed at generating and executing goals. Motivated behavior at the team level emphasizes the co-ordination of effort among team members, whereas individual motivation emphasizes effort that may or may not be exerted in concert with other individuals. That is, there is a larger social component to team motivation, and a larger cognitive component to individual motivation. Indeed, teams must agree, at least to some extent, on their goals and task strategies, and then coordinate their effort to accomplish their collective goals. Thus, individual and team goal generation and goal striving are functionally similar, yet are manifested through mostly *cognitive*-behavioral processes at the individual level and mostly through *social*-behavioral processes at the team level (cf. Morgeson & Hofmann, 1999). Accordingly, we advance the following proposition regarding the similarity in the *functional content* of motivational processes at the individual and team levels.

Proposition 1. Individual motivation processes and team motivation processes are homologous (i.e., functionally similar), in that they are captured by similar individual- and team-level relationships among similar motivational states and goal generation and goal striving processes.

WHAT'S DIFFERENT ABOUT MOTIVATION IN TEAMS?

The preceding discussion posits an isomorphic parallel in the micro-analytic processes underlying individual- and team-level motivation, but does not address the interconnectedness *between* individual members and the team as a whole. Indeed, most organizational scholars and practitioners agree that it is precisely these interconnections that make motivation in teams so different from motivation in individualistic contexts (e.g., Kozlowski & Bell, 2003). It is also widely acknowledged that these interconnections are the most complex and least well understood aspects of motivation in teams. Nonetheless, it is relatively easy to illustrate the critical role that these cross-level linkages play in motivation and performance at both the individual and team levels. Post-hoc, motivational process explanations for the loss or win of a football game, for example, frequently focus on individual–team linkages, such as how the team's game plan (e.g., high scoring versus strong defense) influenced goal striving activities and persistence of individual team members (e.g., effort versus caution), how the performance goals of various team players (e.g., to play aggressively) affected team goals and strategies used to accomplish the goals (e.g., type of plays made during the game), or how the execution of team strategies (e.g., running) affected individual player performance (e.g., most valuable player). In contrast to motivation in the individualistic context, motivation in the team context is critically affected by the form and intensity of the psychological links that bind the individual and the collective.

It is exceedingly difficult, if not impossible, to address the question of what makes motivation different in teams without adopting a multilevel, systems perspective. Attempts to capture the cross-level influences of individuals and teams on motivation by extending individual-level theories of work motivation have been only partially successful. As Weick (1979) noted when he coined the term "double interact," there is a mutual dependence between individual members and the team as a whole such that individual behaviors influence collective processes, which in turn affects individual processes and behavior. More recently, DeShon et al. (2004, p. 1051) have made a similar argument, noting that "team performance contexts present individuals with the challenge of regulating their intentions and actions in ways that contribute to both individual and team effectiveness." That is, individual team members must balance between performing their own role within the team and helping the team accomplish its collective tasks. Accordingly, individuals must choose goals that are in concert with other member's goals, as well as with the team's collective goals. For instance, the goal of a software development team may be to write programming code that meets the functional purpose of the software, within a project timeline and budget. However, the personal goal of a member of the team for writing a specific portion of the code by a specific date must be determined jointly based on the coordination of personal and team goals dictated by the team's strategy (e.g., how writing is distributed across members, and the timing of each member's tasks throughout the project). That is, individual goals in the team must be aligned both *horizontally* (i.e., with other members' individual goals), and *vertically* (i.e., with the team's goals).

Not surprisingly, most individual-level theories of motivation – even those that include explicit social-situational determinants of work motivation – do little to help understand the influence of the individual on the team, or the emergent influences of the person–team transactions on the individual. In expectancy and goal setting theories, for example, motivation is studied in terms of its direct influence on individual performance, but not in terms of its effects on the setting in which performance takes place. As such, these theories predict that higher levels of effort lead to higher levels of job performance, but they do not take into account the more immediate influence of an individual's effort on the setting (team) in which performance takes place. That is, these motivation theories have largely considered individual-level criteria, but not criteria at higher levels of analysis, such as the individuals' direct or indirect influences on team-level outcomes. In work teams, a team member who demonstrates a low level of motivation may generate negative affective reactions among other team members (even unintentionally), and so decrease team-level motivation, lower morale, disrupt task performance, and alter leader behaviors (e.g., LePine & Van Dyne, 2001). Similarly, the development of strong affective bonds among team members over time may disrupt and/or augment individual-level motivation (e.g., Janis, 1972). That is, in a way similar to the function of the family unit in society, teams serve as both the source and recipient of motivated action.

As implied by the Salas et al.'s (1992) definition of work teams, such collectives represent unique social settings for action. In these interdependent contexts, created and sustained formally or informally within the larger organization, an individual's cognition, affect and emotion, and motivation serve as both determinants and consequences of motivational processes operative at the team level. Accordingly, we suggest that a multilevel study of motivation in team contexts may enrich extant work motivation approaches by identifying unique conditions and processes that cannot be detected when focusing solely on individual *or* team motivation (Ambrose & Kulik, 1999; Kozlowski & Bell, 2003). As suggested by Chen and Klimoski (2003), interdependent team contexts intensify the influence of situational variables, such as group norms and climate. Likewise, individual influences on collectives may also be more powerful in interdependent teams (e.g., see Chen, 2005). Thus, the specific content or manifestations of goal generation and striving, as well as their sources and outcomes, are likely to be quantitatively and qualitatively different in teams.

The reciprocal, multi-layered and proximate nature of influence between the team as a whole and its individual members creates potentially powerful micro-environments that may facilitate or hinder individual and/or team performance. Micro-environments that empower team members, for example, may entrain corresponding patterns of high individual and team-level motivation for goal accomplishment (Chen et al., in press; Kirkman & Rosen, 1999). In contrast, micro-environments that inhibit or threaten team members may create maladaptive patterns of individual- and/or team-level motivation. Delineating the critical transactions that promote or hinder the development of adaptive patterns of individual- and team-level motivation can only be accomplished by considering the structure of the interface between the individual and his/her micro-environment. The need for individual team members to regulate their effort toward accomplishing both individual and collective tasks clearly results in added complexity in understanding individual motivation in teams. In particular, due to the inherent and continuous need to balance between focusing on individual and team goals, there is likely to be strong coupling between individual and team motivation in team context, as the goals individuals generate and pursue are likely to be highly related to the goals teams collectively generate and pursue. Consequently, the influences of individual motivation on collective team motivation, and of collective team motivation on individual motivation, are likely to be quite pervasive.

TOWARD A MULTILEVEL PERSPECTIVE

A comprehensive conceptualization of motivation in teams thus requires a multilevel approach. Such a model offers several advantages, including (1) meaningful comparisons between individual and team motivational processes, (2) investigation of the generalizability of individual-level motivational constructs, principles and findings to the team level, and (3) identification of unique person–team transactions that may exert strong influence on performance outcomes (Chen et al., 2004, 2005a). Moreover, initial multilevel research focusing on motivational concepts such as efficacy beliefs, empowerment and goals indicates that factors motivating individual team members may not as strongly or directly motivate the team as a whole, and vice versa (e.g., Chen & Bliese, 2002; Chen et al., in press; Gibson, 2001).

A multilevel approach to motivation in teams is also concordant with broader general systems theorizing (Prigogine & Stengers, 1984) that emphasizes the patterns of exchange between the individual and the collective, as well as the relationships between the individual and the team with the contextual environment. Over the past two decades, a growing number of scientists have used the general systems paradigm to understand the organization and interconnectedness of components in a variety of biological and physical systems, ranging from interaction of neurons in the visual system to the self-organizing coordination of movement in schools of fish (see, e.g.,

Behrmann & Kimchi, 2003; Camazine et al., 2001; Clark, 1997; Kossman & Bullrich, 1997; Thelen, 1995). The emphasis in general systems approaches on understanding multilevel processes in the context of purposive outcomes offers a potentially powerful paradigm that goes beyond current approaches that investigate the determinants and consequences of one or more specific cross-level pathways (e.g., Chen & Klimoski, 2003; Seibert, Silver, & Randolph, 2004) without specifying system goals and processes. In the following sections, we consider features of general systems approaches to further guide our development of a multilevel model of motivation in teams.

Cross-Level Architecture in Biological Systems

Models that seek to explain complex human functions, such as vision, typically emphasize the architecture by which molecular components, such as individual neurons, and molar systems interact to organize, interpret, decide, and implement courses of action with respect to input from the external world. Such models are typically found in basic theory and research on human sensation and perception systems (e.g., hearing, vision, movement). In the area of object recognition, for example, recent theorizing suggests that individual neurons operate in unison to achieve object recognition (e.g., Behrmann & Kimchi, 2003). Each neuron has specific qualities or characteristics that affect their receptivity to being set off by other neurons, as well as qualities or characteristics that relate to the system as a whole. Dysfunction of particular neurons, for example, may or may not yield visual impairments (i.e., affect the system as a whole) depending on both external demands, the compensatory influence of other neurons, and the extent to which dysfunction in an individual neuron remains localized.

In addition, the system of object recognition is affected by external factors that place demands on the system as a whole, such as poor light. Differences in light conditions, or the amount of light that individuals are exposed to, are posited to affect particular neurons (e.g., changing their activation set points) as well as the system as a whole (e.g., activating different sets of neurons to fire in a particular sequence). As such, the molar system by which objects are recognized is affected by external factors that differentially energize individual neurons, the system-level activation of neural firing sequences, and the interdependent molecular activities among individual neurons that aggregate in complex ways to affect the molar visual system.

In an analogous fashion, individual team members function like individual neurons in the visual system. Each team member operates within a personal zone of plasticity that is conditioned by internal (individual) factors as well as by social system demands (i.e., the team). Team motivation, analogous to the molar vision system, is affected not only by the demands made by the environment, but also by the operation of the constituent elements of the system – i.e., its individual members. For example, just as one dysfunctional neuron may impair the operation of a set of neurons and so disrupt object recognition, so can one indifferent or disruptive team member interfere with the successful generation of team goals. Consider, for example, a Special Forces team that must generate specific team goals and an associated strategy for neutralizing the destructive potential of an enemy ship. If one member of the team strongly opposes on-board disabling of the ship (versus destroying the ship), goal generation processes at the team level may lead to a different tactical goal and strategy than if there is consensus for ship disablement among all team members. Similarly, changes in the emergent motivational state of the team brought about by external conditions (e.g., heightened team efficacy for undetected ship boarding, brought about by the acquisition of better equipment) may directly affect team-level goal generation processes, as well as individual members' goals.

The systems perspective as applied to object recognition suggests two features of cross-level influences for our multilevel model of motivation in teams. First, it seems reasonable to expect that the individual and the collective exert reciprocal influence on each other at corresponding points in the motivation system, just as individual neurons affect and are affected by the molar visual system. That is, positive motivational outcomes in teams require horizontal as well as vertical alignment of motivational states and goal generation and striving processes. Second, contextual factors or antecedents to motivational processing appear to exert selective influences on individual- and team-level motivational processes, such that some contextual factors may affect motivation of only some individuals, whereas other factors may influence the motivational state for the collective, as well as all individuals in the team.

Self-Organizing in Groups

Another important aspect of general systems theorizing pertains to the autonomous organization of activities within a system, or *self-organization*. In their review of the literature on self-organization, Camazine et al. (2001, p. 8) define self-organization as "the process in which the pattern at a global level of a system emerges solely from numerous interactions among lower-level components of a system." In the context of a group of individuals or organisms, self-organization refers to the processes by which individual members of the group form a mutual understanding by which to work together in the absence of explicit external orders (cf. Camazine et al., 2001). Among schools of fish, for example, the school's movement may be explained by the information sharing and coordination of movements that occur at the individual fish level. That is, by each fish responding to what their nearest neighbors are doing. The emergent molar pattern of locomotion, in turn, exerts influence on the subsequent activities of the individual fish in the school. Other examples of group activities that involve at least some degree of self-organization include termite mound building, ant raids, and orchestra performances.

From a multilevel motivation perspective, the principle of self-organization and emergent team processes closely resembles Weick's concept of a double interact, in that activities of the individual influence the collective, which in turn influence the individual. Consider, for example, a rowing team competing in a race. Although contextual factors (e.g., good weather, strong past record, clear contest structure) may promote strong individual self-efficacy and team efficacy and cohesive individual and team goal states (to win), the accomplishment of team goals (team goal striving) requires self-organizing processes to achieve rowing synchrony, coordinated team member actions, and monitoring of team-level progress to the finish line. Self-organizational failures at the team level can be expected to affect not just individual goal striving, but individual- and team-level performance. In other words, team motivational processes (e.g., team goal striving) are expected to exert immediate and feed-forward (top-down) influences on individual-level motivational processes and performance.

The Contextual Environment and Multilevel Motivational Antecedents

As we noted previously in our vision example, it is important to recognize that individual team members (or the "parts" analogues to individual neurons) and the team (or the "whole" analogue to the complete vision system) represent distinct elements within a multilevel system that are potentially differentially amenable to various external and internal influences. For instance, moving from a dark room to an outside setting in a bright sunny day would likely affect the complete visual system, given the system as a whole would need to adapt to the extreme change in lighting. On the other hand, particular chemical or hormonal changes in the blood system may affect particular parts of the visual system more than other. Likewise, some contextual factors may exert their strongest influence on collective team motivation, while other factors may primarily affect motivation of some but not all individual team members.

Hackman (1992) provides support for this notion of differential impact of contextual factors in his review of social psychological research on team influences. As Hackman (1992, p. 201) states, "One's group membership largely defines one's "social universe" ... [and] being a member of some groups ... restricts and specifies the domain of stimuli to which individuals are exposed." Hackman suggests that person and situation stimuli affect motivation by providing team members with informational, attitudinal, and behavioral cues (e.g., by informing members regarding appropriate and inappropriate attitudes and behaviors). To organize these diverse influences, he further posits a distinction between two types of stimuli: (a) *Ambient stimuli*, or team-oriented stimuli that pervade the team as a whole, and (b) *Discretionary stimuli*, or person-oriented stimuli directed or presented to specific team members, rather than the team as a whole. Examples of ambient stimuli include the socio-technical aspects of work, such as work design and group norms. Examples of discretionary stimuli include personalized feedback leaders may provide individual members, as well as individual differences in personality and motivational traits, activated by the environment, that predispose the individual to particular patterns of goal choice and striving behaviors. This distinction between ambient and discretionary stimuli provides a powerful framework for considering how person and situation influences affect multilevel motivational processes in and of teams. In particular, discretionary stimuli can be conceptualized as influences that primarily trigger individual-level actions and reactions (much the same way that genes predispose individuals to act and react in certain ways). In contrast, ambient stimuli are directed at affecting team-level action and reactions (similar to how environments predispose individuals within them to act and react in similar ways).

The conceptualization of external contextual influences on motivation in and of teams using Hackman's (1992) input classification scheme raises an important issue about specific pathways of antecedent influences. In particular, a number of presumably important contextual variables, such as leadership and feedback, reflect broad multidimensional constructs that likely encompass both ambient and discretionary inputs to the motivation system. Leadership climate, for example, may be best conceptualized as an *ambient* input that exerts influence on both team- and individual-level motivation, while leader–member exchange seems likely to be more accurately classified as a *discretionary* input that differentially affects different members of the team. With few exceptions (Chen & Bliese, 2002; Chen et al., 2005b, in press; DeShon et al., 2004; Hofmann, Morgeson, & Gerras, 2003), previous work has yet to delineate the dimensionality of key contextual influences on motivation in teams or to sufficiently consider plausible synergistically and complimentary ways in which ambient and discretionary inputs combine to affect to individual and team motivation. Such delineation is critical to our understanding of how simultaneously to facilitate individual and team motivation.

Summary

To account for motivation in and of teams, we must recognize individual-, team-level processes, and, perhaps most importantly, the multiple cross-level processes between individual and team processes. More specifically, we need to understand the coupling of individual- and team-level goal generation and goal striving processes. Just as we cannot fully understand vision without considering how individual neurons function individually and in concert in response to environmental stimuli, we also cannot fully appreciate team functioning without adopting a multilevel, systems approach that takes into account both the individual members and the social system or team they compose and operate within (cf. Katz & Kahn, 1978). Indeed, coordination of activities at the team level may facilitate or hinder the impact of individual level self-regulatory influences on performance. Likewise, effective or ineffective individual regulation processes can greatly affect team-level motivation and performance.

To this point we have provided discussion of the three major issues that confront our development of a full account of motivation in and of teams. Specifically, we reviewed conceptual and empirical evidence to support the identification of major system components of individual and team motivation and their isomorphic parallels. Next, we identified distinctive features associated with motivation in the team context and implications of general systems theorizing for specifying the nature of cross-level influences between the individual and the team as a whole. Finally, we considered contextual antecedents to individual and team motivation using Hackman's (1992) organizational scheme, and have begun to consider potential multilevel pathways of influence for multidimensional input factors, such as leadership. In the next section, we build upon this foundational work to describe, in greater detail, the basic tenets of our integrative multilevel model of motivation in and of teams.

AN INTEGRATIVE MULTILEVEL MODEL OF MOTIVATION IN TEAMS

As shown in Fig. 1, our proposed model builds upon contemporary views of individual-level motivation and assumes isomorphism in individual and team-level motivational processes. Consistent with a general systems perspective, however, we also delineate a set of theoretical propositions regarding the multilevel influence of the context in which the system operates and the interplay between individual and team motivation processes as they affect individual and team performance outcomes. Specific propositions derived from the model and supporting evidence from the organizational literature are described below.

Interplay between Individual and Team Motivational Constructs

Given that individual and team motivational processes can be presumed not to occur in isolation of each other, the next question to address is how they interact. To date, most multilevel theorizing on the topic has suggested that top-down effects (i.e., effects of team-level variables on individual-level variables) are more pervasive, powerful, and immediate than bottom-up effects (i.e., effects of individual-level variables on team-level variables) (see Kozlowski & Klein, 2000). In part, this asymmetry in the pattern of cross-level influences has been attributed to the fact cognitive, affective, and behavioral change occurs faster at the individual level than at higher (system) levels of analysis. From a general systems perspective, this asymmetry is also consistent with the notion that the molar system affects molecular components of which it is comprised more often than singular changes at the molecular level alter the molar system (e.g., the impact of a single dysfunctional neuron in object recognition may be compensated by neighboring neurons). That is, the influence of team goal generation and goal striving processes on individual-level motivation is more frequent and potent than the influence of individual motivation processes on team processes. DeNisi (2000, p. 138) has gone so far as to argue, "It is almost impossible to change the "behavior" of an organization, whereas it is relatively straight forward to change the behavior of an individual."

To reflect this asymmetry in cross-level effects, we propose below that the top-down effects of team variables on individual variables includes both direct effects between different components of team and individual motivation (e.g., between team motivational states and individual goal generation) and cross-level relationships between isomorphic components of individual and team motivation (e.g., between individual and team motivational states). In contrast, we propose that bottom-up effects of individual variables on team variables are subsumed primarily by cross-level relationships likely to occur between isomorphic components in the model. Nonetheless, it is important to note that there may be occasions when bottom-up effects exert a significant impact on team functioning. Indeed, a single team member who fails to accomplish his/her role in the team could adversely affect the likelihood that other team members would accomplish their respective individual goals, as well as the team's overall success. In highly specialized emergency response teams, for example, a single nurse's failure to self-regulate sufficient attention to the monitoring of a patient's blood pressure could lead to ineffective goal striving at the team level and subsequently poor individual and team performance should the patient die.

Cross-Level Relationships
Consistent with a general systems approach, our proposed model posits the co-occurrence of direct top-down effects and direct bottom-up effects of individuals and teams across all phases of motivational processing. As hypothesized below and shown in Fig. 1, these cross-level recursive effects are captured by cross-level relationships in motivational states, goal generation processes, and goal striving processes.

As Shamir (1990) suggests, individual-level motivational states should be positively related to team-level emergent motivational states. Consider, for example, the cross-level relationship involving self- and team efficacy beliefs. This cross-level relationship can be partially explained by a top-down process involving the influence of members' team efficacy beliefs on members' self-efficacy beliefs. Specifically, when members believe their team is composed of capable members who can collectively accomplish the team's mission, they are also likely to believe they can effectively perform their role in their team, given that their role is highly dependent on other team members' roles – a phenomenon Eden (2001) has dubbed means efficacy. For example, a leading prosecutor in a legal team is likely to be personally efficacious regarding cross-examining defense witnesses effectively if she shares the collective (team efficacy) belief that her team is collectively capable to investigate well that particular case, and is highly knowledgeable of broad array of previous relevant cases. Bottom-up processes can also account for the cross-level relationship between individual and team motivational states, given members who feel they can contribute effectively to their team by performing their role well (i.e., have high self-efficacy) also feel their team is more likely to perform better as a result (i.e., have high team efficacy). In fact, several studies have detected moderate to strong correlations between self- and collective efficacy beliefs (e.g., Chen & Bliese, 2002; Feltz & Lirgg, 1998; Jex & Bliese, 1999; Kark, Shamir, & Chen, 2003). Similarly, Chen et al. (in press) have found a positive relationship between individual and team empowerment in teams. Accordingly:

Proposition 2a. Individual motivational states positively relate to team motivational states.

We also propose that cross-level relationships occur between individual and team goal generation and goal striving processes. Such cross-level relationships capture a "double-interact" process (Weick, 1979) in which individual behavior influences the collective (team) context, which in turn affects individual behavior within the context. In advertising project teams, for example, the adoption of a difficult team goal to win an account by creating a new advertising campaign directly influences what goals and how much effort will be required of team members. Conversely, individual member activities that support the adoption of goals that demand low levels of individual effort directly affects the likelihood that the collective will adopt the new campaign team goal (as opposed to less effort-intensive goals such as modifying an old campaign). Also, individual-level behaviors involving goal generation and goal striving are likely to aggregate and form team-level goal generation and goal striving processes, respectively, given teams whose members work harder on developing and executing plans are more likely to exhibit effective team motivational processes (cf. Marks et al., 2001). Moreover, teams who engage in effective team goal generation and goal striving processes are likely to encourage and motivate their members to contribute to these processes (e.g., through processes such as modeling, persuasion, or vicarious experiences; cf. Bandura, 1997).

The general systems paradigm further suggests that successful systems require the content, or architecture, of individual and team motivation processes to be closely aligned. Thus, individual team members must align personal goals and self-regulatory activities with team goals and strategies for goal accomplishment. Pharmaceutical research teams, for example, are unlikely to be productive in formulating new drugs rapidly for market if team members seek different objectives with respect to performing research tasks (e.g., testing new research methods rather than testing drug properties) and/or perform multi-part drug tests in an uncoordinated fashion. Therefore, there is a need for individual and teams to work closely together when generating and striving towards goals and plans.

Preliminary evidence supporting these expectations is provided by Chen and Kanfer (2005), in a study of individual and team motivation processes during team performance of a computerized flight simulation task. Following a team planning session, individual team members were asked to report personal as well as their team's goal generation activities. Following team task performance, individuals were asked to report personal and team goal striving activities. Subject matter expert ratings were also obtained of team-level goal generation and goal striving processes. Results obtained showed a significant pattern of positive cross-level relationships for both individual and team goal generation activities and for individual and team goal striving activities, irrespective of whether team activities were assessed by self-report or subject matter experts. Thus:

Proposition 2b. Individual goal generation positively relates to team goal generation.

Proposition 2c. Individual goal striving positively relates to team goal striving.

Top-Down Effects
In addition to cross-level relationships, motivational processes in teams are likely to involve unique top-down effects of team motivational states on subsequent individual goal generation and of team goal generation on subsequent individual goal striving. These reflect in part the asymmetry between top-down and bottom-up effects discussed by multilevel theorists (Kozlowski & Klein, 2000). Specifically, given that teams' influences on individual members are more powerful than the effects of individual members of their teams, it is likely that team motivational states (e.g., team efficacy and team empowerment) would uniquely affect individual goal generation over and above individual motivational states, and that team goal generation would uniquely affect individual goal striving over and above individual goal generation. In contrast, the bottom-up effects (i.e., individual motivational states → team goal generation, and individual goal generation → team goal striving) are likely to unfold more slowly, and therefore are indirect and less powerful (Kozlowski & Klein, 2000).

The unique top-down team motivational states → individual goal generation effect is likely because the content (i.e., direction) and characteristics (e.g., difficulty) of the goals and plans individuals generate are likely dependent on whether they believe their team is capable of performing effectively (i.e., have high team efficacy) and, more broadly, whether they believe their team has the autonomy and capability to perform meaningful and influential tasks (i.e., have high team empowerment). For instance, members of a service team who believe in the team's collective capabilities to sell certain merchandise are more likely to work individually and collectively to generate effective quarterly sales goals and plans. More generally, empowered teams often face more complex tasks, which require that team members generate more challenging individual goals as means of meeting their challenging tasks. Of course, individuals are also more likely to generate effective goals when they have high levels of self-efficacy and individual sense of empowerment, but knowing that their team, not just them personally, is efficacious and empowered is also important determinant of individual activities contributing to developing team plans. In contrast, individuals who are personally efficacious and empowered are unlikely to exert as much effort on behalf of their team if they believe their team is incapable of handling challenging tasks (Shamir, 1990). Accordingly:

Proposition 3a. Team motivational states positively affect individual goal generation.

Finally, teams engaging in effective goal generation develop challenging goals and effective strategies that can facilitate the work of team members working on accomplishing these goals. Specifically, in combination with individual goal generation processes, team goal generation processes provide a more complete and appropriate "roadmap for action" that directs, energizes, and sustains members' individual efforts allocated toward individual goal accomplishment (i.e., individual goal striving processes) (cf. Locke & Latham, 1990; Weingart, 1992). Stated another way, individual effort directed at generating goals is insufficient – what is needed are *both* individual effort *and* collective team effort to generate an appropriate "architecture" of horizontally and vertically aligned goals and plans that enable more effective individual and team goal striving. Some support for these expectations was found in Chen and Kanfer's (2005) study who showed that team goal generation (through team goal striving) and individual goal generation uniquely and positively predicted individual goal striving. Hence:

Proposition 3b. Team goal generation positively affect individual goal striving.

Effects of Motivational Processes on Performance

There is voluminous evidence documenting the positive influence of motivation on performance – at both the individual and team levels (see, e.g.,

Kanfer, 1990; Marks et al., 2001; Mitchell, 1997). Results of several meta-analyses also show a strong, positive relationship between efficacy beliefs, goals and performance at individual and team levels (Gully et al., 2002; Locke & Latham, 1990; O'Leary-Kelly et al., 1994; Stajkovic & Luthans, 1998), and recent studies by Chen et al. (2005b, in press) and DeShon et al. (2004) have found that motivational states influence performance at least partially through motivational processes at both the individual and team levels of analysis.

Yet, there have been surprisingly few studies investigating possible *cross-level* effects involving individual and team motivation and performance. In particular, very little research in teams to date has considered how individual motivation might aggregate up to affect team performance, or how team motivation might affect individual performance in team settings. Our proposed model suggests that, in addition to the traditional, direct influence of individual and team motivation on their respective levels of performance, performance at both levels may also be importantly influenced by cross-level motivational processes. Thus, we suggest the following, more complete set of propositions regarding the proximal motivational determinants of individual and team performance:

Proposition 4a. Individual goal striving positively influences individual performance.

Proposition 4b. Team goal striving positively influences individual performance both directly and indirectly, through individual goal striving.

Proposition 4c. Team goal striving positively influences team performance both directly and indirectly, through individual performance.

Propositions 4b and 4c expand on current conceptualizations of motivational processing in two important ways. First, we posit that the way teams organize and coordinate member activities to accomplish team performance affects individual-level goal striving and performance. In serially coordinated elementary school teaching teams, for example, effective teaching performance requires close attention to what the previous day's teacher covered and accurate self-monitoring of one's own progress in covering assigned material in the allotted time. Moreover, when teaching objectives are met through "team teaching" methods in which multiple teachers instruct the class at the same time, individual goal striving and performance may be enhanced by team processes such as back-up behaviors and coordination. Likewise, in basketball teams, the direction and allocation of each individual member's effort (e.g., scoring) is largely affected by coordinated team effort (e.g., effectively coordinating screening and passing of the ball, so that the individual player could make the shot and score). Such cross-level effects, of team goal striving processes on individual performance, were in fact supported by results obtained by Chen and Kanfer's (2005) study of simulated flight teams.

Proposition 4c also posits two pathways of influence for the effects of team-level goal striving on team performance. Consistent with most team models, team-level motivation processes are posited to exert a direct effect on team performance, such as when a lack of coordination among ants retards the building of a mound. In addition, however, we suggest that the top-down effect of team-level goal striving on individual performance may exert an indirect effect on team performance. In performing flight teams, such as the Blue Angels, for example, team-level strategies for completing complex and dangerous maneuvers (e.g., follow your neighbor's wing) crucially determines each team member's performance. Even more important, the failure of any one team member to perform successfully has a direct and immediate (and potentially disastrous) impact on the team performance.

An alternative, more positive example of the effects of individual performance aggregating up to affect team-level performance may be provided by considering the assumption of most staffing theories (e.g., DeNisi, 2000; Ployhart & Schneider, 2002). A recent study by Chen (2005) on newcomer (individual) effectiveness in project teams found that newcomers who felt more empowered (i.e., were more motivated) performed better, and that newcomer performance positively contributed to subsequent team performance, even when controlling for prior team performance. Findings by Chen and Kanfer (2005) and Chen et al. (in press), in different contexts, provide additional and similar support for the cross-level relationship between individual and team performance, and suggest that such motivational pathways represent an important, but as yet somewhat neglected, determinant of team performance.

Antecedents of Motivational Processes

No account of motivation in and of teams can be considered complete without addressing the impact of the contextual environment on system components. Indeed, work motivation theory and research has long emphasized the roles that person characteristics (e.g., team member abilities and personality traits) and/or situational factors (e.g., work design) play in individual- and team-level motivation (see for reviews Chen et al., 2000; Feldman, 1984; Hackman, 1992; Hackman & Oldham, 1976; Kanfer &

Heggestad, 1997). However, much less is known about how these factors influence motivation that is conceptualized from a multilevel, systems perspective. In order to understand the impact of personal and contextual antecedents from this perspective, we make two assumptions. First, in accord with Marks et al. (2001), we assume that the multilevel motivational processes we have delineated are dynamic, cyclical, and unfold over time. Thus, as reflected in Fig. 1, the effects we hypothesize are expected to occur throughout the motivational process (i.e., prior to, during, or in-between task engagements).

Our second assumption pertains to how best to conceptualize the multitude of contextual features that impact motivation processes. As noted previously, modern theories of work motivation have typically emphasized the role of either individual-level factors (e.g., personality traits) or team-level factors (e.g., work design, group norms), but there have been few attempts to integrate person and situation perspectives. We assume that a multilevel, systems conceptualization of motivation requires consideration of both types of influences, and that such an interactionist approach can help account for additional variance in individual and team motivation. To enable such an approach, we propose a reorganization of person and situational influences according to their stimulus characteristics, not their impact. That is, following Hackman (1992), we organize contextual and personal factors into two types; namely, ambient (team-oriented) inputs and discretionary (person-oriented) inputs. Fig. 1 provides a partial listing of common and specific examples of ambient and discretionary inputs, and their proposed relations to individual- and team-level motivational processes.

In work settings, leadership arguably represents the most important of all contextual factors, which might affect individual and team motivation. Poor team performances are frequently attributed to leader deficiencies in creating a favorable climate for performance and/or providing insufficient direction or structure to team activities. Similarly, poor individual team member performances are also often attributed to poor leadership related to the way that the leader encourages and interacts with team members. Indeed, several scholars have noted the multitude of critical leadership functions in teams, including team design, staffing, and coaching (e.g., Hackman, 2002; Wageman, 2001; Zaccaro & Marks, 1999). Most researchers agree that leadership is more usefully construed as multidimensional construct, in which some dimensions represent ambient inputs and other dimensions represent discretionary inputs. Leadership behaviors and practices may be delineated into different types of ambient inputs directed toward the team as a whole that develop the leadership climate within the team (e.g., Chen & Bliese, 2002; Shamir, Zakay, Breinin, & Popper, 1998), group norms (Feldman, 1984), design characteristics of the team (Campion, Medsker, & Higgs, 1993; Campion, Papper, & Medsker, 1996), and team feedback. What is common to these kinds of inputs is that they involve social, informational, or task-related factors that have the potential to motivate the team as a whole – i.e., inputs that affect all team members rather than a specific individual or a few members of the team (Hackman, 1992).

For example, transformational leadership theory suggests that effective leaders motivate their group of followers by transforming the values and priorities of followers and motivating them to perform beyond their expectations (Bass, 1985). Indeed, research has shown that transformational leaders often achieve superior results by creating a shared sense of social identity within their group (e.g., Kark et al., 2003). Similarly, Feldman (1984) argues that group norms involve informal rules established by leaders and members of the group to regulate and regularize the behavior of all members belonging to the group. Feldman argues further that group norms are quite powerful in establishing a common code of conduct in groups (see also Hackman, 1992). In addition, work by Campion et al. (1993, 1996) suggests that work team design (e.g., level of interdependence among teammates, extent to which the team is provided with autonomy) helps differentiate between teams, even teams within the same organization, and that design characteristics of teams can motivate the team as a whole. Furthermore, Wageman (2001) has shown that effective design of teams can even facilitate leaders' influences on teams; specifically, leaders' coaching practices were found to be more successful when teams were designed more appropriately.

In contrast, leadership may also be manifested through discretionary inputs, which are directed at particular team members and thus are likely to affect specific individuals in the teams, but not necessarily the team as a whole. For instance, according to leader–member exchange theory (e.g., Dansereau, Graen, & Haga, 1975), leaders develop different relationships with different followers, and thus differentially affect members within their group. Likewise, performance feedback leaders may direct at a particular team member is likely to affect that particular member, but not other members in the team. Finally, leaders may also staff their teams with members who differ on various individual differences, such as motivational traits (Kanfer & Heggestad, 1997) and work experience (Tesluk & Jacobs, 1998). Such individual differences are also consistent with the notion of discretionary inputs, in that they pre-dispose individuals, but not teams, to behave in certain ways.

While it is also possible for ambient inputs to affect individuals in the team, and for discretionary inputs to affect the team as a whole, we argue that what is most important for understanding their effects on motivation in teams is their *relative influence* across levels. Specifically, given that ambient inputs are directed at the team as a whole, they are likely to more strongly affect the team, but yet to also have a (somewhat weaker) top-down effect on individuals within the team. Similarly, given that discretionary inputs are intended to most strongly affect individual team members, they are likely to influence the manner in which the individuals contribute to their team, and thus also have a weaker, indirect bottom-up effect on the team. Further, given that top-down effects tend to be stronger and more immediate than bottom-up effects (Kozlowski & Klein, 2000), we would expect that am bient inputs would incrementally influence individual motivational processes over and above discretionary inputs, but that discretionary inputs (when aggregated across team members) would not affect team motivational processes over and above ambient inputs. As such, leaders can utilize various ambient and discretionary inputs to differentially influence individual and team motivation.

Note that we generally expect the influences of these inputs on motivational processes to be positive, since our focus is on inputs that have high "motivating potential" (cf. Hackman & Oldham, 1976). However, we certainly recognize that various ambient and discretionary inputs can also carry negative consequences on teams. For instance, laizze-faire team leaders can create de-motivating (ambient) climate that adversely affects team motivation (Bass, 1985). This is particularly true in teams facing challenging and uncertain situations (e.g., military teams during combat, production teams in manufacturing organizations that face potential downsizing), where direction and support from leaders is especially critical.

Several studies provided initial support for the theoretical assertions above. For instance, a study by Feltz and Lirgg (1998) on colligate sports teams found that previous team performance (a form of ambient input) affected subsequent team efficacy more strongly than subsequent self-efficacy. In addition, studies dealing with feedback in teams (e.g., Barr & Conlon, 1994; Pritchard, Jones, Roth, Stuebing, & Ekeberg, 1988; Saavedra, Earley, & Van Dyne, 1993) suggest that feedback provided to the team as a whole (an ambient input) is more effective in promoting teamwork than discretionary individual feedback, but that both team and individual feedback contribute to individual motivation. Similarly, a study by Hofmann et al. (2003) showed that leadership climate (a team-level variable) and followers' perceptions of leader–member exchange (an individual-level variable) uniquely contributed to soldiers' motivation to behave safely at work. Further, Kark et al. (2003) have found that transformational leadership (an ambient input) positively predicted collective efficacy to a greater extent than it did self-efficacy. Likewise, a study by Chen and Bliese (2002) found that an ambient group-level input (leadership climate) predicted collective efficacy to a greater extent than it did self-efficacy, whereas several individual-level discretionary stimuli (work experience, role clarity, and psychological strain) predicted self-efficacy, but not collective efficacy. Finally, Chen et al. (in press) found that empowering leadership climate more strongly predicted team empowerment, whereas team members' individual perceptions of leader–member exchange more strongly predicted individual empowerment. Collectively, these studies and theoretical assertions provide support for the following set of propositions:

Proposition 5. The impact of discretionary inputs on motivational processes (relative to ambient inputs) is greater at the individual level than the team level; in contrast, the impact of ambient inputs on motivational processes (relative to discretionary inputs) is greater at the team level than the individual level.

Proposition 5a. Discretionary inputs directly and positively affect individual motivational processes, and indirectly affect team motivational processes through their effects on individual motivational processes.

Proposition 5b. Ambient inputs positively affect individual motivational processes both directly and through their effects on team motivational processes.

Proposition 5c. Ambient inputs positively affect team motivational processes both directly and through their effects on individual motivational processes.

In addition to their "main effects," ambient inputs may also interact with discretionary inputs to affect individual motivational processes. Work motivation theories highlight the importance of situational affordances, or the "motivational fit" between the person and his/her environment (Kanfer & Heggestad, 1997; Mitchell, 1997). That is, individuals who are pre-disposed to be motivated (e.g., have higher levels of achievement motivation) are unlikely to be motivated in situations that do not allow them to express their motivational tendencies. For instance, Hackman and Oldham's (1976) Job Characteristics Model asserts that employees with higher growth needs strength would react more positively to more complex and challenging jobs than those lower on growth needs strength. We submit that such person-by-situation interactions are particularly prevalent in team settings, where the environment (i.e., the team) can have powerful effects on individual team members.

From a motivational-fit perspective, the most likely nature of interaction between ambient and discretionary inputs will involve positive effects of ambient inputs on the positive discretionary inputs → individual motivational processes effects. For instance, as shown in Fig. 2, leadership climate (an ambient input) is likely to enhance the positive influence of need for achievement (a motivational trait, or a discretionary input) on individual motivational processes. This interaction suggests that a good fit between an individual predisposition to be motivated (i.e., need for achievement) and situational cues that support that predisposition (e.g., a motivating climate developed by the leader) would result in the highest possible motivation, whereas low levels of any input can lead to substantially lower motivation. Note that this kind of motivational-fit interaction can generalize to other discretionary inputs, beyond individual differences inputs. For instance, Hofmann et al. (2003) have found a very similar interaction effect involving leader–member exchange and leadership climate. In Hofmann et al.'s study, the positive effect of leader–member exchange on motivation to act safely increased as leadership safety climate increased. Thus, such

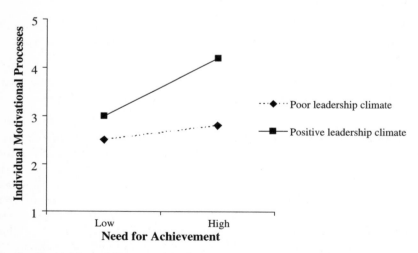

Fig. 2. Interaction of Team and Individual Predictors of Individual Motivational Processes.

person-by-situation (or ambient X discretionary inputs) interactions again reflect the powerful top-down effects of ambient stimuli on individual motivational processes in teams.

Proposition 5d. Ambient inputs moderate the effects of discretionary inputs on individual motivational processes, such that the effects of discretionary inputs on individual motivational processes become more positive as ambient inputs become more positive.

DISCUSSION

This chapter sets out the foundations and outline of a multilevel approach for studying motivational processes in teams. We suggest that this approach provides a more comprehensive account of the complex interplay between the individual and the team as a whole, the manner by which diverse context affects individual and team motivation processes, and the intertwined effects of these processes on individual and team performance. The overarching advantage of the multilevel approach over the more limiting single-level approach includes the ability to examine motivational processes *in and of* teams, as well as their antecedents and outcomes, in a more comprehensive and precise fashion. As such, studies following the new approach are likely to account for additional variance in both individual and team performance that would not otherwise be tapped by single-level studies, given they would consider unique cross-level (i.e., individual and team) effects on performance in and of teams. Moreover, the theoretical model we delineate can help inform organizations and managers about how to effectively motivate simultaneously individual team members and teams a whole.

Implications for Future Research

The integrative multilevel model of motivation delineated in this chapter yields three more immediate implications for the way we study motivation in modern work organizations, as well how motivational processes operate in the context of work teams. First, the proposed model is consistent with the vital need to better understand individual and team work behaviors over time (e.g., Ancona, Goodman, Lawrence, & Tushman, 2001; George & Jones, 2000; Harrison, Price, Gaven, & Florey, 2002; Kozlowski, Gully, Nason, & Smith, 1999). Although the temporal dimension has long been recognized in individual theories of motivation (see Kanfer, 1990) and group theories of performance (e.g., Gersick, 1988; Tuckman & Jensen, 1977), few studies have examined motivation from an integrated perspective. Our multilevel model suggests that one way to coordinate these perspectives is by conducting longitudinal studies on a time scale that allows us to account for individual and team phenomena, as well as unique cross-level phenomena and other changes in individual–team interconnectedness as they naturally unfold over time (e.g., Chen & Kanfer, 2005; Chen et al., 2005b). In particular, to fully capture the individual and team motivational processes that we have delineated, researchers should at a minimum measure goal generation processes prior to task engagement and measures of goal striving processes during or following task engagement. In addition, researchers may find that individual performance at Time 1 may serve as a discretionary input for team members performing at Time 2, and, likewise, team performance at Time 1 may serve as an ambient input for teams performing at Time 2. Studying motivational processes as they unfold over time and across multiple performance episodes can enrich our understanding of behavior in complex social systems such as organizational teams (Marks et al., 2001; Lindsley, Brass, & Thomas, 1995).

The second implication of our model for future research pertains to how we conceptualize relationships between the individual and the collective. In accord with general living systems approaches, we emphasize the operation of motivational processes in terms of the multiplicity of pathways (i.e., direct, indirect, and interactive bottom-up and top-down effects) by which individual team members and the collective are interconnected and influence individual and team effectiveness. As discussed, a number of potentially promising areas for future research may be derived from our adaptation of general systems perspectives, including for example, understanding the ambient antecedents that facilitate or hamper dominant top-down influences, the influence of team member diversity on goal generation effectiveness, and identification of potential natural substitutes or neutralizers (cf. Kerr & Jermier, 1978) of self-organizing processes during team goal striving.

A third fertile area for future research pertains to the boundary conditions that could affect the generalizability of our model, such as our implicit assumption that the proposed processes and relationships generalize across different types of teams and organizational contexts. Several authors have noted that team and leadership processes differ across different types of teams, such as action, management, production, project, and service teams (Sundstrom, 1999; Zaccaro & Marks, 1999). Whether or not the underlying motivational processes generalize across different teams remains an open question that deserves empirical investigation. While the theoretical processes we have delineated may generalize well, their manifestations and the relative importance of different motivational processes may vastly differ across different types of teams. For instance, in management teams, it is more difficult to distinguish between goal generation and goal striving processes, given these teams engage mostly in establishing *organizational* strategies and plans, as opposed to merely team goals and plans. In particular, top-management teams' main task involves setting the vision, direction, and objectives for the organization, the implementation of which is often left to a host of other teams within the organization. Goal striving activities of management teams may entail monitoring of how other teams (e.g., project and sales teams in high-tech firms) implement the organizational goals the management team has generated. Therefore, the extent to which members of top management teams engage in effective goal generation processes, rather than goal striving processes, is more likely to directly affect their performance, and the firm's performance.

In addition, while work design in most teams is common to all team members (Campion, et al. 1993, 1996), it is possible that in cross-functional project teams or in certain action/performing teams (e.g., surgical teams) work design vastly differs across members, and thus it reflects discretionary, as opposed to ambient input. For instance, job characteristics dimensions such as task significance are likely much higher for neurosurgeons than nurses who assist the surgeon during brain surgeries. Therefore, researchers should carefully choose the most relevant ambient and discretionary inputs in their particular study contexts. As a general guide, relative to discretionary inputs, ambient inputs are likely to have greater between-team variance and smaller within-team variance (as reflected by the intra-class correlation; cf. Chen et al., 2004). Furthermore, it is possible that explicit testing of propositions 5a–5d would reveal that different ambient and discretionary inputs would affect different components of the motivational process, and that only some, but not all discretionary and ambient inputs would interact to affect individual motivation. Testing such possibilities would no doubt result in greater generalizability and refinement of the multilevel theoretical model we proposed.

Finally, another important boundary condition for our model is the extent to which the team is actually interdependent. As suggested by Kozlowski and Bell (2003), different forms of interdependence in teams (e.g., task, reward, or goal interdependence; cf. Saavedra et al., 1993) can greatly affect the validity and impact of team-level phenomena. For instance, in Chen et al.'s (in press) study, the extent to which team empowerment related to team performance, and the relationship between team and individual performance, varied greatly depending on the extent to which team members had to work closely with each other to accomplish their team's task. In particular, the team-level and cross-level relationships involving empowerment and performance were significant and positive in highly interdependent teams, but were generally non-significant in low interdependent teams. Clearly, more research is needed to test these and other potential boundaries of our model.

Throughout this chapter, we have cited several studies that lend initial support to most of the propositions in our theoretical model. Obviously, however, the viability of the full model and its ability to complement and extend existing theories of leadership, work design, individual and team motivation remains an empirical question. Thus, studies to provide more complete tests of our theoretical propositions vis-à-vis other models and in various organizational settings are especially important at this stage.

Managerial Implications

Our explicit treatment of individual and team motivational processes as separate, yet inter-linked entities has important implications for managerial practices directed at facilitating effectiveness in teams. Perhaps the most important practical implication pertains to the relative efficacy of organizational interventions targeted at the team as a whole compared to individuals who comprise the team. Our model suggests that organizational interventions and managerial practices directed at teams as a whole (e.g., team re-design, improvement of leadership climate, development of a team performance feedback system) have a stronger initial influence on team motivation than on individual motivation. Over time, however, cross-level influences of team-level interventions on individual motivational mechanisms may operate to increment and sustain both team and individual motivation. Work design interventions, for example, may enhance team member motivation by promoting individual and team goal setting, increasing self- and team-regulatory activities, and/or enhancing self- and team efficacy.

In contrast, organizational interventions designed to enhance team motivation through individual motivational processes alone (e.g., selection of individuals with higher levels of motivational traits, developing better leader–member relationships, and providing employees with individual feedback) may result in more motivated individual team members but not necessarily more motivated teams. For instance, team leaders who develop high mutual trust with some team members, but low trust with others, may find that their team has a few motivated individuals, but that members in the team are unwilling to coordinate and cooperate with each other. Likewise, staffing a team with experienced members who are high on achievement motivation may not lead to improved individual or team motivation unless leaders develop a positive leadership climate that empowers the team to collectively self-manage their work, given such members expect (and rightfully so) to be empowered with high levels of authority and to perform meaningful work (cf. Chen et al., in press). Thus, in the worst case scenario, strategies which rely too much on managing the team via discretionary inputs, and not enough on ambient inputs, may even operate paradoxically by raising negative affect and reducing team motivation. Still, discretionary inputs (e.g., individual feedback) may work very effectively in some situations, such as handling a disruptive or a poorly performing member of a team (LePine & Van Dyne, 2001). Ideally, our model implies that managers should ensure that a good fit exists between ambient- and discretionary-oriented practices.

Consistent with extant models of individual motivation, our integrative model explicitly recognizes the dynamic nature of motivation. As such, another important practical implication of the theoretical model developed in this article is that the efficacy of a given intervention may depend on timing vis-à-vis the team's history. Managers should carefully consider when to target interventions to individual team members, and when to target them to the team as a whole. For instance, integrating our theoretical model with Kozlowski et al.'s (1999) theory of team compilation, we would expect that managerial practices utilizing discretionary input (e.g., developing good leader–member relationships, providing individual feedback) would be more critical during early stages of team development, when individuals learn to perform individual roles and thus focus on self-regulation more than team regulation. In contrast, managerial practices that use ambient inputs (e.g., helping the team process information inputs, providing team feedback) would be more beneficial during later stages of team development, when members are more concerned with the regulation of team goals and tasks. Thus, an important implication of our model is that managers must attend more closely to the type and functional purpose of various practices and interventions in order to manage individuals and teams more efficiently. Managers who focus their efforts mostly on motivating individuals or solely on motivating teams are unlikely to produce the best possible results with their teams.

CONCLUSION

Interdependent work teams are a ubiquitous feature of today's organizational landscape. Understanding motivation in these teams is not simply a matter of understanding the dynamics of individual motivation or of team motivation, but rather understanding the development, maintenance, and repair of multi-level motivational processes "in situ." Our model builds upon theories of individual and team motivation, as well as broad general systems and multi-level perspectives, to provide a preliminary model of motivation in the team context. Three key features of this model include: (1) the proposed parallelism between individual and team motivational processes, (2) the operation of the "double interact" in cross-level influences between individual and team motivation, and (3) the common organization of person and situational/contextual factors in terms of their impact selectivity. Obviously, the proposed model is new and remains to be empirically evaluated and subsequently revised. Nonetheless, there is one implication of this perspective that is unlikely to change – namely, the importance of individuals in teams. In contrast to managerial practices that follow the common "there is no 'I' in 'TEAM'" attitude, our model suggests that managers should allocate resources to motivating *both* the individual and the collective to maximize their teams' potential. The critical question for future research is not whether or not managers should motivate the individual, but *when* and *how* effective managers achieve a seamless integration of motivational practices across levels.

NOTES

1. Consistent with others (e.g., Kozlowski & Bell, 2003), we use the terms teams and groups interchangeably throughout the manuscript, though we recognize that interdependence is higher in teams than in groups in general.

ACKNOWLEDGEMENT

The authors thank Phillip Ackerman, Barry Staw, and Patrick Stubblebine for their helpful comments and insights. Partial support for the writing of this chapter is provided by the Army Research Institute for the Behavioral and Social Sciences (contract #W74V8H-04-K-0002) and National Institute on Aging (AG16648), to the first and second author respectively. Views reflected in this chapter are the authors', and not those of the institutions supporting this work.

REFERENCES

Ambrose, M. L., & Kulik, C. T. (1999). Old friends, new faces: Motivation research in the 1990s. *Journal of Management, 25*, 231–292.

Ancona, D. G., Goodman, P. S., Lawrence, B. S., & Tushman, M. L. (2001). Time: A new research lens. *Academy of Management Review, 26*, 645–663.

Austin, J. T., & Vancouver, J. B. (1996). Goal constructs in psychology: Structure, process, and content. *Psychological Bulletin, 120*, 338–375.

Bandura, A. (1986). *Social foundations of thought and action: A social cognitive theory.* Englewood Cliffs, NJ: Prentice-Hall.

Bandura, A. (1997). *Self-efficacy: The exercise of control.* New York, NY: Freeman.

Barr, S. H., & Conlon, E. J. (1994). Effects of distribution of feedback in work groups. *Academy of Management Journal, 37*, 641–655.

Bass, B. M. (1985). *Leadership and performance beyond expectation.* New York: Free Press.

Behrmann, M., & Kimchi, R. (2003). What does visual agnosia tell us about perceptual organization and its relationship to object perception? *Journal of Experimental Psychology: Human Perception & Performance, 29*, 19–42.

Camazine, S., Deneubourg, J. L., Franks, N. R., Sneyd, J., Theravlaz, G., & Bonabeau, E. (2001). *Self-organization in biological systems.* Princeton, NJ: Princeton University Press.

Campbell, J. P., & Pritchard, R. D. (1976). Motivation theory in industrial and organizational psychology. In: M. D. Dunnette (Ed.), *Handbook of industrial and organizational psychology* (pp. 63–130). Chicago, IL: Rand McNally.

Campion, M. A., Medsker, G. J., & Higgs, A. C. (1993). Relations between work group characteristics and effectiveness: Implications for designing effective work groups. *Personnel Psychology, 46*, 823–850.

Campion, M. A., Papper, E. M., & Medsker, G. J. (1996). Relations between work team characteristics and effectiveness: A replication and extension. *Personnel Psychology, 49*, 429–452.

Carver, C. S., & Scheier, M. F. (1981). *Attention and self-regulation: A control-theory approach to human behavior.* New York: Springer-Verlag.

Chan, D. (1998). Functional relations among constructs in the same content domain at different levels of analysis: A typology of composition models. *Journal of Applied Psychology, 83*, 234–246.

Chen, G. (2005). Newcomer adaptation in teams: Multilevel antecedents and outcomes. *Academy of Management Journal, 48*, 101–116.

Chen, G., & Bliese, P. D. (2002). The role of different levels of leadership in predicting self and collective efficacy: Evidence for discontinuity. *Manuscript submitted for publication, 87*, 549–556.

Chen, G., Bliese, P. D., & Mathieu, J. E. (2005a). Conceptual framework and statistical procedures for delineating and testing multilevel theories of homology. *Organizational Research Methods, 8*, 375–409.

Chen, G., Gully, S. M., Whiteman, J. A., & Kilcullen, R. N. (2000). Examination of relationships among trait-like individual differences, state-like individual differences, and learning performance. *Journal of Applied Psychology, 85*, 835–847.

Chen, G., & Kanfer, R. (in press). Multilevel longitudinal examination of the interplay between individual and team motivation. *Manuscript submitted for publication.*

Chen, G., Kirkman, B. L., Kanfer, R., Allen, D., & Rosen, B. (in press). A multilevel study of leadership, empowerment, and performance in teams. *Journal of Applied Psychology.*

Chen, G., & Klimoski, R. J. (2003). The impact of expectations on newcomer performance in teams as mediated by work characteristics, social exchanges, and empowerment. *Academy of Management Journal, 46*, 591–607.

Chen, G., Mathieu, J. E., & Bliese, P. D. (2004). A framework for conducting multilevel construct validation. In: F. J. Yammarino & F. Dansereau (Eds), *Research in multilevel issues: Multilevel issues in organizational behavior and processes*, (Vol. 3, pp. 273–303). Oxford, UK: Elsevier.

Chen, G., Thomas, B. A., & Wallace, J. C. (2005b). A multilevel examination of the relationships among training outcomes, mediating regulatory processes, and adaptive performance. *Journal of Applied Psychology, 90*, 827–841.

Chen, G., Webber, S. S., Bliese, P. D., Mathieu, J. E., Payne, S. C., Born, D. H., & Zaccaro, S. J. (2002). Simultaneous examination of the antecedents and consequences of efficacy beliefs at multiple levels of analysis. *Human Performance, 15*, 381–409.

Clark, A. (1997). The dynamical challenge. *Cognitive Science, 21*, 461–481.

Cohen, S. G., & Bailey, D. E. (1997). What makes teams work: Group effectiveness research from the shop floor to the executive suite. *Journal of Management, 23*, 239–290.

Dansereau, F., Graen, G., & Haga, W. J. (1975). A vertical dyad linkage approach to leadership within formal organizations. *Organizational Behavior and Human Performance, 13*, 46–78.

DeNisi, A. S. (2000). Performance appraisal and performance management: A multilevel analysis. In: K. J. Klein & S. W. J. Kozlowski (Eds), *Multilevel theory, research, and methods in organizations: Foundations, extensions, and new directions* (pp. 121–156). San Francisco, CA: Jossey-Bass.

DeShon, R. P., Kozlowski, S. W. J., Schmidt, A. M., Milner, K. R., & Weichmann, D. (2004). A multiple goal, multilevel model of feedback effects on the regulation of individual and team performance in training. *Journal of Applied Psychology, 89*, 1035–1056.

Dweck, C. S. (1986). Motivational processes affecting learning. *American Psychologist, 41*, 1040–1048.

Eden, D. (2001). Means efficacy: External sources of general and specific subjective efficacy. In: M. Erez, U. Kleinbeck & H. Thierry (Eds), *Work motivation in the context of a globalizing economy* (pp. 65–77). Mahwah, NJ: Erlbaum.

Feldman, D. C. (1984). The development and enforcement of group norms. *Academy of Management Review, 9*, 47–53.

Feltz, D. L., & Lirgg, C. D. (1998). Perceived team and player efficacy in hockey. *Journal of Applied Psychology, 83*, 557–564.

George, J. M., & Jones, G. R. (2000). The role of time in theory and theory building. *Journal of Management, 26*, 657–684.

Gersick, C. J. G. (1988). Time and transition in work teams: Toward a new model of group development. *Academy of Management Journal, 31*, 9–41.

Gibson, C. B. (2001). Me and us: Differential relationships among goal-setting training, efficacy and effectiveness at the individual and team level. *Journal of Organizational Behavior, 22*, 789–808.

Gollwitzer, P. M. (1990). Action phases and mind-sets. In: E. T. Higgins & R. M. Sorrentino (Eds), *Handbook of motivation and cognition: Foundations of social behavior*, (Vol. 2, pp. 53–92). New York: Guilford Press.

Gully, S. M., Devine, D. J., & Whitney, D. J. (1995). A meta-analysis of cohesion and performance: Effects of levels of analysis and task interdependence. *Small Group Research, 26*, 497–520.

Gully, S. M., Incalcaterra, K. A., Joshi, A., & Beaubien, J. M. (2002). A meta-analysis of team-efficacy, potency, and performance: Interdependence and level of analysis as moderators of observed relationships. *Journal of Applied Psychology, 87*, 819–832.

Hackman, J. R. (1987). The design of work teams. In: J. W. Lorsch (Ed.), *Handbook of organizational behavior* (pp. 315–342). Englewood Cliffs, NJ: Prentice-Hall.

Hackman, J. R. (1992). Group influences on individuals in organizations. In: M. D. Dunnette & L. M. Hough (Eds), *Handbook of industrial and organizational psychology*, (Vol. 3, pp. 199–267). Palo Alto, CA: Consulting Psychologists Press.

Hackman, J. R. (2002). *Leading teams: Setting the stage for great performance.* Boston, MA: Harvard Business School Press.

Hackman, J. R., & Oldham, G. R. (1976). Motivation through the design of work: Test of a theory. *Organizational Behavior and Human Performance, 16*, 250–279.

Harrison, D. A., Price, K. H., Gavin, J. H., & Florey, A. T. (2002). Time, teams, and task performance: Changing effects of surface- and deep-level diversity on group functioning. *Academy of Management Journal, 45*, 1029–1045.

Higgins, E. T. (1997). Beyond pleasure and pain. *American Psychologist, 52*, 1280–1300.

Hinsz, V. B., Tindale, R. S., & Vollrath, D. A. (1997). The emerging conceptualization of groups as information processes. *Psychological Bulletin, 121*, 43–64.

Hoffmann, D. A., & Jones, L. M. (2005). Leadership, collective personality, and performance. *Journal of Applied Psychology, 90*, 509–522.

Hofmann, D. A., Morgeson, F. P., & Gerras, S. J. (2003). Climate as a moderator of the relationship between leader–member exchange and content specific citizenship: Safety climate as an exemplar. *Journal of Applied Psychology, 88*, 170–178.

Janis, I. L. (1972). *Victims of groupthink.* Boston, MA: Houghton Mifflin.

Jex, S. M., & Bliese, P. D. (1999). Efficacy beliefs as a moderator of the impact of work-related stressors: A multilevel study. *Journal of Applied Psychology, 84*, 349–361.

Kanfer, R. (1990). Motivation theory and industrial and organizational psychology. In: 2nd ed. M. D. Dunnette & L. M. Hough (Eds), *Handbook of Industrial and Organizational Psychology*, (Vol. 1, pp. 75–170). Palo Alto, CA: Consulting Psychologists Press.

Kanfer, R. (1992). Work motivation: New directions in theory and research. In: C. L. Cooper & I. T. Robertson (Eds), *International review of industrial and organizational psychology*, (Vol. 7, pp. 1–53). New York, NY: Wiley.

Kanfer, R., & Ackerman, P. L. (1989). Motivation and cognitive abilities: An integrative/aptitude-treatment interaction approach to skill acquisition. *Journal of Applied Psychology [Monograph], 74*, 657–690.

Kanfer, F. H., & Erez, M. (1983). The role of goal acceptance in goal setting and task performance. *Academy of Management Review, 8*, 454–463.

Kanfer, R., & Heggestad, E. D. (1997). Motivational traits and skills: A person-centered approach to work motivation. *Research in Organizational Behavior, 19*, 1–56.

Kanfer, R., & Kanfer, F. H. (1991). Goals and self-regulation: Applications of theory to work settings. In: M. L. Maehr & P. R. Pintrich (Eds), *Advances in motivation and achievement*, (Vol. 7, pp. 287–326). Greenwich, CT: JAI Press.

Kark, R., Shamir, B., & Chen, G. (2003). The two faces of transformational leadership: Empowerment and dependency. *Journal of Applied Psychology, 88*, 246–255.

Katz, D., & Kahn, R. L. (1978). *The social psychology of organizations.* New York, NY: Wiley.

Katzell, R. A., & Austin, J. T. (1992). From then to now: The development of industrial-organizational psychology in the United States. *Journal of Applied Psychology, 77*, 803–835.

Kerr, S., & Jermier, J. M. (1978). Substitutes for leadership: Their meaning and measurement. *Organizational Behavior and Human Performance, 22,* 375–403.

Kirkman, B. L., & Rosen, B. (1999). Beyond self-management: Antecedents and consequences of team empowerment. *Academy of Management Journal, 42,* 58–74.

Kossmann, M. R., & Bullrich, S. (1997). Systematic chaos: Self-organizing systems and the process of change. In: F. Masterpasqua & A. Phyllis (Eds), *The psychological meaning of chaos: Translating theory into practice* (pp. 199–224). Washington, DC: American Psychological Association.

Kozlowski, S. W. J., & Bell, B. S. (2003). Work groups and teams in organizations. In: W. C. Borman, D. R. Ilgen & R. J. Klimoski (Eds), *Comprehensive Handbook of Psychology: Industrial and Organizational Psychology,* (Vol. 12, pp. 333–375). New York: Wiley.

Kozlowski, S. W. J., Gully, S. M., Nason, E. R., & Smith, E. M. (1999). Developing adaptive teams: A theory of compilation and performance across levels and time. In: D. R. Ilgen & E. D. Pulakos (Eds), *The changing nature of work performance: Implications for staffing, personnel actions, and development* (pp. 240–292). San Francisco, CA: Jossey-Bass.

Kozlowski, S. W. J., & Klein, K. J. (2000). A multilevel approach to theory and research in organizations: Contextual, temporal, and emergent processes. In: K. J. Klein & S. W. J. Kozlowski (Eds), *Multilevel theory, research, and methods in organizations: Foundations, extensions, and new directions* (pp. 3–90). San Francisco, CA: Jossey-Bass.

Latham, G. P., & Pinder, C. C. (2005). Work motivation theory and research at the dawn of the twenty-first century. *Annual Review of Psychology, 56,* 485–516.

LePine, J. A., & Van Dyne, L. (2001). Peer responses to low performers: An attributional model of helping in the context of groups. *Academy of Management Review, 26,* 67–84.

Lewin, K. (1951). *Field theory in social science.* Oxford, UK: Harpers.

Lindsley, D. H., Brass, D. J., & Thomas, J. B. (1995). Efficacy-performance spirals: A multilevel perspective. *Academy of Management Review, 20,* 645–678.

Locke, E. A., & Latham, G. P. (1990). *A theory of goal setting and task performance.* Englewood Cliffs, NJ: Prentice-Hall.

Marks, M. A., Mathieu, J. E., & Zaccaro, S. J. (2001). A conceptual framework and taxonomy of team processes. *Academy of Management Review, 26,* 356–376.

Mitchell, T. R. (1997). Matching motivational strategies with organizational contexts. *Research in Organizational Behavior, 19,* 57–149.

Morgeson, F. P., & Hofmann, D. A. (1999). The structure and function of collective constructs: Implications for multilevel research and theory development. *Academy of Management Review, 24,* 249–265.

Naylor, J. C., Pritchard, R. D., & Ilgen, D. R. (1980). *A theory of behavior in organizations.* New York: Academic Press.

O'Leary-Kelly, A. M., Martocchio, J. J., & Frink, D. D. (1994). A review of the influence of group goals on group performance. *Academy of Management Journal, 37,* 1285–1301.

Parker, S. K., & Wall, T. D. (2001). Work design: Learning from the past and mapping a new terrain. In: N. Anderson, D. S. Ones, H. K. Sinangil & C. Viswesvaran (Eds), *Handbook of industrial, work and organizational psychology,* (Vol. 1, pp. 90–109). Thousand Oaks, CA: Sage.

Ployhart, R. E., & Schneider, B. (2002). A multilevel perspective on personnel selection: When will practice catch up? In: F. J. Dansereau & F. Yammarino (Eds), *Research in multi-level issues: The many faces of multi-level issues,* (Vol. 1, pp. 165–175). Elsevier Science Ltd: Oxford, UK.

Pritchard, R. D., Jones, S. D., Roth, P. L., Stuebing, K. K., & Ekeberg, S. E. (1988). Effects of group feedback, goal setting, and incentives on organizational productivity. *Journal of Applied Psychology [Monograph]*, *73*, 337–358.

Prigogine, L., & Stengers, I. (1984). *Order out of chaos: Man's new dialogue with nature.* New York: Bantam Books.

Saavedra, R., Earley, P. C., & Van Dyne, L. (1993). Complex interdependence in task-performing groups. *Journal of Applied Psychology*, *78*, 61–72.

Salas, E., Dickinson, T. L., Converse, S. A., & Tannenbaum, S. I. (1992). Toward an understanding of team performance and training. In: R. W. Swezey & E. Salas (Eds), *Teams: Their training and performance* (pp. 3–29). Norwood, NJ: Ablex.

Seibert, S. E., Silver, S. R., & Randolph, W. A. (2004). Taking empowerment to the next level: A multiple-level model of empowerment, performance, and satisfaction. *Academy of Management Journal*, *47*, 332–349.

Shamir, B. (1990). Calculations, values, and identities: The sources of collectivistic work motivation. *Human Relations*, *43*, 313–332.

Shamir, B., Zakay, E., Breinin, E., & Popper, M. (1998). Correlates of charismatic leader behavior in military units: Subordinates' attitudes, unit characteristics, and superior appraisals of leader performance. *Academy of Management Journal*, *41*, 387–409.

Stajkovic, A. D., & Luthans, F. (1998). Self-efficacy and work-related performance: A meta-analysis. *Psychological Bulletin*, *124*, 240–261.

Staw, B. M. (1984). Organizational behavior: A review and reformulation of the field's outcome variables. *Annual Review of Psychology*, *35*, 627–666.

Stokes, D. E. (1989). *Pasteur's quadrant: Basic science and technological innovation.* Washington, DC: Brookings Institution Press.

Sundstrom, E. (1999). The challenges of supporting work team effectiveness. In: E. Sundstrom & Associates (Ed.), *Supporting work team effectiveness: Best management practices for fostering high performance* (pp. 3–23). San Francisco, CA: Jossey-Bass.

Tesluk, P. E., & Jacobs, R. R. (1998). Toward an integrated model of work experience. *Personnel Psychology*, *51*, 321–355.

Thelen, E. (1995). Motor development: A new synthesis. *American Psychologist*, *50*, 79–95.

Thomas, K. W., & Velthouse, B. A. (1990). Cognitive elements of empowerment: An interpretive model of intrinsic task motivation. *Academy of Management Review*, *15*, 666–681.

Tuckman, B. W., & Jensen, M. C. (1977). Stages of small-group development revisited. *Group and Organization Studies*, *2*, 419–427.

VandeWalle, D., Cron, W. L., & Slocum, J. W., Jr. (2001). The role of goal orientation following performance feedback. *Journal of Applied Psychology*, *86*, 629–640.

Wageman, R. (2001). How leaders foster self-managing team effectiveness: Design choices versus hands-on coaching. *Organization Science*, *12*, 559–577.

Weick, K. E. (1979). *The social psychology of organizing* (2nd ed.). Reading, MA: Addision-Wesley.

Weingart, L. R. (1992). Impact of group goals, task component complexity, effort, and planning on group performance. *Journal of Applied Psychology*, *77*, 682–693.

Zaccaro, S. J., & Marks, M. A. (1999). The roles of leaders in high-performance teams. In: E. Sundstrom & Associates (Ed.), *Supporting work team effectiveness: Best management practices for fostering high performance* (pp. 95–125). San Francisco, CA: Jossey-Bass.

CODE BREAKING: HOW ENTREPRENEURS EXPLOIT CULTURAL LOGICS TO GENERATE INSTITUTIONAL CHANGE

Hayagreeva Rao and Simona Giorgi

ABSTRACT

If institutions are durable, how do they change from within and from without? We build on the emerging synthesis of social movement theory and institutional theory and articulate how institutional entrepreneurs from within and without deploy pre-existing cultural logics to push forward their institutional projects. We develop propositions, which show how the success of these framing activities is contingent on political opportunity, and illustrate them with a wide range of extreme cases.

"Economics is all about how people make choices; sociology is all about why they don't have any choice to make" (Dusenberry, 1960, p. 233). This stereotypical portrait of sociology by an economist becomes even more mordant when we approach a prominent branch of sociology, namely, neo-institutional theory. In the neo-institutional world, institutions constrain human action; scripts, norms, and rules concatenate to form cultural logics

Research in Organizational Behavior: An Annual Series of Analytical Essays and Critical Reviews
Research in Organizational Behavior, Volume 27, 269–304
Copyright © 2006 by Elsevier Ltd.
ISSN: 0191-3085/doi:10.1016/S0191-3085(06)27007-2

that constrain action (Friedland & Alford, 1991; Scott, 1995). In short, cultural logics have a *code*-like character, wherein, they prescribe and proscribe behaviors. Thus, DiMaggio and Powell (1983) in their celebrated article, suggest that as organizations respond to coercive rules, rely on professional norms, and imitate peers, they only succeed in becoming homogeneous, thereby, tightening the bars of an iron cage.

If cultural logics have a code-like character that constrain human action and denote durability, then how is institutional change possible (Clemens & Cook, 1999)? This question constitutes the raison d'etre of the present chapter. Drawing on an emerging synthesis of social movement theory and neo-institutional theory, we focus on institutional entrepreneurs and how they generate change through the deft deployment of pre-existing cultural logics. We build on the idea that social logics are mutable to the extent till they are rife with ambiguity and contradiction (Clemens & Cook, 1999), and liken institutional innovation to code-breaking. We suggest that institutional entrepreneurs may be "insiders" or "outsiders" to a social system who can either exploit the pre-existing logic within the social system, or import a logic from a different domain.

These dimensions enable us to develop a simple yet powerful matrix with four quadrants of code-breaking: subversion (insiders using a pre-existing logic), appropriation (outsiders exploiting a pre-existing logic in the social system), integration (insiders importing a logic from outside and welding it to the pre-existing logic), and insurgency (outsiders importing a logic from the outside and undermining the existing logic). Thereafter, we draw on diverse cases from different time periods and different nations to derive general propositions about how the effectiveness of code-breaking hinges on political opportunity and mobilizing structures. We begin by elaborating how cultural logics are mutable, and then develop our typology of code-breaking.

CULTURAL LOGICS AND CODE-BREAKING

An useful starting point is to conceive of an institution as the reproduction of behavior, and then study the conditions under which reliable reproduction is disrupted, the sources of disruption, and responses to disruption by actors (Clemens & Cook, 1999, p. 441). If institutional change is defined as an exit from one state and entry into another state, three processes of institutional change merit attention. The formation of institutions entails an exit from social entropy or non-reproductive behavior patterns and entry into a system of taken-for-granted behaviors reproduced over time. Deinstitutionalization embodies an exit from one set of taken-for-granted behaviors and an entry into social entropy or deliberate action needed to maintain those behaviors. Finally, reinstitutionalization encapsulates an exit from one set of taken-for-granted behaviors and entry into a new set of taken-for-granted behaviors (Jepperson, 1991, p. 152). Of these three processes, reinstitutionalization embodies a sequence of deinstitutionalization and institution-building, and hence, is the most comprehensive process of change, and therefore, will be the object of our study.

How is re-institutionalization possible in a world where cultural logics constrain human action? Early writers sought to explain institutional change as the outcome of exogenous shocks emanating from outside the institutional system in the form of wars or social crises (see Powell, 1991, pp. 181–200). However, these initial arguments glossed over how actors from within or without the social system could exploit the social logic(s) governing a social system and generate institutional change. As Becker (1963, p. 162) argued, "rules are not made automatically ... . People must be made to feel something ought to be done ... . Someone must call the public's attention to these matters, supply the push to get things done." Seo and Creed (2002, p. 26) describe the problem of institutional change from within as a problem of embedded agency. Greenwood and Suddaby (2006) draw our attention to field-level contradictions and suggest that elite/central players are exposed to these contradictions and thereby, are in a position to develop the awareness, motivation, and openness necessary to initiate change.

However, institutional change from within (or for that matter without) need not to depend on elites and institutional entrepreneurs can also arise from the periphery of a social system. A burgeoning synthesis of neo-institutionalism and social movement theory suggests that re-institutionalization is a political process in which social movements play a double-edged role: they deinstitutionalize existing beliefs, norms, and values embodied in extant social structures and establish new structures that instantiate new beliefs, norms, and values. Crucial in these processes are institutional entrepreneurs who lead efforts to identify political opportunities, frame issues and problems, and mobilize constituencies. By doing so, they spearhead collective attempts to infuse new beliefs, norms, and values into social structures, thus creating discontinuities in the world of organizations (Davis & McAdam, 2000; Rao, Morrill, & Zald, 2000; Rao, Monin, & Durand, 2003; McAdam & Scott, 2005). In contrast to economic entrepreneurs who bear uncertainty in return for profit by establishing new organizations, institutional entrepreneurs are ideological activists who take risks and invest themselves in fighting for a larger cause or a public good, and deftly use cultural logics to advance their cause (DiMaggio, 1988, p. 18).

Students of social movements have suggested that ideological activists engage in "meaning-work." Snow, Burke, Worden, and Benford (1986) emphasize that the first step for ideological activists is to provide a frame for actors' interpretations that either identifies the problem at hand (diagnostic framing) or suggests a solution (prognostic framing). Frames play an important role in creating meaning because they "denote schemata of interpretation that enable individuals to locate, perceive, identify, and label occurrences within their life space and world at large. By rendering events or occurrences meaningful, frames function to organize experience and guide action, whether individual or collective" (Snow et al., 1986, p. 464). Thus, the "meaning-work" of ideological activists consists of actively seeking to frame an issue, making diagnostic and prognostic attributions, and arraying events and experiences in cognitive packages. Suddaby and Greenwood (2005) suggest that framing is part of a rhetorical strategy and direct attention to the use of institutional vocabularies that expose contradictions and theorization or the use of templates.

Framing by itself or meaning-work is not adequate to bring about institutional change. The consensus in the social movement literature is that the ability of institutional entrepreneurs/activists to bring about institutional change also depends upon political opportunities and mobilizing structures (McAdam, McCarthy, & Zald, 1996; McAdam, Tilly, & Tarrow, 2001). Several studies suggest that organized attempts to transform institutions requires political opportunity, that is, access to the political system, the existence of allies, instability in the elite, and the absence of repression from state authorities or those in power (Tarrow, 1989). Moreover, collective vehicles through which people mobilize supporters for collective action are also essential for social movements; such structures include formal social movement organizations (McCarthy & Zald, 1977), work and neighborhood organizations, and informal friendship networks.

However, the dialogue between neo-institutionalists and social movement theorists has yet to delineate how entrepreneurs seeking to re-institutionalize a social field skillfully use or undermine pre-existing logics in the field. Moreover, they also have yet to delineate how insiders and outsiders use pre-existing cultural logics, and how the success of these framing endeavors is contingent on political opportunity, and mobilization. In this chapter, we restrict ourselves to illuminating how the success of framing is contingent on the nature, extent, and scope of political opportunity.

By emphasizing how cultural logics regulate action by furnishing practical guidelines for behavior (Friedland & Alford, 1991; Scott, 1995), cultural-frame institutionalists have focused on the *code-like* character of logics. In a parallel vein, organizational ecologists have also taken a cultural turn, and suggested that organizational forms are based on codes, especially, a genetic code – that is, a set of competences – and a penal code – that is, a set of rules of conduct, whose violation invites penalties (Polos, Hannan, & Carroll, 2002). However, cultural logics also presuppose semiotic codes. Cultural sociologists contend that semiotic codes are collectively known systems of meaning that regulate social action. As a result, "one is constrained not by internal motives, but by knowledge of how one's actions may be interpreted by others (Swidler, 2001, p. 163)." Put another way, it is not the inability to imagine an alternative that constrains institutional change, but rather, the latitude to get away with a framing of a problem and its attendant solution that influences the success of institutional entrepreneurs.

More formally, we propose that institutional entrepreneurs may be "insiders" or "outsiders" to a social system. They can either exploit the pre-existing logic within the social system, or import a logic from a different domain. For the purposes of our paper, an insider is one who started in a focal industry and is a member of the focal industry, and is perceived by industry critics and by established players to be part of the focal industry or domain. We defined logic as "the socially constructed, historical pattern of material practices, assumptions, values, beliefs, and rules by which individuals produce and reproduce their material subsistence, organize time and space, and provide meaning to their social reality" (Friedland & Alford, 1991; Jackall, 1988, p. 112).

Table 1 shows the resulting matrix with four quadrants of code-breaking: subversion (insiders using a pre-existing logic, quadrant 1), appropriation (outsiders exploiting a pre-existing logic in the social system, quadrant 2), integration (insiders importing a logic from the outside and welding it to the pre-existing logic, quadrant 3), and insurgency (outsiders importing a logic from the outside and undermining the existing logic, quadrant 4). In each

Table 1. Code-Breaking Processes.

	Insider	Outsider
Existing logic	Q1 Subversion	Q2 Appropriation
Imported logic	Q3 Integration	Q4 Insurgency

quadrant, we develop propositions delineating the conditions under which re-institutionalization is likely to be successful and then illustrate them using examples of successful and unsuccessful changes. By design, we use "extreme cases" in different contexts and time periods (Eisenhardt, 1989) as illustrative devices.

Q1. SUBVERSION

The Merriam Webster dictionary defines subversion as a "systematic attempt to overthrow or undermine a government or a political system by persons working secretly from within." In our context, subversion implies that insiders skillfully deploy an existing institutional logic in an existing organizational field or domain to promote radical institutional innovation. Successful subversion consists of precluding controversy and conflict, and indeed, eliciting the support of key constituencies in a field or a profession. By contrast, subversion becomes unsuccessful when insiders are hampered by conflict and controversy from achieving their goal of institutional innovation from within. In both cases then, framing is critical to the eventual success of the institutional project. How does it depend on political opportunity? What influences the success of framing endeavors?

P1. The more ambiguous a code or logic, the greater the political opportunity and the more likely is subversive framing to be accepted.

In order to understand the emergence of new rules in an institutional field, we must understand how rules are encoded. Crawford and Ostrom (1995) outline a grammar of institutions, which allows us to generate descriptions of institutional statements. The syntax of the grammar of institutions consists of five elements; (a) attributes which describe the members of the group a given statement applies to, (b) deontic elements which specify what must be done, what must not be done, and what is permitted, (c) aim, the action to which the deontic elements apply, (d) conditions which identify the conditions when a statement is operative, and (e) an or else which defines the sanction to be applied for non-compliance to rules. These elements are not constraints as much as tool-kits for actors (Swidler, 1986), and so ambiguity with respect to any of the elements creates semantic opportunities for insiders to frame appeals for institutional change and innovation. Thus, unclear group boundaries, vague proscriptions and prescriptions, poorly defined sanctions and criteria for enforcing them all enhance opportunities for code-breaking.

P2. The more ambiguous a code or logic, the less members of the elite are committed to the status quo, and the easier it is for insiders to mobilize them, and the greater is the success of subversive framing.

The ambiguity of a code or logic imposes constraints on the degree to which members of the elite are committed to status quo rules. Ostrom (1986) defines seven different rules: (a) position rules that specify roles of actors, (b) boundary rules that delineate the conditions for entry and exit, (c) scope rules that list appropriate outcomes for actions, (d) authority rules that lay out duties and obligations, (e) aggregation rules about ways of collective decision making, (f) information rules about how information is to be collected and shared, and (g) payoff rules which state the costs and benefits of actions. When actors have vague roles, unclear criteria for membership in a social system, murky information and criteria for distributing payoffs, elites are less committed to the status quo, and insiders can subvert the system more easily.

An Example of Successful Subversion: Techno-Cuisine and Ferran Adria

A striking example of how ambiguity in codes provided semantic opportunity and an open-minded elite for successful subversion is Ferran Adria, the chef at El Bulli, and his successful effort to develop conceptual cuisine, and to dismantle nouvelle cuisine.

A beach bar until 1980, El Bulli was bought by Julio Soler, who 3 years later hired the then 23 year old Ferran Adria. Adria had started working in the restaurant kitchen as a college student on a holiday job, but Soler was so impressed with Adria's enthusiasm to offer him the partnership in the business. In the 1980s Adria and Soler traveled from one grand French restaurant to the next, making friends and learning from the giants of nouvelle cuisine – Troisgros, Blanc, Guerard, and Chapel. In 1984, Adria went to a class given by Jacques Maximum, then the chef of the two-star Chantecler at the Hotel Negresco in Nice. Someone in the audience asked Maximum what it meant to create in the canons of nouvelle cuisine and he responded, "Not to copy." According to Adria, that comment represented a turning point in his career (Hesser, 1999).

Adria quickly rose through the ranks of gastronomy and soon garnered two stars. Although a high-status insider, he sought to develop a new type of conceptual cuisine and subvert nouvelle cuisine. As Adria commented later, the "French were culinary has-beens" that invented good cooking, but "now they didn't know what to do with (Wells, 1997)." The basic elements of nouvelle cuisine, as encapsulated in the Ten Commandments of Nouvelle Cuisine reflect four values – Truth, Lightness, Simplicity and Imagination – and urge chefs to be inventive, not to be prejudiced, and not to cheat in terms of their presentation. Elite chefs who were exponents of nouvelle cuisine were also keen to experiment, and indeed, rushed to learn from Adria. The ambiguous rules of nouvelle cuisine also meant that elite chefs were open to experimentation. Both of these were crucial for Adria successful challenge of nouvelle cuisine as an orthodoxy in its own right, and these very rules also inured him against criticism from other chefs.

A comparison of two dishes featuring the same ingredient (rouget) between 1987 and 2003 highlights the extent of subversion. In 1987, "Salmonetes Gaudi" featured two fillets that were sautéed and covered with a colorful, Gaudi-like mosaic made of finely diced vegetables; they were garnished with a cool red pepper jelly, and a salad of spring onions and pine nuts. This dish adhered to nouvelle cuisine – the name of the dish is contemporary, it conjoins fish and vegetables (a combination rare in classical cuisine) and embodies simplicity. By contrast in 2004, the rouget is "like an X-ray. Adria calls it "the mummy." All that is served of the fish is its skeleton, deep-fried whole, wrapped in a shroud of pale cotton candy whose fleeting flavors are sweet and briny. The bones are crunchy, salty, certainly edible, and arguably tasty. This movement in the rouget dishes – from one based on traditional flavor combinations but enlivened by a playful allusion to Gaudi to one that is a conceptual statement first, something to eat second – exemplifies what Adria calls the "cocina de vanguardia" (Matthews, 1998). Its fundamental aspect is a belief that taste is not the only sense that a restaurant should engage. The "sixth sense" is equally important. Adria explains the "sixth sense" as the role of the intellect in the appreciation of gastronomy – the use of humor, of shock (as in the bones of the fish), of memory to stimulate the diner to reflect on what he is eating.

According to Adria, his recipe for innovation is "cold and methodical," and starts with "information, information, information." He has an extensive gastronomic library installed in his new "laboratory workshop" in nearby Barcelona, and claims to have memorized thousands of tastes on his "psychological palate." Adria contrasts nouvelle cuisine with his own conceptual cuisine; "Nouvelle cuisine was creative. My approach is to investigate. It's not the same. This takes a team, equipment, money, and time. We have one rule here: It has to be new. It may be good, but if we've done it before, it doesn't matter." Adria estimates that from 5000 experiments in his laboratory – El Taller – the team might create some 500 dishes, which will then be distilled into the 25 to 50 dishes that will make up the year's core degustation menu at El Bulli. In many of these dishes, flavors are distilled from their natural forms, and infused into ephemeral new textures – foams, mousses, sorbets, and ravioli with skin barely thicker than a bubble's. It seems to move from traditional food to something you might imagine as antifood. In short, Adria has made the cook into a scientist than an artist. Often, his servers instruct diners on how to consume the foams presented in test tubes and other flamboyant dishes.

In 1997, the Guide Michelin promoted El Bulli in Rosas, northeastern Spain, to three stars, an honor enjoyed by only 32 restaurants in the world, 19 of which in France, thereby, implying that the El Bulli offered "exceptional cuisine, worth a special journey (Hesser, 1999)." El Bulli is a commercial success. In 2003, the restaurant bought in slightly more than 1 million euros ($1.25 million), according to its partner Soler. A wide range of related activities added another 3.4 million euros ($4.2 million). But even more importantly, its influence is being felt far and wide. In the late 1990s, the foams, as Adria put it, were a scandal, but by now they are routine, and imitated in France. Senior chefs from Joel Robuchon to Michel Bras, Charlie Trotter, Todd English, Norman Van Aken, Roberto Donna, Jean-Louis Palladin and Douglas Rodriguez, visited El Bulli to discover Adria's new paths (Friedrich, 1999) and hailed him as the progenitor of a new type of cuisine – one where the chef is a scientist rather than an artist.

P3. The greater the degree of contradiction between a code and a system of production, the greater the opportunity for subversive framing.

P4. The greater the incompatibility between a subversive framing and a code or logic, the greater is the degree of instability, and the higher the risk of failure.

A staple proposition in sociological theory since Marx's work on dialectics is that internal contradictions within social systems generate social change within the system (Clemens & Cook, 1999; Sewell, 1992). For instance, systems of classification that delineate minorities may become the basis of ideological challenges to the central state (Brubaker, 1992). Although contradictions within a code may trigger institutional change, an excessive incompatibility between a code or logic and subversive framings by insiders can lead to instability (Sewell, 1992) and failure.

An Example of Failed Subversion: Samurai Vs. Entrepreneur at
Arthur Andersen

The case of Arthur Andersen is interesting because high-status insiders sought to subvert the model of an "accountant as samurai" with that of an "accountant as entrepreneur." Elite partners were open to change and not committed to status quo, and their openness stemmed from contradictions between the code that governed public accounting firms, and the growth of consulting business. However, the logic of the accountant as entrepreneur was incompatible with the logic of the accountant as samurai at Andersen, and led to the eventual collapse of the firm.[1]

Under the logic of the accountant as samurai, the accountant's role was to preserve the integrity of the reports, and insist upon absolute independence of judgment and action. Andersen was organized on the basis of three principles: serving the client, think straight talk straight, and the best and the brightest. The best and the brightest meant that the best people were selected, put through a rigorous program of training that taught them how to do an audit, how to document it, and later, rewarded and developed. Auditors were expected to serve the customer by thinking straight and talking straight. This ethos was symbolized a sturdy set of mahogany doors which embodied confidentiality, privacy, security, and orderliness.

The culture of vigilance, independence, and honesty was maintained not only through rigorous training, but also by a small group, Andersen's most experienced and technically astute partners that later was called the Professional Standards Group (PSG). In the early 1970s, the group was headed by George Catlett and his office was never more than 50 feet away from that of the managing partner of Andersen. The PSG's handpicked members would usually congregate at their regular table in the Midday Club atop the First National Bank Building in Chicago's Loop, and over a lunch of club sandwiches and iced tea, they would chart Andersen's positions on hundreds of complicated accounting issues, from leasing transactions to depreciation rules. For instance, when firms were purchasing IBM 370 mainframes in the late 1970s, they were deducting the cost of the machines over a 10-year period. Andersen's PSG decided that those computers were obsolete after only 5 years, and insisted their clients spread the cost over the shorter term, which cut into profits. Andersen's "line" partners also challenged clients and upheld the standards set forth by the PSG. Andersen would walk away from clients based on risk and ranked clients according to a complex formula that determined their potential to go bankrupt. For example, the head of the thrift practice for Andersen, based in Dallas, Bob Kralovetz dropped Lincoln Savings and Loan, managed by Charles Keating, even when it accounted for 20% of the Phoenix office, because he was concerned about its possible bankruptcy.

By contrast, the emphasis on consulting meant that the accountant was an entrepreneur. As Gresham Brebach, a former head of consulting for Andersen opined, "a consultant is there to influence change, to convince the client to do something different, not to conform or comply. It's a different mindset, a different attitude." Beginning in the early 1990s, all of the audit partners in the Big 6 public accounting firms faced increasing pressure for revenue generation. The pressure was severe in Arthur Andersen due to an internal schism. Earlier, Andersen had a large consulting practice, and the consultants felt that although they earned the bulk of the revenue, the majority of partners were auditors, and wondered as to why they were subsidizing the less profitable audit side of the house. Both split in 2001. The consultants formed a new venture called Accenture and the auditors at Andersen sought to expand their consulting base. This was especially so since the advent of paperless audit had reduced costs of the audit, and therefore, fees for partners. One option was to get large clients, but this was difficult because large clients were reluctant to change auditors. Moreover, since large firms tended to staff their finance and internal control positions with ex employees of their auditor, these functions had a built in bias in favor of the current auditor.

Larry Weinbach, the managing partner of Anderson, and Dick Measelle, the world-wide head of Andersen's tax and audit practice, sought to replace the vigilant and independent auditor with an "Eye of the Tiger" accountant keen to seize opportunities and sell services to clients. At Andersen pressure was put on individual partners to increase revenue and this pressure was intense. Published reports (Delroy, et al., 2002) indicate management set a standard of 20,000 h per year for a partner and his supporting staff. Measelle and other leaders hoped to accomplish the goal of each partner handling 20,000 h of work, without compromising on the basic principles.

Over time, Andersen changed its symbol from a pair of doors symbolizing confidentiality and orderliness to an orange globe signaling its aspirations. More importantly, the PSG also changed and lost its stature. As early as 1989, Larry Weinbach, the managing partner was in New York, but the PSG remained in Chicago. In 1992, top management, for the first time, rejected a key ruling of the PSG on whether stock options should be counted as an expense. As the head of the PSG, Arthur Wyatt, was leaving, he told his successor "The game is over …. . You guys are never going to have the authority within the firm that you once had" (Delroy et al., 2002). Soon there were seven levels between the head of the PSG and the managing partner of Andersen.

The tension between the account as samurai and accountant as entrepreneur logics reached a zenith in the case of Enron, and led to the collapse of Andersen. In 1994 as part of a five-year, $18 million contract, Andersen took over Enron's internal audit functions and the woven sweater's pattern began. During the 1990s, however, Enron was growing by leaps and bounds and the Andersen fees charged to Enron grew as well. Enron initially outsourced internal audit to Andersen (so Andersen was left with the task of auditing its own work). Soon Andersen employees – partners, managers, and staff – were eager to explore and nurture their relationships with Enron, a potential client and a cash cow, with the hopes of career advancement as a by-product. Many of Andersen and Enron employees vacationed together, played golf, attended baseball games at Enron field, frequented the local restaurants and bars, attended charity events, and played fantasy football. By 2000, the annual client fees paid to Andersen by Enron had grown to $58 million and Enron was by far the largest client in the Andersen Houston office. The size of the client fees and the zealous friendships and ties across the two companies impeded Andersen's judgment. Instead of being an unbiased, independent auditor who objected strenuously when asked about questionable and suspect accounting procedures and holding firm to the decision, Andersen was an intimate confidant that searched for creative and innovative justification to assure a friend with lucrative pockets again and again and again. One executive at Enron described the magnetism as follows: "It's like Patty Hearst, you start identifying with your kidnappers." Eventually, Enron's bankruptcy triggered Andersen's own civil liability suit, and its collapse. The leaders of Andersen had subverted the model of the accountant as samurai and won the battle, but lost the war of survival.

Q2. APPROPRIATION

The term "appropriation," according to the Merriam-Webster dictionary, derives from the Latin *appropriare* and means "to take exclusive possession of" and to "take without authority or right." In our context, appropriation implies that outsiders take hold of an existing institutional code/logic in an existing organizational field to promote radical institutional innovation. Appropriation is successful when conflict and controversy are minimized, and counter-mobilization from insiders is rendered redundant. Once again, framing is central to the success of the institutional project, but hinges on political opportunity and mobilization.

P5. When a spin-off movement stemming from an initiator movement enters an institutional domain, the greater the political opportunity for outsiders to engage in appropriation, and succeed in institutional change.

P6. When outsiders are able to mobilize elite support, the greater the political opportunity for outsiders to engage in appropriation, and succeed in institutional change.

McAdam (1995) distinguishes between rare, but exceedingly important, initiator movements "that signal or otherwise set in motion an identifiable protest cycle" and more populous spin-off movements "that, in varying degrees, draw their impetus and inspiration from the original initiator movement." Spin-off movements represent the diffusion and customization of the initiator movement's master logic. Initiator movements pertain to a master domain (e.g., civil rights) and spin-off movements to more specialized domains (e.g., elder rights, disability rights). Thus, the civil rights movement was an initiator movement that provided the basis for a spin-off movement geared to the expansion of rights for the disabled. Spin-off movements derive substantial legitimacy through their affiliation with initiator movements. When initiator movements enter an institutional field via a spin-off movement, outsiders have ample opportunity to enter the field, use the language deployed by insiders and justify their own innovation as a much needed response to the problems articulated by activists in the spin-off movement. Such appropriation is also likely to be more successful when outsiders are able to recruit members of the elite, and thereby, gain access benefits.

An Example of Successful Appropriation: Prisons as a Private Enterprise

A telling example of a spin-off movement and elite recruitment by outsiders leading to successful appropriation was the privatization of prisons. Historically, prisons originated as private endeavors. For example, in England the earliest type of closed incarceration facility was the house of corrections, known as a *bridewell*. The managers of these prisons received their incomes not from government, but from offender fees and contracts from other businesses making use of inmate labor. Similarly, in the United States, in the 18th century states entered agreements with private parties to lease inmates' labor and prisons came under government control only after the Revolution War (Hirsch, 1987). The shift of imprisonment to the government also marked a transition in the philosophy of corrections. Not only detention, but also rehabilitation and reintegration of the inmates became central concerns of the state.

During the 1980s, the conservative movement that brought Margaret Thatcher and Ronald Reagan to power in Britain and in the U.S. was an initiator movement that presaged the growth of many spin-off movements ranging from right-wing radio to the downsizing of government. The anti-government sentiment found fertile ground in the context of a prison reform movement beset by growing incarceration rates and increasing debt that lead state governments to look for new strategies to deal with offenders. By 1985, there were 500,000 inmates in federal and state prisons.

As state governments struggled with shrinking resources and mounting incarceration rates, supporters of private prisons enthusiastically embraced the idea of increasing prisons' space while lowering costs. They claimed that the private sector could build prisons faster and cheaper, since there was no need for bond issues from voters and private parties operated without the burden of bureaucracy and according to the logic of the market. In addition, since private prisons charged a daily fee per inmate, the cost of the correction system was a variable, rather than a fixed cost, for the government (Tolchin, 1985). Dissenters questioned whether private prisons would short-circuit rehabilitation, reduce the tax base, and raise prices with impunity once they were entrenched.

These objections were rendered moot as legislatures and governors rather than correctional agencies were at the fore-front of the effort to outsourcing prison management to private industry (McDonald, Fournier, Russell-Einhourn, & Crawford, 1998). The first prison company, Corrections Corporation of America (CCA), was set up in the 1980s by Thomas Beasley and R. Crantz with support from Jack Massey, previously successful with Kentucky Fried Chicken and Hospital Corporation of America. Beasley, a former chairman of the Tennessee Republican Party, said that the idea came originally from "his activities in Republican politics which taught him the benefits of the absence of bureaucracy." For assistance in running the new organization he hired Don Hutto, then president of the American Correctional Association, which set the standards for government run prisons (Clifford, 1985). In 1985, CCA proposed to pay $250 million to the state of Tennessee to operate its overcrowded penal system and build new prisons to meet federal court inmate-level standards. In the negotiations Tom Ingram, a former aide to the governor, acted as a consultant to the Nashville-based CCA (Rawlins, 1985). While some state officials questioned the legality of the lease-purchase proposal, Beasley noted that prison court orders in 34 states as well as increasingly tight state budgets were forcing new directions in the operation of prisons and that a shift from public to private operation was "not an ideological question, [but] a management decision (Stutz, 1986)."

In the 1980s several other companies followed suit, including Pricor, Buckingham Security Company, and Wackenhut Corrections Corporation (WCC) – a subsidiary of the Wackenhut Corporation, a global security and investigative organization listed on the New York Stock Exchange and active in five continents. In 1988, CCA operated nine prisons, three of which were based in Tennessee. By the end of the 1990s, the private sector housed almost 70,000 inmates – of which CCA held 54 percent and WCC another 27 percent. CCA was the ninth largest prison system; only seven states and the Federal Bureau of Prisons were larger (Camp & Camp, 1998).

P7. The more significant "authenticity" is in an institutional domain, the harder it is for outsiders to appropriate, and the easier it is for insiders to mobilize and thwart outsider attempts at appropriation.

A significant constraint on appropriation by outsiders is the emphasis on authenticity in production. A number of writers have pointed out that authenticity contains two meanings – authentic products and performances are (a) original and (b) credible representations of some cultural form (Peterson, 1997). In general, performers are assessed "in reviews by critics both in terms of known standards and in terms of originality and freshness of interpretation. It is exactly in this contradictory situation that there is room for coding to develop" (White & White, 1993, p. 10). However, Peterson (Peterson, 1997, pp. 150–154) points out that *one need not conform to all the conventions of a genre all the time, instead, what is important is to conform to some of the conventions most of the time.* The key question is what the critical conventions in a social field are, and who enforces conformity to these critical conventions. When critical conventions exist, and conformity to them is deemed to be a signal of authenticity, and it is enforced by either critics or audiences, outsiders may find it very difficult to appropriate a code or logic and can even be penalized.

An Example of Failed Appropriation: Contract Brewers in America

A striking example is the attempt by contract-brewers to appropriate the identity of micro-brewers in America, and the consequent penalties visited on contract brewers. In the 1980s microbreweries and brewpubs emerged as small, specialty beer brewers due to the micro-brewing movement (Carroll &

Swaminathan, 2000). Historically, micro-breweries were not new. Many small breweries flourished before the Prohibition era. For example, in the 19th century, in Pennsylvania alone, there were over 800 micro-brewers. With the Industrial Revolution and better refrigeration and packaging, beer could be held longer and shipped greater distances. A few well-managed companies became very successful; they acquired smaller companies that could not continue to compete. Further, prohibition dramatically reduced the number of the smaller competitors, whose facilities could not be converted to produce nonalcoholic products.

By 1980s, the U.S. beer industry was divided into domestic beers, which were light and inexpensive, and imports, which came in green bottles and had more flavor. The large domestic beer producers controlled virtually all of the beer market due to enormous economies of scale of their production, distribution, and marketing. Micro-breweries and brewpubs were outcroppings of a craft movement that arose in reaction to the "industrial beer" produced by the dominant firms in the beer industry – especially Anheuser Busch, Miller, and Coors.[2]

Beer aficionados were discontented due to the lack of choice, and the dearth of fresh and tasteful beer sold onsite at bars, restaurants, and other gathering places. "Pro-choice" aficionados, such as Fritz Maytag, the owner of Anchor Brewing (producers of "Anchor Steam" beer), exploited this discontent and began to produce small quantities of tasteful beer using traditional methods, and targeted consumers searching for such options. Soon, other micro-brewers and brewpubs commenced production of small quantities of beer using craft methods. The Great American Beer Festival, established in 1982, drew about 40 brewers and 700 beer enthusiasts. These first shots sparked a revolt against the "beer establishment" and other enthusiasts started brewing in small quantities using traditional methods. By 1994, there were close to 500 establishments that are part of the $400 million craft beer movement in the United States. At the same time, craft beer is still a drop in the mug, so to speak, of the beer industry: in 1994, micro-brewers crafted more than two million barrels of beer, which produced revenues much less than the total sales of Michelob Light.

As a craft movement, then, the micro-breweries were by definition, less about scale and more an expression of a new identity. The identity of micro-brewers was premised on small scale, authentic and traditional methods of production, and fresh beer with a myriad of tastes. As aficionados armed with small kettles, fresh ingredients, and unique recipes began to produce a stunning variety of beers, other beer lovers sought to solidify the identity of craft brewing by establishing an infrastructure to support the craft-brewing movement.

A mainstay of the craft-brewing movement was the Institute for Brewing Studies (IBS). An association dedicated to craft brewing, it was founded in 1983 to provide technical data, the most recent statistics, updates on both local and federal regulations, and to distribute a magazine, *New Brewing*, to members. Craft-brewing aficionados also sought to educate the consumer. Festivals, such as the Great American Beer Festival or the Texas Brewing Festival, started to educate consumers about the choices available in the market and provided a platform for aficionados to assess how their beer fared vis-à-vis other specialty beers. The Great American Beer Festival initiated a consumer poll designed to choose the best five beers in 1983, and continued this poll until 1989. The poll was replaced by the Professional Blind Taste Test that chose winners, and grew to become the most prestigious contest in the U.S. By 1998, the craft-brewing movement consisted of more than 1306 micro-brewers and brewpubs.

The growth of the craft-brewing movement did not go unnoticed by the dominant industrial beer producers, who responded by establishing "specialty beer" divisions. "Contract brewers," who sub-contracted the production of beer, also grew. Contract brewers like Boston Beer Company and Pete's Brewing Company positioned themselves as members of the craft beer industry, charging similar price premiums. However, contract brewers' beer was not produced in house, but was produced by mass production breweries with excess capacity. The press initially used the terms "brewpub," "microbrewery," and "contract brewer" interchangeably to qualify a brewery with a limited production per year. By the mid-1990s most magazines and newspapers resolved the lexical impasse by reporting the Association of Brewers' definitions, which distinguished between authentic craft brewers that produced in house small batches of beer and contract brewers that were "a business" that hired a brewery to produce its beer (Kreck, 1995).

This terminological confusion was part of a "marketing ploy," contract brewers advertised their products as local beers to attract local drinkers, but actually paid a large commercial brewery somewhere else to make the beer. Federal law required that labels say where the beer was brewed. Generally, the notices were in small print or lost in a long paragraph of information. Nathan Hale Golden Lager, for example, was marketed by Connecticut Brewing Co. as a local beer, but was actually produced in Wilkes-Barre, PA.; the lettering indicating the production facility was dark on a black background and stood less than 1/16th of an inch tall (Alexander, 1989).

Although the practice was legal, many of the authentic microbrewers rejected the practices of contract brewers and labeled them as "marketing people" and as faux, fraudulent brewers. Contract brewers argued that they planned to eventually own the production facilities and that their beer was local since the work force of the company was local. Jim Koch, president and founder of Boston Beer Co., which marketed Sam Adams, defined the purists' reaction to his beer as a whispering campaign: "We get grief about Pittsburgh [where most of the beer is actually produced], but not from people who drink our beer. It's a great beer. You drink what's in the bottle. If you want to drink the label, you're a fool. I don't want idiots as customers (Rouvalis, 1993)."

In his early ad campaign Koch, a Harvard MBA, accused imported brands such as Heineken and Beck's of shipping inferior formulations to U.S. consumers. In his radio ads, Koch portrayed himself as a microbrewer, who hand-crafted his beers using the recipe of his great-great grandfather. Despite initial announcements of moving production in house, Koch used the company's small red brick brewery in Boston mostly for developing and testing beer brands and for tours. Similarly to Boston Beer Co., Pete's Brewing Co. was founded in 1986 by a business executive, who attributed his company's success to marketing and sales. Accused of not being an authentic microbrewer, he declared, "We are not a contract brewer … . The government defines us as a brewer, we define ourselves as a brewer."

Micro-brewers who hand crafted their beer expressed their contempt for "marketing companies that hold themselves out as micro-brewers" and that "bastardize the term micro-beer to take advantage of a certain amount of customers (Kennedy, 1994)." In 1996, Anheuser Busch and several Pacific Northwest microbreweries filed a complaint with the Bureau of Alcohol, Tobacco and Firearms (BATF) alleging that the labels on Samuel Adams' beer were misleading because the labels stated that Boston Beer Company brewed Samuel Adams. Microbrewers took issue with both the misleading labeling and the inaccurate advertising. Microbrewers believed that the formula of success consisted in "established identities, a strong lead brand, and an established foothold in local markets (Theodore, 1998)."

Despite their significant investments in marketing and sales, contract brewers failed to reap the benefits associated with being an authentic microbrewer or brewpub. Carroll and Swaminathan (2000) showed that from 1985 to 1995 the number of microbreweries and brewpubs grew at a much faster rate than the number of contract brewers and that contract brewers also had higher failure rates and poorer outcomes than other specialist breweries over most of the time period. Thus, the saga of attempts to impersonate micro-brewers suggests that when claims to authenticity are salient in a domain, attempts to appropriate authentic traditions and techniques are thwarted by insiders.

Q3. INTEGRATION

The term "integration," according to the Merriam-Webster dictionary, derives from the Latin *integrare* and means "to form, to coordinate, or blend into a unified functioning whole." In our context, integration occurs when insiders import new institutional codes/logics and connect them with a pre-existing logic. Once again, framing is central to the success of the institutional project, but hinges on political opportunity.

P8. Attempts to import a new logic and integrate it with the existing logic are successful if elements of continuity between the existing and the new logic are emphasized by institutional entrepreneurs.

Insiders are able to successfully bring and blend new logics and codes if there is continuity and consistency with the existing logics and codes. Thus, if the new code or logic is at a higher level and subsumes the existing logic, then integration is likely to be successful and effective (Friedland & Alford, 1991). Alternately, the diagnostic framing (culprits or causes of the problem) may be retained, but the prognostic framing may be changed (Snow & Benford, 1992). Equally important, entrepreneurs seeking to instigate institutional change face multiple audiences, and the greater their ties to these audiences, the more successful is the effort at integration.

An Example of Successful Integration: Slow Food – From Taste to Ecology

The Slow Food movement is a compelling instance of how an entrepreneur was able to achieve integration. The Slow Food movement traces its origin in 1986 to Bra, in the north of Italy, as "a movement for the protection of the right to taste" (Slow Food's website, 2003). Its founder, Carlo Petrini, was a journalist and activist who, disenchanted by the world of politics, wanted to preserve local gastronomic traditions that had been endangered by standardization and industrialization (Stanley, 1989). Slow Food was created as an antidote to the success of fast food and was aimed at rediscovering the "flavors and savors of regional cooking (Slow Food Manifesto, 1989)." An emblem of slowness – the snail – was chosen as the movement's symbol. Among its members there were the French historian Jacques Le Goff, the British wine expert Hugh Johnson, and the Italian playwright-actor Dario Fo, recipient of the Nobel Prize for Literature.

According to Renato Sardo, president of Slow Food International, two events favored the growth of the movement: the methanol scandal, which crushed the Italian wine industry in the 1980s and led to a renewed interest in traditional gastronomic values, and the opening of a McDonald's store in a historical landmark in Rome (Sardo, 2004). Although in its early stage the movement was essentially a gourmands' club, different members had different visions of the direction of the movement. For example, while Folco Portinari, the author of the movement's manifesto, wanted to promote a return to a "realistic cuisine" and saw the movement as a reaction to the sophistication of nouvelle cuisine (Fabricant, 1991), other members were more concerned about educating people – especially children – about nutrition.

Petrini believed that Slow Food was all about gastronomy and conviviality; in the 1980s he met with Ralph Nader in Washington and realized the importance of an economically solid and self-sufficient organization. In 1990, the publishing arm of the movement, Slow Food Editore, was created. Its publications on wines and restaurants became the Italian Michelin guide: a top ranking virtually guaranteed that a vintage would sell out almost instantly. In 1994, Slow Food decided to support its international expansion through the creation of an international office, a magazine, and local units called *convivia*. The convivia relied mostly on voluntary work and were therefore "less expensive than a national association (Sardo, 2004)." The founders of the convivia were mostly gastronomic experts, journalists that published on food and wine magazines, and restaurateurs. The convivia grew slowly and mainly by word of mouth.

In 1996, Slow Food started the Ark of Taste project to document and catalog animal breeds, cheeses, meats, fruits, grains, and herbs whose existence was threatened by the "supermarket culture" and industrialization (Singleton, 1998). To support the Ark Project, the movement created *presidia*, which provided local growers with marketing resources, technical support, apprenticeship training, and assistance in navigating governmental regulatory systems (Kummer, 2002). Restaurants were also encouraged to include an endangered product in their menu. The movement's attention to the discovery and the preservation of flavors was transforming it into a "Noah's ark for taste" (Shriver, 1998), or a "great cuisine with a conscience (Houston, 1999)." According to Petrini, the idea was "to extend the kind of attention that environmentalism had dedicated to the panda and the tiger to domesticated plants and animals."

In 1999, during a visit in the United States, Petrini discussed the necessity to integrate gastronomical and ecological concerns: "the Slow Food movement is different from ecological movements and from gastronomical movements. Gastronomical movements don't defend the small producers and their products, and ecological movements fight the battles, but can't cook. You have to have both at the same time (Brennan, 1999)." The defense of food did not imply, however, a militant style a la Greenpeace, but it worked more like a "homeopathic medicine," to be taken every day in small quantities (Bates, 1999). The concept of slowness had to be applied not only to the consumption, but also to the production of food, and implied the defense of organic methods of agriculture to produce "good" food.

By 1999, Slow Food had grown rather quickly to a membership of more than 70,000 members, with supporters in 35 countries. Its quarterly magazine, "Slow," was published in English, Italian, German, French, and Spanish. As the movement was growing, its membership base was expanding to include even activists such as José Bové, the French farmers' leader who had directed an assault on a McDonald's in Southern France (Owen, 2000). In an interview, Kelly Gibson, co-founder of the Chicago convivium, explained how even geographically proximate convivia could differ in their membership base and in their activities. For example, while "the Chicago convivium's members were mainly chefs and food people, the one in southern Illinois, situated in a rural area, was made up mostly of local farmers (Gibson, 2004)."

Since 2000, Slow Food had achieved its fastest growth in the United States, "a natural Slow Food territory, because of a huge movement of organic food, the phenomenon of the microbreweries, the rise of farmers' markets, and community-supported agriculture (Stille, 2001)." Petrini attributed the movement's success to its combination of gastronomic and ecological concerns. By 2004, Slow Food had 80,000 members in more than 100 countries, organized into almost 800 local convivia. It was also planning the creation of a university in Italy, whose faculty included feminist philosopher and scientist Vandana Shiva, social and cultural historian Victoria de Grazia, Fast Food Nation author Eric Schlosser, wine expert Jancis Robinson, and chef Alice Waters, who had played a key role in the movement's growth in the United States.

P9. When multiple audiences have to legitimate change, the higher the number of ties with allies in these multiple domains (for example, restaurateurs, farmers, journalists), the more likely is framing to be accepted.

An Example of Failed Integration: Consumer Union

If the Slow Food Movement is a telling exemplar of successful integration, the failure of Consumers Union to blend the logic of product testing with the logic of worker rights provides a compelling contrast.[3] In the 1930s two issue entrepreneurs, Stuart Chase and Frederick Schlink, attempted to improve the protection of consumers through the establishment of a new mechanism of control – the Consumer Watchdog Organization (CWO). Chase, an accountant by profession, had written two polemics entitled *The Challenge of Waste* (1922) and *The Tragedy of Waste* (1925) to warn consumers against products that were superfluous and detrimental. Schlink had worked for the National Bureau of Standards and the National Standards Association; together with Chase, in 1927, he published *Your Money's Worth*, in which manufacturers were blamed for creating wasteful variety and advertisers were accused of deceitful claims.

Building on his experience with a consumer's club established in a church in White Plains, New York, Schlink created Consumer Research (CR), whose Bulletin would "investigate, test, and report reliably hundreds of commodities (Silber, 1983, p. 18)." The goal of CR – a nonprofit organization that distanced itself from any political party – was to protect consumers by pushing manufacturers to reduce wasteful variety and keep fair prices through standardization. Scientific analysis, and not emotions, had to guide consumption. CR shielded itself from the opposition of manufacturers and advertisers by building on the ideas of "service" to the customer and truth in advertising – concepts that firms were implementing to professionalize their trade and as a competitive weapon – and by emphasizing standardization and testing. CR grew quickly: in 1927, it had 656 subscribers, but by 1933, there were 42,000 subscribers (Silber, 1983). In 1935 the readership of the Consumers Research Bulletin reached a circulation of 55,000. CR's growth was also fostered by the Depression, which forced consumers to pay more attention to price/quality ratios, and by a wave of books that run exposes of manufacturing and advertising practices.

As CR grew, new activists joined, while some older activists – among which Chase – left the organization because of disagreements with Schlink. These disagreements stemmed from different perspectives on the scope of CR – Chase and other members wanted to deal with social questions concerning wages and working conditions, while Schlink and his supporters believed that these concerns could not be scientifically tested and therefore were outside the boundaries of CR's responsibilities towards consumers. In 1935, Arthur Kallett, an ex-colleague of Schlink at the American Standards

Association and then member of the board of CR – founded a new organization called Consumer Union (CU), which aimed at protecting both consumers and workers. The founders of CU defined the consumer as a worker who was concerned not only about wasteful variety and deceitful advertising but also about wages and income. Living standards could be improved through standardization, product testing, and control of labor conditions. Labor concerns also influenced purchasing choices; for example, CU urged members to boycott anti-union manufactures. Labor legislation that created a favorable environment for labor unions – for example, the Norris–La Guardia Act in 1932 and the Wagner Act in 1935 – stimulated CU's growth: by the end of 1936, it had 20,700 members, and by 1937, it had close to 40,000 members.

CR and CU provided two different models for a consumer watchdog organization. While the concepts of rational decision making, standardization, and scientific testing that were initially promoted by CR spread to governmental agencies and professional societies, small, newly founded consumer groups were modeled after CU. These endorsements stimulated CU's founders to increase circulation of the organization's bulletin, Consumers Union Reports. However, CU's radical agenda encountered resistance from diverse institutional actors: in 1939 the postmaster general of New York banned the bulletin and 62 newspapers, including the New York Times, refused to sell advertising space to CU because of its attacks on industries. Professional journals such as Science and the Journal of Home Economics declined space to CU because CU's claims could not be scientifically substantiated. In 1937, a new watchdog organization began to publish Consumer Bureau Reports, which provided favorable ratings in return for free samples from manufacturers. Both the similarity of the name of the bulletin and its format could confuse the readers and weaken CU's reputation.

Further, CU was directly smeared as a Communist newspaper by the Hearst newspapers, due to a series of CU's exposes of Hearst's Good Housekeeping Institute (so much so, that the Federal Trade Commission launched an investigation against the institute). A few years later, in 1938, a House committee on subversive activities chaired by Congressman Dies sought to investigate whether CU was engaged in un-American activities harmful to the national interest. J. B. Matthews, an associate of Schlink at CR, served as counsel for the Select Committee on Un-American Activities and suggested that Kallett's writings and the fact that a CU ex-employee, Susan Jenkins, had admitted to being an employee of a Communist newspaper (the Daily Worker) were proof that the organization was a Communist front. The Hearst newspapers printed Matthews's accusations in full.

Although there was no systematic investigation of the charges leveled at CU, the Dies Committee's allegations became a matter of concern to the founders and supporters. This spate of attacks from multiple actors led CU's founders to disengage from their radical agenda. Reports on labor conditions were no longer included in CU's bulletin, which more conservatively focused on product testing and ratings, establishing CR as a reference model for nonprofit watchdog organizations.

Q4. INSURGENCY

The term "insurgency," says the Merriam-Webster dictionary, derives from the Latin *insurgere* and means "to rise up" and an insurgent is one "who rises up against a civil authority or established government." In our paper, insurgency exists when outsiders import new institutional codes/logics and confront a pre-existing logic/code. Once again, framing is central to the success of the institutional project, but hinges on political opportunity.

P10. When a domain is closed to change, outsiders seeking to import a new logic are successful if they are able to secure the support of third parties, and expand political opportunity.

An example of Successful Insurgency: From Châteaux to Garages,
a Revolution

The rise of the garagistes in response to the hegemony of the Bordeaux producers is a recent example of insurgency in an institutional domain. In the 1990s Saint Emilion in Bordeaux, France, became the epicenter of a wine revolution. Some local wine-makers pioneered a new, rich flavored wine making style of predominantly Merlot-based red wines. These wines were dubbed "vins de garage," or garage wines, because they were not produced in the great châteaux. However, as they became more popular among connoisseurs and consumers, a price explosion followed that threatened the high-end market. This market in Bordeaux was traditionally represented by more subtle Cabernet-Sauvignon based wines produced in the region of Medoc. The old guard of wine-makers in Bordeaux adhered to a classification of wines introduced for the 1855 Exposition Universelle de Paris. Upon request of Napoleon III, brokers in the wine industry had then ranked the wines according to a chateau's reputation and trading price. The result was the Bordeaux Wine Official Classification. Red wines that made the list all came from the Médoc region with the exception of the Château Haut-Brion from Graves. The wines were ranked descending from first to fifth growths, called crus. According to this official classification, which has been changed just once in 1973 (when Château Mouton-Rothschild was elevated from a second growth to a first growth vineyard), there are five grand crus chateaux in the region of Bordeuax: Château Margaux (Margaux), Château Latour (Pauillac), Château Haut-Brion Pessac (Graves), and Château Mouton-Rothschild (Pauillac). A newcomer to the region that wanted to produce a classified wine had just the option to buy one of these chateaux (Isark, 2001).

Bordeaux's traditional wine-making technique was based on large yields of unripe grapes that, since they had not reached their full flavor, produced a bitter aftertaste and sometimes required more than a decade of aging to become drinkable (Echikson, 2001). Since speculation in Bordeaux wines took off in the 1980s, the wine aristocracy had not modified its traditional way to do business. For example, wines had to pass through several tiers on the way to market, and each step of the process added cost to the final price. The best wines were even sold as "futures," two years in advance of release (DeBord, 2004). An industry expert commented, "That approach was fine when these wines were drunk largely by the English upper class, who favored many of the funky aspects that fine old "claret" could develop (bitter, astringent notes and age-defeated fruit to go along with the seductive tobacco and leather aromas). But wine has changed. Modern palates, for whom Robert Parker is Virgil, crave sweeter, richer wines – so-called "fruit bombs" – that can be drunk right away (DeBord, 2004)."

The garagistes were "new" winemakers and came from families with deep roots in the wine business, such as the Thienponts, the makers of Le Pin, who had owned châteaux in Bordeaux since the 1920s, or Count Stephan von Neipperg, who produced La Mondotte (Prial, 2000). To produce a garage wine, the grapes had to be ultra-ripe and flavors were further concentrated by cold-fermenting wine. Traditional estate owners pejoratively called this wine "jam" because of its sweetness and claimed that it would not age as well. Until 1999, the chateaux owners of Medoc, the left bank, dismissed garage-type wines as just wines from the peasant farmers of Saint-Emilion, the right bank.

The well-known wine critic Robert Parker supported the garagiste revolution with his enthusiastic reviews in praise of garagistes' exceptionally small productions of mostly Merlot-based wines. By 2000 the most prized garage wines were selling for more than Petrus (Prial, 2000). One of the first garage wines – Le Pin – came from a five acre vineyard, which rarely produced more than 600 cases of wine a year, in Pomerol, the home of

Petrus. New "garages" were subsequently established in St. Emilion, in the Graves, and even in Medoc – the most traditional of all the Bordeaux regions. Initially the garagistes aimed at updating the 1855 classification system that stood between them and formal recognition and struggled with the complexity of the establishment's pricing and sales system. When that failed, they simply established alternate pricing, sales, and distribution channels that cut the old guard off. For example, in Fronsac, a group of 15 garagistes created a group – called Expression de Fronsac – to market their garage wine together. Its members came from different backgrounds, from investment banking to a plastics and packaging business (Echikson, 2003). In a 2001 tasting held in Japan, the garage wine of Michel Garcia earned the top rank, finishing ahead of even the famed Chateau Cheval Blanc. Garcia's construction company had recently renovated Cheval Blanc's buildings; he recalled that "when his clients, the aristocrats, first found out that he also made wine, they laughed. They no longer are laughing (Echikson, 2001)." Due to the garagiste revolution in Bordeaux, "what counts is not the history or grandeur of the chateau, but the care of the winemaker (Echikson, 2001)."

P11. Insurgencies are likely to fail when their code/logic is co-opted by the dominant players in the institutional domain.

An Example of Failed Insurgency: Dogme95 and the Attack on Hollywood

Insurgencies seek to attack a dominant category or organization. When dominant players or category co-opts cognitive elements of the critique leveled against them, insurgents lack an issue and may have well have to concede defeat (Pfeffer, 1992). A nice example is the case of the Dogme movement in film, which sought to inveigh against Hollywood, but was disarmed when many Hollywood directors started to embrace the Dogme critique.

On March 20, 1995, the Danish filmmaker Lars von Trier stood up at the Odeon Theatre in Paris – a key location in the May 1968 uprisings – on the 100th anniversary of the cinema and tossed handfuls of pamphlets into the audience. On the flyers he spelled out the rules of Dogme95, the collective of film directors founded in Copenhagen in spring 1995, with the expressed goal of countering "certain tendencies" in cinema (Dogme's website, 2005). According to the Dogme95 manifesto:

> In 1960 enough was enough! The movie was dead and called for resurrection. The goal
> was correct but the means were not! The new wave proved to be a ripple that washed

ashore and turned to muck. Slogans of individualism and freedom created works for a while, but no changes ... . The anti-bourgeois cinema itself became bourgeois, because the foundations upon which its theories were based was the bourgeois perception of art. The auteur concept was bourgeois romanticism from the very start and thereby ... false!

Dogme95 was founded as a "rescue action against predictable storytelling, superficial action and emotional manipulation of mainstream cinema," especially Hollywood (Rosenthal, 2004). Dogme95 saw films as a collective, impersonal effort and the introduction of digital technology as the ultimate democratization of the cinema, since anyone could then make movies (Dogme's website, 2005). Since the tricks and the movie cosmetics of Hollywood created an illusion of pathos and love and did not communicate emotions, Dogme95 wanted to counter the film of illusion by the presentation of an indisputable set of rules known as the Vows of Chastity.

The movement's Vows of Chastity – which had been likened to Martin Luther's 95 theses at Wittenberg for their "back to basics" philosophy – prescribed shooting on location, with a handheld camera, and forbade easy plots (for example, no murders and no guns), precluded temporal and geographical alienation (the film has to take place now and here), and inveighed against artificial props and sets on location, special lighting, optical work, filters, and music (unless it occurred where the scene was being shot). Finally, the director could not be credited.

Lars von Triers and three Danish directors – Thomas Vinterberg, Soren Kragh-Jacobsen, and Kristian Levring – signed the manifesto as a way to escape Hollywood genre films and to give characters and dialogue absolute precedence over spectacle and incident, generating documentary-level realism (Rosenthal, 2004). Of the four signatories on that first film-making manifesto, only one was familiar. Lars Von Triers had in fact achieved an enormous success with "Breaking the Waves," which earned him an Oscar victory. Vinterberg had graduated from Denmark's National Film School in 1993 and his graduation short, the "Last Round," received an Oscar nomination. Soren Kragh-Jacobsen, who started out as a musician and was known as the Danish Bob Dylan, and Kristian Levring were both neophytes in the film industry.

According to Vinterberg, "the rules [of Dogme95] were drawn up partly out of boredom, partly in jest. But the group was serious in its goal to make better films. We were trying to break conventions in filmmaking, trying to avoid this growing mediocrity in filmmaking. And what we did was sit down at a coffee shop in Copenhagen for an hour, and said what we normally do when we make a film. Then we forbade it (Chollet, 1998)." The language of the Dogme was informed by religious terminology: commandments to be followed, vows to be taken, confessions to be made, and reprimands and blessings to be received. The Dogme directors also referred to each other as "brethren," like crusaders in quest of a spiritual goal (Kehr, 2004).

The Dogme brothers were initially inspired to contemplate dark subjects, involving incest, suicide, mental retardation, prostitution, and schizophrenia. The first Dogme film, Festen (The celebration), was shot on a hand-held, $1700 DVD camera and represented, according to its director Thomas Vinterberg, "a layer of evil and abomination he had never been to before (Dogme's website, 2005)." The second Dogme film, Idioterne (The idiots), concerned a group of men pretending to be mentally handicapped. When the film was shown at the Cannes Film Festival, it turned out to be a disaster.

According to Dogme films' producer Peter Jensen, "it was when Soren Kragh-Jacobsen's Mifune was shown at the Berlin festival a year after the launching that people really got crazy about the Dogme movies" (Colton, 1999). Both Mifune and Dogme's fourth film by Kristian Levring – The King is Alive – confronted less debatable themes than its Dogme predecessors and demonstrated that Dogme was not just "a manifesto for migraines," as it had been dubbed by one critic (Jensen, 2002).

Because of the productions' simplicity, all three of the completed Danish Dogma films cost less than $1 million each, slightly below the average cost for films in Denmark. Early on, as Vinterberg said in an interview, "Dogme was very much a product of Danish film culture and generated a Scandinavian renaissance, with little or no impact on Hollywood." In the United States, Dogme was perceived as a low-budget, independent method of filmmaking that did not attract establishment artists like Francis Ford Coppola or Martin Scorsese nor the American independent scene, such as the Sundance film festival. To spread the Dogme gospel, von Trier and Vinterberg set up an association, Dogme Brothers, which would provide training to new Dogme directors, starting with seminars in Argentina. After The Idiots, Von Triers received a letter from Jean Luc-Godard saying he felt the director was "really on to something." Godard himself had pioneered the use of small crews, natural light, and acrobatic camerawork, but the tenth Dogme rule sternly repudiated the core New Wave's concept of the centrality of the auteur, since the director could not be credited for the film.

However, over time Dogme was slowly becoming a "brand." In the United States, more than a dozen directors were planning to shoot a Dogme film. In October 1999, at the Universal Pictures Film Conference, Steven Spielberg spoke enthusiastically about Dogme and announced his intention to make a Dogme film. Martin Scorsese called Von Trier "wonderful film-maker ... who got furious, threw everything up in the air, and said, Look, let's start from nowhere now (Jensen, 2002)." In August 2002, Lars von Trier and his three co-signatories of the Dogme 95 manifesto – Vinterberg, Kragh-Jacobsen and Levring – issued a statement saying they were "alarmed by the success of their revolutionary method of film-making" and decided that they would no longer authorize new Dogme films (Jensen, 2002). The brothers wanted to prevent Dogme from "becoming a commercial concept used to market movies rather than a creative principal used to redefine film-making." According to Vinterberg, Dogme died because it had been "accepted and corrupted" and "the whole idea was to create renewal. Dogme had become bourgeois" (Hofmann, 2002). For his part, Von Trier suggested that "the more fashionable Dogme had become, the more boring."

CONCLUSIONS AND IMPLICATIONS

Our paper asked, "if institutions are durable constraints on human action, how do they change from within and from without?" Instead of taking recourse to explanations based on external shocks, we sought to build on the emerging synthesis of social movement theory and institutional theory and wanted to articulate how institutional entrepreneurs from within and without deployed existing cultural logics to push forward their institutional projects. While such activities are recognized as framing activities, we wanted to understand how the success of framing was contingent on political opportunity. We suggested that logics were semiotic codes, and as a result, the constraint on institutional change was not the inability to conceive of alternatives as unthinkable, but instead the ability to get away with framing innovations.

We focused on the origins of institutional entrepreneurs (insiders or outsiders in an institutional domain), whether they used an existing logic/code or imported a logic/code from another domain and developed a four-fold typology. We distinguished among subversion (insiders undermining an existing code), appropriation (outsiders exploiting an existing code), integration (insiders importing a code from a different domain), and subversion (outsiders championing an external code/logic to a field). We developed a number of propositions to show the scope conditions under which subversion, appropriation, integration, and insurgency would succeed; in particular, we showed how the success of framing activities was contingent on political opportunity and mobilization. We then illustrated these propositions using a number of rich examples.

Thus, we depicted the El Bulli restaurant of Ferran Adria in Spain as the successful subversion of nouvelle cuisine, and compared it with Anderson's failure to subvert its auditor as samurai logic that eventually led to its collapse. Similarly, we contrasted the successful growth of private prisons in America with the failure of contract brewers to understand when appropriation of microbrewers' identity was likely to be effective. Likewise, we compared how the Slow Food movement in Italy was able to transform itself into an eco-gastronomic movement with the inability of Consumer Union to illuminate the conditions under which the integration of product evaluation and advocacy for worker rights could be successful. Finally, we contrasted how the garagiste movement in France was able to successfully challenge the dominant wine châteaux of Bordeaux with the inability of the Dogme movement to transform filmmaking.

Our paper focused on the linkage between framing and political opportunity – our goal was to understand the conditions under which activists could get away with innovation from within and without institutions. However, logics and codes, and alterations therein, do not endanger large-scale change – they create openings, and scale shift is required for movements to cumulate and have lasting impact (McAdam et al., 2001). This is where mobilization plays a crucial role (McCarthy & Zald, 1977), especially, social networks, formal and informal organizations, and conduits for contagion.

Indeed, many of our case examples spotlight the salience of structures of mobilization. For example, Ferran Adria succeeded in subverting nouvelle cuisine in part because of his tour of nouvelle cuisine chefs in France. In his *voyage de formation* Adria not only learnt the state of the art from the masters of nouvelle cuisine, but also built a network of friends and potential allies who came to respect him first as a chef of *nueva cocina*. This respect as a nouvelle cuisine chef shielded Adria from subsequent criticism for his techno-cuisine. Adria's shift was then interpreted as an evolution rather than a revolution in full observance of the principle of experimentation championed by nouvelle cuisine chefs. The freedom to experiment, originally espoused in opposition to the constraints of traditional French cuisine, was taken by Adria to a new level and his kitchen became a lab in which to experiment with shapes, tastes, and consistencies. Adria's kitchen also became the epicenter of a pilgrimage of chefs who wanted to be trained in conceptual cuisine and who then applied some of Adria's techniques and principles in their own restaurants, augmenting his base of influence.

On the other hand, the Andersen case provides an interesting example of how the channels of mobilization available can hinder the attempts of change even of high-status insiders. The consulting arm of Andersen – Andersen Consulting – enjoyed the highest margins and every year showered the accounting partners with rich bonuses. The cause of the consultants also benefited from external validation from the media, which eagerly monitored this internal struggle and depicted the accountants' position as inadequate and not up-to-date with the changing nature of Andersen's business. However, the consultants could "win" their battle for the subversion of the existing "accountant as samurai" model only by obtaining the majority of votes in the general meeting of partners, where the supporters of the model in place outnumbered its detractors. Since, this channel of mobilization was dominated by the accountants, the consultants' project of change failed and the consultants had to create a new company to establish new rules of the game.

The structures of mobilization emerged as an influential force even in our analysis of cases of appropriation. In the instance of private prisons, similarly to Adria's *tour de France*, the entrepreneurs at the head of these companies skillfully created a web of elite allies among government officials by recruiting them as consultants or supporting their campaigns. These entrepreneurs did not confront the opposition coming from the media, which raised issues of economic sustainability and of psychological rehabilitation of the inmates, but focused their attention in building consensus among the decision makers and in eliciting favorable legislation.

In contrast, the contract brewers who mimicked the identity of microbrewers failed to establish alliances with the critics of this niche and the microbrewers themselves, who then voiced their concerns and labeled as fraudulent the contract brewers' attempts. The ownership of the brewing facilities and production in small batches became the hallmarks of authenticity of a microbrewer and all those beer companies who failed to comply on these two criteria could not legitimately label themselves microbrewers.

Along similar lines, the success of the Slow Food movement partially depended on the local roots of the convivia, who recruited journalists, restaurateurs, and later organic farmers. On the other hand, Consumer Union and its model of a Consumer Watchdog Organization that championed the causes of both the consumers and the workers faced attacks of anti-Americanism of the Hearst newspapers and magazines in reaction to CU's series of exposes of Hearst's Good Housekeeping Institute. A few years later, Consumer Union found in the Congressional hearings of a House committee a venue of even more serious opposition in which its critics could coalesce and gain further strength. As a result, Consumer Union progressively abandoned its emphasis on labor conditions and retreated to scientific testing of products, decreeing the failure of the radical product-testing model.

Finally, in our analysis we found that even the success of insurgency rests on the channels of mobilization. In the region of Bordeaux the garagistes initially tried to sell their wines through the existing distribution channels, but faced the strong opposition of the established high-status players and their intricate distribution system. The garagistes then relied on other networks – international distributors and the Internet – to bypass the existing system and gain popularity. The garage wines ended up commanding even higher prices than the chateaux wines. On the contrary, the absence of barriers to the diffusion of the Dogme style of filmmaking led to its commercialization and therefore to the corruption of its original intents of purity, simplicity, and frugality. The experiment was then pronounced dead by its own founders.

In conclusion, the analysis of these eight cases has provided some interesting insights, but has at the same time opened a new set of questions that merit further exploration. For example, subsequent research could explore the conditions under which informal networks facilitate or hinder the success of institutional change. For example, why did the informal network of Adria shield him from criticism, while the informal networks of the Dogme brethren or of the Andersen's consultants hindered their success?

It is not also clear what role formal organizations play in stimulating or supporting institutional change and in what circumstances this role eventually matters. Similarly, the role of incubator organizations such as churches and universities merits further exploration to pinpoint if these organizations influence attempts of institutional change by providing cadres or by cross-fertilization of models of success across distinct domains.

While our attention has been focused on the relationship between framing and political opportunity, a pressing task for future research is then to understand the relationship between framing and resource mobilization and between resource mobilization and political opportunity. Only then can we have a complete account of change from within and without institutions.

NOTES

1. This example is drawn from the case "A Tale of Two Cultures: Arthur Andersen and Deloitte & Touche," Kellogg School of Management, written by Robert Dewar and Hayagreeva Rao.

2. The description of the micro-brewing movement leans heavily on the account provided in "Power Plays: Social Movements, Collective Action and New

Organizational Forms," Hayagreeva Rao, Calvin Morrill, and Mayer Zald, *Research in Organizational Behavior*, 2000.
   3. This section is based on Hayagreeva Rao, Caveat emptor: The construction of nonprofit consumer watchdog organizations, *American Journal of Sociology, 103(4)*, 912–961.

ACKNOWLEDGMENT

We are thankful to Barry Staw for his incisive suggestions to improve the paper.

REFERENCES

Alexander, S. (1989). Is a Beer Local If It's Produced Not So Locally. *The Wall Street Journal*.
Bates, T. (1999). The Slow Revolution. *Portland Oregonian*.
Becker, H. S. (1963). *Outsiders: Studies in the sociology of deviance*. New York: Free Press.
Brennan, G. (1999). Slow food followers target fast-food nation. *The San Francisco Chronicle*.
Brubaker, R. (1992). *Citizenship and nationhood in France and Germany*. Cambridge, MA: Harvard University Press.
Camp, C. G., & Camp, G. M. (1998). *The corrections yearbook: 1998*. Middletown, CT: Criminal Justice Institute.
Carroll, G. R., & Swaminathan, A. (2000). Why the microbrewery movement? Organizational dynamics of resource partitioning in the U.S. brewing industry. *American Journal of Sociology, 106*.
Chollet, L. (1998). *A microscopic look at family deception using new film rules*. The Record.
Clemens, E., & Cook, J. (1999). Politics and institutionalism, explaining durability and change. *Annual Review of Sociology, 25*, 441–466.
Clifford, C. (1985). The corrections corporation of America. *The Sunday Times*.
Colton, M. (1999). N.Y. moviemakers korine. *New York Observer*.
Crawford, S. E. S., & Ostrom, E. (1995). A grammar of institutions. *American Political Science Review, 89*(3), 582–600.
Davis, G., & McAdam, D. (2000). Corporations, classes, and social movements after managerialism. *Research in Organizational Behavior, 22*, 195–238.
DeBord, M. (2004). The accidental connoisseur: An irreverent journey through the wine world. *The Nation*.
Delroy, A., Burns, G., Manor, R., McRoberts, F., & Torriero, E.A. (2002). The fall of Andersen. *Chicago Tribune*.
DiMaggio, P. J. (1988). Interest and agency in institutional theory. In: L. G. Zucker (Ed.), *Institutional patterns and organizations: Culture and environment*. Cambridge, MA: Ballinger.
DiMaggio, P. J., & Powell, W. W. (1983). The iron cage revisited: Institutional isomorphism and collective rationality in organizational fields. *American Sociological Review, 48*, 147–160.
Dogme's website. (2005). dogme95.dk.
Duesenberry, J. G. (1960). *Comment on economic analysis of fertility. Demographic and economic change in developing countries*. NBER, Princeton: Princeton University Press.
Echikson, W. (2001). Wines: A French revolution. *BusinessWeek*.

Echikson, W. (2003). Wine: St.-Emilion style at a nicer price in nearby locale. *The Wall Street Journal.*

Eisenhardt, K. M. (1989). Building theories from case study research. *Academy of Management Review, 14*(4), 522–550.

Fabricant, F. (1991). Slow Food Congress fights for culinary culture. *Nation's Restaurant News.*

Friedland, R., & Alford, R. R. (1991). Bringing society back symbols, practices, and institutional contradictions. In: W. W. Powell & P. DiMaggio (Eds), *The new institutionalism in organizational analysis.* Chicago: University of Chicago Press.

Friedrich, J. (1999). A restaurant of culinary surprise. *The Wall Street Journal.*

Gibson, K. (2004). *Telephone interview.*

Greenwood, R., & Suddaby, R. (2006). Institutional entrepreneurship and the dynamics of field transformation. *Academy of Management Journal, 49.*

Hesser, A. (1999). In Spain, a chef to rival dali. *The New York Times.*

Hirsch, J. (1987). What's new in private prisons. *The New York Times.*

Hofmann, K. (2002). Heir of the dogme. *Financial Times.*

Houston, S. (1999). Quality time. *The News & Observer Raleigh.*

Isark, M. (2001). *Garage sale. Scotland on sunday.*

Jackall, R. (1988). *Moral mazes: The world of corporate managers.* New York: Oxford University Press.

Jensen, J. R. (2002). Dogme is dead. *The Guardian.*

Jepperson, R. (1991). Institutions, institutional effects, and institutionalism. In: W. W Powell & P. DiMaggio (Eds), *The New institutionalism in organizational analysis* (pp. 143–163). Chicago: University of Chicago Press.

Kehr, D. (2004). Dogme: still strong, less dogmatic. *The New York Times.*

Kennedy, T. (1994). Competition brewing: Summit girds for fight with mass-produced brands. *Star-Tribune.*

Kreck, D. (1995). Craft craze taps biggest of the big. *Denver Post.*

Kummer, C. (2002). *The pleasures of slow food.* San Francisco: Chronicle Books.

Matthews, T. (1998). The big Appetite. *Wine Spectator.*

McAdam, D. (1995). 'Initiator' and 'Spin-off' movements: Diffusion processes in protest cycles. In: M. Traugott (Ed.), *Repertoires and cycles of collective action* (pp. 217–239). Durham, NC: Duke University Press.

McAdam, D., McCarthy, J. D., & Zald, M. N. (1996). Introduction: Opportunities, mobilizing structures, and framing processes – toward a synthetic, comparative perspective on social movements. In: D. McAdam, J. D. McCarthy & M. N. Zald (Eds), *Comparative perspectives on social movements: Political opportunities, mobilizing structures, and cultural framings.* Cambridge, England: Cambridge University Press.

McAdam, D., Tilly, C., & Tarrow, S. (2001). *The dynamics of contention.* New York: Cambridge University Press.

McAdam, D., & Scott, W. R. (2005). Organizations and movements. In: G. Davis, D. McAdam, W. R. Scott & M. Zald (Eds), *Social movements and organization theory* (pp. 4–40). New York: Cambridge University Press.

McCarthy, J. D., & Zald, M. N. (1977). Resource mobilization and social movements: A partial theory. *American Journal of Sociology, 82,* 1212–1241.

McDonald, D., Fournier, E., Russell-Einhourn, M., & Crawford, S. (1998). *Private prisons in the United States.* Abt Associates Inc., Executive Summary.

Ostrom, E. (1986). A method of institutional analysis. In: F. Kaufman, G. Majone & V. Ostrom (Eds), *Guidance, control, and evaluation in the public sector* (pp. 459–475). Walter de Gruyter: New York.

Owen, R. (2000). A slow death for fast food? *The Times*.

Peterson, R. A. (1997). *Creating country music: Fabricating authenticity*. Chicago: University of Chicago Press.

Pfeffer, J. (1992). Understanding power in organizations. *California Management Review*.

Polos, L., Hannan, M. T., & Carroll, G. R. (2002). Foundations of a theory of social forms. *Industrial and Corporate Change, 11*, 85–115.

Powell, W. W. (1991). Expanding the scope of institutional analysis. In: W. W Powell & P. DiMaggio (Eds), *The new institutionalism in organizational analysis* (pp. 183–203). Chicago: University of Chicago Press.

Prial, F. (2000). $1,000 Wines you never heard of. *The New York Times*.

Rao, H., Monin, P., & Durand, R. (2003). Institutional change in Toque Ville: Nouvelle cuisine as an identity movement in French gastronomy. *American Journal of Sociology, 108*, 795–843.

Rao, H., Morrill, C., & Zald. M. (2000). Power plays: how social movements and collective action create new organizational forms. In: *Research in organizational behavior* (pp. 239–282).

Rawlins, B. (1985). Company offers $100 million to operate Tennessee prisons. *The Associated Press*.

Rosenthal, D. (2004). Dogme still has its day. *The Times*.

Rouvalis, C. (1993). Boston Beer's 'breWhaha': Competitors cringe at Samuel Adams' patriotic image. *Pittsburg Post Gazette*.

Sardo, R. (2004). *Telephone interview*.

Scott, W. R. (1995). *Institutions and organizations*. Thousand Oaks: Sage.

Seo, M.G., & Creed, W. E. D. (2002). Institutional contradictions, Praxis and institutional change: A dialectical view. *Academy of Management Review, 27*, 222–247.

Sewell, W. H., Jr. (1992). A theory of structure: Duality, agency, and transformation. *American Journal of Sociology, 98*, 1–29.

Shriver, J. (1998). At slow food fest, taste trumps time. *USA Today*.

Silber, N. (1983). *Test and protest: The influence of consumers union*. New York: Holmes & Meier.

Singleton, K. (1998). The slow food movement is gearing down to a Snail's pace. *International Herald Tribune*.

Slow Food Manifesto. (1989). slowfood.com.

Slow Food's website. (2003). www.slowfood.org.

Snow, D. A., Burke, E., Jr., Worden, R. S., & Benford, R. D. (1986). Frame alignment processes, micromobilization, and movement participation. *American Sociological Review, 51*, 464–481.

Snow, D. A., & Benford, R. D. (1992). Master frames and cycles of protest. In: A. D. Morris & C. Mueller (Eds), *Frontiers in social movement theory* (pp. 133–155). New Haven, CT: Yale University Press.

Stanley, A. (1989). The militant epicures: Even the barricades groan. *The New York Times*.

Stille, A. (2001). Slow food: An Italian answer to globalization. *The Nation*.

Stutz, T. (1986). Director opposes privately run prisons in Texas. *The Dallas Morning News*.

Suddaby, R., & Greenwood, R. (2005). Rhetorical strategies of legitimacy. *Administrative Science Quarterly, 50*, 35–67.

Swidler, A. (1986). Culture in action: Symbols and strategies. *American Sociological Review, 51*, 273–286.

Swidler, A. (2001). *Talk of love*. Chicago: University of Chicago Press.

Tarrow, S. (1989). *Democracy and disorder: Protest and politics in Italy, 1965–1975*. Oxford, England: Oxford University Press.

Theodore, S. (1998). Still crazy about craft beer. (Boston Beer Co.'s Jim Koch). *Beverage Industry, 89*(1), *26*(4).

Tolchin, M. (1985). Private Prisons Operators: The benefits promised are dubious. *The New York Times*.

Wells, P. (1997). People. *International Herald Tribune*.

White, H., & White, C. (1993). *Canvases and careers: Institutional change in the French painting world*. Chicago: University of Chicago Press.

ROADS TO INSTITUTIONALIZATION: THE REMAKING OF BOUNDARIES BETWEEN PUBLIC AND PRIVATE SCIENCE

Jeannette A. Colyvas and Walter W. Powell

ABSTRACT

We analyze the process of institutionalization, arguing that it is the out-come of the self-reinforcing feedback dynamics of heightened legitimacy and deeper taken-for-grantedness, using novel techniques to document and trace this change over a 30-year period. Our focus is the remaking of the boundaries between public and private science, an institutional transfor-mation that joined science and property, two formerly distinct spheres. The setting is Stanford University, an early adopter and pioneer in the formulation of policies of technology transfer. We illustrate how archival materials may be systematically assessed to capture notable changes in organizational practices and categories, reflecting both local and field-level processes. The paper concludes with a set of indicators that gauge low, medium, and high elements of institutional change. We argue that this approach allows for more precision in measurement and enables

Research in Organizational Behavior: An Annual Series of Analytical Essays and Critical Reviews
Research in Organizational Behavior, Volume 27, 305–353
Copyright © 2006 by Elsevier Ltd.
ISSN: 0191-3085/doi:10.1016/S0191-3085(06)27008-4

comparisons across studies, two standard critiques of the institutional approach.

1. INTRODUCTION

Despite broad appeal and wide application in studies of the diffusion of managerial practices, the adoption of organizational structures, and even the global spread of managerialism, institutional theory has lacked agreement about several of its core concepts. This approach to organizational analysis has had a "big tent" attitude, welcoming social scientists with interests as varied as discourse analysis and critical realism to comparative researchers studying the world polity. While having galvanized interest, this broad embrace comes at the expense of precision in measurement (Haveman, 2000). This difficulty in conceptual fidelity is not surprising, given that institutionalization is both a multi-level process as well as an outcome. Nevertheless, several of the core ideas associated with the institutional approach, specifically legitimacy and taken-for-grantedness, have not been characterized in a way that allows for ready comparisons across studies. Thus, our goal in this chapter is to facilitate agreement about these central concepts in institutional analysis.

We argue that institutionalization is driven by the self-reinforcing feedback dynamics of heightened legitimacy and enhanced taken-for-grantedness. Consequently, the expansion and deepening of these constructs are the motors of a wider process of institutionalization, which we break down and analyze. We illustrate how practices can be more or less legitimated and assess how taken-for-grantedness changes through time, as well as show how both can be assessed and measured. To accomplish this, we use archival materials from the technology transfer office at a leading research university, Stanford, and draw on these materials in a way that provides metrics of low, medium, and high legitimacy and taken-for-grantedness. One of the criticisms of institutional research has been a lack of attention to how elements of the social order can be pre-, semi-, or fully institutionalized (Tolbert & Zucker, 1996; Strang & Sine, 2002). We address this shortcoming directly by spelling out the gradations and scale of a process of institutionalization.

Our empirical focus is the remaking of the boundaries between public and private science, and the joining of science and property, two spheres that were formerly distinct. The subject of the commercialization of science is highly apt for our theoretical aims because of the institutional transformation that has transpired over the past four decades. We begin in an era, the

1970s, when academic entrepreneurship was unfamiliar, technology transfer practices were highly idiosyncratic and not formalized, and the commercialization of science was even actively resisted. Over time, entrepreneurial activity became more familiar and commonplace on some university campuses, and was eventually buttressed in the early 1980s by federal law encouraging these efforts. By the late 1990s, technology transfer was celebrated and championed. Consider two indicators of this institutional change. Technology transfer offices on U.S. campuses numbered only in the 20s in 1980, but exceeded 200 by the year 2000 (Mowery, Nelson, Sampat, & Ziedonis, 2004). From 1980 to 2000, the number of patents assigned to research universities rose 850% (Owen-Smith, 2003). The great majority of this increase is driven by patenting in the biomedical field (Ganz-Brown, 1999; National Science Board, 2000); hence our focus is on the life sciences.

Stanford University was an early champion of technology transfer, which was initially pursued by multiple units on the campus, ranging from the sponsored research office, to the technology licensing office, to the laboratories of individual researchers. Through time, the practices were consolidated in a single high-profile office, and greatly elaborated and routinized, making this office a critical site for the locus of institutionalization. We make extensive use of rich archival materials from this office, and illustrate how researchers can draw on documents to provide concrete evidence of the changing nature of organizational practices, and to gauge how familiarity with specific practices evolves and is reproduced through time. We show how the development of categories and classifications at Stanford had ramifications well beyond the boundaries of the university.

The chapter is not intended as an empirical analysis of the commercialization of university science; we take up that task in related work. Rather, our aim is to demonstrate how archival materials from the university office that helped pioneer the field of technology transfer can be utilized to study paths to institutionalization. We offer our argument both as a theoretical contribution, where we analyze taken-for-grantedness and legitimacy as constituent components of a sequence that can lead to institutionalization, and a methodological exemplar, which shows how primary documents can be used and indicators derived from careful readings.

Through analysis of the practices of technology transfer, we enrich the conception of legitimacy by showing how procedures and definitions that initially require a great deal of effort, explanation, and translation become more codified over time, as the range of possible options becomes narrower. In a cognitive sense, a great deal of compression occurs, which allows participants to understand both meaning and nuance in a rapid fashion.

We show how taken-for-grantedness is the outcome of purposive action, the refining of skills, and the development of reflexivity on the part of participants. Our view of taken-for-grantedness is very much embedded in practices and categories that are associated with different degrees of understanding that change through time.

We turn next to a discussion of our key concepts – legitimacy and taken-for-grantedness, highlighting their central features. The research site, the Office of Technology licensing at Stanford University, which served as a bridge between the worlds of the academy and commerce, is then described. We review the archival materials next, then turn to a detailed analytical narrative of source materials. We conclude the narrative discussion with more general observations on the institutionalization of academic entrepreneurship. We then discuss implications of our approach, suggesting possible applications of our tools to other empirical settings. To encourage such efforts, we abstract from the context of science and commerce and suggest a number of more general organizational indicators of the process of institutionalization. We offer at the end a framework based on our findings that provides a foundation for comparative and complimentary research.

2. CORE CONCEPTS

Legitimacy is perhaps the most central concept in institutional research (Meyer & Rowan, 1977; Zucker, 1977; DiMaggio & Powell, 1983; Scott & Meyer, 1983) and has been crucial to various lines of work in organizational theory more generally (Hannan & Freeman, 1989; Hannan & Carroll, 1992; Aldrich & Fiol, 1994; Dacin, Goodstein, & Scott, 2002). As defined by Suchman (1995, p. 574), legitimacy is "a generalized perception or assumption that the actions of an entity are desirable, proper, or appropriate within some socially constructed system of norms, values, beliefs, and definitions." Given the centrality and importance of legitimacy in organization studies, it is curious that more attention has not been devoted to analyzing its constituent elements, and capturing how legitimacy is acquired, replicated, and even lost (Baum & Powell, 1995).

A first step involves specifying the core components of legitimacy. Almost all institutional theories argue that once particular practices or outcomes become legitimated, they are "built into" the social order, reproduced without substantial mobilization, and resistant to contestation (Jepperson, 1991). Greif (2006) captures this endogenous element nicely with his definition of an institution a "as system of rules, beliefs, norms and organizations that can jointly generate a regularity of behavior in a social situation." Thus, a key feature of legitimacy is its self-reproduction, reflected in the conception of a practice, belief, or rule as desirable, appropriate, and comprehensible. As people act collectively toward a common purpose, legitimated activities are reciprocally interpreted and become habitualized.

Selznick (1957, p. 17) observed that tasks can become imbued with social meaning, "infused with value beyond the technical requirements of the task at hand." Organizational ecologists have also drawn on this cognitive conception of legitimacy, arguing that legitimacy stems from endogenous population dynamics and represents a stage when "there is little question in the minds of actors that it serves as a natural way to effect some kind of collective action" (Hannan & Carroll, 1992, p. 34). A central feature of legitimacy, then, is that it resides in collectivities as a widely shared presumption. The basis for the presumption can vary – it can be embedded in culture, sanctioned by law, or championed by proselytizers – but the collective consciousness element is critical.

The extant literature highlights several aspects of legitimacy, which should, in principle, be analytically separable. One idea is relational embeddedness, referring to the extent to which a practice or rule is in use within an organizational field, and how such diffusion generates interdependence and self-reinforcement (Baum & Oliver, 1992). Aldrich and Fiol (1994) draw a useful distinction between socio-political legitimacy, where practices or rules are either permitted, mandated or sanctioned by the state, and cultural-cognitive legitimacy, in which ideas are more constitutive, laden with meaning, and used widely in sense-making. In her study of the evolution of technology transfer at Stanford University, Colyvas (2007) observed three stages of legitimation. There was an initial period, 1970–1980, of idiosyncratic, variegated practices, or pre-legitimacy. The second stage, 1980–1993, was marked by the passage of the Bayh–Dole Act in 1980 (formally referred to as Public Law 96–517, the Patent and Trademark Law Amendment Act), which permitted universities to retain intellectual property rights to inventions that resulted from government-funded research. This legislation was based on a rather diffuse notion that technology transfer would enhance U.S. competitiveness against foreign competition (Mowery et al., 2004). This era was a period of growing standardization, marked by the stamp of socio-political legitimacy. The third stage, 1994 to the present, is a period of broad institutionalization ushered in by a growing cultural-cognitive legitimacy, reflected in the acceptance that academic entrepreneurship is desirable and to be venerated.[1] While Stanford was a leader in promoting academic entrepreneurship, during this period technology transfer became an accepted managerial activity on university campuses, and this professionalization greatly increased relational embeddedness.

Berger and Luckman (1967, pp. 94–95) describe legitimation as a process whereby comprehensibility deepens and crystallizes. In their work, the initial stage represents incipient legitimacy, or a growing awareness that "this is how things are done," and these routines take on a persistent or enduring quality. The second involves the development of causal imageries, as lay theories in a rudimentary form are developed and elaborated more formally. The third involves expanded legitimation by reference to a differentiated body of knowledge. The fourth level entails creation of a symbolic universe, so that symbols, beliefs, and practices are deeply situated and take on moral force. We add that as this crystallization process unfolds, vulnerability to social intervention lessens. Moreover, we stress that the practice or structure that is becoming legitimated can be transformed in the process. An important aspect of this transformation is the degree and form that taken-for-grantedness can take.

Taken-for-grantedness has been central to sociological institutionalism, providing the cognitive element in explaining the reproduction of the social order (Zucker, 1977). Berger and Luckman (1967) stress, for example, the taken-for-grantedness of language, and one's mother tongue, and the extent to which many of the realities of everyday life become objectified. Jepperson (1991) emphasizes standardized interaction sequences or chronically repeated activities as having strong taken-for-grantedness features. In their elaboration of a logic of appropriateness, March and Olsen (1989) describe how individuals inculcate duties and expectations of conduct. Long ago, Veblen (1899) discussed settled habits of thought, in which surely he had in mind a form of taken-for-grantedness.

The key to developing a metric of taken-for-grantedness is to not view such activity as unreflexive, and thus portray humans as over-socialized cultural dopes, but to recognize that skill, effort, and practice are necessary elements in the process by which an activity or convention becomes taken-for-granted (DiMaggio & Powell, 1991). The institutionalization of principles and practices initially requires the mindful engagement of individuals in organizations. Our intention is to reveal the manner in which complicated mosaics of routines, categories, and identities are converted into rules of action in particular situations. We also note that even as taken-for-grantedness deepens, it can still be subjected to external scrutiny.

Whether taken-for-grantedness represents pre-conscious understandings, pre-set expectations, a schema or script for guiding interaction, a highly efficacious routine, a deeply felt value, or a widely prevalent and strongly embedded practice, the resilience of an activity or belief is enhanced through practice and replication. In Berger and Luckman's (1967) formulation, becoming taken-for-granted entails search for pre-existing templates for thought and action. Such sense-making efforts can be efficacious as they reduce the cognitive load associated with decisions, as well as decrease risk by providing well-rehearsed modes of communication and action and ready-made categories for resolving uncertainties (Weick, 1995).

Thus, a key metric of taken-for-grantedness is the extent to which practices become embedded in organizational routines and become largely unquestioned. This is the process we illustrate in this paper. But it is important to stress that experience with routines does not necessarily equate with competence or with consensus. Nelson and Winter (1982) emphasized that routines can represent organizational memory, a political truce, a target, or a skill. Routines may embody accumulated or organizational experience, a "ceasefire" between opposing coalitions, an aspiration level, or an organizational capability.

An apparent tension that exists in the literature is the assumption that institutionalization often represents greater codification, more specification of rules or procedures or more pages in a manual, while taken-for-grantedness can entail condensation as practices are so well understood they can become unspoken. We suggest that compression and elaboration complement one another, with elaboration expanding before compression can set in, and compression, in turn, enabling further elaboration. In his magisterial treatment of the history of manners from the 13th century to the present, Elias (1978) used etiquette guides to extract descriptions of table manners, bodily functions and sleeping habits.[2] One of the compelling points he illustrates is that in early guides there was extensive discussion of how to use a fork, but by the 19th century, such discussion had grown silent. In our view, this dropping off of the discussion reflects taken-for-grantedness. In contrast, notes about bedroom manners and whether adults should sleep with children and how people of the same sex should appropriately share a bed became more detailed. The abbreviation of table manners and the expansion of bedroom manners were both part of the rise of an ethos of Western civility. By the 1800s, table etiquette had been mastered by the literate middle classes and hence further explanation was no longer necessary. But the creation of conventions for rearing children and interacting "appropriately' with other adults in the bedroom needed more attention. Thus, compression suggests a widely shared symbolic or moral universe, while elaboration of more capacious rules and procedures reflects attempts to formulate that symbolic or moral code.

Similarly, some practices can be routinized and taken-for-granted through compliance to external pressures, but fail to become deeply cognitively embedded. In such cases, there may be widespread public compliance, but privately individuals or organizational representatives can challenge or grumble over the value of particular practices. For example, we will see in our case that the taken-for-granted assumptions about the convention of who deserves to be listed as an author on a scientific paper are not congruent with the legal requirements for who qualifies as an inventor on a patent. In contrast, normative pressures, which rely on cultural and moral understandings, can operate in a proselytizing manner, enrolling more members of a community in a practice or belief in a cooperative, collective endeavor, even if the activity is not formally permissible. Such normative effort is very much facilitated by discursive claims (Suddaby & Greenwood, 2005; Lawrence & Suddaby, 2006). Consequently, we do not expect that taken-for-grantedness and legitimacy always advance at the same pace or to the same degree. Our goal is to capture a process of institutionalization, with all of its fits and starts and partial steps and missteps, through which legitimacy and taken-for-grantedness advance and reinforce one another. In our case, university practices evolved into routines and became taken-for-granted, and were replicated with relative ease. As these activities became widely accepted and considered legitimate, they were deemed desirable and appropriate.

3. THE RESEARCH SETTING: UNIVERSITY–INDUSTRY INTERFACES AND TECHNOLOGY TRANSFER

Technology transfer at Stanford is an apt setting for analyzing levels of legitimacy and taken-for-grantedness. First, the development of technology licensing at U.S. universities is a reflection of a broader process of institutional change whereby the realms of public and private science have become integrated into a common domain (Owen-Smith, 2003; Sampat & Nelson, 2002). Technology transfer offices are boundary spanning units that join together the academic and commercial worlds, providing a ripe context for observing the mixing of public and private science (Guston, 1999; Owen-Smith, 2005). Second, this transformation takes place both at multiple levels (i.e. individuals, departments, and organizations) and across multiple organizational forms (i.e. university, industry, and government sectors). The ramifications of these changes enable us to consider both local and field-level processes. We are able to observe the importation and development of new practices into existing organizational forms, as well as the reconstitution of an organizational field.

While U.S. universities have a long history of relations with industry (Geiger, 1993; Nelson & Rosenberg, 1994), the commercialization of basic science is a fairly recent phenomenon. Acquiring resources and financial incentives are a component of this development, but not a primary factor. Powell and Owen-Smith (1998), for example, demonstrate that large-scale entry by universities into attempts at income-generating activities is more an effort to signal legitimacy than a sign of commercial acumen. Most university technology offices barely break even, and the majority of invention disclosures do not culminate into a license (Mowery et al., 2004). Nor is legislation the driving factor that many casual observers claim. Even though the *Economist* (2002, p. 3) proclaimed that federal legislation authorizing university technology transfer was "possibly the most inspired piece of legislation to be enacted in America over the past half century," more informed scholars have shown that this legislation was only a small part of overall government involvement in basic research, and more an authorization than a catalytic intervention (Eisenberg, 1996; Mowery et al., 2004; Powell, Owen-Smith, & Colyvas, 2007).

Stanford was among the first initiators of a technology transfer program, long before federal legislation in the early 1980s mandated such activity. We focus on the life and medical science disciplines to control for variation in disciplinary, market, and institutional environments.[3] Moreover, in the early 1980s the biotechnology industry was just emerging. We are thus able to observe the earliest features of an institutional transformation, precisely when states of legitimacy and taken-for-grantedness were very low. Stanford became one of the more successful technology transfer offices, frequently touted as a model for emulation in both the U.S. and abroad. According to the 2002 annual survey of the Association of University Technology Managers, Stanford University rates among the top 5 universities across numerous key technology transfer performance metrics, including license income received, invention disclosures, U.S. patents issued, start-up companies formed, and licenses executed with equity (AUTM, 2002).

Stanford's Office of Technology Licensing (OTL) was founded in 1969 by an engineering-trained industrialist, Neils Reimers, who had worked for a short time in the university sponsored research office and believed that there were numerous opportunities where the university would be able to capture the commercial benefits of academic research (Reimers, 1997; Weisendanger, 2000).[4] In the life sciences, faculty were only just beginning to become involved in consulting with fledgling commercial enterprises, many of which emerged from university discoveries and a healthy number were founded by academicians (Powell, 1996). Within the university, much of the impetus behind disclosing inventions was driven by the sponsored research office because life science-related federal funding agencies had developed institutional patent agreements that required notification of any potentially patentable invention. At this time, federal research agencies had requirements that universities report inventions, state a plan for dissemination, and request permission to patent.

While involvement with commercializing science today is attributed to entrepreneurship and part of an overall professional *modus operandi* of involvement with industry (Shane, 2004), early participation in the technology transfer program came largely through coincidence with other professional activities. Typically, life science faculty who submitted invention disclosures became involved through consultative ties to industry and the resultant company interest in acquiring proprietary access grew out of this relationship. On occasion, some scientists were approached by the technology transfer office with a query about marketing their inventions. Most of the early inventions at Stanford came from just a handful of research programs. Thus, early steps toward commercial involvement were not triggered by prospects of monetary gain, but stemmed from the ongoing relationships of laboratory leaders and their means of involving their technicians and collaborators in the goals of the research (Colyvas, 2006). Only over the past 15 years, with the explosion of the biotechnology industry, has commercial involvement on the part of biomedical faculty become the norm rather than the exception.[5]

The OTL had modest beginnings with only two staff, but grew rapidly. By 1975, it had a gross annual revenue of over $1 million and had already received two invention disclosures that would be among their most lucrative and well-known patented inventions. Today, the OTL has more than 25 employees with annual gross royalty income of almost $50 million.[6] Despite high profile breakthroughs and lucrative licensing agreements, financially successful technology transfer as measured through licenses and income is, nevertheless, relatively unusual. The Stanford OTL reports that only 20–30% of invention disclosures make it to the stage of a license, and among these, most active licenses do not earn any net income. In fiscal year 2003–2004, of the 436 inventions that generated funds, only 44 made over $100,000, and but six of these produced $1 million or more (Stanford, 2004).[7] Tech transfer is clearly a process involving a good deal of luck, as a few winners generate the bulk of the revenues.

4. METHODS AND MATERIALS

We follow the suggestions of Ventresca and Mohr (2002) and Schneiberg and Clemens (2006) who call for a more considered approach to archival analysis and historical inquiry. Schneiberg and Clemens (2006) argue that accounts of institutions are "discursive constructions that incorporate cultural models in their telling." Consequently, researchers must infer meanings as authors frequently reveal habits of mind and assumptions only indirectly, through their use of emphasis, quotations, and questions. They also caution that once a practice or regime acquires legitimacy, debates cease and conflicts or questions wither (Zelizer, 1979; Schneiberg, 1999). Thus, the presence, absence, onset, and cessation of commentary can be utilized to periodize the development of an institutional rule or organizational form and to develop simple categorical measures of legitimacy.

Mohr (1994, 1998) has been in the forefront of efforts at illustrating how cultural meanings and social structures are mutually constitutive. Drawing on organizational records at four key time periods, Mohr and Guerra-Pearson (2006) analyze how charitable organizations developed vocabularies that both interpreted social problems as well as staked claims to solve problems. They demonstrate how social work bureaucracies won out in a battle with settlement houses to become the dominant force in social welfare services in the early 20th century. Ventresca and Mohr (2002) champion a new archival tradition characterized by formal methods that treat archives as data to be collected, analyzed, and measured directly.

Several recent empirical studies advance these new methodological claims. In their analysis of the decline of classic French cuisine and the growth of nouvelle cuisine, Rao, Monin, and Durand (2003) link changes in cooking to broader social transformations while simultaneously using texts and interviews to chart the redefinition of French cuisine. Suddaby and Greenwood (2005) analyze rhetoric at public commissions over the appropriateness of combining the accounting and legal professions into a multi-professional organization, and vividly capture the heated contests between competing professional logics. We enter this line of research by using correspondence to trace the changing meanings and organizational practices associated with technology transfer.

We utilize an archival dataset based on a systematic review of life science discoveries that were inventions submitted to Stanford from 1970–2000 (Colyvas, 2007). The sample of disclosures by faculty, staff, and students affiliated with a basic life science department, as well as co-inventors from other departments, total 218 inventions between 1970 and 2000.[8] The university's inventions are organized into dockets, reflecting an instance of disclosing an invention by a scientist to the university. The dockets contain a chronology of the commercialization process, including legal and contractual documentation as well as hand written notes, notations in the margins, personal correspondence, and recordings of personal interactions and opinions. While the legal correspondence is often documented and preserved in its final form and may include public records (i.e. patent or licensing agreements), the informal side is often reflected in letters and memoranda written to the file, and, more recently, e-mails. The dockets also reveal many failed alternative ideas and approaches as well as disputes that are not included in the final results of a commercialization arrangement. For example, there is evidence of numerous licenses and interactions with industry that did not result in a completed agreement. Finally, particularly in the early years when practices were not fully formed, the advisory and consultative aspects of handling sensitive issues or making sense of new situations comes through in archival documentation, such as memos written to the files.

We utilize correspondence we have selected from the OTL, identifying letters and memos from these dockets as "exhibits" for our purposes. The letters and memos represent traces of organizational memory. We think of them as a longitudinal conversation. We select correspondence about administrative procedures involving relationships with individuals and organizations that are central to the tech transfer process. These artifacts have been modified, with the identifying information removed to preserve the anonymity of the participants. We use only the relevant parts of letters and memos to avoid unnecessary length. The correspondence was chosen to illustrate the concepts of legitimacy and taken-for-grantedness, not as a documentary representation of the larger body of materials in the Office of Technology Licensing. This analysis is offered as an existence proof of the features and processes we wish to highlight, not as a comprehensive sampling of the university archives.

The initial coding scheme classified invention disclosures in terms of practices and meanings associated with features of the technology transfer process, including the reduction of a research finding or program into a description of an invention, the determination of inventorship, the terms of licensing, and the conditions for disbursement of real or potential income. This initial classification suggested three time periods: (1) idiosyncratic, when practices and arrangements were determined on a case-by-case basis; (2) standardized, as rules and routines became developed and codified; and (3) institutionalized, once commercializing science was self-replicating and

Table 1. Invention Disclosures by Time Period.

Year	Practice of Commercializing Academic Research	Stage of the Technology Transfer Program	Number of Invention Disclosures	Number of Individual Inventors
1970–1980	Introduction	Idiosyncratic	31	47
1981–1993	Implementation	Standardized	64	85
1994–2000	Expansion	Institutionalized	123	150

largely invulnerable to contestation. Table 1 provides the frequency counts of invention disclosures and inventors within each period. The growth in numbers did not trigger more personnel and more formalization in the OTL, rather the process worked in reverse. The OTL "scaled up" and developed standards under the leadership of Niels Reimers, the organization's founder, so that it could more proactively tutor and educate campus inventors in hopes of securing more invention disclosures.

We reviewed the disclosures from each time period and extracted exhibits that reflected critical features of legitimacy and taken-for-grantedness. Our analytic approach was to identify the definitions and debates found in the disclosures (Suddaby & Greenwood, 2005), and to discern patterns in the development of practices and their meanings (Mohr, 1998).

5. NARRATIVE ANALYSIS

We begin with a discussion of legitimacy, using the correspondence to illustrate how the commercialization of university science at Stanford became more accepted, comprehensible, and diffused across the university over time. We then discuss how discrete elements of this process became taken-for-granted. We begin with specific pieces of correspondence, and build our analysis directly from them, then conclude with a more general abstract assessment. Our goal is to detail an analytic narrative that interprets the documents and provides more general insights into how legitimacy and taken-for-grantedness can be gauged through textual analysis.

Legitimacy and the Commercialization of University Science

We first address the initial contact between public and private science, and turn to the growing acceptance of commercializing university science. The first set of documents (Exhibits A, B, and C) are internal university correspondence dealing with faculty and commercial engagements regarding licensing opportunities. We offer them as examples of low to high levels of legitimacy of technology transfer at Stanford. Exhibit A is a 1971 memo written to the disclosure file by the director of the OTL, documenting a meeting where terms of interaction with a company are discussed with respect to its effects on faculty and their research. Exhibit B is a late 1970s memo from a faculty member to an OTL associate expressing specific concerns about the university's licensing of an important technology, wherein he attempts to draw clear personal boundaries between the university and his science. Exhibit C consists of two letters, both having to do with conflict of interest guidelines for faculty and start-up companies. Both address the respective scientists' high degree of involvement in the commercial transfer of their research. These exhibits illustrate both organizational and field-level emergence of language and shared understandings that become embedded in the norms and practices of the academy.

Standards of Desirability and Appropriateness
Perhaps the clearest indicator of the novelty of commercializing basic science, and its attendant low level of legitimacy, is the difficulty that participants had in categorizing or labeling behaviors as acceptable or routine in the context of academic research. The first memo (Exhibit A) contains extensive discussion of contingencies and procedures, from how potential disputes with respect to revenue disbursement may be resolved, to the degree of involvement of faculty members with the licensing organization. " ... *(N)o person connected with the project would receive personal remuneration. The "inventor's" share of royalty income would be added to the standard department share ...* " (quotation marks in original). The explicit elaboration of these details reflects the extent to which the organization and the individuals within it sought to mitigate the tension between what may be beneficial and what may be objectionable. As Suchman (1995) noted, the pragmatic element of legitimacy depends on rendering activities unsurprising. For example, the frequent mention of the word "appropriate" indicates that there is a question over whether this activity is suitable from the perspective of the university and the faculty, hence the status of commercialization demanded explicit justification. "*It was considered appropriate that the proposed program be entered into ...* " and "*necessary in this specific case for development of a beneficial and useful [technology] for the public.*" Entering into an agreement with a company required a clear rationale and, notably a statement of necessity, rather than just a statement of benefit. Furthermore, the

Exhibit A. Commercialization of University Science.

Code: Low legitimacy

Source: July, 1971 Memo to file written by Director of Technology Licensing program

Dr. [Department Chair Name], Dr. [Faculty Member in the Department], Dr. [Principal Investigator] and Mr. [Technology Licensing Associate] met on Tuesday, July 20, to discuss the above proposed license agreement between university and [company name].

The [Department] research personnel, along with Dr. [Faculty Collaborator] (who would provide research inputs in regard to ... properties), agreed that no person connected with the project would receive personal remuneration. The "inventor's" share of royalty income would then be added to the standard department share. It was agreed that only specifically named individuals could be bound by this arrangement, and it was agreed that it would be appropriate to list these specific people in the agreement with [Company Name]. It was discussed and considered inappropriate in connection with the project for any individual to have a separate consulting agreement with [company] in the specific technological area of the proposed research program.

The question of maintaining [Company Name] marketing, trade secrets, manufacturing, or other proprietary information confidential was discussed at length. It was agreed that for the personnel involved on the project to maintain such information confidential it would have to be so indicated by [Company Name] prior to disclosure to the individual. Scientific information would be openly exchanged without any restriction on further dissemination. No express or implied restrictions by [Company Name] on publication of scientific discoveries in scientific journals would be accepted. It was acknowledged that the portion of the project concerning properties of cells was largely conceptual at this time, and it was therefore not clear the extent of contribution of this portion to the total program. This posed a problem regarding the division of royalties between [Department] and the [Laboratory]. It was agreed that third parties, namely Mr. [licensing associate] and possibly an outside attorney, would adjudicate the division of departmental royalties if the proper division of royalties was not clear from the extent of contribution of the two groups.

It was considered appropriate that the proposed program be entered into since such a collaboration between a scientific [company field] and the University would be necessary in this specific case for development of a beneficial and useful [technology class] for the public. Mr. [Licensing Associate] agreed to contact [Company Name] to commence detailed negotiations and will coordinate appropriate reviews or consultations during the progress of discussions.

Copies to: [7 faculty members in the department]

Exhibit B. Commercialization of University Science.

Code: Medium legitimacy

Source: Late 1970s memo from faculty member to OTL associate regarding notable invention

Dear [Name],

Several months ago when Stanford began discussions with [Name] Corporation and with one of their competitors about possible licensing of the [Named invention], I indicated my wish to remain uninvolved in and uninformed about the University's activities in this area. As you know, I made this request because I have been serving as a scientific consultant to [Company Name], and I was eager to avoid any appearance of potential conflict of interest.

Subsequent events have led me to reconsider this earlier position. The extensive discussions about patents that have been held both within and outside of the university have persuaded me that any steps taken by the University in licensing this patent will unavoidably have significant fallout on me. I believe that my potential risk from the University's licensing activities is greater risk than the risk from the appearance of conflict of interest; therefore, I now ask to be completely informed about University's plans, goals, proposed licensing arrangements, etc. with regard to this patent – as is the standard practice with other patents at Stanford.

Our recent discussion in which you indicated that Stanford has been considering an exclusive short-term licensing agreement with one particular company provides an example of the basis for my concern. The question of exclusivity is perhaps the most sensitive issue associated with this patent so far as the scientific community is concerned. If Stanford were to proceed with an exclusive agreement, I believe that both the University's image and my personal image as a scientist would be affected. Until our recent telephone discussion, I had no information about these plans, which have a potential for being detrimental to me.

For the record, I want to state that my relationship with [Company Name] is as a scientific consultant; I hold no equity in the company and I do not give [Company Name] business advice. My scientific consultations to date have been primarily in areas other than [named invention] and [science related to named invention]. I expect that it will be possible for me to effectively separate my relationship with Stanford as the inventor, from my relationship with [Named Company] as a scientific consultant. I am acutely sensitive to the potential problems inherent in this situation; for this reason, I plan to be especially scrupulous in avoiding any action whatsoever that might possibly be construed as involving a conflict of interest.

Sincerely,

[Scientist Name]

criteria for partnering with a company included an invocation of the greater social good, as opposed to mere personal or university gain. Here the perception of science as an opportunity for serving the public is invoked to justify this particular engagement with industry (Sarewitz, 1996). This move represents considerable reach into the larger society to attempt to justify a new practice. Note also how the message was made clear that this situation was more an exception rather than a rule. This letter reflects that technology transfer is new, unfamiliar, and not well established within the university. Thus, when legitimacy was low, there was a need to draw from outside the university and buttress the activity with an argument about public benefit.

As the practice of technology transfer becomes more legitimate, the existence of the activity requires less justification. A set language begins to emerge to identify which features of the activity are deemed desirable and

Exhibit C. (C1, C2) Commercialization of Science.

Code: High legitimacy

Source: June, 1993 memo from OTL licensing associate to department head

This memo is provided as background relating to the licensing of inventions from Prof. X's lab to [company name], pursuant to the conflict guidelines for licensing arrangements involving faculty holding equity in a prospective licensee. We feel licensing all three inventions to [company] is most appropriate for developing this technology effectively for a number of reasons.

[Company] has proven to be a good licensee. They are progressing rapidly with the commercialization of this technology. They began Phase 1 clinical trials, and appear to be fully committed to the projects associated with Professor X's technology. [Company] was founded in 1988, and has since completed 3 rounds of venture financing, one round of exercised warrants, and a corporate partnership with [a large pharmaceutical corporation]. They are planning an initial public offering later this year. All of these activities should put them on strong financial footing to continue to aggressively develop the technology.

Please let me know if I can provide any further information, which would help your evaluation.

Cc: Professor X, Head of OTL

————————————————————————————————————

Source: September, 1996 letter from assistant professor to associate dean asking for conflict of interest permission

Dear [ ],

As you are aware we have had previous discussions regarding my starting of a company surrounding technology developed in my laboratory. As you are also aware I disclosed the essential aspects of this technology in the Spring of 1993. Since that time I have started a company around the technology and have assigned my interest in the patent to the Company. For conflict of interest it is necessary for you to know that I am a Founder, hold equity in the Company, and will serve as Consultant and the Chair of the Scientific Advisory Board for the

Company. I am fully aware of the time limitations inherent in my obligations to Stanford and will uphold them appropriately.

I am also aware that my laboratory is not to become the research arm of the Company. I can assure you I fully understand the need to separate my lab from the Company. It is for this reason that I have hired only the most able CEO and law firm to represent the Company and to seek significant financing to ensure that the Company can stand alone, independent of research efforts from my group. The targets for the company are those defined by the market place. The targets of interest to my lab group are those defined academically and will be kept distinct.

Please let me know if there are any other issues that need to be addressed.

Sincerely,

[Faculty Name]

---

what context or contingencies make the practice appropriate. Viewed more abstractly, an institutional vocabulary develops. As Mills (1940) noted long ago, language provides a vocabulary of motives in which words and expressions carry and articulate distinctive logics of action. Consider the study of the transformation of health care by Scott, Reuf, Mendel, and Caronna (2000), where they illustrate a change in logics with the shift of the doctor/patient relationship to health care provider/consumer. Similarly, in the second letter (Exhibit B) the discussion of propriety turns from the overall general activity to the particular nature of engagement, detailing case-specific aspects of the practice. Whereas in the first letter (Exhibit A), there is a clear articulation of broad (normative) concerns associated with secrecy and potential constraints that may be associated with an industrial partner, this letter from a faculty member to an OTL associate highlights the move toward classification of problems and the standardization of solutions. The clear language around "conflict of interest" and the "question of exclusivity" exemplifies this shift. As the scientist writes, "*[t]he question of exclusivity is perhaps the most sensitive issue associated with this patent so far as the scientific community is concerned.*" The tone of the discussion changes from a broad debate about the appropriateness of the activity to a somewhat narrower one of whether the license should be open or exclusive. More specifically, in this context, the debate is over whether a single company can have the license, and potentially preclude others from using the technology, or whether any company could license the technology for a fee. The faculty member refers to the issues with little elaboration, yet places extensive emphasis on the personal hazards: "*I believe that my potential risk from the University's licensing activities is greater than the risk from the appearance of conflict of interest ...* " Thus, the faculty member redraws the line between science and commerce: "*therefore, I now ask to be completely informed about University's plans, goals, proposed licensing arrangements, etc. with regard to this patent – as is the standard practice with other patents at Stanford.*"

Efforts at mitigating concerns over a potential spoiled identity, or the new problems that arise in the context of commercial involvement, emerge through trial and error learning. The letter from the scientist (Exhibit B) shows that technology transfer routines were becoming standardized. The individual 'offended' scientist's actions and the meanings associated with them in the context of the wider community of science are not well understood, hence the situation causes him considerable concern. Although the practice of patenting and licensing university research has become more familiar within the university, the scientist attempts to create an arms-length distance from this process to preserve his academic reputation and to signal disassociation from the university's efforts. The scientist begins with a strategy of remaining "*uninvolved and uninformed about the University's activities in this area,*" and then through an assessment of risk to his personal reputation, as the university proceeds with licensing efforts, requests to be "*completely informed.*" Thus, while the perception of the problems are increasingly clear, the solutions are still very much in flux.

We regard this correspondence as indicative of middle-stage legitimacy because the activities are becoming both more explicated and familiar within the organization, and the scientist is cognizant of possible risks to his reputation. Yet the means by which to deal with controversy and possible damage to one's reputation are not apparent. But rather than choose distance and deflection, he opts for deeper knowledge and engagement. Moreover, this is a highly prestigious scientist, and had he chosen to disengage or deflect, such a move would have been consequential. More generally, we know that the greater the prestige of a defector, the more an activity is delegitimated (Podolny, 1993; Strang & Soule, 1998; Rao et al., 2003). But the growing legitimacy of the commercialization of science is signaled by this scientist's decision to closely monitor the university's actions and to attempt to account for them in the wider republic of science.

As an activity becomes more legitimated, the standards become more available, contingencies articulated, and responses much more scripted. Consider the high-level of candor and transparency in the second letter in Exhibit C (C2). This is a letter from a young professor to an associate dean, which emphasizes that the process has been bureaucratized and pushed down to lower levels in the university. "*For conflict of interest it is necessary for you to know that I am a Founder, hold equity in the Company, and will serve as Consultant and the Chair of the Scientific Advisory Board for the Company.*" Whereas the letter in Exhibit B evinced awareness of specific problems, this letter reflects that conflicts are now standardized through a reporting procedure and a statement of the type of interactions that a scientist has with companies. Note also the compact nature of the language: "*I am fully aware of the limitation inherent in my obligations with Stanford and will uphold them appropriately... I am also aware that my laboratory is not to become the research arm of the Company.*" Two decades earlier, such engagement would have required pages of documentation and debate, and involved top university officials. Now it appears in two short sentences. When legitimacy is high, very little articulation is necessary to accompany the reference to which behaviors are acceptable. The language in Exhibit A discusses at length the features of the situation that would or would not be "appropriate," while Exhibit B draws the distinction between norms governing action for the individual scientist compared to the university. The culmination of the process is illustrated in the two Exhibits C1 and C2, where what is appropriate is determined by the best way to achieve success in commercializing a technology. Thus, once the legitimacy of an activity is high, norms are compressed into succinct pre-set routines and procedures.

The letters reveal discussion about not only the specification of actions, but contain debate about whether such actions are normatively suitable in the context of academic science. There are numerous invocations of appropriateness, even though its meaning and origin varies. In the early years, the criteria for what is or is not suitable commercial engagement by the university is hammered out in the context of individual cases, involving scientists and practitioners in the details of each specific interaction. By the middle stages of legitimacy, as more standards for commercializing science are instantiated, the early tone of propriety based on ideas about necessity turns to questions of risk, harm, and detriment. The scientist avers that "... *I believe that both the university's image and my personal image as a scientist would be affected.*" As legitimacy grows and deepens, what is appropriate moves from a question of whether or not to commercialize to which industry partner is preferred. Thus, the activity is no longer problematic, only the mechanics of whom to commercialize with are. This transformation is nicely illustrated in Exhibit C1, a letter from an OTL associate to the department head, where the language focuses on the capability of a startup firm: "*We feel licensing all three inventions to [company] is most appropriate for developing this technology effectively for a number of reasons ...* " Previously, attention was focused on whether a university invention should be marketed, now the concern is whether the company is a model startup firm with venture capital backing.

These examples suggest that the process of legitimation may not necessarily be smooth or linear. Early case-specific congruence can be challenged as a practice spreads and gains credibility. But rather than defection or opposition, a notable scientist opts to be engaged and regulative. A possible breach is lessened, and subsequent contests are over details, not fundamental debates over appropriateness. Thus, as a practice achieves an initial state of legitimacy and is codified into a set of standards that identify what constitutes desirable action, perceived problems and issues congeal and can possibly become amplified. If contestation is to occur, the middle period is a likely stage. But when a practice becomes highly legitimate, problems and issues become embedded in organizational routines and procedures, designed to mitigate concerns and render them tractable and comprehensible. In effect, the concerns become institutionalized as they are labeled, clarified, and hashed out, and become less vulnerable to contestation.

Boundary Formation and Development

Another element of legitimation concerns the maintenance and dissolution of boundaries. When the legitimacy of technology licensing was low, the boundaries between university and industry were sharp and coherent. Within the ivory tower, both the activities of individual scientists and the university were perceived as a common set of practices, representing the same institutional field (Merton, 1973; Gieryn, 1983). In contrast, industrial science was regarded as a different domain, with distinctive career ladders, incentives, and reward structures (Marcuson, 1960; Kornhauser, 1963; La Porte, 1965; Allen & Katz, 1986; Lam, 2005). As the legitimacy of commercializing science grew, however, there emerged a cleavage between the individual scientist and the university as an organization interacting with companies. Note how in Exhibit A, faculty consulting activities were considered linked to the commercialization of science on the part of the university. In Exhibit B, the scientist draws a distinction between himself and the university, signaling his membership in a larger community of academic science, concerned that the university has traversed into the domain of industry. Nevertheless, in this middle stage of legitimation, consulting activities do not constitute a boundary as they represent a separate, unrelated activity for the scientists. By the latter stage, consulting is one of the many forms of engagement that a scientist openly has with a company. The boundary with industry has been bridged, as the university licenses, partners, and collaborates, while the individual scientist is now a scientific advisory board member and even founder.

When the legitimacy of commercializing science was low, the idea of a scientist consulting in the same area to a licensing company was anathema. The memo (Exhibit A) states, "*It was discussed and considered inappropriate in connection with the project for any individual to have a separate consulting agreement with [company] in the specific technological area of the proposed research program.*" When legitimacy develops and reaches the middle stage, such extreme steps were less necessary, as the technology licensing office grew more autonomous and scientists could separate themselves as individuals from the technology transfer process. Serving as a scientific consultant to a licensing company is no longer inappropriate, yet engagement in the negotiations of the terms of technology transfer signals a distance and means of avoiding perceived conflicts of interest. Note also the shifting locus of decision-making – from a collective discussion among peers to a dyadic conversation between two individuals representing different parties with deep knowledge of the interaction rituals. By the final stage of legitimacy, transparency becomes the currency for mitigating problems. The scientist lists multiple forms of involvement with the licensing company, reflecting a deep engagement with industry that needs no apologies and is widely accepted.[9]

Taken-for-Grantedness

A critical component of legitimacy is taken-for-grantedness, a micro-level process that complements legitimacy, and, in turn, furthers institutionalization. The idea was developed by Berger and Luckman (1967) as a means by which the social order is reproduced as human activity is shaped into patterns and shared meanings and becomes repeated, habitualized actions, which are subsequently externalized as objective reality. Scholars in organizational analysis drew on these insights to develop their ideas about cognitive aspects of legitimacy, whereby a behavior or a practice becomes embedded in taken-for-granted routines and assumptions (Zucker,1977; Meyer & Rowan, 1977; DiMaggio & Powell, 1983). The key element of taken-for-grantedness is the development of shared activities and conventions that define the way things are or should be done (Scott, 1987).[10] We elaborate below on these themes, demonstrating their manifestations in both practice as well as social and technical categories.

Interaction Rituals Between the University and Industry

We begin with letters (Exhibits D, E, and F) between the university and companies, using them to illustrate the development of routines and norms of engagement between the worlds of university science and commerce. The letters selected from the OTL files concern initial efforts to market and license university inventions. This "shopping" correspondence captures, we believe, the process by which an activity moves from a state of ambiguity and unfamiliarity to highly routinized, prescribed, and well-understood. We code steps along the process as low, medium, and high taken-for-grantedness. Exhibit D is a letter from the OTL manager to the president of a technology company expressing confusion around the norms of disclosure prior to a licensing agreement. Exhibit E is a letter from a company to the technology licensing manager stating their understanding of the terms of disclosure when evaluating a university invention. Finally, Exhibit F is a more contemporary, standard exchange between the OTL and a company, exemplifying a highly scripted mode of contact. Together, these letters reflect the changing patterns of interaction among faculty, administrators, and companies as the university technology transfer program develops and becomes institutionalized.

In the early period of university–industry contact, there is a lack of clarity and common agreement about key terms of engagement with industry in the context of technology transfer. Over time, rules and conditions become standardized and interaction highly routinized. The concern over confidentiality when disclosing university inventions to industry illustrates this process. Initially, the form and amount of information about a scientific technology that should be shared with potential licensees was not agreed upon, rendering the distinction between what is or is not confidential unclear to the university. Also unfamiliar were the guiding principles of when to provide confidential information and when to offer non-confidential information. See, for example, the tone of perplexity as the technology licensing associate questions the non-compliance of the company to which the university tried to market an invention: "*I am curious to learn why [company name] did not sign and return the confidential disclosure agreement promptly*" (Exhibit D). This letter from the technology licensing associate

Exhibit D. Relations between University and Companies.

Code: Low taken-for-grantedness

Source: February, 1979 letter to president of a technology company from OTL Manager

Subject: [title of invention]

Dear [Name]:

I am responding to your letter of January 24 [which declined interest due to lack of evidence of commercial utility]. We did not receive from [company name] our copy of the Confidential Disclosure Agreement provided to you during our meeting in November. We assumed a lack of interest on [company name] part and are now in the process of concluding license arrangements with another company. I will appreciate your returning the material, which we provided to you.

It is not often that we will have completely adequate data when we submit an invention disclosure to a company so that it can make a no-risk decision regarding collaboration with the University. Of course, that means that many of our option and license agreements eventually do not result in a commercial product or process, and expenditures at risk of time and money by a company are thereby lost. That is simply the nature of a university technology licensing situation.

I am curious to learn why [company name] did not sign and return the confidential disclosure agreement promptly. In retrospect, it may not have been prudent on my part to provide the invention disclosure without first obtaining the signed confidential disclosure agreement. As Dr. [X's] work has not yet been published, I would appreciate very much your doing what you can to have the invention disclosure returned.

I'm sorry things didn't work out. Perhaps we can do better next time.

Best Regards,

[Name]
Manager, Technology Licensing

Exhibit E. Relations between University and Companies.

Code: Medium taken-for-grantedness

Source: December, 1979 letter to OTL Manager from large corporation

Dear [Name],

You have indicated a willingness to display an apparatus termed [description of invention] to myself and other representatives from our firm. I have contacted Dr. [professor's name] and we shall shortly be visiting her laboratory in the Stanford School of Medicine where the apparatus is in operation.

We require that for this visit the conditions of non-confidentiality contain:

1. Stanford University will not submit any information to us in confidence.
2. No confidential relation shall exist between us.
3. Stanford University has the sole and legal interest in and is free to disclose to our company any information, which you may discuss with us.
4. We will have the sole and unrestricted right and license to use any information so disclosed by you as it may see fit.
5. Your sole legal remedy against us for allegedly unauthorized or unlicensed use of ideas, which you may disclose to us shall be only as provided by applicable patent laws.

If Stanford University agrees to the foregoing, please indicate your acceptance of these conditions by signing in the space below and returning a signed copy to me.

Sincerely,

[Name]
[company name]

expresses regret at having approached the interaction informally by sending the invention disclosure before obtaining what was perceived to be the appropriate documentation. *"In retrospect, it may not have been prudent on my part to provide the invention disclosure without first obtaining the signed confidential disclosure agreement.*" Ironically, the informality is not at issue, rather the choice of routines and prescribed interactions. Note the vocabulary: "*curious, promptly, prudent.*" The etiquette of exchange is nebulous and not well worked out. In that same year, a company provides an explicit listing of the terms of engagement, written in almost contract form, signaling that a first-step interaction involves the disclosure of non-confidential information: "*Stanford University will not submit any information to us in confidence … no confidential* relation *shall exist between us*" (Exhibit E). While the university side seeks confidentiality in disclosure and informality in exchange, the industry side requires non-confidentiality in disclosure and formality in exchange.

As the practice of marketing academic technologies becomes routinized, university and industry develop considerable congruence in their *modus operandi.* University technologies are shopped to a designated individual within a company, by providing proscribed abstracts containing only non-confidential information. The letter from a large pharmaceutical firm is to the point: "*Thank you for the opportunity to review the information you forwarded to me at [company name]. I have forwarded the information to our scientists for their review and response … Please forward all future non-confidential disclosure to me at [email address]*" (Exhibit F). Compared to the first two letters, little is explained or made explicit with respect to the nature of technology transfer or the terms or conditions involved in the exchange. Confidentiality and its ramifications, which initially required a good deal of explication, over time become well understood and the discussion highly compressed.

Social Learning and the Development of Collective Understanding

A key feature of taken-for-grantedness is the development of common patterns of communication among members of a field as information is filtered and attended to in comparable ways by individuals in different organizations (DiMaggio & Powell, 1983). Such field-level learning greatly enhances the ability to transmit information across organizational boundaries without extensive discussion, and dampens contestation as well. As practices become habitual across organizations, and reciprocally interpreted, a common mind set evolves that deepens commitment to such activities by members of a field (Galaskiewicz, 1985; Miner & Haunschild, 1995).

Thus, as university and industry were pulled together in a common pursuit, routines, norms, and terms of engagement were imported and interacted with extant logics in the context of the Office of Technology Licensing. Network ties among inventors, companies, and licensing associates help

---

Exhibit F. Relations between University and Companies.

Code: High taken-for-grantedness

Source: June, 2001 letter from licensing staff member to staff member at large pharmaceutical company

[Name],
Licensing Liaison
Stanford University
Office of Technology Licensing
[address]

Dear [First Name],

Thank you for the opportunity to review the information you forwarded to me at [company name]. I have forwarded the information to our scientists for their review and response. Should there be any interest on the part of our scientists, I will contact you directly.

Thank you for your time and consideration in this matter. Please forward all future non-confidential disclosures to me at [email address]. Please feel free to contact me at [phone number] if you wish to discuss this matter further, or identify other potential opportunities, which you believe may be of interest to [company name].

Best regards,

[Name]
U.S. Academic Coordinator
Genetics and Discovery Alliances
[company name]

***Letter also has hand written note that reads as follows: [first name], Thanks again for the high-priority status! Talk to you soon. [first name]

---

thicken the infrastructure of technology transfer (Powell, 1996). Thus, despite starting from different locations and understandings in their respective organizational environments, companies and universities became involved in a joint activity, eventually developing common understandings and shared membership. Consequently, a community of common interests formed and the daily practices of how to transfer university technologies became well understood. As the taken-for-granted understandings deepened, the field was drawn more and more closely together. In this respect, these shared typifications help knit the licensing field together.[11]

The first letter (Exhibit D) demonstrates the initial discordance between the university and a company over an evaluation of an invention. The company, apparently concerned about risk and expenditures, requests further data and demonstration of validity of the research findings. The OTL responds with a statement about the inherent uncertainty associated with university technology transfer. "*Of course ... many of our option and license agreements eventually do not result in a commercial product or process, and expenditures at risk of time and money are thereby lost.*" The tone of the message reflects current knowledge at the time: "*That is simply the nature of a university technology licensing situation.*"

Similarly, the potential licensee imparts information about norms of appropriate exchange from a commercial perspective. For example, Exhibit E, a letter from a potential industrial licensee, demonstrates a clear articulation of the terms of engagement around confidentiality, reflecting a standard set of criteria and routines common among commercial enterprises. Exhibit D, however, written in the same year, demonstrates the university's growing pains in both conforming to these norms of appropriate exchange among companies and asserting matter-of-factly the uncertain nature of "a university technology licensing situation." Exhibit E demonstrates a clear sense of a convention from the company's point of view, emphasizing that they review technologies on a non-confidential basis and that there are sharp, codified rules that information is not submitted to the firm "in confidence."

Here we observe medium taken-for-grantedness as categories are distinguished (confidential and non-confidential disclosure) and steps taken to match them to specific rules of exchange. The level of taken-for-grantedness is not highly established, however, as both consequences and enforcement require an explicit specification. "*Your sole legal remedy against us for allegedly unauthorized or unlicensed use of ideas which you may disclose to us shall be only as provided by applicable patent laws*" (Exhibit E). Exhibit F reflects the development of a concise exchange whereby categories are distinct, practices are mutually understood, and the interaction, to borrow from Selznick (1957), is infused with meaning and value.

In these letters we observe the mutual learning taking place between university and industry as this new mode of interaction between the two realms emerges and becomes institutionalized. In the first decade of the program we see industry's request for a more compelling demonstration of the scientific findings or value of a technology, prompting a response from the university about the uncertain nature of early stage basic research. Similarly, note the subsequent absorption by the university of norms of secrecy and routines that are already established within industry. This transfer of standards and norms suggest that field-level learning and diffusion is occurring. Not only is there learning inside the technology transfer office, but these new practices are transmitted to university officials and diffused to faculty as well. Even faculty in disciplines that do not patent come to accept patenting as a routine part of academic life.[12] Moreover, this new competence is not a simple case of organizational learning because the rules of engagement with industry are being co-created and reflect a deepening joint involvement in a common endeavor.[13]

Elaboration of Roles and Activities

Another mechanism that promotes taken-for-grantedness and provides co-herence to an emerging organizational field is the establishment of compa-rable job positions in different organizations (DiMaggio & Powell, 1983). These common career statuses greatly facilitate communication and lubri-cate exchange among members of a field. We see in the correspondence files that, by the year 2000, exchanges now occur between staff members who are counterparts within their respective organizations and designated to con-duct this particular activity. The university licensing 'liaison' corresponds with industry's 'academic coordinator' (see Exhibit F). A position has been established whose task is to notify companies about new technologies and an industrial counterpart either expresses interest or declines. Moreover, responsibility has been delegated well down the hierarchy of the respective organizations. The task at hand is now well defined to the point that the terms of engagement require little explication. Whereas in Exhibit D, there is an extensive articulation of risk and the low likelihood that licenses will result in a commercial product, the same practice two decades later indicates no discussion of risk, no reference to data or demonstration of value.

Thus, a critical element of taken-for-grantedness is the extent to which roles develop to handle particular types of knowledge and information (Berger & Luckman, 1967, pp. 72–79). Roles are developed and elaborated as a common stock of knowledge expands and becomes more "objective." In the early years of technology transfer, the correspondence takes place between senior executives – the presidents of companies and the executive director of the OTL. In Exhibit F the formalities of job titles are softened and personalized with a hand-written note at the bottom of the page: "*thanks again for the high-priority status! Talk to you soon*" (Exhibit F). The two junior-level correspondents acknowledge their similar status and roles and add a personal touch to the formalities and boiler-plate language of the correspondence.

Social and Technical Categories

Our analysis of how routines became taken-for-granted illustrates how initially there was variety and ambiguity, then this heterogeneity was negotiated and encoded through the creation of categories and typifications, and eventually condensed into clear routines that are infused with meaning and value. A similar process occurs with important social and technical categories. We turn to a discussion of the development of the norms and routines of technology transfer in the context of the establishment of intellectual property in academic science. Specifically, we show how the idea of what constitutes an invention and who is an inventor follows a comparable process from variability into compression.

This group of letters (Exhibits G, H, and I) is a series of interactions within the university between scientists and administrators over particular inventions. Exhibit G contains two memos.

The first is from the OTL manager to university scientists and the legal council within the Sponsored Projects Office about funding agencies' requirements for intellectual property. The second memo documents a conversation between an SPO administrator and a scientist trying to ascertain the appropriate list of inventors for a patent. Taken together, these memos demonstrate considerable lack of understanding and confusion around the definitions of inventor and invention. Exhibit H is a letter from a faculty scientist to a technology licensing associate referring to an explanatory discussion about intellectual property and suggesting additional work that may be patented. Exhibit I is a letter from the OTL to a scientist assigning tasks necessary to begin marketing an invention. As with the development of organizational routines, the crystallization of categories entails heightened understanding of expectations and values. Thus, we demonstrate how the classificatory features of technology transfer become condensed and infused with meaning, value, and expectations.

From Ambiguity to Compression

In the early stage of low taken-for-grantedness, the classifications of invention and inventor were vague and arbitrary. No common institutional vocabulary was in place as a reservoir for participants to draw on. In exhibits

Exhibits G. (G1, G2) What is an Invention? Who is an Inventor?

Code: Low taken-for-grantedness

Source: March, 1979 memo from Director of Office of Technology Licensing to lawyer in Sponsored Projects Office and two faculty in Life Science Department.

Regarding the above invention sent to you on March 1, 1979, the clause covering patent rights is contained in our [government agency] Institutional Patent Agreement. The IPA requires that Stanford submit a written invention report of each subject invention promptly after conception or first actual reduction to practice and that the report specify whether or not we intend to file a patent application.

Invention disclosures do not necessarily have to be on a patentable item. We are required to submit a disclosure on any "subject invention," which means any process, machine, manufacture, composition of matter or design, or any new or useful improvement thereof, which is or may be patentable. Also, to be recognized legally, a coinventor must have conceived of an essential element of an invention, or contributed substantially to the general concept. It is not sufficient to have merely participated in creation of the system as a whole. This may help you to determine appropriate persons to be listed as coinventors.

———————————————————————————

Source: April, 1980 memo to invention file from university patent engineer, concerning a discovery that subsequently proved to be instrumental in the development of the biotechnology industry.

I spoke with [professor A]'s secretary, who conveyed to me that [professor A] thought [technology] was "an invention" so I proceeded to obtain the information necessary for a disclosure. [Professor B] said that he developed the technique, [professor C] helped, but wasn't sure whether [professor D] or [professor A] should be listed as "inventors." Then, I spoke with [professor C] who was trying to get a hold of [professor A] to see what [professor A] thought about being an "inventor"... [professor C] hadn't gotten in touch with [professor A] but had gotten some message that [professor A] didn't feel this should be patented (something like that). I have not heard from either of them and am sending [professor B] the disclosure without [professor A]'s name. I have asked that he check all information, including inventors, on the form.

Exhibit H. What is an Invention? Who is an Inventor?

Code: Medium taken-for-grantedness

Source: October, 1986 letter from faculty member to OTL licensing associate

Dear [First Name],

Thank you for the informative discussion regarding patents. I have an appointment to talk with [a colleague] this afternoon. I will keep you informed of my plans as they develop.

I have an idea for another patent which I would like to pursue with the office of Technology Licensing. It is an algorithm, which I have developed for characterizing [organ mechanism]. I have enclosed a paper, which describes it. This paper has been accepted for publication but has not been published yet.

The acceptance of the paper should give some indication of the validity of the technique. However, I do not really know whether or not companies would be interested. I imagine that this idea would be similar (in terms of company interest) to another patent which we discussed, that characterizes the [organ with technology].

I would be glad to discuss this idea with you.
Sincerely,

[Faculty Member]

D1 and D2, we see extensive use of quotations marks around the words invention and inventor. "*I spoke with [professor A]'s secretary, who conveyed to me that [professor A] thought that [technology] was "an invention" ... [professor B] said that he developed the technique, [professor C] helped, but wasn't sure whether [professor D] or [professor A] should be listed as "inventors ... "* Eventually (Exhibit F) the quotations disappear, suggesting the development of a common vocabulary and shared meaning. "*We'd like to begin marketing your invention to companies ... please send me a list of companies that you think might be interested .... [w]e have found that our inventors are often our best source of licensees.*"

Exhibit I. What is an Invention? Who is an Inventor?

Code: High taken-for-grantedness

Source: August, 2000 letter from OTL licensing associate to university inventors

Dear [Name] and Dr. [Faculty Name],

We'd like to begin marketing your invention to companies to get some feedback, gauge interest, and find potential licensees. Can you please create a non-confidential marketing abstract for your invention and send me an electronic copy? Also, please send me a list of companies that you think might be interested in this technology. We have found that our inventors are often our best source of licensees.

If you have any questions, please let me know. For your reference, I've attached a sample marketing abstract.

Thanks,

[First Name]
Licensing Associate

The correspondence suggests that initially there was considerable latitude in interpreting who was an inventor or what constitutes an invention. In the first two letters (Exhibits G1 and G2), the scientists themselves are asked to determine first whether or not their scientific finding or artifact is an invention. Then the scientists are consulted over which of their collaborators are actually co-inventors. The OTL is searching for an authoritative source to assist in this classification. For example, the guidelines from the government funding agency provide some basis for establishing what determines an invention: "*Invention disclosures do not necessarily have to be on a patentable item. We are required to submit a disclosure on any "subject invention," which may mean any process, machine, manufacture, composition of matter or design, or any new or useful improvement thereof, which is or may be patentable.*" But the government criteria are amorphous and almost contradictory, reflecting more the idiosyncrasies of administrative routines than a specific regulatory (e.g. legal) definition or convention. The labels and categories of "subject inventions" have very little purchase in the new field of the life sciences. Scientists confronted with the task or opportunity of commercializing their science had few anchors, especially in new areas such as biological materials or process-related techniques, such as cloning, that had scant legal precedent.[14]

The definition of inventor is similarly plagued initially by a lack of clarity or standard definition. The scientists are not only consulted to adjudicate a concept they hardly understand, but also are provided with vague and indistinct criteria for doing so. *"Also, to be recognized legally, a coinventor must have conceived of an essential element of an invention, or contributed substantially to the general concept. It is not sufficient to have merely participated in the creation of the system as a whole."* Despite the elaborate language, there is little in terms of analogy or prior examples to guide these scientists. Compare this memo to Exhibit I, which provides an attached example of the "marketing abstract" the licensing associate requests.

Eventually, we see the emergence of a finite range of possible definitions that are contingent on a set of particular circumstances or examples. In Exhibit H, the scientist refers to a tutorial from the OTL, which provided a basis for determining what other inventions may be generated from one's research program. The scientist remarks, *"thank you for the informative discussion regarding patents ... I have an idea for another patent which I would like to pursue ... "* The scientist here draws on specific guidelines to formulate what may be a potential invention – something patentable, not yet published, and an indication of validity. *"I have enclosed a paper which describes [the idea]. This paper has been accepted for publication but has not been published yet. The acceptance of the paper should give some indication of the validity of the technique."* A scholarly paper serves as the currency for codifying and sharing the potential invention (compared to a marketing abstract in Exhibit H), and analogy directs attention to what also may be commercializable: *" ... I do not really know whether or not companies would be interested. I imagine that this idea would be similar (in terms of company interest) to another patent which we discussed, that characterizes the [functioning of a specific organ]."* The professor is not sure whether his research output is commercially viable, but he is certainly interested in developing connections.

In the latter period, the bandwidth of definitions narrows and becomes less contingent, or associated with context. In the letter to a scientist (Exhibit I), the OTL associate conveys very explicit expectations to the faculty member with respect to the role of the inventor. *"We would like to begin marketing your invention to companies ... Can you please create a non-confidential marketing abstract for your invention and send me an electronic copy?"* Moreover, there is no longer any elaboration of the term invention, the details have disappeared. Rather, the word now invokes a set of practices and routines associated with technology transfer, including the generation of a marketing abstract and contacting companies. Minimal explanation of the procedures are necessary; there is no discussion of what non-confidentiality in the context of a marketing abstract would entail. In the early stage, when taken-for-grantedness was low, there was a broad, expansive search for how to classify what an invention was and who ought to be included as an inventor. In the middle stage, tutorials are developed and enthusiastic faculty attempt to match their research output against the criteria specified for eligibility for a patent. Once the concepts of invention and inventor become highly taken-for-granted, they became reified and more abstract, and encode a good deal of information. An inventor should do certain things and an invention has particular characteristics.

A distinguishing feature of high taken-for-grantedness is the inter-subjectivity that is involved. Descriptions are concise and packaged. Inventor and invention are meaningful terms in multiple senses now – legally, procedurally, and the categories are increasingly celebrated as both commercially valuable and prestigious within the university. The last letter captures how the schemas for the commercialization process have become set: " ... [P]lease send me a list of companies that you think might be interested in this technology. We have found that our inventors are often our best source of licensees." The label of inventor has become central to the technology transfer process, infused with value as the source of not only patentable knowledge, but also a means of identifying a licensee. Furthermore, the status of an inventor carries a set of understood and accepted expectations in the commercialization process. Compare this status to Exhibit H, where the mention on the part of the scientist to any potential industrial interest was a basis for identifying an invention – an invocation of analogy and reference, rather than an enactment of a role in a known and understood process.

Summary

We have used the correspondence of the Stanford Office of Technology Licensing to show how scientific entrepreneurship became more legitimate, activities and categories taken-for-granted, and the overall process institutionalized. The correspondence reflects new vocabularies that convey important organizational changes. As the vocabulary evolved, the categories of invention and inventor shifted from diffuse to settled. Some topics that were intensely discussed in the early years became conventional and were rendered silent and invisible, reflecting both their legitimation and the extent to which contested classifications were made ordinary (Bowker & Star, 1999). Faculty who did not patent did not know the details of specific OTL procedures or categories, but over time they took for granted that such things were properly in place. Thus, increased taken-for-grantedness and legitimacy permitted the expansion of the organizational reach of the OTL and its operations.[15]

During the OTL's early years, decisions were made on a case by case basis, and these decisions required the input of multiple units on campus, with top echelon approval usually needed to resolve matters. The categories of inventor and invention were inchoate, and the search for authoritative guidelines was continuous. New ideas proliferated, stemming from many sources, and many plans and schemes were considered and hatched but never followed through. As the legitimacy of technology transfer grew, attention turned to implementing a more standardized set of routines. Most licensing activity became consolidated within the OTL; and within this unit, a career ladder developed as the number of staff expanded. Decisions no longer needed the involvement of top executives as more standard activity could be delegated. As categories were established and data used as evidence, the bandwidth for disagreements narrowed. New situations or unfamiliar cases came to be viewed as an opportunity to expand the reach of existing routines or the occasion to create new standards. Consider the novel issue of how to share biological materials. Stanford had to redefine an older category called tangible research property, which previously referred to equipment, in order to facilitate and harmonize the sharing of biological research tools with other scientists. This routine extended the informal practice of scientific collaboration to a formal policy that applied the same rules to both academic and industrial scientists.

Once legitimacy became strong, and support for technology transfer diffused widely across the campus, the procedures for commercializing science became highly elaborated. Currently, all responsibility is consolidated within the OTL, which is highly visible on campus, and widely emulated nationally and even internationally. Key decisions are now made with dispatch by lower level personnel, and when anomalies occur, these staffers can handle exceptions readily. Surprises have become rare, as most situations and solutions have become classified and routinized and disputes are accommodated and contained. We see, then, that compression and elaboration through the development of categories and procedures are not contradictory trends, but rather complements. As the legitimacy of technology transfer expanded, academic entrepreneurship became widely embraced and required little justification. Thus, acceptance triggered greater procedural rationality as various questions, challenges, and opportunities provided occasions to deepen and expand the repertoire of routines associated with technology transfer.

The analytic narrative we have presented is neither linear nor conflict-free. The institutionalization process was fraught with disputes, misunderstandings, and some effort at distancing. Legitimacy and taken-for-grantedness increased over time in this particular case, but this trend was neither inevitable nor without debate. Recall the case of the eminent scientist who initially did not want to be informed about the OTL's commercial efforts but then turned to active monitoring. He showed awareness of the possible risks that exclusive licensing might have to his scientific reputation. Put differently, he perceived that the identities of ivory-tower scholar and scientist entrepreneur were mutually exclusive. Moreover, people who attempt to cross categories or identities are often penalized, as Zuckerman, Kim, Ukanwa, and Ritter (2003) have shown in their study of Hollywood actors and film genres. But precisely because a number of high-status scientists became actively involved in commercializing science, a strong signal was sent that such activity did not detract from one's scientific reputation (Zucker, Darby, & Brewer, 1998; Owen-Smith & Powell, 2001). And concurrently with sending this signal, it was these prominent scientists that were able to provoke discussion, mollify disputes and concerns, and ultimately play a hand in constructing the normative architecture of participation in commercial activities.

The changes we discern in the correspondence over three decades underscore the growing legitimation and taken-for-grantedness of commercial applications of university science. With respect to legitimacy, we clearly see how the activity becomes more comprehensible (Suchman, 1995). Initially, when legitimacy was low, the move was to reach into the larger society and borrow the template of the public good (and mark the activity as an exception rather than a rule). This unfamiliar activity of commercializing science had to be justified by an argument that economic growth and job creation would be generated. In the middle stage, a new institutional vocabulary develops that incorporates private sector orientations and activities. In the high stage, routines are skillfully executed and their attendant meanings widely understood. The transformation moves from high elaboration (i.e. details, debates, clarifications) and low classification (e.g. categories, definitions) to low elaboration (i.e. little need to spell out how to do things, descriptions are highly condensed) and high classification (e.g. conflict of interest forms, job categories, and intellectual property).

At a more micro level, taken-for-grantedness deepens as the community of participants expands. Consider, for example, the discussion of confidentiality where the university absorbs practices from commercial partners. More broadly, as relations between the OTL and technology companies thicken, a shared sense of membership in a common technological community develops. In the 1990s, faculty begin starting companies based on their research discoveries, and a considerable number of licenses go to university spinoffs or startups where Stanford inventors hold key executive positions or serve on scientific advisory boards. The categories of inventor and invention become highly taken-for-granted, reified and celebrated as entrepreneurial activity is rewarded and becomes a basis for a common identity in the larger high-tech community of Silicon Valley.

6. DISCUSSION AND IMPLICATIONS

Much of the literature in institutional analysis has emphasized external influences and exogenous shocks as the key motor of institutional change. Whether the trigger is legislative mandate, as in affirmative action law or the creation of the European Union, political ideology, such as neo-liberalism or the oppositional role of social movements, or disputes over professional jurisdiction, as in studies of contests between physicians and managers or accountants and lawyers, much of the analytical weight for explaining institutional change has been placed on external forces. This attention is not surprising. If institutions are regarded as durable and self-reinforcing, then the question of what factors create change or rob them of their staying power is a vexing one. Hence the attention to outside influences that jolt institutions and prompt changes. Our contribution is to develop an endogenous account of institutionalization, by attending to how an activity moved from unfamiliar to accepted to venerated. We focus on internal work practices, attending to local processes in which routines and categories are developed through trial and error efforts, and borrowed with modifications from partners in the private sector. This local process proved to be highly consequential in creating a broader field of technology management, as Stanford's OTL became one of the most active participants in the building of this larger community.

Perhaps more than most other elite universities, Stanford has had a strong "knowledge-plus" orientation, and played an important role in the development of Silicon Valley's high-tech community (Kenney, 2000; Rowen, Hancock, Lee, & Miller, 2000). Nevertheless, the linkage between academic science and technology application has not been without conflict. Consider the different vocabularies and role identities that had to be bridged – from unfettered inquiry, knowledge for knowledge's sake, science is not for sale, knowledge has a public purpose and ivory-tower academic to engaged scientist linking basic and translational science, solving pressing biomedical problems and curing diseases, academic entrepreneurship, and universities as engines of economic growth. Similar to Rao et al's (2003) study of the replacement of classic French cooking by nouvelle cuisine, we see new roles, language, and values emerge that help cement the institutionalization of technology transfer. Moreover, this compilation of roles, languages, and values becomes imbricated into a new identity of scientist-entrepreneur.

Thus, institutionalization produced a practical form of legitimacy in which statuses were formalized, boundaries redefined, access to resources reinterpreted, and even the nature of resources reconstrued. Taken-for-grantedness entailed the creation of routines and the classification of identities and discoveries. Recall the first set of exhibits where administrators and scientists tried to sort out appropriate contingencies together, then a middle level where the university as a corporate actor and the scientist as a member of an intellectual community were separate, eventually culminating into the third level with a new hybrid classification of scientist-inventor-entrepreneur. At this latter point, the proprietary features of academic work are handled through conflict of interest statements. This process is deeply mindful, and not a case of mindless replication. The activity becomes habituated, but only through considerable effort at creating standards and establishing norms of appropriateness.

One objective of our effort is to provide a framework for analyzing processes of institutionalization in other empirical settings. We recognize that other researchers may not have access to a treasure trove of documents spanning three decades. Nevertheless, other process studies with longitudinal data could draw profitably on our work. To this end, we highlight general features of taken-for-grantedness, legitimacy, and institutionalization, characterizing potential indicators of low, medium, and high states, in Fig. 1.

Recall that we argued that institutionalization is a product of the coincident expansion of heightened legitimacy and deeper taken-for-grantedness. To be sure, we are not claiming the two processes march in lock step with another. Below we discuss cases where the two could diverge. But in this context institutionalization occurs through the collated embedding of practices, meanings, expectations, and values. Fig. 1 abstracts from the technology transfer context and suggests an ensemble of indicators that reflect, in our view, a more general process of institutionalization. While these metrics may not apply in every context, we think they offer fertile tools for the

	Low	Medium	High
Institutionalization			
organizational structure	decisions made by top-echelon	career ladder develops & delegation takes place	lower-level personnel afforded discretion to solve problems
practical action	multiple means to achieve new goals	coherence around goals develops & means are restricted	means-ends calculation well-understood
reproduction	learning by doing	tutorials, training programs, strong socialization	outreach & evangelism via flourishing professions & new identities
self-reinforcement	vulnerable	anchored	resilient
Legitimacy			
standards	symbols & vocabularies drawn externally to invoke support	institutional vocabularies develop	rich, local language becomes widely accepted & emulated
norms of appropriateness	trepidation over adoption prompts high articulation	values become more clear but can provoke opposition	norms & values venerated & objectified
boundaries	existing boundaries well-defined, cross-traffic requires approval	boundaries blur, cross-traffic more accepted	boundaries redrawn & integrated into community with common interests
Taken-for-Grantedness			
practices	idiosyncratic & developed on a case-by-case basis	consolidation occurs	scripted & well rehearsed, little need for articulation
roles	ambiguous	varying conventions offered, some trigger debate	defined & steeped with expectations
categories	diffuse	classifications emerge	settled & infused with value

Fig. 1. Indicators of the Process of Institutionalization.

analysis of both thorough and extensive or incomplete and partial institutionalization. Our indicators are built out of our case, but the ambition of
Fig. 1 is to make them portable.

Fig. 1 allows for examination of the multi-level process of institutionalization, its bottom-up emergence and top-down consolidation, as well as
local manifestations of field-level processes. Reading down the columns, we
see low, medium, and high states for each theoretical construct. We organize
the figure in the context of elements associated with each construct based on
our case. Our column descriptions should be useful for analyses of qualitative data at either one, a few, or many points in time. Reading the figure
vertically captures the nested elements of the overall phenomenon, with
taken-for-grantedness focusing on organizational routines, roles, and
categories, and legitimacy a broader concept invoking public standards,
norms, and the boundaries of a field. Institutionalization refers to the formal
instantiation of organizational structures, reflected in careers and administrative levels, as well as mechanisms at each stage that sustain and reinforce the process.

Viewed horizontally, our indicators capture the processual aspects of institutionalization as the constituent elements change through time. Here we
see the feedback dynamics as roles and categories develop, vocabularies
are constructed, career ladders grow, and socialization expands. Reading the
rows, then, provides stepping stones toward the settling of categories, the
reconfiguration of boundaries, and the comprehension of clear means-end
calculations. For example, at a low stage, institutionalization is not easily
self-reinforced. As it grows it becomes anchored in specific practices, and as
it deepens, it is resilient to alternatives and robust to challenges.

Again, we stress that the component parts and stages need not fit together
as coherently as we have depicted. The process can be halted, for example,
due to contestation. We suggest this is particularly likely at the middle stage
as new practices or values can prompt reaction from incumbents. Or the
constructs can evolve at different speeds. Consider an activity, such as internet pornography or organized crime, that may have acquired medium or
high taken-for-grantedness but low legitimacy. In cases where such activities
are not aligned in a nested fashion, we contend that institutionalization is
incomplete. Indeed, social life is abundant with cases of partial institutionalization. Consider efforts at legalizing cannabis as medical marijuana,
transposing organized crime into family business, attempts at clinical testing
for herbal supplements, or on-line gambling.

In our case, the expansion of the commercial application of science
may well lead to the de-institutionalization of open science (Owen-Smith &

Powell, 2001; R. R. Nelson, 2005). As technology transfer becomes more conventional and appropriate, an older model of an ivory-tower, unfettered view of science is robbed of its hold on the academy. Indeed, the institutionalization of entrepreneurial science may signal the demise of disengaged science for science's sake (Powell et al., 2007). Thus, processes of institutionalization can also be cases of de-institutionalization.

Our objective with Fig. 1 is to establish proof of concept with respect to taken-for-grantedness, legitimacy, and institutionalization through direct examination of archival materials. While the sources from which the exhibits were drawn are rich in content and comprehensive over time, there are limitations to our analyses. We have emphasized developing abstractions from selected archival materials to derive indicators. We have not attempted to systematically code the entire set of OTL correspondence. We choose instead to select a diversity of letters and memos rather than focus on the same type of correspondence through time. More consideration could also be paid to the matrix of participants, notably the mix of faculty, students, and staff, and analyze whether increasing diversity among them prompts a return to earlier states of institutionalization, or whether new entrants enter the process at midstream. Similarly, two external aspects of institutionalization merit further attention. One feature is the involvement of Stanford in creating a professional association that serves as a canopy for the field and Stanford's active role in tutoring other universities, in the U.S. and abroad, in the mechanics of tech transfer. The other aspect concerns legislative decisions – both inside the university at the faculty senate, but more notably at the federal level, that legitimated and consolidated the efforts of such universities as MIT, Stanford, the University of California-San Francisco, and Wisconsin.

Our research calls for an application of contemporary tools of archival analysis toward more direct, process-oriented metrics for institutionalization, allowing for more conceptual precision in understanding both the endogenous dynamics of institutionalization and the roads that lead to it. A core issue here is the determination of what the 'units' of legitimation or taken-for-grantedness are, and the form they take in specific contexts. For example, in this study we follow discrete states of low, medium, and high taken-for-grantedness in the *practice* of marketing a technology, and the *social and technical categories* of inventor and invention as constituent parts of legitimacy. In our examples, the classifications were pre-existing and imported to the organization, requiring considerable sense-making and field-level learning. We show how practices and meanings develop recursively. We also demonstrate how the objects we observe are transformed as their degree of taken-for-grantedness deepens. Further research could examine more internally developed practices and classifications such as the development of revenue disbursement models within universities, the growing use of for-profit activities to cross-subsidize charitable activities in nonprofit organizations, or considerations of outsourcing formerly core activities in commercial enterprises. We hope our approach provides further insight to how taken-for-granted understandings knit communities of participants together and provide institutional vocabularies that become the *lingua franca* of different fields.

NOTES

1. The period at Stanford was distinguished by the enactment of a rule requiring mandatory disclosure by all university personnel of all patentable inventing. Previously faculty disclosed on the basis of the requirements of federal funding agencies, thus the 1994 campus decision greatly expanded the mandate of disclosure and was not met with any protest. We take this acceptance as a clear sign that technology transfer had been integrated into the mission of the university. See, for illustration, the OYL's website: "The mission of Stanford University's OTL is to promote the transfer of Stanford technology for society's use and benefit while generating unrestricted income to support research and education." (http://www.otl.stanford.edu/about/why.html).

2. We thank Huggy Rao for suggesting the parallels between Elias' work and ours.

3. We draw from the larger research project of Colyvas (2007), which addresses the development and diffusion of commercialization activities among scientists at Stanford from 1970 to 2000.

4. From the university administration's perspective, the creation of an office of technology transfer was intended to recruit faculty, especially junior scientists, and build on the connections with industry that were developing in the computer and engineering sciences.

5. For example, in 1980, after a decade of the operation of the technology transfer program, there were only three faculty inventors from the life science department we are studying. By 2000, there were 20, more than 75% of the faculty in the department.

6. Interestingly, the OTL has never employed any attorneys, opting instead to rely on outside counsel when needed (Fischer, 1998).

7. While the earned income from the OTL is relatively modest compared to sponsored research expenditures ($50,176,009 in gross licensing income compared to $573,416,214 expended in sponsored research funds in fiscal year 2002), the amount disbursed to units within the university is not trivial. Fifteen percent of the total revenues are administered under the discretion of the technology transfer office in conjunction with the Dean of research. The remaining 85% of the gross royalties are disbursed in 1/3 increments to the school, the department, and the individuals that generated the invention. In fiscal year 2003–2004, $12.7 million went to departments, $12.5 million to schools (with more than $10 million to the school of medicine), and

$11.8 million was paid to individual inventors, including faculty, students, and staff of the university. Such funding is discretionary and not tied to a particular project or burdened with stringent reporting requirements or outcome measures as is the case with sponsored research at universities.

8. Of the 35 faculty members who held an appointment in the sampled department during this period, 24 appear as inventors. Including co-inventors on the disclosures, there are 250 individuals in total. Of course many faculty disclose multiple times. The most prolific inventor in the department had 35 disclosures.

9. Our colleague, Gili Drori, has observed that many contemporary discussions of transparency contain elements of modern secular religiosity. In her work on corporate social responsibility, she observes cases of corporate self-reports of labor code violations. Drawing on Jacques Ellul's work, she notes that such confession and ratcheting up of labor standards are steps on a path to "moral recovery."

10. We stress that this process of becoming more taken-for-granted is not deterministic or uni-directional, and need not lead to inevitable constraint. Contestation, as we discussed above, can certainly occur and shape how things come to be accepted as natural, and social meanings always have an element of plasticity, such that even enactment and reinforcement can lead to change.

11. At the field level, a professional association is formed – AUTM, Association of University Technology Managers, and MIT and Stanford play a critical role in its creation and development. The Association grows from 7 members in 1974 to more than 3000 by 2002. Such growth reflects the expansion of professional expertise, and the development of field-wide scripts and standards. Moreover, membership is not restricted to university personnel. Industry associates, government and nonprofit institutes, and non-U.S. members are welcomed. And, of course, academic researchers begin studying technology transfer as well.

12. At Stanford, the range and diversity of departments where patenting occurs is quite extensive. One of the more entrepreneurial units is the music department, and its program CCRMA, Center for Corporate Research in Music and Acoustics (A. J. Nelson, 2005). The founder of CCRMA, John Chowning, developed an algorithm for FM synthesis, which Yamaha developed into the DX synthesizer, the largest selling set of musical instruments ever made, and one of Stanford's most lucrative licenses. These early revenues were plowed back into subsequent multiple efforts at commercializing computer-generated music.

13. In other correspondence not presented here, we find cases of the university and long-term commercial partners working jointly to "tutor" younger start-up companies or non-U.S. companies on the mores of appropriate licensing behavior. Similarly, the Stanford OTL provides tutorials to U.S. and foreign universities, and the OTL and experienced faculty inventors run workshops for younger faculty and graduate students. More recently, the OTL has developed a training module available for purchase on DVD.

14. The parallels with Edelman's (1992) discussion of the legal ambiguity that surrounded equal opportunity law are striking. Here there was considerable confusion surrounding legal definitions and legislative dictates, which was mitigated through interpretive efforts by companies and universities, which then in turn reform the legal definitions of invention and inventor.

15. We thank John Meyer for emphasizing this point.

ACKNOWLEDGMENTS

We thank the States and Markets program at the Santa Fe Institute, supported by the Hewlett Foundation, the Columbia-Stanford Consortium on Biomedical Innovation, funded by the Merck Foundation, and the Association for Institutional Research for research support. We are especially grateful to the Office of Technology Licensing at Stanford University, which has afforded us unrestricted access to their archives. We are also grateful to Helena Buhr, Gili Drori, Hokyu Hwang, John Meyer, Andrew Nelson, Jason Owen-Smith, Charles Perrow, Huggy Rao, Marc Schneiberg, Laurel Smith-Doerr, Barry Staw, and David Suarez for comments on an earlier draft. We have benefited from comments made at seminars at MIT's Sloan School and the University of Alberta.

REFERENCES

Aldrich, H. E., & Fiol, C. M. (1994). Fools rush in? The institutional context of industry creation. *Academy of Management Journal, 19,* 645–670.

Allen, T. J., & Katz, R. (1986). The dual ladder: Motivational solution or managerial delusion? *R&D Management, 16*(2), 185–197.

AUTM. (2002). Licensing Survey: FY. Association of University Technology Managers.

Baum, J. A. C., & Oliver, C. (1992). Institutional embeddedness and the dynamics of organizational populations. *American Sociological Review, 57,* 540–559.

Baum, J. A. C., & Powell, W. W. (1995). Cultivating an institutional ecology of organizations: Comment on Hannan, Carroll, Dundon and Torres. *American Sociological Review, 60,* 529–538.

Berger, P. L., & Luckman, T. (1967). *The social construction of reality.* Garden City, NJ: Doubleday.

Bowker, G. C., & Star, S. L. (1999). *Sorting things out: Classification and its consequences.* Cambridge, MA: MIT Press.

Colyvas, J. A. (2006). From divergent meanings to common practices: The institutionalization of technology transfer at a research university. Working Paper, Stanford University.

Colyvas, J. A. (2007). Institutionalization processes and the commercialization of university research. Doctoral Dissertation, Stanford University School of Education.

Dacin, T. M., Goodstein, J., & Scott, W. R. (2002). Institutional theory and institutional change: Introduction to the special research forum. *Academy of Management Journal, 45*(1), 45–57.

DiMaggio, P. J., & Powell, W. W. (1983). The iron cage revisited: Institutional isomorphism and collective rationality in organizational fields. *American Sociological Review, 48,* 147–160.

DiMaggio, P. J., & Powell, W. W. (1991). Introduction. In: W. W. Powell & P. J. DiMaggio (Eds), *The New Institutionalism in Organizational Analysis* (pp. 1–38). Chicago, IL: University of Chicago Press.

Economist. (2002). Innovation's golden goose. Economist, December 14, p. 3.

Edelman, L. (1992). Legal ambiguity and symbolic structures: Organizational mediation of civil rights. *American Journal of Sociology, 95,* 1401–1440.

Eisenberg, R. (1996). Public research and private development: Patents and technology transfer in government-sponsored research. *Virginia Law Review, 82,* 1663–1727.

Elias, N. (1978). *The civilizing process: The history of manners.* New York: Urizen Books.

Fischer, L. M. (1998). Technology transfer at Stanford University. *Strategy and Business, 13*(4), 76–85.

Galaskiewicz, J. (1985). Professional networks and the institutionalization of a single mind set. *American Sociological Review, 50,* 639–658.

Ganz-Brown, C. (1999). Patent policies to fine tune commercialization of government sponsored university research. *Science and Public Policy, 26*(6), 403–414.

Geiger, R. L. (1993). *Research and relevant knowledge: American research universities since world war II.* New York: Oxford University Press.

Gieryn, T. (1983). Boundary work and the demarcation of science from nonscience. *American Sociological Review, 48,* 781–795.

Greif, A. (2006). *Institutions and the path to the modern economy: Lessons from Medieval trade.* Cambridge University Press.

Guston, D. (1999). Stabilizing the boundary between U.S. politics and science: The role of the office of technology transfer as a boundary organization. *Social Studies of Science, 29,* 87–111.

Hannan, M., & Carroll, G. (1992). *Dynamics of organizational populations: Density, legitimation, and competition.* New York: Oxford University Press.

Hannan, M., & Freeman, J. (1989). *Organizational ecology.* Cambridge, MA: Harvard University Press.

Haveman, H. (2000). The future of organizational sociology: Forging ties among paradigms. *Contemporary Sociology, 29,* 476–486.

Jepperson, R. L. (1991). Institutions, institutional effects, and institutionalism. In: W. W. Powell & P. J. DiMaggio (Eds), *The new institutionalism in organizational analysis* (pp. 143–163). Chicago: University of Chicago Press.

Kornhauser, W. (1963). *Scientists in industry: Conflict and accommodation.* Berkeley: University of California Press.

Kenney, M. (Ed.) (2000). *Understanding Silicon Valley: The anatomy of an entrepreneurial region.* Stanford: Stanford University Press.

La Porte, T. R. (1965). Conditions of strain and accommodation in industrial research organizations. *Administrative Science Quarterly, 10*(1), 21–38.

Lam, A. (2005). Work roles and careers of R&D scientists in network organizations. *Industrial Relations, 44*(2), 242–275.

Lawrence, T., & Suddaby, R. (2006). Institutions and institutional work. In: *Handbook of Organization Studies,* 2nd edition, Forthcoming.

March, J. G., & Olsen, J. R. (1989). *Rediscovering institutions: The organizational basis of politics.* New York: Free Press.

Marcuson, S. (1960). *The scientist in American industry.* Princeton: Industrial Relations Section, Princeton University.

Merton, R. K. (1973). *The sociology of science.* Chicago: University of Chicago Press.

Meyer, J. W., & Rowan, B. (1977). Institutionalized organizations: Formal structure as myth and ceremony. *American Journal of Sociology, 83*(2), 340–363.

Mills, C. W. (1940). Situated actions and vocabularies of motive. *American Sociological Review, 5,* 904–913.

Miner, A. S., & Haunschild, P. R. (1995). Population level learning. In: L. L. Cummings & B. M. Staw (Eds), *Research in Organizational Behavior*, (Vol. 17, pp. 115–166). Greenwich, CT: JAI Press.

Mohr, J. W. (1994). Soldiers, mothers, tramps, and others: Discourse roles in the 1907 New York City charity directory. *Poetics, 22*, 327–357.

Mohr, J. W. (1998). Measuring meaning structures. *Annual Review of Sociology, 24*, 345–370.

Mohr, J., & Guerra-Pearson, F. (2006). The differentiation of institutional space: Organizational forms in the New York social welfare sector, 1888–1917. In: W. W. Powell, & D. L. Jones (Eds), *How institutions change*. University of Chicago Press.

Mowery, D. C., Nelson, R. R., Sampat, B., & Ziedonis, A. (2004). *Ivory tower and industrial innovation*. Stanford, CA: Stanford University Press.

National Science Board. (2000). *Science and engineering indicators – 2000*. Washington, DC: NSB.

Nelson, A. J. (2005). Cacophony or harmony? Multivocal logics and technology licensing by the Stanford University Department of Music. *Industrial and Corporate Change, 14*(1), 93–118.

Nelson, R. R. (2005). Basic scientific research. In: R. Nelson (Ed.), *The Limits of Market Organization* (pp. 233–258). New York: Russell Sage Foundation.

Nelson, R. R., & Rosenberg, N. (1994). American universities and technical advance. *Research Policy, 23*, 323–348.

Nelson, R. R., & Winter, S. (1982). *An Evolutionary Theory of Economic Change*. Cambridge, MA: Harvard University Press.

Office of Technology Licensing (2004). Celebrating Stanford inventors. Annual report 2003–2004, Stanford University.

Owen-Smith, J. (2003). From separate systems to a hybrid order. *Research Policy, 32*, 1081–1104.

Owen-Smith, J. (2005). Dockets, deals, and sagas: Commensuration and the rationalization of experience in university licensing. *Social Studies of Science, 35*(1), 69–97.

Owen-Smith, J., & Powell, W. W. (2001). Careers and contradictions: Faculty responses to the transformation of knowledge and its uses in the life sciences. In: S. Vallas (Ed.), *The transformation of work* (pp. 109–140). Elsevier Science.

Podolny, J. M. (1993). A status-based model of market competition. *American Journal of Sociology, 98*, 829–872.

Powell, W. W. (1996). Inter-organizational collaboration in the biotechnology industry. *Journal of Institutional and Heoretical Economics, 120*(1), 197–215.

Powell, W. W., & Owen-Smith, J. (1998). Universities and the market for intellectual property in the life sciences. *Journal of Policy Analysis and Management, 17*(2), 253–277.

Powell, W. W., Owen-Smith, J. and Colyvas, J. A. (2007) Innovation and emulation: Lessons from the experiences of U.S. universities in selling private rights to public knowledge. *Minerva*, forthcoming.

Rao, H., Monin, P., & Durand, R. (2003). Institutional change in Toque Ville: Nouvelle cuisine as an identity movement in French gastronomy. *American Journal of Sociology, 108*, 795–843.

Reimers, Niels (1997). *Niels Reimers*. Regional Oral History Office, The Bancroft Library, University of California, Berkeley. Available from the Online Archive of California, http://www.ark.cdlib.org/ark:/13030/kt4b69n6sc.

Rowen, H., Hancock, M. G., Lee, C.-M., & Miller, W. F. (2000). *Silicon Valley edge: A habitat for innovation and entrepreneurship*. Stanford, CA: Stanford University Press.

Sampat, B., & Nelson, R. R. (2002). The evolution of university patenting and licensing procedures: An empirical study of institutional change. *Advances in Strategic Management, 19*, 135–164.

Sarewitz, D. (1996). *Frontiers of illusion: Science, technology, and the politics of progress.* Philadelphia, PA: Temple University.

Schneiberg, M. (1999). Political and institutional conditions for governance by association: Private order and price controls in American fire insurance. *Politics and Society, 27,* 67–103.

Schneiberg, M., & Clemens, E. (2006). The typical tools for the job: Research strategies in institutional analysis. In: W. W. Powell, & D. L. Jones (Eds), *How institutions change.* Chicago: University of Chicago Press.

Scott, W. R. (1987). The adolescence of institutional theory. *Administrative Science Quarterly, 32,* 493–511.

Scott, W. R., & Meyer, J. W. (1983). The organization of societal sectors. In: J. W. Meyer & W. R. Scott (Eds), *Organizational environments: Ritual and rationality* (pp. 129–154). Beverly Hills, CA: Sage.

Scott, W. R., Reuf, M., Mendel, P., & Caronna, C. (2000). *Institutional change and health care organizations.* Chicago: University of Chicago Press.

Selznick, P. (1957). *Leadership in administration: A sociological interpretation.* Evanston, IL: Row, Peterson.

Shane, S. (2004). *Academic entrepreneurship: University spinoffs and wealth creation.* London: Edward Elgar.

Stanford University. (2004). Annual Report of the Office of Technology Licensing 2003–2004. Available at http://www.otl.stanford.edu/about/resources/otlar04.pdf.

Strang, D., & Sine, W. D. (2002). Inter-organizational institutions. In: J. A. C. Baum (Ed.), *Companion to Organizations* (pp. 497–519). Oxford: Blackwell Publishers.

Strang, D., & Soule, S. A. (1998). Diffusion in organizations and social movements: From hybrid corn to poison pills. *Annual Review of Sociology, 24,* 265–290.

Suchman, M. C. (1995). Managing legitimacy: Strategic and institutional approaches. *Academy of Management Review, 20,* 571–611.

Suddaby, R., & Greenwood, R. (2005). Rhetorical strategies of legitimacy. *Administrative Science Quarterly, 50*(2005), 35–67.

Tolbert, P. S., & Zucker, L. G. (1996). The institutionalization of institutional theory. In: S. R. Clegg, C. Hardy & W. R. Nord (Eds), *Handbook of organization studies* (pp. 175–190). London: Sage.

Veblen, T. (1899). *The theory of the leisure class: An economic study of institutions.* New York: The Macmillan Company.

Ventresca, M. J., & Mohr, J. (2002). Archival methods in organization analysis. In: J. A. C. Baum (Ed.), *Companion to organizations* (pp. 805–828). New York: Blackwell.

Weick, K. (1995). *Sense-making in organizations.* Thousand Oaks, CA: Sage.

Weisendanger, H. (2000). A History of the OTL. Available at http://www.otl.stanford.edu/about/resources/history.html.

Zelizer, V. (1979). *Morals and markets: The development of life insurance in the United States.* New York: Columbia University Press.

Zucker, L. G. (1977). The role of institutionalization in cultural persistence. *American Sociological Review, 42*(5), 726–743.

Zucker, L., Darby, M., & Brewer, M. (1998). Intellectual human capital and the birth of U.S. biotechnology enterprises. *American Economic Review, 88,* 290–306.

Zuckerman, E. W., Kim, T.-Y., Ukanwa, K., & Ritter, J. V. (2003). Robust identities or non-entities: Type-casting in the feature film labor market. *American Journal of Sociology, 108,* 1018–1075.

THE STEWARDSHIP OF THE TEMPORAL COMMONS

Allen C. Bluedorn and Mary J. Waller

ABSTRACT

The contemporary move toward privatization has led to the assigning of property rights to many intangible public resources. One shared intangible resource swept up in this marketization is, we argue, the temporal commons – the shared conceptualization of time and temporal values created by a culture-carrying collectivity. As a result, the stewardship, or management, of the temporal commons is judged exclusively by the market-sanctioned metric of efficiency. We suggest that metrics based on the stakeholder approach to organizational effectiveness are more appropriate than the sole reliance on market efficiency criteria for judging the stewardship of a temporal commons, and offer several examples of stewardship evaluated by such metrics from the perspectives of a variety of stakeholders. We close with a call for more cognizant agency and wider participation in temporal commons stewardship.

INTRODUCTION

They hang the man and flog the woman
That steal the goose from off the common

Research in Organizational Behavior: An Annual Series of Analytical Essays and Critical Reviews
Research in Organizational Behavior, Volume 27, 355–396
Copyright © 2006 by Elsevier Ltd.
ISSN: 0191-3085/doi:10.1016/S0191-3085(06)27009-6

But let the greater villain loose
That steals the common from the goose.

The Law demands that we atone
When we take things we do not own
But leaves the lords and ladies fine
Who take things that are yours and mine.

The poor and wretched don't escape
If they conspire the law to break;
This must be so but they endure
Those who conspire to make the law.

The law locks up the man or woman
Who steals the goose from off the common
And geese will still a common lack
Till they go and steal it back.

English folk poem, ca. 1764 (Bollier, 2002)

Thus was the sentiment of many in 18th century England as they saw much of their public land – their "commons" – unilaterally enclosed and controlled by more powerful private entities for the sake of production efficiency (Boyle, 2003). True, when previously public land was so enclosed and managed, the economics of the situation changed dramatically; absent the potential overuse of the land by the public in the traditional "tragedy of the commons" sense (Hardin, 1968), it was believed the land could be made more productive, ultimately feeding and clothing more people. However, while this "enclosure movement" touted its aim as increased efficiency, its by-products were to further enrich a select echelon, increase the dependence of peasants on wages earned from that echelon (Humphries, 1990), eventually extinguish much of the public's collective memory of and desire for a commons, and arguably hinder its efficacy in managing shared public assets as well.

Like the early enclosure movement, contemporary efforts to enclose not public greens but *intangible* public resources such as cyberspace, information, and elements of culture have been increasingly successful, but not without a heated debate (see Bollier, 2002; Brown, 1998). On one side of the debate is the argument that without such appropriation by private ownership, these intangible resources will suffer in terms of efficiency. The general belief in this area is that assigning property rights to intangible resources that now exist in the public domain will ultimately give the owners of those rights more capital and incentives to further develop those resources for the betterment of all. On the other side of the debate are those in favor of intangible resources remaining in the public domain, accessible to all. The underlying logic here is that assigning property rights will constrain creativity and further development of resources to only those who hold the leverage of legal ownership, shutting out any other possibility of creative extension, or improvement by members of the public at large – in sum, that creativity and innovation can flourish by building on past innovations *if* the past is not monopolized (Lessig, 2004).

The point of this article is not to take sides in the debate, but to train focus on one particular intangible public resource which, we believe, has been swept along largely unnoticed by the contemporary enclosure movement. We suggest here that this silent and ubiquitous enclosure, made in the name of efficiency, has resulted in the enclosure of the *temporal commons*. This enclosure has fundamentally affected how we regard and use time, and its effects have reverberated through our families, our work groups, our organizations, and our culture.[1] Like Hardin's (1968) assertions regarding the overpopulation of the planet, we assert that the enclosure of the temporal commons is a problem for which there is no technical solution, but for which there may be a social one.

Our aim in this article is two-fold: first, to introduce the notion of the temporal commons and its enclosure; and second, to suggest that active stewardship of the temporal commons may not only be possible but also be both desirable and achievable. We argue that the public has accepted the enclosure of the temporal commons based on a judgment of efficiency, but that other metrics are better suited to judge the management of this commons. Using these metrics, we provide four examples of active temporal commons management and evaluate the outcomes of that management from the perspective of a variety of stakeholders. If we are successful in achieving our aim, we hope to have supplied those who study a variety of social issues, including stress, life satisfaction, and tensions between work and family, with a means to consider and evaluate temporal stewardship in the future.

THE TEMPORAL COMMONS AND ITS ENCLOSURE

The term "temporal commons" was introduced by Bluedorn (2002, pp. 255–256) as a metaphor that emphasized human agency in the conceptualization of time. We build on that use here with the following formal definition: *The shared conceptualization of time and the set of resultant values, beliefs, and behaviors regarding time, as created and applied by members of a culture-carrying collectivity, constitute a temporal commons.* Although a full philosophical and rhetorical discourse on the nature of time is beyond our scope here (see McGrath & Rotchford, 1983, for an organizationally focused discussion of such matters), it is important to note the pivotal role time plays in culture. Hall (1983) suggests that time and culture are inextricably linked, with time playing a fundamental role in the "hidden cultural grammar [that] defines the way in which people view the world, determines their values, and establishes the basic tempo and rhythms of life" (p. 6). Different cultures create and hold different ideas about what time is and how it should be used; for example, the overall pace of life, the measurement of time (i.e., with clocks or events), and what constitutes tardiness varies from culture to culture (Bluedorn, 2002; Levine, 1997). These value differences cannot be judged as right or wrong, for they help form the basis of cultural distinctiveness. As other elements of culture, such as law, religion, music, stories, wisdom, and communities constitute intangible resources created by a people and embodied in their culture (Geertz, 1977), so too is a temporal commons an integral, intangible part of that culture. What time is and the values associated with it are deeply held assumptions in the core of cultures – so deeply held, that they may be only rarely articulated, if at all (Hall, 1983, p. 6).

As many have noted, a new enclosure movement has unfolded during the last quarter century, blurring the lines between the market and the public domain (Boyle, 2003; Safrin, 2004) and enveloping many intangible aspects of culture – including, we assert, the temporal commons. The move toward enclosure of more and more intangible assets from the public domain has been spurred on by two central factors. First, the U.S. and several other governments have embraced a market-driven course of privatization (Henig, 1989) or "hyperownership" (Safrin, 2004), selling, giving, or (in a *de facto* sense) assigning common public resources to private entities. For example, new portions of the public broadcast spectrum, worth an estimated $70 billion, were given to broadcasters by the U.S. government in the hopes of motivating high-definition television development (Brinkley, 1998). Likewise, as government funding sources such as the National Endowment for the Arts have dwindled over the past two decades, many artists and museums have turned to corporate sponsorship of artistic expression, leading to issues of censorship by sponsors (Schiller, 1991). Even public spaces themselves, once part of a civic cultural experience and funded by public resources, are now claimed and named by sponsorship. Stadiums and other public venues, public broadcasting time, and even public events now bear the name of corporations, but while the funds received by selling off naming rights to cultural elements seem to vanish into bureaucracy, the privatized label remains embedded in culture (Bollier, 2002, p. 157). Those supporting the ownership movement label any resistance as a childish "romantic" view of the benefits of common public resources (Chander & Sunder, 2004), and invariably cite Hardin's (1968) pessimistic view of the ability of people to collectively manage resources at all, even though many problems with Hardin's view have been identified, including counterexamples (Ostrom, Burger, Field, Norgaard, & Policansky, 1999). Labeling resistance to enclosure movements as "childish" or "romantic" hastens the departure of common public resources from the collective memory of what Zerubavel (2003) described as "mnemonic communities," or groups with shared memories of the past (p. 4). A great irony associated with this process is that it diminishes the range of strategic options available to organizations and industries. For example, one attribute of a temporal commons is the extent to which it emphasizes speed and values it positively (an attribute to be considered at length later in the article). Yet Ancona and Chong (1996) provide an example of one industry that deliberately and strategically tried to slow the pace of new product development, which in the context of contemporary temporal commons seems iconoclastic, perhaps in part because the virtue of working and progressing at a slower pace has all but vanished from the collective memories of industrial nations.

The second factor leading to a new enclosure movement is technology, which has helped create (e.g., cyberspace) or make accessible (e.g., the human genome) many intangible public resources. Private entities ranging from multinational corporations to aboriginal organizations (Brown, 1998) have taken action to legally claim and own these intangible resources. For example, some argue that ownership of gene sequences or even individual genes should be allowed in a free market as a return on research investment (Haas, 2001) – a position that dates back to 1774, when powerful London publishers argued they would be financially ruined without permanent copyrights to protect their investments in typesetting and printing original works. The House of Lords opted for limited-term copyrights anyway, and as a result, more publishers were able to provide copies of popular books throughout the country after original copyrights expired, and the London publishers "could no longer control how culture in England would grow and develop" (Lessig, 2004, p. 93).

In contrast, the current move to assign ownership rights to information and ideas that would otherwise exist in a freely accessible public domain is unprecedented (e.g., the Sonny Bono Copyright Term Extension Act, which allows Congress to extend existing copyrights into perpetuity). Further, if innovation builds on past creative efforts that are accessible, the rampant and protectionist enclosure of information and ideas may serve to stunt future creative and economic growth (Boyle, 2003). For example, the Walt Disney Corporation, an organization that has clearly profited by claiming ownership to numerous folk tales that once existed as intangible elements of culture in the public domain (e.g., Snow White, Pinocchio, Aladdin, etc.), vigorously fought against Mickey Mouse being added to the public domain after 75 years of copyright protection (Bollier, 2002, p. 123).

Thus have many intangible elements of culture come to be owned. Governments and technology have facilitated the private ownership of intangible public assets in the contemporary enclosure movement. Given that the public has, so far, allowed the private claiming of pieces of culture that it recognizes as such, it comes as little surprise that the public has not resisted the claiming of an intangible asset it seems not to recognize as such: the temporal commons. Historically, the public does not act to protect resources it does not recognize (Bollier, 2002, p. 5) or that it does not perceive to be defensible (Neeson, 1984). This facilitates private entities or corporations to make claims for specific components of the temporal commons, albeit they may not conceptualize what they are doing as enclosing a temporal commons. Nevertheless, and regardless of how such entities frame their actions and intentions, we argue that a new enclosure movement has occurred, and has by default already enclosed the temporal commons by using market-driven values to fundamentally change how we experience time. The claiming of the temporal commons by the market is manifested by the acceptance of the public (1) that time – *any time* – is available for market transactions, and (2) that the value of time should be based solely on its transaction potential. Additionally, the *quality* of one's experiences of time is not quantifiable and in comparison does not add up favorably to the benefits of enclosure under a system that reifies transactions and efficiency. As a result, economics in general tends to devalue the non-quantifiable aspects of any commons, including the temporal commons.[2]

Consequences of Marketization

What are the outcomes of the "marketization" of the temporal commons? Time once quiet, such as time spent on trains or buses, is now filled with LCD screen advertisements and riders handling their business affairs on mobile telephones. Waiting rooms are filled with the babbling of televisions, and children sit in classrooms exposed to advertising on "educational" Channel One broadcasts (De Vaney, 1994), or in the back-seats of vans, pacified by DVD players showing movies saturated with "product placement" advertising (see Graser, 2005). Time once spent away from work is now interrupted with continuous wireless access to the Internet and e-mail, and is filled with either work or advertisements. Less time is available for what Robert Levine terms "time-free thinking" – being totally immersed in an activity without noticing the passage of time, a state particularly important for creative thinking (1997, p. 46) and for developing relationships with others. Even romance has been relegated to the likes of "speed dating" (DiGrazia, 2003).

Regarding how we value time, physicians tied to efficiency plans are penalized for time spent building relationships with patients and rewarded for maximizing the number of patient "transactions" per unit of time. Some physicians fear the creation of "beeper medicine" – a "medical culture built on the quick fix" (Honore, 2004, p. 148; see also Gleick, 1999, p. 85). Likewise, employees increasingly place little value on relationship-building and attachment in organizations, seeing themselves instead as part of a labor market, frequently "transacting" themselves for new and higher-paying positions in other organizations (Kanter, 1989). In markets moving at the speed of computerized transactions, there is no time to mull the implications of decisions – only time to make and implement them (Waller & Roberts, 2003), possibly helping lead to the numerous publicized ethical breeches by corporate executives. Time to reflect is not regarded as economically defensible in a market-driven value system. Speed – fitting more market transactions into every slice of time – has become paramount (Gleick, 1999). Setting time equal to money depreciates other (qualitative) ways to value and experience time, and the market-oriented valuation of time has steadily replaced non-market-oriented temporal values.

An important alternative view to the one just presented here must be addressed: that before the contemporary enclosure movement, the temporal commons – the way we use and value time – was already securely market-oriented. However, a national public opinion study in the U.S., based on a random-sample survey and in-depth focus groups across the country, found that Americans "believe materialism, greed, and selfishness increasingly dominate American life, crowding out a more meaningful set of values centered on family, responsibility, and community," but are ambivalent about the conflict between the desire for material wealth and their deepest aspirations, which are non-material (Merck Family Fund, 1995). Similarly, although the relationship between wealth and perceived well-being is complex, market-driven values such as material wealth have been shown in some cases to be negatively related to individual perceptions of well-being, at least in part due to the psychological tension produced by values conflict (Burroughs & Rindfleisch, 2002). Likewise, work–family conflicts are not necessarily moderated for those who make more money, but are moderated for those workers who have closer ties with the community (Martins, Eddleston, & Veiga, 2002). The small-but-growing movement in popular culture for voluntary simplicity (e.g., Pierce, 2000) and slowness (e.g., Honore, 2004) may signal efforts to counteract what some see as a society at odds with its values. It is precisely this values-based discord which leads us to the conclusion that market-oriented temporal values have replaced alternative ways to value time, but not by the hand of the public. We, like others, assert that market and public can achieve a balance of co-existence (Bollier, 2002), but that the nearly unchecked privatization of public resources has in effect allowed powerful market stakeholders to *dictate* market values to the public (Barnes, Rowe, & Bollier, 2004), and thus trump non-market-oriented valuations of time. As related to a temporal commons, we shall see this impact of market values most clearly when we encounter the English Temporal Revolution later in the article.

Clarification of Purpose

To this point, we have defined and discussed the concept of a temporal commons, and we have argued that some sectors of society have more power and thus have been more able to achieve changes in the temporal commons they believe will enhance their well-being. Furthermore, such changes to the temporal commons have been but one part of a more general trend to convert intangible publicly shared resources to private control. These are serious claims, and before we proceed to discuss examples that will support them, a few mitigating points should be made.

First, we will argue that both advocates of specific changes in a temporal commons and "innocent bystanders" (i.e., those not involved in the debate as well as those who may not even be aware of the debate) are usually consciously *unaware* of the larger combination of temporal dimensions and attributes that comprise their temporal commons. The two sets of people will often be similarly clueless that a greater temporal commons exists and that the proposed change will likely affect other elements of it, often unpredictably. Further, proponents will often make claims about the effects of specific proposed temporal changes. However, given that most people are usually unaware of the overall temporal commons, the changes advocated tend to be specific and focused rather than omnibus, and the unintended effects wrought by overall changes to the commons often go unexamined.

Second, we believe everyone has a legitimate claim on the temporal commons in which they take part, so we will not argue that some voices should be silenced in favor of others. Our point is that some voices have had a disproportionate say in deliberately changing some parts of the temporal commons, while others, often equally affected, have had no voice at all nor at times even realized that it would be legitimate to have a voice. The call then is not so much "workers of the world unite," as it is for the workers of the world to realize the temporal commons exists and is a shared resource, and to speak up when changes to that commons are proposed. It is a call for the participants in a specific temporal commons to develop an understanding of proposed changes and to make known their feelings regarding how changes to the commons will affect their lives.

Third, certainly not all social change is consciously ordained or directed, and this applies to the temporal commons as much as it does to any other aspect of human cultures and social life. Some changes are likely to be completely unintended and mandated by no one in particular, yet they occur nevertheless. This is true of change in a temporal commons as well. Our task is not to ferret out the conspirators and dispatch them; rather, it is to make it legitimate for all of us to become co-conspirators, really co-stewards, in the management and maintenance of our temporal commons.

Finally, we are not temporal Luddites: we do not reject the idea of changes in the temporal commons per se. Like changes in anything, we view some changes as generally beneficial; others, as generally harmful; and still others are difficult to evaluate, so we do not advocate suspending any temporal commons in a stasis field, placing it as an ant in amber, so to speak. We do believe, however, that it is fair to address any proposed change in a temporal commons with questions such as: Beneficial to whom? Harmful to whom? Beneficial and harmful to what (i.e., other dimensions of the temporal commons, other aspects of the culture)?

As we see it, our task now is to clarify the concept of the temporal commons and its stewardship, in part because both ideas are new, and in part because they deal with a domain of culture that has been neglected by the social sciences in general and the organization sciences in particular. We see this domain, the temporal commons, as a combination, a system of dimensions and attributes that is both socially constructed and open-ended. By socially constructed our point is that the temporal commons held by a group, be that group a set of friends who meet regularly for dinner or the thousands of people who comprise a large corporation, is the product of human interaction among the members, past and present, of that group. Certainly the past and present members of a group are directly involved in constructing their temporal commons, but so may be people and groups outside the focal group. This can occur when the members of one group imitate the practices of other groups in order to achieve greater legitimacy, something new groups are especially prone to do. Bluedorn (2002, pp. 8–9) provides an example of this kind of social construction of a temporal commons attribute in his interpretation of both early Christianity's and early Islam's selection of Sabbath days as examples of the institutional theory process of mimetic imitation (DiMaggio & Powell, 1983).

But a temporal commons is never constructed once and for all. As we shall see, many aspects of a temporal commons may tend to persist for centuries, but a temporal commons is always an ongoing creative process (see Fraser, 1999, pp. 26–29, on the open-ended nature of time). And this process is open-ended in that new temporal forms, certainly attributes and even dimensions perhaps, can be added to the mix of dimensions and attributes that constitute a specific temporal commons. To further complicate things, sometimes the new attributes may replace the old, but at other times the new will be added to the previous mix to create new combinations and linkages. For this reason, it is impossible to create an exhaustive list of all the dimensions and attributes that may combine to form a temporal commons because new ones may always potentially be created. Nevertheless, there are some dimensions that appear to be universal, several of which we will be discussing, and these include temporal depth, polychronicity, punctuality, and the speed or pace of activities, all of which will be explained when these dimensions are presented later in our discussion.

Our purpose in what follows is to clarify the temporal commons concept and its importance by presenting several examples of successfully advocated changes in temporal commons, not all of which were unopposed. In the course of presenting the examples, we will discuss the impacts on other temporal and non-temporal aspects of human life. We will also discuss the concept of temporal stewardship – the active management of a temporal commons – and issues such as who has responsibility for this stewardship. As we shall see, all of these examples involve the agency of organizations in some way, acting either alone or in concert to achieve the changes being advocated. As such, we will discuss how the changes affected various stakeholder groups as well as provide theoretical interpretations of these situations.

TEMPORAL STEWARDSHIP

What is stewardship? This question must be answered before we can address the issue of *temporal* stewardship, so to try to answer this question, we shall refer to the more generic dictionary definition which tells us that stewardship is *the conducting, supervising, or managing of something; esp: the careful and responsible management of something entrusted to one's care* (*Merriam-Webster's Collegiate Dictionary*, 10th ed.). Moreover, the *sine qua non* of this definition is the "esp," the careful and responsible management of something entrusted to one's care. This element is key because it is what provides the term with its positive connotation, and the temporal commons is something that has been entrusted to people's care, albeit usually tacitly.

Obviously, everyone is in favor of careful and responsible management, that is, of stewardship, yet how can we know if a manager is behaving carefully and responsibly? At the organizational level, the answers are normally sought in two domains: effectiveness and efficiency. Although these criteria overlap to some extent, they differ fundamentally. Effectiveness is the extent to which an organization (or group, person, etc.) achieves its goals, and efficiency is the ratio of a system's output to its input (Price, 1972, p. 101; Price & Mueller, 1986, p. 205). This difference becomes clearer with a concrete example. Health care effectiveness can be measured by how many lives the system saves (assuming the goal is to save lives), whereas its efficiency is the average cost of saving each life. The debatable nature of the relative importance of each potential criterion is illustrated well by a physician at a ThedaCare hospital. The hospital was implementing procedures developed at Toyota to increase efficiency, and in a discussion of these procedures the physician said: "Sure, there is value to getting through a visit faster [efficiency], but what about the value of getting better [effectiveness]? Why not measure that?" (Wysocki, 2004, p. A6). Yet just as obviously, one of these criteria is ultimately more important and compelling than the other, the more important being the saving of lives, which is effectiveness (see Drucker's, 1974, pp. 45–46, discussion of the relative importance of efficiency and effectiveness). And the following statement helps one discern the difference as well as see the point about which is more profoundly important: "Efficiency is about how; effectiveness is about why. Efficiency is to effectiveness what intelligence is to wisdom" (Bluedorn, 2002, p. 105).

The health care example oversimplifies the problem of measuring or assessing effectiveness because there may be many goals for organizations, some seemingly in conflict, and that messiness and ambiguity may be at least one reason why efficiency often trumps effectiveness, at least in the short term. As we discussed previously, the efficiency or worth of time is in many ways today measured by the worth of transactions conducted or savings accrued, rather than the quality of experience, during that time. In other words, the worth of time in our market-driven culture is measured by its efficiency, to the exclusion of practically all other metrics. And a specific temporal commons example illustrates efficiency's ascendancy well.

The example concerns a phenomenon experienced every year by much of the world that resides outside the tropics: the shift into daylight saving time. Late in 1973, the U.S. Congress passed legislation designed to deal with the energy crisis brought on by an oil embargo. The subject of the legislation was daylight saving time, and the new law radically increased the portion of the year during which the country would operate under daylight saving time because it was felt that living and working under daylight saving time would conserve energy. Conserving energy means the country would have continued to function as before, but would do so consuming less energy (an input). In other words, the country would operate more efficiently. Undoubtedly this efficiency was seen as a means to other ends, but it seems easy for such means to become ends in themselves. We will return to the question of daylight saving time later in the article.

The problem remains, though, by what criteria are an individual or group deemed a good steward of anything, let alone of a temporal commons? The two criteria just suggested may provide general guidance, even metrics, but if the argument is accepted that effectiveness is more important than efficiency, assessing effectiveness alone will not suffice because some satisficing level of efficiency is always necessary too. To choose one to the exclusion of the other is a false choice because the two are not mutually exclusive. The proper question is, what should be the balance between efficiency and effectiveness? Part of the answer to this question will always be debatable, though, because it will deal with fundamental value questions. And intertwined with this value question is a fundamental temporal quality: *temporal depth*.

Temporal Depth

Temporal depth is the temporal distances into the past and future that individuals and collectivities typically consider when contemplating events that have happened, may have happened, or may happen (Bluedorn, 2002, p. 114). It is often discussed under the time horizon label, though this label almost always refers to distances into the future rather than into the past.

Future temporal depth deals with temporal distances into the future and past temporal depth describes temporal distances into the past. Overall or total temporal depth is the sum of the temporal distances into the past and the future an individual or collectivity typically considers. Indeed, several studies reveal a consistent positive correlation between the lengths of past and future temporal depths for individuals (Bluedorn, 2002; Bluedorn & Richtermeyer, 2005; El Sawy, 1983) and companies (Bluedorn & Ferris, 2004), with the length of the past temporal depth apparently having a causal impact on the length of future temporal depth but not vice versa (El Sawy, 1983). Yet both efficiency and effectiveness are silent regarding temporal depth, especially future temporal depth, but neither can be assessed without future temporal depth being specified. For without knowing the specific temporal interval over which either is to be assessed, it is impossible to do so. The assessor needs to know if the efficiency is to be calculated as the number of college graduates produced this semester or this year, if profitability is for the next quarter or the next year.

Certainly, the omission of explicit references to temporal depth can be addressed by specifying the time period for which the assessment will be made. But even if this is done, both efficiency and effectiveness can still be contested matters. Even efficiency, a seemingly straightforward mathematical ratio, can be problematic because what to count as system outputs and inputs can be contentious issues. And effectiveness is usually a contentious issue by its nature as various organizational stakeholders can hold widely divergent goals for the organization, hence arrive at very different assessments of its effectiveness (Connolly, Conlon, & Deutsch, 1980).

Our goal is not to eliminate such contention and debate, nor to suggest unambiguous empirical metrics. We are not even sure that would be possible since this appears to be a staggeringly difficult issue, even at the conceptual level (e.g., Bluedorn, 1980; Campbell, 1977; Hannan & Freeman, 1977; Steers, 1975; Quinn & Rohrbaugh, 1983; Scott, 2003, pp. 350–372), although some have tried (e.g., Kaplan & Norton, 1996). One course to take would be to abandon effectiveness and efficiency entirely for other possible criteria such as exploitation and exploration (March, 1991). But we believe efficiency and effectiveness more directly address the issue of stewardship quality than other possible criteria, so they are the criteria we will employ in our consideration of the issue. However, our purpose in employing them is not to reach definite conclusions about the quality of stewardship in specific cases; instead, it will be to illustrate the point that different stakeholders have different interests and perspectives, and can, therefore, reach different conclusions about the quality of the stewardship.

So we will use efficiency, and especially effectiveness, from a stakeholder perspective as sensitizing concepts and criteria (Blumer, 1954) to stimulate questions about the stewardship of the temporal commons – questions that usually go unasked.

As sensitizing concepts, we propose neither a list of specific empirical indicators nor a calculus for combining them into quantitative scores. For as we have already noted, even measuring effectiveness, for example, or just trying to specify it conceptually, has been long lamented as a formidable, perhaps impossible, task. The point here is not how to operationalize these criteria. Rather, the point is that questions about the quality of temporal stewardship usually go unasked, and one reason why may be the lack of criteria to assess that quality.

The Spanish Siesta

To illustrate the importance of asking the question about the quality of temporal stewardship as well as the difficulty of answering it unambiguously, we will consider the case of the Spanish siesta. The siesta is an attribute of the temporal commons in Spain, an attribute whose origins extend over 2,000 years into the past back to the Roman era (Vitzthum, 2004). The siesta is the custom of taking a nap after lunch for one or two hours, and today this custom is disappearing in Spain, especially in the large cities such as Madrid. The question of temporal stewardship regarding the siesta is intertwined with the question of why the siesta is disappearing. And it is disappearing for a variety of reasons.

One reason appears to be the growth of cities and housing patterns within them. As the cities have gotten larger, many people now live farther from their places of employment than they did previously. This adds a significant amount of commuting time to the one or two hours required for the siesta (*Wall Street Journal*, 2005b), creating a total time commitment which is often impractical in a modern economy.

A second reason is government efforts to establish a 9-to-5 workday, as revealed by the desire for such work hours expressed by officials like the minister of employment and women's affairs in the regional government of Madrid (Vitzthum, 2004). The siesta was possible traditionally because people would return to work afterward and work for several more hours. This meant that organizations, public and private, were often open for business well into the evening hours. Thus, a law that went into effect in late December of 2005 requiring Spanish government ministries to close by 6:00 p.m. (*Wall Street Journal*, 2005b, p. A9) will hasten the demise of the siesta because the ministry employees will be unable to work after 6:00 p.m., by that putting pressure on them to work during the traditional siesta period.

Since government is a key factor in contemporary societies, the schedule of its operations, in this case the daily rhythms of its operations, will likely affect the schedules of other organizations who must deal with the government ministries. This suggests the daily schedules of the government ministries may serve a zeitgeber (pacing) role for other organizations by providing this explicit signal in the form of hours of operation. For this reason, we would anticipate the work hours of other organizations to gradually become aligned with the ministry hours, especially the work hours of organizations that deal directly and regularly with the government ministries. But the effects will likely spread further, for even organizations that do not come into direct contact with the government ministries will have dealings with other organizations that do. And the organizations that deal with those organizations, in turn, will likely realign their schedules as well. This is actually an example of entrainment, the process by which the rhythms of systems come into alignment with those of other systems (Ancona & Chong, 1996), and it provides a third reason the siesta is disappearing: the alignment of organizational rhythms with those of the government ministries. Indeed, part of the movement to establish something like 9-to-5 work schedules is the Spanish effort "to bring its practices in line with other European countries" (*Wall Street Journal*, 2005b), which may indicate entrainment with the work schedules of other European countries.

So here we see several reasons why the siesta is disappearing in the Spanish temporal commons, but none of these reasons explicitly addresses the original question of the quality of the temporal stewardship involved in this change. From the standpoint of efficiency, it is likely the officials who advocate this change, and in this sense are the stewards of this portion of the Spanish temporal commons, would claim that average employee productivity, hence the overall efficiency of the organization, would increase because everyone's work hours would be more consistent and predictable, people would be present to do the work as it needs to be done, and so forth. But the elimination of the siesta may produce just the opposite effect due to reduced amounts of sleep. For the Spanish now sleep about 40 minutes less each day than other Europeans (Vitzthum, 2004), and Spanish employees, even though they work long hours compared to people in most countries, are characterized by relatively low productivity (*Wall Street Journal*, 2005b). The low productivity could be generated by the sleep deficiency given what is known about the negative effects of sleep deprivation (Coren, 1996), such as poorer decision making, accidents, and other problems.

The reason for the reduction in sleep appears to be due, not just to the elimination of the siesta, but to the connection between the practice of siestas and other elements of the Spanish temporal commons. Actually, it is the severing of those connections with the elimination of the siesta that may be the problem. The other key attribute of the Spanish temporal commons involved is the Spanish pattern of continuing the daily cycle of activity far into the night, producing a nation of night owls. For example, customers for their evening meal usually go to restaurants at 10:00 p.m. or later, but people are still in the morning rush hour by 7:30 a.m. (Vitzthum, 2004). With a siesta in mid-afternoon, this pattern was sustainable without net sleep loss, but subtract the siesta and maintain the late-night pattern of activities combined with the same starting times the next morning, and a sleep deficit occurs. Something had to give, and so far Spaniards have been more willing to reduce their sleep than to give up the late-night pattern of daily activity. Will this trade-off continue or will the siesta be reinstituted, which would be difficult given the commuting constraint, or will the pattern of daily life activities gradually shift to earlier hours? Examining this situation from the standpoint of effectiveness, one group of stakeholders, the general citizenry, might argue that the old pattern – siesta and late nights – was preferable, even if other stakeholders such as organizational managers and organizations in other countries (suppliers and customers) might find the new siesta-less pattern preferable.

As noted earlier, we propose no calculus for reaching a normative decision about which pattern is better and note that even if such a calculus were available, *better* is always a value judgment anyway. For example, Judge and Spitzfaden (1995) reported the intriguing finding that the greater the diversity of time horizons used by managers in firms, the better their firms seemed to perform financially. So it would be easy to conclude that a temporal commons with a greater diversity of temporal depths would be better for organizations. But since we are using the stakeholder approach to effectiveness, the question really should be, better for whom? Perhaps better for groups such as stockholders, but for all stakeholders? That could be possible, but it would be dangerous to assume this to be the case.

And managers are not the only stewards of temporal depth in a temporal commons. Singapore's Minister of Education, Tharman Shanmugaratnam, noted the need for such stewardship when he said, "Someone in society has to be focused on the long term … " (Zakaria, 2006, p. 37). He further noted that in the United States foundations and a "tradition of civic-minded volunteerism" often "fulfill this role" (Zakaria, 2006, p. 37). If Shanmugaratnam is correct, we see not just examples of temporal stewardship but examples of who such stewards might be.

We will now illustrate how efficiency and effectiveness can be used in a sensitizing, question-generating manner to address the stewardship of a temporal commons, and we shall do so by examining temporal commons and their stewardship at four levels of phenomena: the civilization, the society, the organization, and the work group. And we shall proceed to these examples, not just to illustrate the question of stewardship, as useful as that may be, but to reveal several important dimensions and attributes of temporal commons, and by that add greater clarity to the temporal commons concept itself.

ILLUSTRATIVE STEWARDSHIP OF TEMPORAL COMMONS

As just indicated, we will examine commons at several levels – civilization, society, organization, and group – and in the choice of these illustrations we have found it useful to identify examples involving deliberate efforts to change these commons. Such cases are especially useful because any attempt to change even one part of a temporal commons is clearly an example of stewardship of that commons, as would be active resistance to any such proposed changes. This is true even if the proponents of the change are unaware of the overall commons they will be affecting. We will begin our consideration of these illustrations at the level of the civilization.

Civilization

On February 24, 1582, a decision was announced that proposed an adjustment in the temporal commons of Europe, parts of the Middle East and Africa, as well as parts of North and South America. The announcement was in the form of a papal bull issued by Gregory XIII stating that October 4 that year would be followed by October 15 (Richards, 1998, p. 251). The bull cancelled 10 days, October 5–14, in order to establish a reformed calendar that would keep Easter in what was climatically spring, for due to the cumulative effect of small inaccuracies in the Julian calendar, Easter had been gradually migrating toward the summer climes regardless of what the calendar said (Steel, 2000, p. 166). Canceling October 5–14 corrected all that, and to prevent it from happening again, the bull instituted new rules for determining whether a year ending in zero was a leap year or not. (The new rules did not actually prevent such a migration, but compared to the Julian rules, they slowed it by several orders of magnitude.)

Concern over the flaws in the Julian calendar, which was actually a very good calendar, had been expressed to the church for years, but never before resulting in this form of papal action. This reform produced what we now call the Gregorian calendar, which is used to guide secular affairs throughout much if not quite all of the world today. But the road to such universal usage was a long one because the Protestant countries in Europe declined to change their calendars, at least not immediately. For example, Protestant England did not adopt the Gregorian reformed calendar until 1752, nor did its colonies (Richards, 1998, pp. 248–249). So the birth date of George Washington, which contemporary Americans have lived all their lives knowing as February 22, was actually on February 11 by the Julian calendar, which was in effect at the time of his birth. To help avoid confusion during the period of transition to the reformed calendar, the phrase "Old Style" was often included with dates given in the former calendar system (Wiencek, 2003, pp. 31 and 49). And as indicated, today much of the world uses the reformed calendar for secular matters, even though it took over four centuries to accomplish this conversion.

The calendar system people use is an overt, indeed, tangible part of their temporal commons. But it is not merely a time-reckoning system, as critical as that function may be for coordinating human activities, for it will often form the core of a cultural complex of beliefs and values in its own right. An example of this is the week, which unlike the day, month, and year, corresponds to *no known cycle* in the natural world to which it can plausibly be linked. Lacking a natural anchor, the week is completely a social construction (see Zerubavel, 1985). And the week reveals values and beliefs about the appropriate rhythms of life that are embedded in the calendar. Such beliefs involve sacred issues such as the appropriate days for religious observances and worship as well as secular affairs such as the appropriate number of days one should work before having days off from paid employment. That these beliefs and values are institutionalized and not just the custom of dividing the timeline into seven-day segments is strongly suggested by the deep resistance to major attempts to change the week during the French Revolution and in the Soviet Union during the 1930s (Zerubavel, 1985, pp. 27–43). Hence, the institutionalization of the week as well as the rest of the calendar indicates a complex of beliefs and values accompanies the calendar's more visible manifestation.

So what of Gregory XIII's reformed calendar announced and decreed to be implemented in the bull of 1582? This was a change that certainly affected

Western Civilization as well as, ultimately, other civilizations too. From the standpoint of temporal stewardship, what were its impacts on Western Civilization in terms of efficiency and effectiveness? From today's perspective, we are inclined to intuitively say it must have increased them because this is the scientific, enlightened system of reckoning the months, days, and years that we scientific and enlightened people have used all of our lives. From the standpoint of efficiency, the existence of two calendars, Julian and Gregorian, one used by some countries, the other used in the rest, would have certainly created difficulties in coordinating activities between countries using the different calendars or between groups in the countries such as merchants and businesses trying to coordinate their activities with their counterparts in the other countries. So when the Russian Olympic team missed the entire Olympic Games of 1908, they did so because Russia still used the old style Julian Calendar, but the games were held in London in that year, and England had, of course, been using the Gregorian calendar for over a century-and-a-half at that point (Richards, 1998, p. 247). The Russians had taken the dates to be the dates in their calendar, and when they arrived in England, much to their surprise, the games had concluded. This is undoubtedly but one more example of what must be many examples, large and small, that happened once Gregory XIII unleashed the reformed calendar on Europe. As such, efficiency in the sense of the productive use of resources would have diminished, for such mistakes would surely have reduced the efficiency of these types of (attempted) coordinated activities because greater efforts – transaction costs (Williamson, 1975) in contemporary terminology – would have been required than if everyone had used the same calendar. As for effectiveness, for most stakeholder groups in everyday life the new calendar made little difference. Europe had a common calendar before the Gregorian reform and although it would finally have one again four centuries later, from the standpoint of an individual's lifetime, the Julian calendar was just as good as the Gregorian (the effects of the lesser accuracy of the former taking over a century to really detect). But from the perspective of at least one stakeholder group, the leadership of the Roman Catholic Church, the new calendar would have been seen as more effective than the Julian calendar because it kept Easter during the time of the year where the church leadership wanted it to be located.

But there is one more likely outcome, at least in the first decades following Gregory XIII's declaration of a new calendar. As already mentioned, the Catholic countries adopted the reformed calendar first (even among them some were faster adopters than others), only to be followed, begrudgingly, by their Protestant brethren. In such a mix, with some countries Gregorian, others Julian, which calendar a country used came to be yet one more distinguishing feature, like language, that defined the country, hence who belonged to it and who did not. As such, the differentiation created by the reformed calendar is an example of how time and temporal practices, beliefs, and values distinguish insiders from outsiders. This is a matter readily seen in the observance of Sabbath days and holidays. Where more than one Sabbath exists, those who observe one are clearly differentiated from those who observe another (Bluedorn, 2002, p. 7), and the same holds true for holidays. Similarly, conquerors will change the time of their conquered countries to their own, as Germany did during World War II: the parts of Europe under German occupation were converted to Berlin time (Ambrose, 1994, p. 19). In the same vein, we note that when the Ukraine began to formally break away from the disintegrating Soviet Union in 1990, among the changes enacted by the newly and democratically elected city council in the Ukrainian city of Lvov was the establishment of Lvov time, which was an hour earlier than Moscow time (Sterba, 1990, p. A12), a form of temporal differentiation that obviously proclaimed a new "in group," one that was asserting it was no longer part of the rapidly disappearing Soviet Union.

So temporal differentiation makes it more difficult to coordinate activities in general, which generally leads to a reduction in efficiency, which, in turn, has possible consequences for the effectiveness of the overall system. These impacts of temporal differentiation occur, in part, by reinforcing in-group/out-group distinctions, an outcome consistent with Lawrence and Lorsch's (1967) theoretical statements about the impact of differentiation on organizational performance (i.e., unless additional integrating mechanisms are developed and used, increasing differentiation in an organization is likely to reduce rather than enhance organizational effectiveness because the overall quality of coordination will be reduced in the organization). These principles of organization theory more completely explain, and support, our conclusion that until the conversion to the reformed calendar was more or less completed five centuries after it was initiated, Gregory XIII's introduction of the reformed calendar reduced the level of efficiency within European civilization as a whole because it created a greater state of temporal differentiation without concomitantly creating additional integrating mechanisms that would maintain or enhance the quality of coordination within Europe. From the standpoint of effectiveness, the existence of the two calendar systems may well have promoted sectarian solidarity, which some stakeholders may have regarded as an improvement, hence as an increase in effectiveness. (This would be similar to greater cohesiveness developing within a company's departments if the departments are temporally differentiated from each other, and which some stakeholders in the company may regard as a desired condition.) But from the standpoint of the overall system (Western Civilization as a whole), the existence of the two calendars likely reinforced sectarian strife, which would be seen by those with an ecumenical perspective as a reduction in effectiveness.

Society

The launching of the Gregorian calendar reform had major repercussions for at least one entire civilization, and that was Gregory XIII's intent. More circumscribed is, perhaps, a notable change in one society's temporal commons, albeit this change would ultimately spread to the temporal commons of other societies as well. The change has been described as the instilling of "work discipline" in a society believed to be deficient in this virtue. A large part of what has been called "work discipline" is more generally known as *punctuality*, a dimension about which no temporal commons worthy of the label may remain silent. Not that all such commons extol the virtues of a fastidious timeliness, but all would seem to have norms and values about the importance of punctuality as well as beliefs about what is and is not "on time." And unlike some aspects of culture, these norms and values are likely to be consciously known and held, making them what Schein (1992) described as espoused values. That societies differ in this respect Levine and his colleagues have documented well (Levine, 1997; Levine, West, & Reis, 1980). Arriving for an appointment at a time that would not be considered late in Brazil, would often be considered egregiously late in the United States.

But the change in one society's temporal commons of interest here did not occur in Brazil or in the United States (although it spread to the latter promptly) – it occurred in England and it took many decades or longer to achieve, likely over a century. More specifically, the change in punctuality norms and values occurred hand-in-hand with the change in England from an agrarian and cottage industry-based economy to that inaugurated by the industrial revolution, the change to the factory system. And the inauguration of the industrial revolution seems to have ushered in enclosure movements as well, enclosure movements directed at both tangible and intangible commons, the former involving the land and its use, the latter involving issues such as copyrights and our principal concern in this article, the temporal commons.

These changes were neither instantaneous nor painless, terms that could just as appropriately be applied to the industrial revolution itself. And this change toward norms of increasingly strict punctuality were only made

possible with the invention of the mechanical clock in the latter part of the
13th century (Bluedorn, 2002, pp. 9–10) and its subsequent increasing accuracy for many centuries thereafter. This transition to "work discipline"
has been beautifully described by E. P. Thompson (1967) with a sympathetic
eye for those upon whom it was imposed, for imposed it was, deliberately
and relentlessly. And Thompson identified the reason this discipline, an
orders-of-magnitude increase in the importance attached to being on time,
was consciously imposed on labor: "Attention to time in labour depends in
large degree upon the need for the synchronization of labour" (1967, p. 70).
The more "synchronization of labour" that was required, the more importance and value that was attached to punctuality. Thus, when an individual
family earned its livelihood by farming or by transforming wool into yarn
or cloth, each farmer or spinner made an independent contribution to the
national economy, a level of synchronization that another Thompson (J. D.
Thompson, 1967), would have described as either pooled or rudimentary
sequential interdependence. But with the factories came more multi-linked
chains of sequential tasks and functions, and perhaps even some reciprocal
interdependence as well. Moreover, the linkages between these tasks were
now more tightly coupled than before. The change in the nature of the
technology used in production led to new ways to organize production, and
an important attribute of this organization and the process of production
was the "synchronization of labor" E. P. Thompson described. And that
synchronization required a labor force that would show up on time regularly, and one that would work until quitting time regularly. But such a
workforce apparently did not exist, in the main, at the dawn of the industrial
age. It had to be created.

As E. P. Thompson described the world of work before the factory system, "The work pattern was one of alternate bouts of intense labour and of
idleness, wherever men were in control of their own working lives" (1967, p.
73). Much of that control ended with the factories, where the attempt was
made to remove that cyclic pattern and replace it with an even pace, which
would have as its goal the same quality effort being expended at 3:30 p.m. as
at 10:30 a.m. At least that was the goal, and to approximate it, a punctual
workforce had to be created. Among the earlier practices the owners tried to
abolish was "Saint Monday," which was, in some cases, a centuries-old
routine in some trades and occupations of taking Monday off from work
each week (E. P. Thompson, 1967). The observance of Saint Monday was
obviously incompatible with the kind of time discipline required in the new
factories, and although not extinct today, we suspect this term's use in the
lines above will be the first time many readers will have encountered the

phrase, which indicates the term has fallen into disuse because, in turn, the practice itself has been diminished tremendously, if not entirely.

But Saint Monday was a fairly gross phenomenon, and the new time discipline focused on much more fine-grained temporal behavior. This is illustrated in the following statement from a voluminous set of rules the owner of the Crowley Iron Works promulgated for the Warden of the Mill around 1700:

> Every morning at 5 a clock the Warden is to ring the bell for beginning to work, at eight a clock for breakfast, at half an hour after for work again, at twelve a clock for dinner, at one to work, and at eight to ring for leaving work and all to be lock'd up. (E. P. Thompson, 1967, p. 82)

Aside from the length of the workday revealed in this statement, we see both an emphasis on precision – the phrase is "at" not "at about" or "around" – and synchronization, for the lack of qualifications in this rule implied that this rhythm of work would apply to everyone. It is interesting to note that the Warden was to provide a weekly account of the employees' work times every Tuesday which was to be produced "without favour or affection, ill will or hatred" (E. P. Thompson, 1967, p. 82). This is interesting because it was written two centuries before Max Weber would write his landmark description of bureaucracy, which included this famous description of impersonal bureaucratic action: "without hatred or passion, and hence without affection or enthusiasm" (Weber, 1978, p. 225). Thus, we see developing simultaneously new systems of production, new technology, new forms of organization, and a new temporal commons, all of which likely contributed to and reinforced the development of each other.

With an increasing emphasis on punctuality, we also see a developing emphasis on speed that continues to the present day (Gleick, 1999), especially in the United States. The linkage between speed and punctuality is even incorporated in Levine and Norenzayan's (1999) use of the accuracy of bank clocks – suggestive of how important it is to be on time – as one component of their index of a country's pace (speed) of life. It is only natural that punctuality would bring with it an emphasis on speed because deadlines, the arbiters of punctuality, tend to stimulate activity, especially as they loom near (see Bluedorn & Denhardt, 1988, for a review of this effect). Moreover, speed is the essence of efficiency and in many cases speed defines efficiency in terms of units produced per some unit of time. It is not merely a coincidence, perhaps, that Adam Smith, writing during this same period, would illustrate the efficacy of the new modes of production and organization with the example of pin manufacturing, which with the new mode of organization (a fine-grained division of labor) could produce thousands more pins in a day than could the same company organized around individual craftsmen, each of whom produced an entire pin by themselves (Smith, 1776/1976, pp. 8–9). The more that can be done per unit of time, the more efficient the organization, and since doing things faster results in more being produced per unit of time, it is only natural that speed would be emphasized as a virtue along with punctuality.

So at the same time that the physical commons were being appropriated and re-defined – the original enclosure movement discussed earlier – so too was the temporal commons of that time, for punctuality and, likely, speed were ascendant. And with the same justification: increased efficiency, which from the perspective of one stakeholder group, the owners of enterprises, should lead to greater effectiveness in the form of profitability. So from the standpoint of efficiency, because resources, human and material, were used productively, likely more productively than before, the efficiency of organizations likely increased. Further, this was certainly an era of exper- imentation in both technology and organization, which the recast temporal commons did not seem to impede and likely facilitated. And such exper- iments also had the potential to influence efficiency. For example, Max Weber touted the greater efficiency of the bureaucratic form of organization compared to other generic forms of organization (1978, p. 233) and the bureaucratic form began its ascendancy to become the dominant form during this period.

But if that is all we had to say about efficiency and effectiveness, our discussion would be incomplete concerning the increasing emphasis on punctuality and speed in this temporal commons. This is so because the benefits of efficiency and its effects on profitability (a measure of effective- ness for some stakeholder groups such as owners) produced by the new temporal commons, the new technology, and the new organizational forms were intended to benefit some much more than they were intended to benefit others. But when other stakeholders involved with the new factories are considered, the benefits in terms of effectiveness were differentially distrib- uted indeed.

Apple Computer's CEO Steve Jobs (2004) once noted that "the journey is the reward' (p. 65), but for many of those involved in the journey during the 18th and 19th centuries, the journey offered sparse rewards (low effective- ness). And the workday revealed in the rule quoted from the Crowley Iron Works is but one indicator of how sparse those rewards from the new temporal commons and forms of organization might be for the bulk of the people involved with the new enterprises (i.e., a 15-hour day with only a half-hour given for breakfast and an hour for lunch). Furthermore, that 15-hour day may have differed from traditional agrarian alternatives such as fieldwork not so much in its length, perhaps, but in the nature of the hours themselves. We suspect this because factory work is machine oriented and driven, which tends to make the rank-and-file employees seem like parts of a machine, with the whole organization conceptualized as a machine itself (see Morgan, 1997, concerning the machine metaphor as one of the original ways to conceptualize industrial organizations). Conceptualizing the organization as a machine is important because machines need to be kept running smoothly, meaning at a uniform speed throughout their hours of operation. This contrasts with traditional agrarian tasks, which though involving long hours, did allow individuals to vary the pace of their work as they wished and even to rest for a time when they chose to do so (more autonomy at the micro level in Hackman & Oldham's, 1976, terms). At the level of the hour, the factory was more minutely controlling than the field (less autonomy). Elliott Jaques has stated, "In the form of time is to be found the form of living" (1982, p. 129). If so, and we believe it is so, then the new temporal commons must have been a burdensome mix of beliefs, values, and norms because the form of living can only be characterized as wretched for many of those involved.

Not that the new temporal commons was without resistance at the time – and E. P. Thompson (1967) clearly documented that it was – but the resistance was largely unsuccessful. And today when we hear of the "slowness" movement (e.g., Honore, 2004), we fail to realize that it may be a faint glimmering of a temporal attribute only dimly perceived in the collective memory and is, in fact, a form of resistance to the excesses of a temporal commons with hypertrophied concerns for punctuality and, especially, speed. So we tend to be dismissive ("Oh, how quaint") if not overtly contemptuous ("Flakes"). But is resistance futile? Within certain limits, probably not, just extremely difficult. Yet for a genuine temporal revolution, which is exactly what happened with the radical changes that developed in England's temporal commons in the 18th and 19th centuries, the bounds themselves would have to change. That is, people are nested within a variety of social systems (families, organizations, societies) and these systems themselves are usually nested within each other (a department is nested within a company, the company is nested within an industry, the industry is nested within a society, the society is nested within a civilization, and so forth). And each broader system provides norms, values, and beliefs that constrain or bound the cultural phenomena of the systems nested within them. So the society's values bound or establish parameters within which its nested organizations operate, organizations do the same for the departments nested within them, and so forth. We suspect the slowness movement is likely to be successfully limited by bounds and nesting structures, and that larger forces, forces at least as powerful as the downsizing movement of the late 20th century that has carried over into the 21st, will affect attempts by individuals to change the temporal commons in ways that try to move it outside these cultural and systemic boundaries. The downsizing movement probably added force to the momentum of the centuries-long acceleration of emphasis on speed, because fewer people were left to do the same work, meaning they had to work faster and perhaps longer as well. Is the 15-hour day on its way back into the temporal commons?

If the 15-hour day is returning, it would be the undoing of at least a century or more of successful 19th and 20th century efforts by organized labor to shorten working hours in Europe (Blyton, 1989) and North America (Hunnicutt, 1988), albeit some of these successes had been reversed in North America at various points during the 20th century. These efforts to shorten working hours do illustrate organized labor in the role of a steward for the temporal commons because the lengths of the work week and day provide a core structure for a temporal commons, in this case a society-wide one.

The English Temporal Revolution radically altered England's temporal commons, and these radical changes spread to other parts of the world as well. Such changes make the calendar reform of Gregory XIII, though generating lots of yelling, usually of nonsense, a rather minor cultural event, though useful because all that yelling reveals just how deeply held our beliefs about time are and how institutionalized time-reckoning systems such as the calendar are. We see the Gregorian calendar reform as relatively minor in comparison to the English Temporal Revolution because the new calendar really did not change anything about how people lived and worked. If one approached it from the perspective of the anthropology of everyday life, it was a non-event. The English Temporal Revolution was just the opposite, because before it was through – and it is unclear if it is through yet because the emphasis on speed seems, in particular, to have continued to intensify, at least in the United States – the temporal commons had changed, not just in the workplace, but in all of English society. And one thing is clear, that with enough reinforcement by the technological and organizational forces that comprised the cultural milieu in which this revolution occurred, the changes to the temporal commons were institutionalized and became the new temporal values, dominant and legitimate, for the entire society. And they have persisted for centuries. Consequently, it will be interesting to see if an analogous temporal revolution occurs in China where 114 million people have left the countryside to work in cities where some factories have long work-days (11 hours) and emphasize efficiency as evidenced by the timing of workers with stopwatches and the posting of signs that state the number of seconds it takes a worker to complete a task (Chang, 2004, pp. A1 and A5). But not all changes to a temporal commons become institutionalized, even if they seem to be successful from the standpoint of efficiency or effectiveness, and this point will be illustrated in our example of a temporal commons at the organizational level.

Organization

"If activities have no temporal order, they have no order at all," (Moore, 1963, p. 9), but different temporal orders produce different effects. As will be seen in the organization we are about to examine, the temporal order was often chaotic and dysfunctional for both the company and the people who worked there. The example here does not involve the entire organization, just one section of it: the section of product development engineers studied by Leslie Perlow (1997, 1999). And the example focuses on the field exper-iment Perlow conducted as a deliberate attempt to improve the temporal commons in this section of the company.

What was wrong with the existing temporal commons when Perlow ar-rived? The problem was that the engineers' work required a combination of both collaborative and individual efforts, but the temporal structure of the engineers' daily routines facilitated collaboration, while impeding the en-gineers' ability to perform the individual elements of their work. Specifi-cally, the norms in this section's temporal commons were such that the engineers interacted constantly, and most important, spontaneously. Hence, the norms proscribed any engineer from refusing to interact with a colleague when that colleague needed to discuss an issue involving a product under development. But the large quantity of these seemingly random interactions made it very difficult for the engineers to perform the portion of their work requiring individual effort because attempts to do so were constantly being interrupted. This meant the engineers routinely worked longer hours than they otherwise might have worked (Perlow, 1997, pp. 115–116), and this had a major negative impact on the temporal commons of their respective fam-ilies. While previous research suggests interruptions can often provide pos-itive opportunities to reflect and reframe creative, collaborative work (Okhuysen & Waller, 2002), the number of interruptions experienced by the engineers in Perlow's study went well beyond having an overall positive effect on work or non-work experiences.

Working with the engineers, Perlow introduced a new form of time to the product development engineers along with a new set of norms to accompany it. This new time was *quiet time* (Perlow, 1997, pp. 115–128), and it was designed to address problems created by the old temporal commons, while simultaneously promoting the achievement of the organization's goals (Perlow, 1997, p. 116). What was quiet time? Quiet time was simply a specific time of the day during which the engineers "would be left uninterrupted for blocks of 'quiet time'" (Perlow, 1997, p. 116). In other words, it would be a known time during which spontaneous interactions would be forbidden. As a change in temporal commons, the institution of quiet time was just as revolutionary for this section of the company as the English Temporal Revolution had been for England.

The creation of quiet time *ipso facto* created a second form of time, "interaction time." Prior to the change, almost all of work time was interaction time, although it had no label. Now there were two forms of time, one in which spontaneous interactions were permitted and actually encouraged, and another form in which all such interactions were forbidden. And once these forms were created, it became necessary to specify the boundaries between them, which provided additional variables to examine during this field experiment. So different times of the day were tried as were different ways of specifying the different time frames. As Perlow noted (1997, p. 120), the purpose of quiet time was not to de-emphasize the importance of the engineers interacting with each other; rather, it was simply to provide the engineers with known periods of uninterrupted time.

From the standpoint of both efficiency and effectiveness, quiet time was a success, a new form of time that substantially improved the temporal commons in this section of the company. Specifically, quiet time seemed to facilitate the engineers' ability to get more of their work done without having to work as much on weekends or late into the evening, which amounts to an increase in efficiency (the same amount of work being accomplished in fewer hours). Further, the division vice-president credited quiet time for the unit being able to launch on time the new product the engineers had developed, which from the standpoint of several stakeholders (e.g., company managers, owners, and customers) would be an indication of effectiveness. So from the standpoint of making productive use of resources – efficiency – quiet time improved the temporal commons. It also increased effectiveness from the standpoint of several stakeholder groups (e.g., managers and owners), and perhaps the stakeholder group comprised the engineers themselves, for the changes in the unit's temporal commons also seemed to enhance their professional work activities, and to some extent, though not for all (Perlow, 1997, p. 126), their personal lives as well. In terms of the latter effects, the quiet time revolution was more positive than the English Temporal Revolution.

But in terms of temporal depth, though, the quiet time change was ineffective because quiet time was never institutionalized in this section of the company, so the practice faded away and would fail the test of effectiveness over the long term (longer temporal depth). Perlow's field experiment did allow, literally, for experimentation with the structural amount of polychronicity in the engineers' workday, and in this respect, it was effective in providing an example of a fundamental dimension in all temporal commons. Polychronicity is about how many things people prefer to be engaged in at once, specifically, how much people (1) prefer to be engaged in two or more tasks or events simultaneously, (2) actually engage in behaviors consistent with these preferences, and (3) believe the best way for people to do things is the way they prefer to engage tasks and events (Bluedorn, 2002, p. 51). Perlow systematically varied the polychronicity structure of the engineers' workday in her experiment – although she did not conceptualize this manipulation in terms of polychronicity – by making it less polychronic. Before she introduced quiet time, the engineers' days were spent "continually flipping back and forth from individual to interactive work" (1997, p. 77). Quiet time reduced the continual flipping back and forth characteristic of a high level of polychronicity (see Bluedorn, 2002, p. 53), at least for parts of the day.

Compared to the English Temporal Revolution, which continues in some ways to the present time (e.g., the emphasis on speed, Gleick, 1999, and speed-based strategies, Blackburn, 1991; Stalk & Hout, 1990), the quiet time change in the temporal commons at this company was short-lived. Although the engineers' and their executives liked the practice of quiet time and the temporal commons it engendered – the engineers even reached a collective agreement to continue it – Perlow (1997, p. 124) noted that after the experiment ended there was "a marked deterioration in the individual's adherences to quiet time," which she attributed to the lack of sanctions for violating it and the absence of any change in the cultural assumptions about what it took to succeed at work (1997, p. 127). Basically, some parts of the organization's culture overwhelmed the nascent beginnings of changes in another part of the culture, the short-lived changes in the temporal commons. It is noteworthy that Perlow herself, in a discursive footnote, relates these causes to the engineers reverting to their pre-experimental behavior, the collective sum of which she likens to the "tragedy of commons" (1997, p. 127), suggesting we identified an apt example, indeed.

But Perlow may have demonstrated not just the impact of quiet time in one unit, but the more general principle that temporal commons can be very difficult to change deliberately. As mentioned earlier, efforts to change the week in France during the French revolution and in the Soviet Union during the 1930s received considerable resistance, even in the context of harsh and repressive political regimes. Perhaps this is because many dimensions and attributes of temporal commons are located at the level of culture Schein labeled "basic underlying assumptions" (Schein, 1992). Two characteristics of basic underlying assumptions may explain the difficulty of changing a temporal commons. First, many of the beliefs and values at this level are held below the level of conscious awareness, which makes them difficult even to discuss. Second, beliefs and values at this level are about the most fundamental aspects of reality, of which time is one. So the specific beliefs and values about time would be, by their nature, held to be beliefs and values about very important aspects of life, and by definition, taken to be true. This would naturally make them difficult to change for who would willingly shift their view to believe and behave in a way understood to be wrong about issues that are also considered fundamental? A temporal commons is not impossible to change, but it is likely there will often be cultural impediments to most changes.

Group

The preceding example involved part of an organization, yet the organization's culture ultimately determined the long-term outcome of attempts to change the temporal commons portion of the culture in one part of that organization. This leads us to a consideration of groups in their own right, albeit within an organizational context. The example we have chosen to illustrate yet more attributes of the temporal commons is Connie Gersick's (1988, 1989) well-known field and laboratory research on the punctuated equilibrium phenomenon in work groups, and in particular for groups with a deadline for accomplishing a single, creative project. A deadline is, of course, a temporal phenomenon, a milestone by which certain tasks are to be performed. As such, a deadline establishes a specific time horizon for not only a group's accomplishments, but, as for many of the groups Gersick studied, the end of the group's existence.

A time horizon, be it that of an individual, group, or organization, has been more formally conceptualized as part of a larger phenomenon, temporal depth, which was discussed earlier in the article, and is "the temporal distances into the past and future that individuals and collectivities typically consider when contemplating events that have happened, may have happened, or may happen" (Bluedorn, 2002, p. 114; see also Bluedorn, 2000, 2005). And as Bluedorn has noted, temporal depth has gone relatively unstudied, although a small amount of work has been done, usually under the label of time or planning horizon, an example of which is the Judge and Spitzfaden (1995) study discussed earlier. Until recently, even descriptive statistics about the lengths of the future horizon of individuals or organizations did not really exist in publicly accessible outlets. Some recent research has reported such statistics for American college students (Bluedorn, 2002), a random sample of Missouri entrepreneurs (Bluedorn & Richtermeyer, 2005), and a random sample of American publicly traded corporations (Bluedorn & Ferris, 2004). Based on the statistics reported in these studies, the deadline-defined time horizons of the groups Gersick studied in the field would all be characterized as either short- or mid-term time horizons, varying as they did from one week to six months (Gersick, 1988, p. 13), while the laboratory groups were given 60 minutes to complete their creative task (Gersick, 1989).

In many ways, the deadline-imposed future temporal depth was the strategic parameter, not just in the groups' temporal commons, but as the central fact of life for the group, because it literally defined the limit of each group's life. Perhaps it is this salience that led the group deadlines to apparently determine the overall pattern through which the groups progressed as they did their work, the pattern that has become famous in organizational behavior and is known as an example of punctuated equilibrium. The pattern that Gersick discovered was that these groups began their work in a certain way, substantially changed their routines and the behavior of individual group members half-way to the deadline at a point known as the "mid-point transition," and then worked to the deadline in fundamentally different ways than they did during the first half of their existence (Gersick, 1988, 1989).

In some ways, this model of the overall process displayed by these groups is similar to Perlow's field experiment with the product development engineers in which she created a new form of time in the engineers' work unit, by that establishing two forms of time rather than the preceding one form. Gersick's punctuated equilibrium model indicates there are at least three forms of time that predictably develop in groups of the type she studied. But unlike the types of time established in Perlow's field experiment, those Gersick observed did not overlap: the process time in Phase 1 (the first half of the group's existence) differed from the process time during the mid-point transition which differed from the process time in Phase 2 (the second half of the groups' existence). Further, with the possible exception of the mid-point transition, the differences that distinguished Phases 1 and 2 were not sufficiently consistent across the groups to easily label them descriptively (c.f., the "quiet time" and "interaction time" labels in Perlow's experiment). Instead, the labels "Phase 1" and "Phase 2" are used, which clearly communicate that the two time periods are different, but really communicates nothing about the nature of the differences. So rather than quiet time or interaction time, or banana time (Roy, 1959–1960), or tea time, prime time, or face time, we simply know that the two times, Phases 1 and 2, will differ, but the specific nature of the differences cannot be completely anticipated beforehand.

Gersick's research demonstrated the central role the groups' deadlines played in determining the general form of the process that would unfold as the groups proceeded with their activities, and as such, provides a specific example of the strong effect the temporal commons has on group activities – temporal depth being one attribute of a temporal commons. In the cases Gersick studied, the impact of this temporal depth factor also seems positive for the groups, the larger organizations of which they were a part, and for their members individually. The deadlines seem to have promoted the development of the process for the groups' work in a way that led to the successful completion of the groups' tasks, which would be an indicator of effectiveness from the standpoint of stakeholders such as the groups' leaders and likely other managers in the organizations of which they were a part. Consequently, this element of the temporal commons clearly promoted the productive use of resources, hence the groups' efficiency, but lacking deadline-free comparison groups we cannot say for sure whether the groups Gersick studied were more efficient than deadline-free groups, even though we strongly suspect they would be more efficient than such groups. We do note that even under unstable deadline conditions, with deadlines being shifted backward or forward in time, groups still seem to engage in a clear transition at the mid-point (Waller, Zellmer-Bruhn, & Giambatista, 2002). And without a deadline, the transition might never occur, or at least take much longer to occur, thus extending the amount of time the group will take to accomplish its work, making it less efficient. So in terms of single-project groups that are given a specific deadline, hence a specific length of the future time horizon in their temporal commons, the impact of the temporal commons, especially the temporal depth component, seems to affect both the groups' efficiency and effectiveness.

As for the more general impact of the temporal depth component on other types of groups (e.g., on-going groups), little evidence has been published. Even the series of experimental studies McGrath and his colleagues conducted (summarized in McGrath & Kelly, 1986) involved fixed time intervals for the groups, hence deadlines. Similarly, there is some evidence to support the claim that a long-term horizon is superior to a short-term horizon for societies (Ashkanasy, Gupta, Mayfield, & Trevor-Roberts, 2004) and for organizations (Bluedorn & Ferris, 2004), but these results are not completely clear cut, certainly not enough to confirm the type of strong claims Ouchi (1981) made for the superiority of a long-term horizon. However, some note that the combination of individuals' temporal perspectives (i.e., past, present, or future orientations) in a group may lead to varying levels of success in completing work under deadline conditions (Waller, Conte, Gibson, & Carpenter, 2001). This idea is supported by Judge and Spitzfaden's (1995) findings. Although they were dealing with entire organizations, the nature of their findings resonates for other levels of analysis as well. As noted in previous discussions in this article, Judge and Spitzfaden found that no single temporal depth was related to organizational performance (effectiveness); rather, it was the mix of time horizons that was related to organizational effectiveness, albeit effectiveness as measured by the traditional owner/manager stakeholder criterion of profitability. Their findings indicate that the greater the variety of future temporal depths employed by the companies' managers, the greater the companies' effectiveness. This suggests the question: Is a long temporal depth generally better in terms of effectiveness? But this misframes the issue, and it is more properly framed as what is the best mix or balance of temporal depths in a given situation? And this framing would seem to apply to individuals and groups, organizations and societies.

CONCLUSION

We have described the idea of a commons as a resource or a nexus of resources held in common by a human collectivity, have shown that a commons can involve intangible resources as well as tangible, have illustrated ways in which actors have asserted ownership of intangible common resources, and then proceeded to define and describe the temporal commons and its enclosure via marketization. We presented one example from each of four different culture-carrying human aggregations – civilizations, societies, organizations, and groups – and these examples illustrated both some of the temporal attributes that comprise such a commons as well as how the management of a temporal commons could be evaluated in terms of efficiency and effectiveness.

A theme underlying all of these discussions is the concept of human agency – not necessarily human agency as manifested in the form of a human leader, although this is possible, but likely more prevalent is an agency manifesting itself collectively and at times not even consciously. The basis for such a thesis is, of course, the point that time and the organization of all its attributes (e.g., systems of time reckoning, punctuality, speed, polychronicity, and temporal depth) by human collectivities is a social construction (Bluedorn, 2002), and like all social constructions, time is amenable to human direction. But this brings us to one last question: direction by which humans? Does everyone have an equal say, or are some voices more persuasive than others?

As political beings, it is unlikely that everyone will have an exactly equal say about anything. Nevertheless, three of the four examples clearly show differential impacts on the temporal commons. Gregory XIII had much more influence on the calendar system than any other person of his time. The factory owners and managers in 18th and 19th century England had much greater power than even Gregory the XIII had when it was their turn to change a temporal commons, in their case the imposition of a time discipline that placed punctuality and speed in the ascendancy. And finally, in the case of Gersick's project groups, whoever delegated the project to the group and set the deadline for completing it had a greater impact than any group member or even the collective action of the groups.

The sole exception to such wide power differentials was observed in the organization Perlow studied in the context of a field experiment to change the temporal commons of one part of it (the unit of the project development engineers). In that case, Perlow worked with the group and reached agreements with them about changing their temporal commons. So in the case of this collectivity, the change was decided by relatively democratic means.

In all these cases, those making the decisions exercised stewardship over their culture's temporal commons, and in these cases they did so deliberately although they probably did not foresee all of the consequences their changes would engender, such as the processes that would unfold in Gersick's groups. It is an appropriate political question to ask, though: are all these stewards the appropriate ones to exercise this voice while others remain silent, or as in the case of the English working class in the 18th and 19th centuries, not silent, but ineffective? To illustrate the question of who should say, we will turn to one final example, for as this analysis was being written the U.S. Congress was debating a deliberate attempt to alter the American temporal commons. The issue under debate was a proposal to lengthen the portion of the year in which daylight saving time would operate. The stated reason for the proposal was to save energy with claims made that electricity use would be reduced by one percent from such an extension (Fialka, 2005, p. D2). The empirical evidence for this claim was shaky at best (*Wall Street Journal*, 2005a), and had even been questioned by a credible authority over 30 years before by an individual the U.S. government had asked to examine the evidence for such a claim the last time the U.S. increased the period of daylight saving time for the same reason. His conclusion: "The interim report before me indicated no overall energy savings linked to advancing the nation's clocks an hour" (Bartky, 2000, p. x).

A number of other voices were heard in the minutes before this change would have slipped through the U.S. Congress little noticed. Several religious groups objected to any lengthening on the grounds that increasing the darkness in the mornings would place school children at greater risk of accidents from school buses and other vehicles as well as make them more vulnerable to "individuals who prey on children" (Fialka, 2005a, p. D2). Software vendors and utilities opposed the change too because they believed "computer software and meters with electronic chips that record time will have to be changed, a project that could take years and cost millions of dollars" (Fialka, 2005b, p. D2). Even the Secretary of Energy urged the Congress to drop the proposal because he believed it would cause "serious international harmonization problems for the transportation industry" (Fialka, 2005a, p. D2) in the words of the Air Transport Association, "throwing U.S. arrivals at foreign airports out of synchronization with European schedules" (Fialka, 2005a, p. D2). These are all legitimate stewardship voices, including those of the representatives who proposed the legislation. Indeed, even the less than profound voices of candy makers excited about the possibility of increased candy sales at Halloween that such a change might generate (Zaryouni, 2005, p. D1) are legitimate, but should other voices be heard as well? The last time the length of the daylight saving time period was increased in the United States, it was increased, at least in part, due to the lobbying efforts of the Daylight Savings Time Coalition, whose members (companies in the fast food, greenhouse, and sporting goods industries) wanted daylight saving time to begin earlier in the spring because they thought it would increase their sales (Varadarajan, Clark, & Pride, 1992, p. 44). The members of this coalition were exercising stewardship from the standpoint of their own self-interests, not those of the country as a whole. But the rest of the country was not similarly organized, so we would argue that when agencies of government control part of the temporal commons, as in the case of daylight saving time, a democratic government has the responsibility to make sure a representative array of voices speak and are heard on the issue.

But the larger part of most temporal commons is not under direct government control (e.g., How would one legislate polychronicity?), so the issue of stewardship is elusive. Perhaps the nascent stewardship theory (Davis, Schoorman, & Donaldson, 1997) proposed as a different approach to organizational governance than agency theory (Jensen & Meckling, 1976) will provide some guidance, but it will need to develop more theoretically in order to do so. So we are not prepared to prescribe who time's stewards should be, other than to say everyone may have a role to play in its stewardship. Time by its nature seems to be conservative, for efforts to change any aspect of a temporal commons are usually met with resistance and often end in failure – notable examples being the failures of both revolutionary France and the Soviet Union to change the length of the week (Zerubavel, 1985, pp. 27–43) and the ultimate outcome of Perlow's experiment with quiet time discussed earlier. But to blithely continue with an "ignorance is bliss" attitude may not be desirable either. Perhaps the foundation of progress is simply the understanding that human beings construct time and its organization and are, hence, to some degree capable of changing it. Achieving this kind of recognition may be what the Norwegian government had in mind when it asked each of its citizens to devote one hour of a working day to the contemplation of time and its use (Kahn, 2000). It may well be that no two people "living *at* the same time live *in* the same time" (Jaques's emphases, 1982, p. 3), meaning that we all create our own times to a certain extent, but all members in a collectivity will be affected by the collectivity's temporal commons, even if not in exactly the same way. We ignore our responsibility for stewardship of our temporal commons at our own risk.

How much we risk is illustrated well in the history of the scientific management movement and the debate over it (Kanigel, 1997). In the early years of that debate, N. P. Alifas, a leader in the American labor movement, made the following statement:

> The people of the United States have a right to say we want to work only so fast. We don't want to work as fast as we are able to. We want to work as fast as we think it's comfortable for us to work. We haven't come into existence for the purpose of seeing how great a task we can perform through a lifetime. We are trying to regulate our work so as to make it an auxiliary to our lives and be benefited thereby.
>
> Most people walk to work in the morning, if it isn't too far. If somebody should discover that they could run to work in one third the time, they might have no objection to have

that fact ascertained, but if the man who ascertained it had the power to make them run, they might object to having him find it out (Commons, 1921, pp. 148–149).

Beliefs, values, norms, and practices about speed are prominent elements of a temporal commons, and this statement illustrates one side of the debate about this aspect of the American temporal commons, at least as it existed in the American workplace early in the 20th century. On the other side, of course, were the disciples of Frederick Taylor, driven by the quest for ever greater production efficiency, hence for an increase in the speed at which workers performed their tasks. In this case, though, there was at least some debate about this issue although it would appear the scientific management side generally prevailed.

Given what we would argue was scientific management's Pyrrhic victory, it is well to be reminded that Max Weber (1904–1905/1958) described the modern economic complex of material goods and the technological and organizational means used to produce them as an "iron cage," which could well lead to "Specialists without spirit, sensualists without heart; this nullity imagines that it has attained a level of civilization never before achieved" (p. 181). If so, using one of the criteria, effectiveness, we have proposed for evaluating the stewardship of temporal commons, it is fair to ask of the technological and organizational developments: to what end? Repeating Steve Jobs' point, the journey is the reward, but how rewarding is it to live in an immutable cage for most of one's life? Who would want Frederick Taylor as a jailer? This is the risk of ignoring our shared responsibility for the stewardship of the temporal commons.

ACKNOWLEDGMENTS

The authors thank Stephen Haggard, Robert Roe, and James Wilbanks for their helpful comments on a previous version of this article.

NOTES

1. We focus attention in the article primarily on modern Western culture, chiefly in the United States; however, given this culture's increasing impact on other cultures of the world, much of the article applies to non-Western cultures as well.

2. See Mohring, Schroeter, and Wiboonchutikula (1987) for an example of the economic valuing of time.

REFERENCES

Ambrose, S. E. (1994). *D-Day, June 6, 1944: The climactic battle of World War II*. New York: Simon & Schuster.

Ancona, D., & Chong, C-L. (1996). Entrainment: Pace, cycle, and rhythm in organizational behavior. In: B. M. Staw, & L. L. Cummings (Eds), *Research in organizational behavior* (Vol. 18, pp. 251–284). Greenwich, CT: JAI Press.

Ashkanasy, N., Gupta, V., Mayfield, M. S., & Trevor-Roberts, E. (2004). Future orientation. In: R. J. House, P. J. Hanges, M. Javidan, P. W. Dorfman & V. Gupta (Eds), *Culture, leadership, and organizations: The GLOBE study of 62 societies* (pp. 282–342). Thousand Oaks, CA: Sage.

Barnes, P., Rowe, J., & Bollier. D. (2004). The state of the commons: A report to owners. Friends of the Commons. Retrieved on May 31, 2006, from http://friendsofthecommons.org/state/index.html

Bartky, I. R. (2000). *Selling the true time: Nineteenth-century timekeeping in America*. Stanford, CA: Stanford University Press.

Blackburn, J. D. (1991). *Time-based competition: The next battleground in American manufacturing*. Homewood, IL: Business One Irwin.

Bluedorn, A. C. (1980). Cutting the Gordian Knot: A critique of the effectiveness tradition in organizational research. *Sociology and Social Research, 64*, 477–496.

Bluedorn, A. C. (2000). Time and organizational culture. In: N. M. Ashkanasy, C. P. M. Wilderom & M. F. Peterson (Eds), *Handbook of organizational culture and climate* (pp. 117–128). Thousand Oaks, CA: Sage.

Bluedorn, A. C. (2002). *The human organization of time*. Stanford, CA: Stanford University Press.

Bluedorn, A. C. (2005). Future focus and depth in organizations. In: A. Strathman & J. Joireman (Eds), *Understanding behavior in the context of time: Theory, research, and application* (pp. 271–287). Mahwah, NJ: Lawrence Erlbaum.

Bluedorn, A. C., & Denhardt, R. B. (1988). Time and organizations. *Journal of Management, 14*, 205–230.

Bluedorn, A. C., & Ferris, S. P. (2004). Temporal depth, age, and organizational performance. In: A. L. Kalleberg & C. F. Epstein (Eds), *Fighting for time: Shifting boundaries of work and social life* (pp. 113–149). New York: Russell Sage Foundation.

Bluedorn, A. C., & Richtermeyer, G. (2005). The time frames of entrepreneurs. Paper presented at the Annual Meeting of the Academy of Management. Honolulu, Hawaii, August 5–10.

Blumer, H. (1954). What is wrong with social theory? *American Sociological Review, 19*, 3–10.

Blyton, P. (1989). Time and labour relations. In: J. Hassard, S. Hill, K. Starkey & P. Blyton (Eds), *Time, work and organization* (pp. 105–131). London: Routledge.

Bollier, D. (2002). *Silent theft*. New York: Routledge.

Boyle, J. (2003). The second enclosure movement and the construction of the public domain. *Law and Contemporary Problems, 66*, 33–74.

Brinkley, J. (1998). *Defining vision: The battle for the future of television*. New York: Harvest Books.

Brown, M. F. (1998). Can culture be copyrighted? *Current Anthropology, 39*, 193–222.

Burroughs, J. E., & Rindfleisch, A. (2002). Materialism and well-being: A conflicting values perspective. *Journal of Consumer Research, 29*, 348–370.

Campbell, J. P. (1977). On the nature of organizational effectiveness. In: P. S. Goodman & J. M. Pennings (Eds), *New perspectives on organizational effectiveness* (pp. 13–55). San Francisco, CA: Jossey-Bass.

Chander, A., & Sunder, M. (2004). The romance of the public domain. *California Law Review*, 92, 1331–1373.

Chang, L. T. (2004). In Chinese factory, rhythms of trade replace rural life. *Wall Street Journal*, December 31, pp. A1 & A5.

Commons, J. R. (Ed.) (1921). *Trade unionism and labor problems (second series)*. Boston: Ginn.

Connolly, T., Conlon, E. J., & Deutsch, S. J. (1980). Organizational effectiveness: A multiple-constituency approach. *Academy of Management Review*, 5, 211–217.

Coren, S. (1996). *Sleep thieves: An eye-opening exploration into the science of mysteries of sleep.* New York: Free Press.

Davis, J. H., Schoorman, F. D., & Donaldson, L. (1997). Toward a stewardship theory of management. *Academy of Management Review*, 22, 20–47.

DiGrazia, C. (2003). I've got a date at 7, but I'll work you in at 7:03. *New York Times*, August 31, section 14CN, p. 1.

DiMaggio, P. J., & Powell, W. W. (1983). The iron cage revisited: Institutional isopmorphism and collective rationality in organizational fields. *American Sociological Review*, 48, 147–160.

De Vaney, A. (1994). *Watching channel one: The convergence of students, technology, and private business.* Albany, NY: State University of New York Press.

Drucker, P. F. (1974). *Management: Tasks, responsibilities, practices.* New York: Harper & Row.

El Sawy, O. A. (1983). Temporal perspective and managerial attention: A study of chief executive strategic behavior. *Dissertation Abstracts International*, 44(05A), 1556–1557.

Fialka, J. J. (2005a). Daylight saving expansion plan is ripped by airlines, churches. *Wall Street Journal*, July 20, p. D2.

Fialka, J. J. (2005b). Daylight-saving plan might be scaled back. *Wall Street Journal*, July 21, D2.

Fraser, J. T. (1999). *Time, conflict, and human values.* Urbana, IL: University of Illinois Press.

Geertz, C. (1977). *Interpretation of cultures.* New York: Basic Books.

Gersick, C. J. G. (1988). Time and transition in work teams: Toward a new model of group development. *Academy of Management Journal*, 32, 274–309.

Gersick, C. J. G. (1989). Making time: Predictable transitions in task groups. *Academy of Management Journal*, 32, 274–309.

Gleick, J. (1999). *Faster: The acceleration of just about everything.* New York: Pantheon Books.

Graser, M. (2005). Product-placement spending poised to hit $4.25 billion in '05. *Advertising Age*, 76(14), 16.

Haas, A. K. (2001). The Wellcome Trust's disclosures of gene sequence data into the public domain and the potential for proprietary rights in the human genome. *Berkeley Technology Law Journal*, 16, 145–165.

Hackman, J. R., & Oldhan, G. R. (1976). Motivation through the design of work: Test of a theory. *Organizational Behavior and Human Performance*, 16, 250–279.

Hall, E. T. (1983). *The dance of life.* New York: Doubleday.

Hannan, M. T., & Freeman, J. (1977). Obstacles to comparative studies. In: P. S. Goodman & J. M. Pennings (Eds), *New perspectives on organizational effectiveness* (pp. 106–131). San Francisco, CA: Jossey-Bass.

Hardin, G. (1968). The tragedy of the commons. *Science, 162*, 1243–1248.

Henig, J. R. (1989). Privatization in the United States: Theory and practice. *Political Science Quarterly, 104*, 649–670.

Honore, C. (2004). *In praise of slowness: How a worldwide movement is challenging the cult of speed.* New York: Harper Collins.

Humphries, J. (1990). Enclosures, common rights, and women: The proletarianization of families in the late eighteenth and early nineteenth centuries. *Journal of Economic History, 50*, 17–42.

Hunnicutt, B. K. (1988). *Work without end: Abandoning shorter hours for the right to work.* Philadelphia: Temple University Press.

Jaques, E. (1982). *The form of time.* New York: Crane Russak.

Jensen, M. C., & Meckling, W. H. (1976). Theory of the firm: Managerial behavior, agency costs, and ownership structure. *Journal of Financial Economics, 3*, 305–360.

Jobs, S. (2004, February). Steve Jobs now and then. *Macworld, 21*, 64–65.

Judge, W. Q., & Spitzfaden, M. (1995). The management of strategic time horizons within high technology firms: The impact of cognitive complexity on time horizon diversity. *Journal of Management Inquiry, 4*, 179–196.

Kahn, J. P. (2000). Till the end of time. *Boston Globe*, June 20, p. D11.

Kanigel, R. (1997). *The one best way: Frederick Winslow Taylor and the enigma of efficiency.* New York: Viking.

Kanter, R. M. (1989). The new managerial work. *Harvard Business Review, 67*(6), 85–92.

Kaplan, R. S., & Norton, D. P. (1996). *The balanced scorecard: Translating strategy into action.* Boston: Harvard Business School Press.

Lawrence, P. R., & Lorsch, J. W. (1967). *Organization and environment: Managing differentiation and integration.* Boston: Harvard University, Graduate School of Business Administration.

Lessig, L. (2004). *Free culture: The nature and future of creativity.* New York: Penguin Books.

Levine, R. (1997). *A geography of time.* New York: Basic Books.

Levine, R. V., & Norenzayan, A. (1999). The pace of life in 31 countries. *Journal of Cross-Cultural Psychology, 30*, 178–205.

Levine, R. V., West, L. J., & Reis, H. T. (1980). Perceptions of time and punctuality in the United States and Brazil. *Journal of Personality and Social Psychology, 38*, 541–550.

March, J. G. (1991). Exploration and exploitation in organizational learning. *Organization Science, 2*, 71–87.

Martins, L., Eddleston, K. A., & Veiga, J. F. (2002). Moderators of the relationship between work-family conflict and career satisfaction. *Academy of Management Journal, 45*, 399–410.

McGrath, J. E., & Kelly, J. R. (1986). *Time and human interaction: Toward a social psychology of time.* New York: Guilford.

McGrath, J. E., & Rotchford, N. L. (1983). Time and behavior in organizations. In: L. L. Cummings, & B. M. Staw (Eds), *Research in organizational behavior* (Vol. 5, pp. 57–101). Greenwich, CT: JAI Press.

Merck Family Fund. (1995). *Yearning for balance: Views of Americans on consumption, materialism, and the environment.* Takoma Park, MD: Merck Family Fund.

Morgan, G. (1997). *Images of organization* (2nd ed.). Thousand Oaks, CA: Sage.

Mohring, H., Schroeter, J., & Wiboonchutikula, P. (1987). The values of waiting time, travel time, and a seat on a bus. *RAND Journal of Economics, 18*, 40–56.

Moore, W. E. (1963). *Man, time, and society*. New York: Wiley.

Neeson, J. M. (1984). The opponents of enclosure in eighteenth-century Northhamptonshire. *Past and Present, 105*, 114–139.

Okhuysen, G. A., & Waller, M. J. (2002). Focusing on mid-point transitions: An analysis of boundary conditions. *Academy of Management Journal, 45*, 1056–1065.

Ostrom, E., Burger, J., Field, C. B., Norgaard, R. B., & Policansky, D. (1999). Revisiting the commons: Local lessons, global challenges. *Science, 284*, 278–282.

Ouchi, W. G. (1981). *Theory Z: How American business can meet the Japanese challenge*. New York: Avon.

Perlow, L. A. (1997). *Finding time: How corporations, individuals, and families can benefit from new work practices*. NY: ILR Press, Ithaca. An imprint of Cornell University Press.

Perlow, L. A. (1999). The time famine: Toward a sociology of work time. *Administrative Science Quarterly, 44*, 57–81.

Pierce, L. B. (2000). *Choosing simplicity: Real people finding peace and fulfillment in a complex world*. Carmel, CA: Gallagher Press.

Price, J. L. (1972). *Handbook of organizational measurement*. Lexington, MA: D. C. Heath.

Price, J. L., & Mueller, C. W. (1986). *Handbook of organizational measurement*. Marshfield, MA: Pitman Publishing.

Quinn, R. E., & Rohrbaugh, J. (1983). A spatial model of effectiveness criteria: Toward a competing values approach to organizational analysis. *Management Science, 29*, 363–377.

Richards, E. G. (1998). *Mapping time: The calendar and its history*. Oxford: Oxford University Press.

Roy, D. F. (1959–1960). "Banana time": Job satisfaction and informal interaction. *Human Organization, 18*, 158–168.

Safrin, S. (2004). Hyperownership in a time of biotechnological promise: The international conflict to control the building blocks of life. *American Journal of International Law, 98*, 641–685.

Schein, E. H. (1992). *Organizational culture and leadership* (2nd ed.). San Francisco: Jossey-Bass.

Schiller, H. I. (1991). Corporate sponsorship: Institutionalized censorship of the cultural realm. *Art Journal, 50*, 56–59.

Scott, W. R. (2003). *Organizations: Rational, natural, and open systems* (5th ed.). Upper Saddle River, NJ: Prentice Hall.

Smith, A. (1776/1976). *An inquiry into the nature and causes of the wealth of nations*. Chicago: University of Chicago Press.

Steers, R. M. (1975). Problems in the measurement of organizational effectiveness. *Administrative Science Quarterly, 20*, 546–558.

Sterba, J. P. (1990). Ukrainian reformers match wits and pluck with party holdouts. *Wall Street Journal*, July 17, pp. A1, A12.

Stalk, G., Jr., & Hout, T. J. (1990). *Competing against time: How time-based competition is reshaping global markets*. New York: Free Press.

Steel, D. (2000). *Marking time: The epic quest to invent the perfect calendar*. New York: Wiley.

Thompson, E. P. (1967). Time, work-discipline, and industrial capitalism. *Past and Present, 38*, 56–97.

Thompson, J. D. (1967). *Organizations in action*. New York: McGraw-Hill.

Varadarajan, P. R., Clark, T., & Pride, W. M. (1992). Controlling the uncontrollable: Managing your market environment. *Sloan Management Review, 33*(2), 39–47.

Vitzthum, C. (2004). In busy Madrid, there's no time now for a midday nap. *Wall Street Journal*, September 22, pp. A1, A14.

Wall Street Journal (2005a). Clockwork blues. *Wall Street Journal*, July 22, p. W13.

Wall Street Journal (2005b). Labor law may portend end of Spanish siesta. *Wall Street Journal*, December 29, p. A9.

Waller, M. J., Conte, J. M., Gibson, C. B., & Carpenter, M. A. (2001). The effect of individual perceptions of deadlines on team performance. *Academy of Management Review, 26*, 586–600.

Waller, M. J., & Roberts, K. H. (2003). High reliability and organizational behavior: Finally the twain must meet. *Journal of Organizational Behavior, 24*, 813–814.

Waller, M. J., Zellmer-Bruhn, M. E., & Giambatista, R. C. (2002). Watching the clock: Group pacing behavior under dynamic deadlines. *Academy of Management Journal, 45*, 1046–1055.

Weber, M. (1958). *The Protestant ethic and the spirit of capitalism* (T. Parsons, Trans.). New York: Charles Schribners. (Original work published 1904–1905).

Weber, M. (1978). In: G. Roth, & C. Wittich (Eds), *Economy and society* (Vol. 1). Berkeley, CA: University of California Press.

Wiencek, H. (2003). *An imperfect god: George Washington, his slaves, and the creation of America*. New York: Farrar, Straus, and Giroux.

Williamson, O. E. (1975). *Markets and hierarchies: Analysis and antitrust implications*. New York: Free Press.

Wysocki, B. Jr. (2004). To fix health care, hospitals take tips from factory floor. *Wall Street Journal*, April 6, pp. A1, A6.

Zakaria, F. (2006, January 9). We all have a lot to learn. *Newsweek, 147*, p. 37.

Zaryouni, H. (2005). The energy bill and your bills. *Wall Street Journal*, July 28, pp. D1–D2.

Zerubavel, E. (1985). *The seven day circle: The history and meaning of the week*. Chicago: University of Chicago Press.

Zerubavel, E. (2003). *Time maps: Collective memory and the social shape of the past*. Chicago: University of Chicago Press.

SET UP A CONTINUATION ORDER TODAY!

Did you know that you can set up a continuation order on all Elsevier-JAI series and have each new volume sent directly to you upon publication? For details on how to set up a **continuation order**, contact your nearest regional sales office listed below.

To view related series in Business & Management, please visit:

www.elsevier.com/businessandmanagement

30% Discount for Authors on All Books!

A 30% discount is available to Elsevier book and journal contributors on all books (except multi-volume reference works).

To claim your discount, full payment is required with your order, which must be sent directly to the publisher at the nearest regional sales office above.